THE COMPANION GUIDE TO

New York

THE COMPANION GUIDES

GENERAL EDITOR: VINCENT CRONIN

It is the aim of these guides to provide a Companion in the person of the author, who knows intimately the places and people of whom he writes, and is able to communicate this knowledge and affection to his readers. It is hoped that the text and pictures will aid them in their preparations and in their travels, and will help them remember on their return.

LONDON • THE SHAKESPEARE COUNTRY • OUTER LONDON • EAST ANGLIA
NORTHUMBRIA • THE WEST HIGHLANDS OF SCOTLAND
THE SOUTH OF FRANCE • THE ILE DE FRANCE • NORMANDY • THE LOIRE
FLORENCE • VENICE • ROME
MAINLAND GREECE • THE GREEK ISLANDS • JUGOSLAVIA • TURKEY
MADRID AND CENTRAL SPAIN

Most of these guides are also available as trade paperbacks

In Preparation

OXFORD AND CAMBRIDGE • PARIS

THE COMPANION GUIDE TO

NEW YORK

MICHAEL LEAPMAN

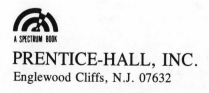

PRENTICE-HALL, INC.
Englewood Cliffs, N.J. 07632

COLLINS
8 Grafton Street, London W1

Library of Congress Cataloging in Publication Data

Leapman, Michael (Date)
The companion guide to New York.

"A Spectrum Book."
Bibliography: p.
Includes index.
1. New York (N.Y.)—Description—1981— —Tours.
I. Title.
F128.18.L38 1983 917.47'10443 82-23092

ISBN 0-13-154682-1
ISBN 0-13-154674-0 (pbk.)

ISBN 0-13-154682-1

ISBN 0-13-154674-0 {PBK.}

ISBN 0 00 216198 2

Trade Paperback 0 00 216394 5

William Collins Sons and Co Ltd
London • Glasgow • Sydney • Auckland
Toronto • Johannesburg
Prentice-Hall Inc
New Jersey
First published in Great Britain and
in the United States 1983

Maps drawn by Constance Dear

The photographs by Edmund Gillon appeared in
THE GREAT SIGHTS OF NEW YORK: A PHOTOGRAPHIC GUIDE
by J. Spero and E. V. Gillon Jr © 1970 Dover
Publications Inc., NY. Used with the permission of
the publisher.

A SPECTRUM BOOK

Printed in the United States of America

10 9 8 7 6 5 4 3 2 1

Prentice-Hall, International, Inc., *London*
Prentice-Hall of Australia Pty. Limited, *Sydney*
Prentice-Hall of Canada, Inc, *Toronto*
Prentice-Hall of India Private Limited, *New Delhi*
Prentice-Hall of Japan, Inc., *Tokyo*
Prentice-Hall of Southeast Asia Pte. Ltd., *Singapore*
Whitehall Books Limited, Wellington, *New Zealand*
Editora Prentice-Hall do Brasil Ltda., *Rio de Janeiro*

For Olga, who has walked every yard of the way, and for Ben, who may feel as though he has

''New York is a stroke of genius . . . a larder for the hungry, a living library for the intellectually starved, a refuge not only for the oppressed but also for the creative.''

Mayor Edward Koch
at his inauguration,
January 1978

Contents

Illustrations

List of Maps

List of Maps

Foreword

UNTIL SCARCELY MORE than a dozen years ago, the reaction of New Yorkers when told you were going to visit their city might have been: 'Why?' They, after all, had to live here and had learned to come to terms with the multiple inconveniences. But to visit? On holiday? Paris, Rome, Athens, London, San Francisco, even Boston — those were cities for tourists. New York was a place from which you fled in the summer because of the heat, in the winter because of the cold, and for the rest of the year because of the dirt, the crime, the noise, the smell, the traffic jams — all the evils created by squeezing too many people trying to do too many things into the same crowded space.

When my wife and I first came here from England in 1967 we also took that view. We did not imagine then that in two years we would be offered the chance to live here, or that we would dream of accepting such an offer should it be made. Yet we were and we did. So pervasive at the time was the negative publicity, especially about crime, that the impression was abroad that anyone who set foot on a New York street in the hours of darkness was more likely than not to be relieved of any valuables he might be carrying, with violence done to his person in the bargain. When friends and relatives expressed dismay at the thought of us living here I would respond, in as confident a tone as I could muster: 'More than eight million people live in New York. It must be a livable city.'

So it is, but at the beginning the disorientation which afflicts the short-term visitor is magnified for intending residents. When people speak about the relentless pace of life they are often boasting, but it does foster a brusque manner with strangers which seems like rudeness but is often not. It is partly the fault of New Yorkers that you hear more about visitors' encounters with con men, pickpockets and the rare taxi-driver who overcharges than about residents banding together to help a young couple who had their car and luggage stolen, a friend who left her handbag in a taxi and had it returned, complete with nearly two thousand dollars in cash and travelers' checks. In the Jack Lemmon film *The*

Out-of-Towners, a pair of visitors are mugged and cheated of all they have, and end up sleeping in Central Park. The film did nothing to improve the city's reputation but in a perverse way New Yorkers loved it. It encouraged their image of themselves as gutsy survivors of some medieval ordeal of chivalry: you may not enjoy the experience but you emerge a better person. The sense of danger is, after all, one of the ingredients of the New York experience.

After three years I was re-assigned to London. So powerful were the withdrawal symptoms that when, five years later, I was given the chance to come back here, I scarcely hesitated. New York and its attitude to visitors have improved since our first uneasy visit. Forced to recognize how important tourists are for its economy, the city makes a great effort to make them welcome and to smooth its harshest edges. 'I Love New York,' affirm the T-shirts, lapel buttons and advertisements aimed at potential visitors. In the television commercials the stress is always on the word 'I'. The translation is: 'In spite of everything, I have discovered how to deal with New York and even to enjoy it. That makes both me and the city lovable.'

The metaphor that many first-time visitors have employed is of the steam which rises from manholes at some street corners — part of an underground heating system for older buildings. They see this as a symbol of the city's latent energy. My own favorite symbol is a grubby sign at the end of the platform at the subway station nearest my office, on 42nd Street near Third Avenue. 'Hold Your Hat,' it reads starkly, presumably warning of strong breezes on the escalator. I like to think of it as a message to someone newly arrived, about to take his first peep above ground at the city swirling furiously about him.

One sunny June evening I was walking with a friend, making his third or fourth visit to New York, up Second Avenue at the tail-end of the rush hour. 'I always like coming here,' he said, as homegoing commuters scurried past. 'There's a tremendous air of excitement, although I'm never quite sure what the excitement is about.' My job, in this book, is to tell you.

THE COMPANION GUIDE TO

New York

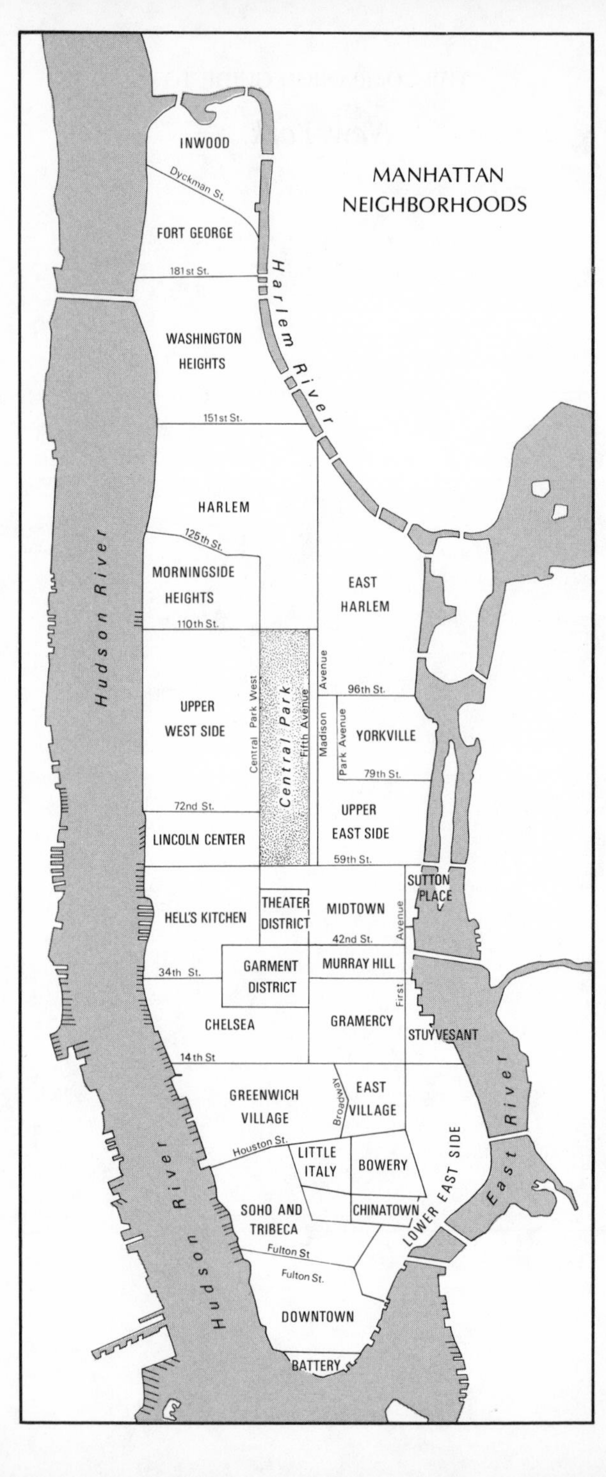
MANHATTAN
NEIGHBORHOODS
INWOOD
Dyckman St.
FORT GEORGE
181st St.
Harlem River
WASHINGTON
HEIGHTS
151st St.
HARLEM
125th St.
MORNINGSIDE
HEIGHTS
110th St.
EAST
HARLEM
Hudson River
UPPER
WEST SIDE
Central Park West
Central Park
Fifth Avenue
Madison Avenue
Park Avenue
96th St.
YORKVILLE
79th St.
72nd St.
UPPER
EAST SIDE
LINCOLN CENTER
59th St.
SUTTON
PLACE
HELL'S KITCHEN
THEATER
DISTRICT
MIDTOWN
42nd St.
First Avenue
GARMENT
DISTRICT
MURRAY HILL
34th St.
CHELSEA
GRAMERCY
STUYVESANT
14th St
GREENWICH
VILLAGE
Broadway
EAST
VILLAGE
East River
Houston St.
LITTLE
ITALY
BOWERY
LOWER EAST SIDE
SOHO AND
TRIBECA
CHINATOWN
Fulton St
Fulton St.
DOWNTOWN
BATTERY

1
Orientation

TO GET THE MOST out of New York, cultivate your imagination. The city as you are going to see it is stunning enough, but unless you know how it was and how it came to be what it is, you will miss much. Many times I shall ask you to picture scenes which have vanished, through the tendency of New Yorkers to pull things down and start again rather than to conserve and adapt what they have. You might conclude that I am adopting the disapproving tone of a native of a country which has been less ready to destroy its past; and in some cases you will be right, for New Yorkers themselves are outspoken in denouncing the more outrageous acts of civic vandalism. Yet it is necessary to understand the motivation of the large-scale demolitions. They derive from the city's comparative youth.

Until the 1820s it was a provincial town of two hundred thousand people. The opening of the Erie Canal in 1825, making it the only Eastern port with a water-borne route to the Midwest, turned it almost overnight into the most important city in the country, the center of American commerce. This triggered a period of exceptionally rapid expansion. There was plenty of room to spread northward, but commerce had to stay near the harbor, on the south-eastern edge of the island, where the old residential buildings were simply too small to be converted to new purposes. Larger offices and warehouses had to be built, and when they in turn became too small they had to be replaced. The pattern was repeated time and again over an increasing area, as the shopping and residential districts were pushed ever farther north, until today the metropolis fills not only Manhattan but an impressive area of territory surrounding it.

Until the last twenty years or so there has been no group of any size campaigning for old buildings to be saved. The wealthy who used to wield economic power would sail to Europe and gaze at the venerable relics of the Middle Ages and the Renaissance: that was culture, that was really old, and there was no means of creating anything comparable in a country which did not start erecting structures of any substantial life expectancy until the nineteenth century. All they could do was to build extravagant modern copies of Gothic and Renaissance monuments, or in a few cases ship the real ones across the Atlantic, stone by stone. There was no point in saving what they felt were their own undistinguished, run-of-the-mill domestic or commercial buildings if by razing them they left space for something more efficient, and more profitable.

This restless compulsion to embellish, to enlarge and to replace is the more noticeable because it contrasts with another characteristic of New Yorkers, their capacity for sentiment and nostalgia. In films, plays, books and especially in popular songs, the city has manufactured instant legends about itself; but the life span of the best songs is longer than that of many of their subjects. The Broadway to which George M. Cohan wished his regards to be given is now a different place from the Great White Way to which the greeting was first sent, about half a mile farther south.

You will find this contrast still more of a puzzle when you first arrive, to be jostled and maybe even abused at the airport or harbor, or in the bus or train station. Only when you begin to discover the solution to the mystery will you start to appreciate and enjoy New York.

I am going to start with a few practical points before beginning the detailed itineraries. You should have reserved in advance somewhere to stay, for in recent years New York's hotels have been filled almost to capacity for most of the year. Few vacationers will be able to afford the big name hotels like the Plaza and the Waldorf Astoria, or the newer Grand Hyatt and Helmsley Palace: these charge more than $100 a night for a single room, without breakfast or other meals. As you move down the hotel price scale, you get, broadly, what you pay for. Many travel agents will have an up-to-date list of hotel charges published by the city's Convention and Visitors Bureau.

A way of keeping down the cost, and getting a more intimate view of New York's day-to-day life, is to rent or exchange a city apartment for a week or two. You could use an agency specializing in holiday house exchange or advertise for yourself in *New York* magazine (755 Second Avenue, New York, NY 10017) or the *Village Voice* (80 University Place, New York, NY 10003).

If you arrive by train, boat or bus the straightforward way of getting to your hotel or apartment is to take a taxi: the terminals for all three modes of transport are near the center of Manhattan. By air, from overseas, you will arrive at John F. Kennedy airport, about fifteen miles from the city center, in the borough of Queens. On a domestic flight, it will be Kennedy or La Guardia (considerably closer to Manhattan in the same general direction) or Newark, across the Hudson in New Jersey. From Kennedy, a taxi to Manhattan will cost about $20. There is an express bus run by Carey Transportation which leaves the airport three times an hour for a terminal at 38th Street and First Avenue and costs $6.00: from the bus terminal you would have to get a taxi to your hotel, unless it is very near and you are travelling light. The whole trip will take about an hour. The fairly recent 'train-to-the-plane' service involves getting a special blue bus from the airport to a nearby subway station, where there is an express service to several points in the city, costing $5.00 and also taking about an hour. If your hotel is near Sixth Avenue (Avenue of the Americas), this might suit you, since most of the Manhattan stops are on that avenue. For the determined skinflint, a green bus runs round the inner perimeter road at Kennedy and takes about half an hour to get to the Union Turnpike subway station on the IND line in Queens. From there you can connect to any subway stop in the city, and the total fare is at present (1983) only $1.50–.75 for the bus (exact change required) and another 75 cents for the subway. It will take you about ninety minutes to Manhattan by this route, allowing for changes and waiting.

From La Guardia a taxi to the city is about half the cost of one from Kennedy, and is probably worth the expense. Carey also runs a regular service from here and there is a $1.50 bus/subway connection, although no 'train-to-the-plane' service. Because Newark is in a different state the taxis are allowed to charge double their metered rate (they are not allowed to pick up return fares in New York), so a cab could cost you nearly $40. A better way is to take the bus to the Port Authority Terminal on 40th Street and Eighth Avenue ($2.25) and get a New York taxi from there.

How to See New York

The book is organized into chapters which, for the most part, describe walks that can be completed in a day, though in a few cases a rather long day. The city is rich in museums, but they will disrupt any strict schedule planning because every visitor will want to spend a different amount of time in each. To explore thoroughly the Metropolitan Museum, for instance, one day is scarcely enough, so the best plan would be to leave it out when you initially tackle the walk in Chapter 12 and go back to it later, when you know how much extra time you have. The same procedure may be applied to other institutions. (Details of opening hours and admission charges are listed at the back of the book.)

I suspect that many writers of New York guides begin with laudable intentions of showing the whole city, the outer boroughs as well as Manhattan, and even parts of adjacent New Jersey and Connecticut. Soon, however, they are forced to recognize the reality that the average visitor simply does not have the time to take in the marginal areas, given the riches of the principal borough. Like the others, therefore, I have concentrated on Manhattan, though there is one walk entirely in Brooklyn which, to my mind, is among the two or three most interesting in the book. I have in the last chapter outlined things to look for in the outer boroughs if you do have time.

Manhattan is reasonably simple to navigate, being planned for the most part on a rigid grid system. The avenues run from north to south and are numbered in ascending scale from east to west, from First to Twelfth. Complications occur when the island bulges: on the Lower East Side four alphabetical avenues, A to D, are added east of First Avenue, and farther north York and East End Avenues make their appearance. The street numbers go up as you go north — hence 'uptown' towards the high numbers in the Bronx and 'downtown' is south, towards 1st Street. The numbering starts at Houston Street: those below there already had names when the City Commissioners drew up the grid in 1811, marking phantom streets on terrain that was almost entirely rural.

To find a particular street address, remember that Fifth Avenue is the divide between the east and west crosstown streets and that the numbers go up in hundreds as they cross the avenues, ignoring Madison and Lexington which respectively divide Fifth and Park (Fourth) Avenues, and Park and Third. Thus 220 East 42nd Street is between Second and Third Avenues, 220 West 42nd Street between Seventh and Eighth. To find numbers on the avenues use the fairly simple table which I have printed as an appendix.

Subways

Most chapters will begin at a point in the city easily accessible by public transport and I urge you to use the buses and subways at least a few times, despite their discomforts and (rare) dangers. Public transport offers a quick way of gaining sharp insights into the nature of a city and its people. Watching New Yorkers on the subways or buses brings into focus their long-suffering air of coping with adversity which I described in the introduction. You will meet the 'subway crazies', demented folk who can be found in any of the city's public places, carrying on loud, animated and often abusive conversations with themselves, gesticulating wildly. You will see bag ladies, who live in shop doorways or the tunnels near Grand Central Station, bearing their possessions in well-worn paper carrier bags. None of these, generally, is a threat.

Not everybody on the subway is demented. On the trains that call at Wall Street you will see businessmen and women, their clothes crumpling in the crush and heat, trying bravely to read the *Wall Street Journal* by folding it neatly in quarters. Younger office workers stare blankly at the bilingual (English and Spanish) advertisements, their minds on something else. Students try to concentrate on textbooks about computer technology or self-improvement. Nobody talks: even if they have someone to talk to, the dreadful din rules it out.

Paul Goldberger, a writer on architecture for *The New York Times*, has written: 'There is no public environment in the United States as squalid as the New York City subway. It is dirty, cramped, smelly and altogether lacking in amenities as basic as a place to sit down. It is efficient — that much can be said for it. But as an object of design, the subway is a lesson in what not to do. No other city has made for its citizens a public place as mean and unpleasant as New York City has made its subway.' While all of this is true, it is also a fact that the only low-priced alternative is the buses, slightly less squalid and without the advantage of being an efficient means of getting speedily from one place to the next.

Because of the long, thin shape of Manhattan, most subway routes go north-south, uptown or downtown. Travelling in those directions is therefore fastest, and trying to go from east to west can cause delay and confusion. A crosstown route on 63rd Street is being built, due to open in 1985. The great asset of the subways is that most of them run on four parallel tracks instead of two, meaning that express and slow trains can follow the same route. If you get on a train at a local (non-express) station, you can change at the first express station, generally by merely crossing the platform, and cover a tremendous distance in a short time.

Whether that tremendous distance will be in the direction you intended travelling will depend on your ability to decode the system map, which you can get free from city tourist offices or from the token booths at the stations — it is a question of asking around until you find one which has maps in stock. The map is of stunning complexity since it portrays a system which is itself incurably complex. This is because the lines were originally owned by three private companies, sometimes competing over parallel routes, and were incorporated into a single, city-run unit only in the 1940s. Old habits die hard and the different routes are still referred to by their old company names — IRT, IND and BMT — both colloquially and in signs at the stations, though gradually these are being replaced by a new color coding scarcely easier to comprehend. The trains are designated by letters (single or double) or by numbers, depending on what company originally owned them.

To get on the subway you must buy a metal token (present price 75 cents) at a booth at the station entrance, and place it in the platform turnstile. (It makes sense to buy a batch of tokens at one time, because the buses also accept them.) Be careful to read the sign over the station entrance which tells you whether it leads to the uptown or downtown trains. Many stations have no internal connection between the two platforms, and if you get on to the wrong side by mistake there is no alternative but to leave the station, cross the road and spend another token to get on to the right platform. If travelling late at night, stick with the crowds near the center of the platform and of the train. This is not only a safety precaution: outside the peak hours the trains are shortened and you can be caught having to sprint up the platform for the end car.

Buses

Most of the north-south avenues except Park, West End, Eleventh and East End have buses running along them and there is also a comprehensive network of crosstown buses. The fare for a single bus ride is 75 cents: the flat bus and subway fares are always the same and the authorities are constantly threatening to increase them. You can use a subway token or pay the exact fare in coins into the box at the driver's right hand. He will not accept paper money. If you are going to change to another bus on the same journey, ask him for an 'add-a-ride' ticket. The buses stop every two blocks. In rush hours they are so slow that it is often quicker to walk.

Not all the buses go straight up and down avenues or cross streets: some turn off when you least expect it, so it is worth asking the driver, before you commit your money to the fare box, if he is going where you want to go. You might be lucky enough to get a bus map at one of the city tourist offices.

At weekends and on public holidays the city runs two pompously named 'culture bus' routes, which between them stop at the main tourist attractions. For a single fare of $1.75 you can get on and off them at will. Pick up a leaflet at a tourist office or phone 330-1234 for details of times and routes. They are not a bad idea if you want to spend a whole day visiting museums and sights some distance apart, but they are based on something of a misapprehension — the belief that riding on a bus is a good way of seeing the city. The vehicles (or at least the old models, slowly being replaced) are cunningly devised so that you can see very little, sitting or standing, even which street you are passing. In a crowded bus watch for pickpockets and bag snatchers, and be specially careful if someone seems to trip in front of you as you alight: the passenger behind you might be rifling your pocket or handbag as you stoop to help.

Taxis

Taxis cost a dollar for the first ninth of a mile and ten cents for each succeeding ninth of a mile and you should add about twenty per cent to the metered fare for the tip. They are more comfortable than buses but often not much faster, because they get stuck in the same traffic jams — and are sometimes just as jerky, depending on the driver. If you are in a hurry, say to get to the theatre, it may be better to grit your teeth and descend into the subway, since long jams build up in the Broadway area at curtain time. All official cabs are yellow and it is a bad idea to get into 'gypsy' cabs of any other color. Vacant cabs have their roof lights lit but it is easy to be fooled by the small 'off duty' or 'on radio call' signs which can be hard to make out beside the larger 'taxi' light. By law, drivers are supposed to take you anywhere within the city limits, including the Bronx, Brooklyn, Queens and Staten Island. Kennedy and La Guardia airports are both within that area. Most will take you where you want to go, but if one of them declines you can do little but threaten to report the refusal. All cab drivers have their picture and license number next to the meter. If you have been overcharged or otherwise abused, take down the number and find a policeman.

The wry, philosophical New York cab driver is a legendary figure but your chance of being driven by one is small; usually the driver just sits there sullenly, occasionally letting out a curse at life in general, the traffic or opposing drivers in particular. Some speak only rudimentary English, many work part-time and not all of them know the city too well. Even if you are making for a famous landmark it is a good idea to give the street co-ordinates. ('Plaza Hotel, please. That's at Fifth and 59th.') If you are going to a street with a name instead of a number, say in Greenwich Village, get precise directions before you get in the cab and relay them to the driver.

Other transport

Bicycling is increasingly popular in Manhattan. You can rent bikes from several shops, including one in Central Park. Consult the Yellow Pages of the phone book. An unusual way of getting a panoramic view of the city is to go for a quick flip in a helicopter. They leave from the heliport at the eastern end of 34th Street. Phone 683-4575 for prices and details.

Food

I have not seen precise figures, but I should imagine that in number of restaurants per head of population New York would be near the top. Yet in part the very multiplicity of places, styles and prices is bewildering. Many visitors end up eating unadventurously at their hotel or in any of the fast food chains which originated here but are now scarcely distinguishable from those in almost every world capital.

I am not going to attempt any kind of comprehensive restaurant listing. For one thing, they are among the least permanent elements in an inconstant city. That amazingly cheap little bistro that I could recommend to you might be amazingly cheap because it is using up the tail-end of a lease, and will have disappeared by the time this book is published. Similarly, the chef at one five-star French restaurant might be bought by a rival, invalidating everything one knew about both establishments. So I shall mention restaurants when they have been there long enough to be established and when they fit naturally into the territory I am describing (you will find these and other restaurants listed alphabetically in the index under the heading 'restaurants'). For the rest, the most useful thing I can do is suggest a few general principles on eating out.

Almost any coffee shop will serve a fine and hearty breakfast cheaper than a hotel, and even fast food chains do a presentable job. You can, at the time of writing, get a sufficiently ample breakfast for around $5 to enable you to skimp on lunch and have a real blowout at dinner. Your coffee cup will generally be refilled as often as you wish. Lunch for many New Yorkers is simply a sandwich at the office desk. While most visitors will have no desk, they can exploit this tradition by buying a fresh, tasty and generously filled sandwich and eating it in a park or at a table in the sandwich shop. Or you can get a couple of slices of pizza from one of the proliferating pizza parlors, which have ledges where you eat standing up. There are plenty of hamburger chains, restaurants and delicatessens. A chain called Lindy's has branches in several convenient places — one at Rockefeller Center and one opposite Grand Central Station. Their prices are a bit more than you ought to pay, but the service and comfort are superior. The name was that of an old Broadway eating-house thinly disguised as Mindy's in Damon Runyon's stories of Manhattan low life, where his demi-mondaine characters would ruminatively drink coffee and eat cheesecake, discussing crime and philosophy in their curious patois. An establishment called Leo Lindy's, on Broadway north of Times Square, is under different ownership but scarcely distinguishable.

For serious evening meals . . . well, it depends how serious. In top-class restaurants you generally get what you pay for, in comfort and quality. For classical French cuisine, Lutèce, La Caravelle and the Palace are excellent and unbelievably expensive. For American style food, the Palm provides an interesting experience, though one you may not want to repeat: not because of the food, which is splendid, but because of the cost, the quantity served and the overwhelming atmosphere of frenzy. Many good judges say the best steaks are to be had at Christ Cella, a block or two from the Palm, and I have eaten a massive and tender flank at the Old Homestead on the outskirts of Greenwich Village. In Brooklyn I enjoy Gage and Tollner's — a fine restaurant with excellent service and a well-preserved Edwardian atmosphere.

For a late-night French snack, the Brasserie, at the foot of the Seagram Building off Park Avenue, is convenient, and so is Richoux of London in the Citicorp Building, Third Avenue and 53rd Street. Some of the best

Chinese restaurants in the world are in New York, both in Chinatown and on the Upper East Side. Indian food is less of a tradition here: you will find one or two quite good restaurants, mostly around the UN Center, but they tend to be more expensive than they should. Central European cooking survives in the old Yorkville section round East 86th Street and at the Ukrainian Restaurant in the East Village. The largest concentration of Latin American restaurants is on the Upper West Side: Victor's on Columbus Avenue is one of the oldest and best of the Cuban variety.

There remain what I call the 'production number' restaurants, where you go for the environment rather than the fare. Sardi's in the Broadway theatre district ranks as one of those. The food is mediocre and overpriced, but if you go in the hope of rubbing shoulders with famous actors, you might just be lucky. You are, however, more likely to find them at Elaine's on the Upper East Side, where whether or not you are allotted a table depends on the whim of Elaine, the proprietress. Mamma Leone's is a cheerful restaurant in the Broadway area where the emphasis is on quantity rather than quality but where the singing waiters make it all seem fun. One way of gauging an unknown restaurant is to read the reviews in its window. Restaurants are never shy of boasting when someone has written well of them. Be selective about which reviews you take at face value. The ones from the *New York Times* are to be respected the most, while *New York* magazine and the *Village Voice* are also reliable.

Until recently, you would have been hard put to it to find much outdoor eating and drinking in New York, except in obvious locations such as the parks and Rockefeller Center. From time to time, though, a fit of collective delusion strikes the citizens, who fantasize about how nice it would be if they lived in Paris or Rome or Juan-les-Pins: a rash of open air cafés then spills out on to the sidewalks. They are not generally to be recommended. The traffic is hard to bear and except for a few weeks in spring or autumn the weather is normally too hot or too cold for comfort.

Ice cream

New Yorkers love ice cream and have invested it with a passionate sensuousness which shows through as they caress a cone and lick the last vestiges of the creamy confection from around their mouths. To be called ice cream it has to be made with fresh dairy produce rather than with animal fats and this is part of the reason why the quality is high. Serious ice cream parlors usually have a selection of twenty or more intriguing flavors, some apparently invented simply because the name sounded snappy. I prefer to stick to the standard coffees and vanillas, the fruit sorbets or the nutty flavors — pecan and almond especially. Devoted ice cream fanciers may turn up their noses at Baskin Robbins, the most prolific of the multi-flavor chains, but I find their product perfectly passable. My favorite is Haagen Dazs, which has an outlet near Alexander's on 59th Street. Their selection is smaller than most but it all tastes tremendous, especially the boysenberry sorbet. Howard Johnson's, among the originators of flavor proliferation, are unfashionable but not at all bad, though some of their outlets in midtown Manhattan are a bit squalid. Those who prefer ice cream fruitier and less creamy should try the italian ices served in paper cones sold from pushcarts on street corners.

Drink

There are thousands of bars in New York, catering to almost every taste and need. The singles bars, mainly on the Upper East Side but increasingly on the Upper West Side and in the Village, constitute the most famous category. The business of mating is carried out in a structured fashion here and these are places where young men and women go specifically to meet partners. Most are hoping to find people with whom they will form long-term liaisons but naturally a great many casual pick-ups and equally casual abandonments occur. As a short-term visitor you may not want to take part in the transactions, but nobody will mind if you go along and watch them happening. Both heterosexual and homosexual pairings are catered for, generally in separate establishments, and it is easy to tell which kind you have wandered into.

For a drink with a view there are bars on top of the RCA Building in the Rockefeller Center, the Gulf and Western Building on Columbus Circle, and the World Trade Center. That on the 15th floor of No 1 Times Square is pleasant for an after-theater drink. The bars in the Wall Street area are, at lunch-time, good places to watch people making deals — or acting as if they are making deals — over a martini or three. There are literary bars (the White Horse, the Lion's Head) in Greenwich Village, and I recommend McSorley's saloon in the East Village as the New York version of an English pub (only beer is served). Newspapermen congregate in bars near the *Daily News* building on East 42nd Street. Costello's, on 44th Street between Second and Third Avenues, is a favorite of the expatriate press, and has wall panels drawn by James Thurber for its original location nearby on Third Avenue. (Many New York bars and some restaurants have their walls covered with the work of cartoonists, possibly the origin of the city's passion for graffiti.) Farther north, on Third Avenue by 55th Street, P. J. Clarke's is a fine old Victorian bar, always crowded.

Nearly all the bars serve food, some of it rudimentary, but you are in no sense obliged to order it. Many singles bars are mysteriously named for fruits (Maxwell's Plum) or days of the week and some are a bit saucy (Knickers). A pleasing feature in many is the incidence of good live music. It can range simply from a tinkly piano to torch singing or a jazz combo. A few bars offer amateur or semi-professional comedians the chance to stand up and work before an often skeptical audience. The most popular of these include Catch a Rising Star on First Avenue near 77th Street, the Improvisation on 44th Street near Tenth Avenue and the Comic Strip on Second Avenue near 81st Street. *New York* magazine, the *New Yorker* and the *Village Voice* contain reliable guides to bar and night club entertainment. With music, drinks are more expensive, or there is a modest cover charge, or both.

Entertainment

The conscientious tourist should always make a point of seeing the distinctive art form of the place he is visiting. You ought, therefore, to see a Broadway musical. If you must see the latest smash hit you will have to pay some $35 for the best seats and not much less for the worst, plus a commission to a ticket agency if, as is probable, you are unable to get seats from any other source. If willing to settle for last season's smash hit or a preview of an unknown quantity you can get seats at half-price from an excellent facility called unpronounceably 'Tkts NY'. Every day the theatres send unsold seats to the Tkts booth on a triangular island between Broadway and Seventh Avenue at the junction with 47th Street. Do not be put off by the long line: there are six windows and they move quite fast, and you will usually strike up impromptu friendships while waiting. A board by the windows announces which tickets are available. If you do not see listed the particular show you want, you could try at the theatre box office for returns, but these will be at full price. Tickets go on sale at the Tkts booth at noon for matinées (generally on Wednesdays, Saturdays and Sundays), and at 3 p.m. for evening performances, most of which begin at 8 p.m. A branch office of Tkts on William Street in the Wall Street area sells tickets only for evening performances and for a more limited selection of shows, but the wait is often shorter. Some shows coming towards the end of their runs give out 'twofers', short for 'two for the price of one'. These are vouchers which can be exchanged at the box office for tickets, again at half-price, avoiding the Tkts lines. Twofers can be picked up at the Visitors' Bureau on Seventh Avenue and 42nd Street and at the City Cultural Affairs Building on Columbus Circle (Broadway and 58th Street), or at some restaurants and shops. Read the small print, which limits the performances for which they are valid, generally excluding Saturday nights.

In recent years straight plays have made a comeback on Broadway, after a period during which almost nothing but musicals had a chance of an extended run. Many serious plays begin in off-Broadway theatres, most in Greenwich Village and a few in a new small-theatre district around 42nd and 43rd Streets west of Times Square. The Tkts booth dispenses tickets for these also and since the original face value is generally a lot less than in fully fledged Broadway theatres they can be exceptionally cheap. On-Broadway, off-Broadway and even off-off-Broadway (shoestring semi-amateur companies playing in tiny halls, many in Soho) you will be struck by the high level of professionalism in the acting and staging. Capsule descriptions of the plays in *New York* magazine, the *New Yorker* and the *Village Voice* will give you some idea of what you might like to see.

The same publications are also reliable guides to films. The main movie district has shifted lately from Broadway to the area around Bloomingdale's department store on Third Avenue and 59th Street. This is where the latest American and overseas hits are shown, and there are often lines for the most fashionable. The theatres here are smaller than the old Art Deco palaces, so harder to get into if the film is a hit. Tickets are around $5. Old Hollywood classics are shown at a few specialist theatres.

The Museum of Modern Art on 53rd Street, between Fifth and Sixth Avenues, shows old feature films which you can attend for the price of museum admission.

Music and dancing

The discotheque has had a long run as the symbol of New York sophistication but is nearing the end of it. In any event it is useless making specific recommendations because these are more ephemeral than almost any other institution in this swiftly changing city. You will have to refer to those city magazines and periodicals I have mentioned, and to the gossip columns of the *Daily News* and the *New York Post*. Do not expect an inexpensive evening: some discos charge an admission fee and drinks can be outrageously priced.

The city magazines also provide guides to jazz and rock music. New York has some of the finest jazz clubs in the world, many in Greenwich Village locations which they have occupied for years. These are more stable institutions than discos and usually better value. You can call Jazzline on 423-0488 for comprehensive information. Performances at the Metropolitan Opera and the City Ballet are generally sold out months in advance, but a theatre agent may be able to find you seats for a shade over the box office price: it is worth enquiring. Watch the papers for details of free opera and ballet in Central Park: you might be too far away to enjoy a supreme visual or auditory experience, but you will enjoy the easygoing atmosphere. For classical music look up programmes at Carnegie Hall and the Lincoln Center (*see index*). Outdoor rock and popular music concerts are sometimes held in the Wollman ice rink in Central Park for a modest admission charge.

Even if you are not an enthusiast for ballroom dancing, a visit to Roseland will acquaint you with a segment of New York social life you will not readily encounter elsewhere. Middle-aged to elderly men with toupées and women with carefully coiffed hair go there from the suburbs to meet partners of their kind and to dance to the deliberate beat of the tango, the foxtrot and the waltz. On Wednesdays, Fridays and Saturdays they slip in an hour of disco dancing to keep up with the times but essentially the place is much as it was when established in 1919. (It moved to its present location on 52nd Street, west of Broadway, in the

1950s.) There are two bars and a restaurant where the food, if undistinguished, is not overpriced.

Shopping

Alexander's, at 59th Street and Third Avenue, is the most conveniently placed of the cheaper stores, though with low prices comes slow service (or no service at all, really: you select what you want and then have to wait in a long line to pay for it). Clothes and bed linens are good value for visitors from Britain. Books can also be cheap, notably at the branches of Barnes and Noble which have sprouted in the last two years in most central parts of the city. Avoid those flashy electronics and camera emporiums that nest like cuckoos in shopfronts along Fifth Avenue, using the tail-end of leases. Generally you will get better value in the department stores or at chains such as Radio Shack or Sam Goody (*see index*). For souvenirs, the shops in the city museums could be your most fruitful source, especially the Museum of the City of New York and Brooklyn Museum (*q.v.*).

Sports

For baseball, the New York Yankees play at Yankee Stadium in the Bronx and the Mets at Shea Stadium in Queens: both are on the subway. Advance tickets cost around $6 and are obtainable from Ticketron outlets and, in the case of the Mets, from branches of Manufacturers Hanover Bank. *New York* magazine and the *New Yorker* print the games a week or two ahead. Between September and January the New York Giants play football at Giants Stadium in New Jersey, and the Jets at Shea Stadium. The most popular indoor winter sports are basketball and ice hockey, which New York's major league teams, the Knicks and the Rangers, play at Madison Square Garden on Eighth Avenue and 32nd Street.

Some of the world's best thoroughbred racehorses are on view six days a week (every day except Tuesday) for the whole year except for three weeks in August, at either Aqueduct (on the subway) or Belmont Park (only slightly farther out: special trains go every race day from Penn Station at Eighth Avenue and 32nd Street). In the autumn there is evening thoroughbred racing at the Meadowlands, next to Giants Stadium in New

Jersey (bus from the Port Authority terminal). For the rest of the year the track is given over to trotting, a colorful sport which also takes place at Yonkers, north of the city, or at Roosevelt Field on Long Island, both a bus ride from the Port Authority terminal.

As for participatory sports, swimming comes expensive in Manhattan: you must get temporary membership at a health club or the YMCA. The few public pools convenient to the city center are dreadfully crowded. The same is true of the public tennis courts in the parks, generally booked far ahead. If you must take exercise, the cheapest and least complicated way is to jog around Central Park with the multitudes before breakfast. For nearby beaches, look up Coney Island, Jones Beach and Rockaway Beach in the index.

If you have absorbed all the foregoing you are probably as ready as you will ever be to experience this tremendous city. So, as the waitress will command tersely, pushing your eggs and English muffins towards you at breakfast: 'Enjoy it.'

2

Southern Approaches

New York is a maritime city and the best way of getting an overall view of it, relating the main parts to the whole, is to take the Circle Line's three-hour boat trip around Manhattan Island. It leaves from the **Hudson River pier** at the western extremity of 43rd Street, beyond Twelfth Avenue, a ten-minute walk from the subway stations at Times Square or 42nd Street and Eighth Avenue. The 42nd Street crosstown bus (M 106) and the 49th Street crosstown (M 27) both go right to the pier; sailing schedules vary with the time of the year.

The boat goes south, passing first on its left the site of the new convention center, under construction between 39th and 34th Streets hard by the river. The city planners hope that, when finished, it will symbolize New York's revitalization, so it is ironically apt that it should be alongside the crumbling old passenger piers that are a symbol of the city's decline in the middle years of this century. Until the 1950s most travellers from overseas arrived by sea and these piers would have been noisy and crowded. Now, although a few liners still cross the Atlantic in summer, it is slow and expensive for the modern traveller, wanting to pack in as much as his time and funds will allow.

If the city can afford it, the ugly piers will be cleaned up and converted to a recreational purpose. The factories on the New Jersey side are scarcely prettier but things improve quickly as we circle the **Statue of Liberty,** enjoying the classic view of the downtown Manhattan skyscrapers, and move into position to enter the East River — not really a river but a channel linking New York Bay with Long Island Sound. In the distance to our south the **Verrazano Narrows Bridge,** which has spanned the narrows since 1964, is a sweeping, dramatic, functional feat of technology, named after the adventurer who, four hundred and forty years earlier, made the first firm record of sighting the mouth of what is now the Hudson River. It is asking a lot of the imagination to strip away the accumulation of man-made objects and to picture the bay, fringed

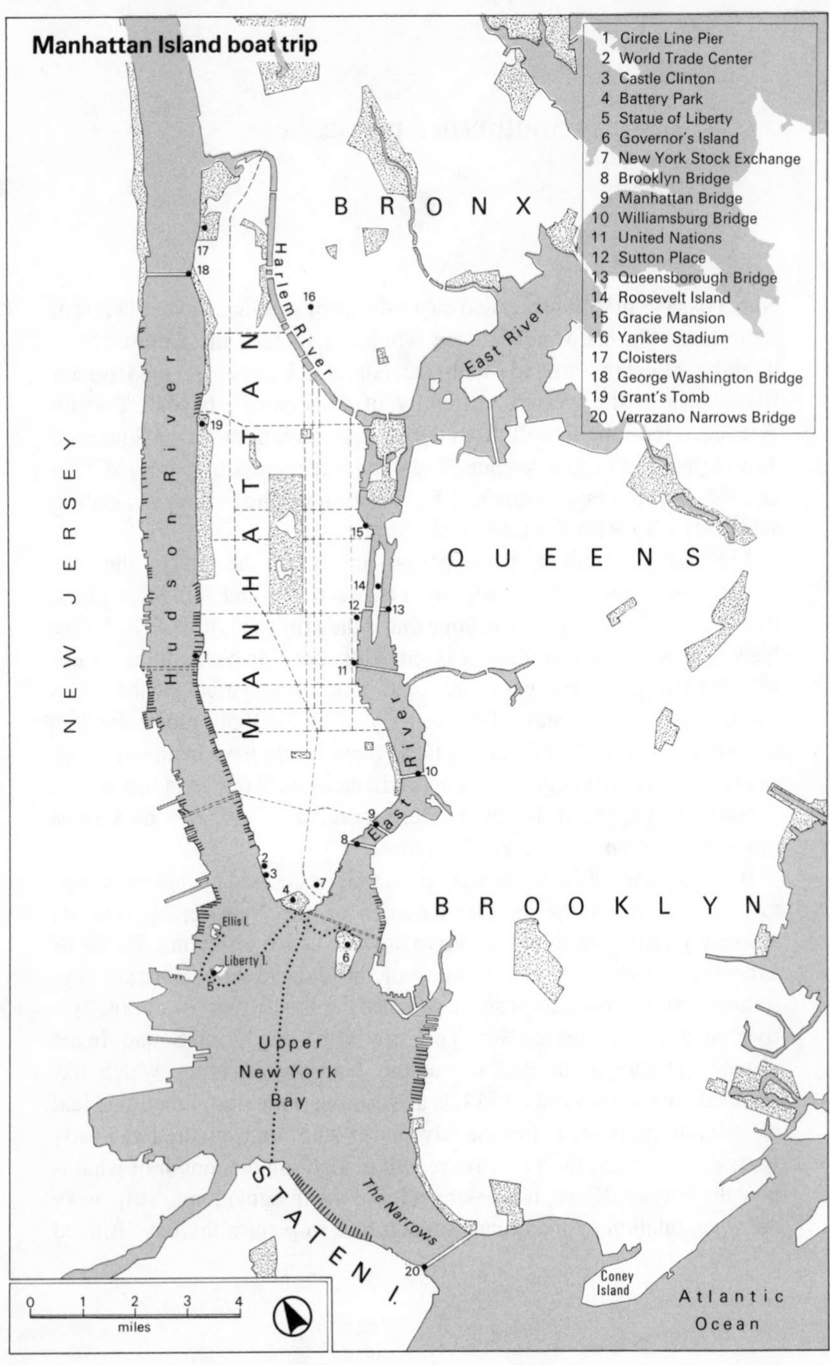
Manhattan Island boat trip
1 Circle Line Pier
2 World Trade Center
3 Castle Clinton
4 Battery Park
5 Statue of Liberty
6 Governor's Island
7 New York Stock Exchange
8 Brooklyn Bridge
9 Manhattan Bridge
10 Williamsburg Bridge
11 United Nations
12 Sutton Place
13 Queensborough Bridge
14 Roosevelt Island
15 Gracie Mansion
16 Yankee Stadium
17 Cloisters
18 George Washington Bridge
19 Grant's Tomb
20 Verrazano Narrows Bridge
BRONX
QUEENS
BROOKLYN
MANHATTAN
NEW JERSEY
Hudson River
Harlem River
East River
Ellis I.
Liberty I.
Upper New York Bay
The Narrows
STATEN I.
Coney Island
Atlantic Ocean
0 1 2 3 4
miles

with forests, as it was when Giovanni de Verrazano's sailing boat first nosed into it. He was a Florentine and, at the behest of King Francis I of France, was seeking the elusive Northwest Passage to the Orient. (Christopher Columbus, during his voyage thirty-two years earlier, had stayed farther south.) Verrazano described his discovery thus:

> We found a very agreeable situation located within two small prominent hills, in the midst of which flowed to the sea a very great river, which was deep within the mouth; and from the sea to the hills, with the rising of the tide, which we found eight feet, any laden ship might have passed. On account of being anchored off the coast in good shelter, we did not wish to adventure in without knowledge of the entrances.[1]*

They took small boats in, whereupon the natives,

> clothed with the feathers of birds of various colors, came toward us joyfully, uttering very great exclamations of admiration, showing us where we could land with the boat more safely. We entered said river, within the land, about half a league, where we saw it made a very beautiful lake with a circuit of about three leagues.

A gale forced the navigators back to their ship, 'leaving the said land with much regret because of its commodiousness and beauty, thinking it was not without some properties of value'.

That prescient observation did not provoke a headlong rush of European sailors. There are sketchy reports of other sorties into the harbor later in the sixteenth century, but the first voyage farther inland of which we have documentary evidence was undertaken in 1609 by Henry Hudson, an English explorer employed then by the Dutch East India Company. By penetrating as far as what is now Albany, and determining that the river did not, as he had hoped, link two great oceans, Hudson earned the right to have this important waterway named after him.

He sailed from Amsterdam in April in the *Half Moon,* only fifty-eight feet long and carrying a mixed Dutch and English crew of about twenty. Though instructed by his company to seek a north-east passage round the Arctic, he encountered thick ice and was persuaded by the disgruntled crew to switch to the warmer waters south and west. By mid-July they had

---

*Supernumerals in the text refer to the source notes at the back of the book.

reached the new continent and anchored off Maine. After a slow progress down the coast they pushed uncertainly into New York Bay on 3 September. 'This is a very good land to fall with,' wrote Robert Juet, Hudson's mate, 'and a pleasant land to see.' Yet Hudson did not linger. Having made quite cordial initial contact with the natives, he rushed up-river until the channel narrowed and the water became fresh, convincing him that there was no second outlet to the sea.

Returning to the mouth, he bartered with the natives for a quantity of furs, but in time relations became less friendly. According to Juet's log, the Indians tried to steal things and in the resulting skirmish several were killed. Having given the natives a foretaste of both the commercial advantages and social drawbacks of European civilization, Hudson sailed home, where he was reprimanded for having made his discovery under the aegis of the Dutch. Hudson agreed to go out on a new mission, this time flying the British flag. He reached Hudson's Bay where his crew, dismayed by the cold and doubting their skipper's ability as a navigator, mutinied. They put Hudson, his son and seven others in a small boat and cast it upon the open water, where they presumably froze to death.

The British were justified in their fear that Hudson's discovery had handed the Netherlands a commercial advantage, and the Dutch were not slow to exploit it. During the next five years other sailors set out from Holland and established the rudiments of a fur trading post on the river at the most northerly point Hudson had reached, calling it Fort Nassau. In 1624, four years after the Pilgrims had gone to Massachusetts, thirty families, one hundred and ten people altogether, left Holland to become New York's first settlers. Most established themselves at Fort Nassau, but eight families plumped for the island just south of Manhattan, called Nut Island because of the proliferation of chestnut and walnut trees: today it is **Governor's Island** and our tour boat is just passing it.

More families joined them, bringing a hundred head of livestock for which there was insufficient grazing on the island; so the settlement moved to the seemingly limitless expanse of Manhattan proper and came to be called New Amsterdam. In 1626 Peter Minuit was sent out as director-general of the settlement, which by then boasted a population of three hundred. He is best known for undertaking the first and most advantageous of the millions of land deals which have been executed in New York, buying Manhattan, the Indian name of the island, from a group of Indians for trinkets worth 60 guilders, then equivalent to about

Ellis Island immigration station, opened in 1892; after its closure in 1954 it was designated as a national monument and awaits restoration, although in the meantime it can be visited by tourists.

'Give me your tired, your poor,/Your huddled masses, yearning to breathe free . . . ' More than twenty million immigrants sailed by Bartholdi's Statue of Liberty in the forty years following its construction.

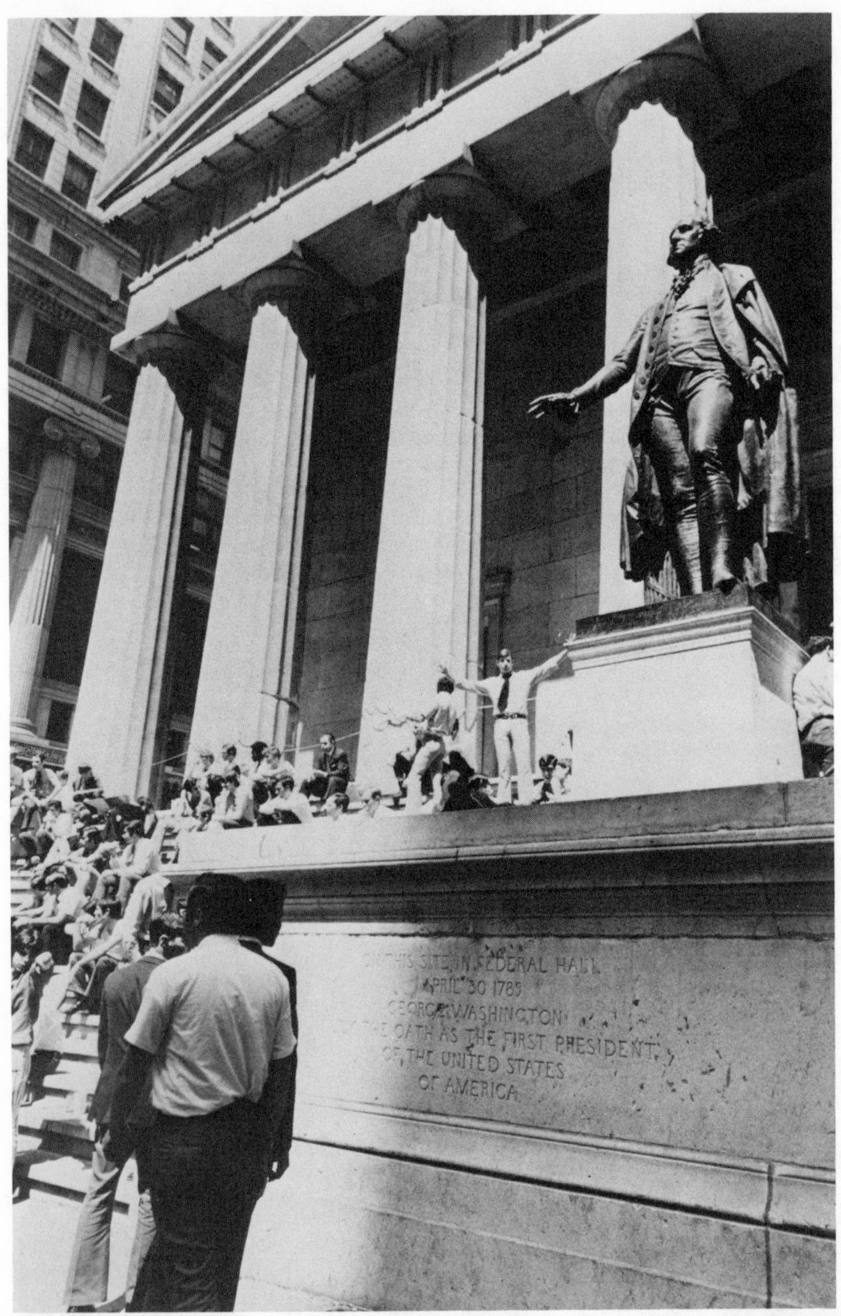

Federal Hall National Memorial and John Q. A. Ward's statue of George Washington, who took his oath of office here in 1789.

£15 ($24). In Manhattan real estate, however, nothing is as simple as it seems and it transpired that the group of Indians with whom he was dealing were not from Manhattan at all. One version of the story has the Dutch repurchasing the land from other Indians a few years later, though history is uncertain about this.

Minuit was succeeded by two incompetent and pettish administrators who engaged in wasteful and destructive wars against the Indians, until in 1647 the most colorful of the Dutch Governors, Peter Stuyvesant — 'Peg-Leg Pete' — came from Curaçao in the West Indies, bent on giving the now seven hundred colonists the tough administration they appeared to need. An irascible autocrat and part-time buccaneer who had lost his right leg in a fight with the Portuguese, Stuyvesant presided over the growth of his dominion until, by the end of his seventeen-year term, it had a population of fifteen hundred, a city charter and some reasonably solid buildings.

The town was dominated by a fort, crudely constructed of stone and earth, jutting into the sea on the site of what is now the old **Customs House**, south of Bowling Green. (The bulk of the land which now surrounds the Customs House to seaward is man-made landfill.) Near that, at the end of Whitehall Street, Stuyvesant had built his official residence and, in the rolling countryside two miles north, he established a farm, in Dutch a bouwerie, at the end of a road called, for that reason, the Bowery. The town had a town hall on Pearl Street, facing the harbor in the East River. A wall of nine-foot wooden stakes along present-day Wall Street marked the northern limit of the settlement. No trace remains of any of these structures.

The British, during much of this time, were preoccupied with the events surrounding their civil war, but they doggedly maintained their claim that all the east coast of North America, from New England to Virginia, was rightly theirs. In 1664 Charles II took it into his head to grant the territories round the Hudson to his brother the Duke of York, and sent Colonel Richard Nicolls out to claim them. Four warships sailed into the harbor and troops were landed on Nut Island and Long Island. The Dutch settlers had by then had their fill of Stuyvesant's tyranny, in particular his imposition of taxes and reluctance to grant effective home rule. They were resentful of the cavalier attitude of the Dutch West India Company, the notional owners of the colony. So, when Stuyvesant appealed for volunteers to defend Dutch rule, nobody responded. Colonel

Nicolls took over unopposed, became governor and named his dominion New York, honouring the duke. Stuyvesant returned to Holland to account for the loss; but he had become fond of the way of life in his bouwerie and returned. When he died in 1672 he left descendants who were to become pillars of New York's high society. The Dutch took over again in 1673 but their second chance lasted only just over a year and in 1674 New York began more than a century of British rule, ending after the revolution of 1776.

Our tour boat, of course, will not pause here for the sake of our history lesson, but the entrance to the East River is also the best spot to ponder New York's important role in the War of Independence. The battles in and around the city in 1776 cannot be said to have had a crucial effect on the outcome of the war, for they were won by the side that was eventually to lose. They were, all the same, the first military engagements between the British and the Americans after that year's Declaration of Independence. The British, driven from Boston the previous winter, resolved that New York would be the point at which they would re-assert their authority over the rebels. In June and July some two hundred ships under the command of Lord Howe arrived and anchored just outside the harbor, beyond where we now see the Verrazano Narrows Bridge. The troops set up camp on Staten Island. On 4 July, while the landings were in progress, the Declaration of Independence was signed, seeming to rule out compromise. Washington hoped that the mouth of the harbor was sufficiently well defended to prevent the British ships from entering it, but Howe managed with some ease to send two frigates up the Hudson to moor north of the city.

Still, the bulk of the fleet remained off Staten Island and Howe decided to make his assault on the city by land. On 22 August he landed fifteen thousand men, nearly half of them Hessian mercenaries, at Gravesend Bay in the south-west corner of Brooklyn. His plan was to occupy Brooklyn and launch his attack on Manhattan from there. The key to this strategy was Brooklyn Heights, the high ground fringed with a tree-lined promenade which we can see just south of **Brooklyn Bridge**.

The action is known as the Battle of Long Island, although it was played out entirely in the present-day borough of Brooklyn. Howe's men penetrated the American forward lines at a number of points, and one important engagement took place in what is now Prospect Park. The Americans fell back to prepared positions between Gowanus Bay and

Wallabout Bay, roughly the stretch of Brooklyn closest to our right as the boat rounds the tip of Manhattan. As the British made preparations to attack the fortifications, Washington could see that his garrison would be outnumbered and defeated. On the night of August 29, under cover of fortuitous rain and fog, he evacuated his men safely to Manhattan from the ferry slip beneath where Brooklyn Bridge now makes its Brooklyn landfall. The fact that he managed to preserve the bulk of his army meant that Washington was later able, when the fortunes of war changed, to defeat the British.

While awaiting the British assault on Manhattan, the Americans took time to launch an ingenious invention which, while having no effect on the outcome of the war, was more than a century ahead of its time. David Bushnell, a Yale graduate, designed and built the world's first submarine, a curious, wooden, hand-cranked craft with a crew of one. One September night it was launched from the end of Whitehall Street on Lower Manhattan. The object was to cross the harbor unseen and to fix an explosive device to one of the British warships off Staten Island. The pilot, Ezra Lee, reached the fleet successfully but the bomb would not stick and he jettisoned it. Returning, his compass failed and he had to surface to find his way back. He avoided capture and landed safely at the Battery.

A few days later Lord Howe's army set out in boats from Green Point and Newtown Creek in Brooklyn, north of the Williamsburg Bridge, the most northerly of the trio now linking Brooklyn with Lower Manhattan. They landed in Manhattan at the foot of 34th Street, today the site of a heliport, a few blocks north of **Waterside Plaza**, the prominent and imaginative brick apartment tower built in the 1970s on a platform of landfill. The defenders of the city retreated north to make their stand at Harlem Heights, between the Harlem and Hudson Rivers, which we shall pass later.

Meanwhile we switch abruptly to modern times and away from warfare to what many hope serves as a substitute for it. On our left we pass the slender box of the **United Nations** secretariat, and beyond it the General Assembly building with its dish-shaped roof, which helped establish the idiom of post-war architecture. The green glass skyscraper just behind them is of the 1970s and houses the UN Plaza Hotel. Next to it, **Tudor City** is a strange complex of the 1920s in which replicas of Elizabethan manor houses were plonked atop tall, vaguely Gothic brick towers. The boat ride affords an unequalled chance to see the bizarre things New York architects have thought appropriate for the roofs of their creations, from the replica of a 1929 Chrysler radiator cap on the Chrysler Building to water towers disguised as Italianate turrets on some West Side apartments. A few have full-scale roof gardens with mature trees: you will notice some in **Sutton Place**, the exclusive residential area just north of the UN, where you can watch out also for a charming row of nineteenth-century town houses.

On the right of the boat now, as we shoot **Queensborough Bridge**, we can see the 1970s apartments on **Roosevelt Island**. This was once Welfare Island, the site of city jails, hospitals and lunatic asylums. Two hospitals remain but in the island's mid-section are four new apartment buildings with a distinctive stepped profile to allow most inhabitants river views. The island is linked to Manhattan by an overhead cable car called an aerial tramway.

Our guide is providing an accurate reflection of New York preoccupations — chiefly about fame and money — by feeding us masses of facts: names of the celebrities who live in this or that building and, in a tone of awe and disbelief, the rents that are paid. 'How much do you think it costs to play there?' she asks rhetorically as we pass some indoor tennis courts. 'Twenty dollars for a half-hour. Hits you right there, doesn't it?'

On our left, nearly opposite the lighthouse on Roosevelt Island's tip, we get an excellent sight of **Gracie Mansion**, the 1799 country seat built for Archibald Gracie, a wealthy shipowner, and now the official home of New York's mayor. In a while we go under **Triborough Bridge**, linking Manhattan with the Bronx and Queens, then fork left up the **Harlem River**, glimpsing an edge of the East Harlem slums.

We are approaching what I regard as the highlight of the trip. As our boat passes under a road bridge carrying the Henry Hudson Parkway north to Westchester, a low railway bridge swings aside to let us back into the Hudson. Looking north, the river broadens between wooded cliffs: this, at last, is close to what Henry Hudson and his crew must have seen on that path-finding voyage. Imagine the excitement they felt as they sailed up towards the Tappan Zee — the river's widest point and surely the beginning of the Northwest Passage which would assure the prosperity of the Netherlands and thus of themselves.

Our boat turns away, though, back past the transplanted medieval

Cloisters and under the tremendous **George Washington Bridge**. On the high ground on either side of the bridge two forts — Fort Lee on the New Jersey side and Fort Washington on the Manhattan side — were the last strongholds of the American defending forces before they ceded all of New York to Howe's invaders in November 1776, three months after the initial landing in Brooklyn. We left Howe's troops earlier marching north up Manhattan's East Side. They defeated Washington's army at Harlem Heights (on our left just south of the bridge), then marched north to another victory at White Plains in Westchester County, before turning south again to enter New Jersey at Fort Lee. Washington was less prudent at Fort Washington than he had been in Brooklyn: by failing to evacuate in time he lost nearly three thousand men, most taken prisoner. It was the low point of American fortunes in the war and they never retook New York militarily. In November 1783, after the signing of the peace treaty, the British sailed away ignominiously from Staten Island — the route by which they had arrived seven years earlier.

Our boat now passes **Grant's Tomb**, monument to a later military success, then the aging apartment houses of the Upper West Side, staring disdainfully at the newer luxury condominiums of New Jersey on the Palisades opposite. We pass the modern passenger terminal on our left where, if it is a weekend, we may see a few cruise liners getting up steam to take their passengers to the warm waters of the Caribbean. Three hours after it began, our own voyage ends back at West 43rd Street; but before we start our exploration on foot, I want to suggest three more short trips by water, that serve to sketch aspects of New York's history of which few traces remain on Manhattan itself. All of them begin from the southern end of Manhattan, a short walk from Bowling Green station on the Lexington Avenue subway. Whitehall Street and South Ferry, on different subway routes, are also close at hand.

Governor's Island

No Dutch building remains on Lower Manhattan and there is precious little trace even of the British colonial period. The most substantial memento of the British is on Governor's Island but to visit it involves some advance preparation. Formerly a military garrison and prison, it has since 1966 been occupied by the US Coast Guard and you must write to the Commanding Officer of USCG Support Center, Governor's Island,

New York, N.Y. 10004, asking for a permit. It is one of the few spots in New York which still relies on the water for its communications with the world at large. There are tours for visitors from April to October or, if you can convince them of your particular interest, the Coast Guard will authorize you to visit at your convenience. If you are in New York for more than a few days it might be worth the trouble to go through this routine for, although it is only a ten-minute ferry ride from the city, a half-day's outing there does offer a complete change of scene and pace. Access is by Coast Guard ferry from the green pier to the left of the Staten Island ferry terminal at the end of Whitehall Street. The ferry is free, but visitors must show their letter of authorization before being allowed to board. The pier, now mouldering, was erected in 1906, in a style which was familiar in the days when ferries to Brooklyn and New Jersey abounded. Straw-colored Guavaschino tiles line the roof of the porch, the same style as those on Ellis Island and at the Oyster Bar in Grand Central Station: evidence that this terminal has seen grander days.

The part of chief interest is just south of where the ferry docks, past the cannon with the British royal insignia that points menacingly at Wall Street. Three of the island's oldest houses stand with their backs to Brooklyn Bridge, their entrances grouped around a pleasant village green dotted with trees and flower beds. The oldest is the **Governor's House**, built for the British governors about 1708. In spite of many subsequent alterations, which have spoiled the balance of the seaward façade, the house has kept its essential character as a Georgian brick country home of modest size and little presumption, in keeping with the small scale of the colony which its occupant then had to administer. Next door is the **Dutch House**, an early nineteenth-century replica of the traditional stepped gabled dwellings the early colonists put up on Manhattan. Next to that is the largest of the group, the **Admiral's House**, built in 1840 with tall Doric columns, stretching two storeys, at its front and rear. When the island was an army garrison its commanding officers — who included Generals Bradley and Pershing — lived in it. At the southern end of the green is the **Block House**, a sober Greek Revival building of 1840 which may owe its severity to the fact that it served as a prison.

North of the green, the golf course is built around **Fort Jay**, whose dry moat forms what must be one of the strangest bunkers in the game. Fort Jay was completed, largely by the volunteer labor of students and others, in 1798, to deter any attempt by Britain to re-take its former colony. Its star-shaped plan was based on the latest French military theories, and there is something Gallic, too, about the heroic sculpture of war-like objects on top of the entrance. A couple of hundred yards to the north-west is another defensive fortification, **Castle Williams**, built in 1811 along with the almost-matching Castle Clinton, across a quarter of a mile of water on the edge of Battery Park, which we shall visit later in this chapter. Castle Williams was used as a military prison from 1912–66. If the gate is open you can climb past the abandoned cells to the promenade on top, where one massive cannon remains and from where there are excellent views of Lower Manhattan, Ellis Island and the Statue of Liberty.

Statue of Liberty and Ellis Island

To understand New York and most other large eastern American cities you have to recognize how much of their present-day character can be attributed to the extraordinary influx of disparate peoples from Europe between 1850 and 1921. I do not mean simply the surface manifestations of a polyglot culture — munching a pastrami sandwich in an Irish bar, washing down a slice of pizza with a glass of beer with a German name. The broader, less tangible attributes of New York's life, the extraordinary intellectual and commercial vitality, the constant drive towards self-improvement and providing for the children a better life than their parents enjoyed — these are immigrant qualities.

The next two waterborne excursions are run by the Circle Line and tickets are obtainable at their booth on the southern edge of Battery Park, west of the Staten Island Ferry pier. The cost of the round trip to both the Statue of Liberty and the Ellis Island immigration station is $1.50, children half-price. Boats for the statue leave every hour on the hour, more frequently on summer weekends. Ellis Island boats leave four times a day and the island is closed altogether from end-October to end-April. You could certainly make both trips on the same day and could even squeeze them in with a Governor's Island excursion, but if you have time it is better to space them for the sake of variety. Phone 269-5755 for the exact timings. For those on a very tight schedule, a glimpse of all these maritime monuments may be had from the Staten Island Ferry, a forty-five-minute return journey.

It is hard to tell the immigration story without descending into sentimentality for it is one which, despite constant retelling, loses none of its power to move. The **Statue of Liberty**, the first landmark seen by those immigrants who came after its completion in 1886, impresses both by its size (305 feet high) and by the simple power of Frederic Auguste Bartholdi's conception of liberty escaping from shackles and holding a beacon to enlighten the world. Few write about it without quoting from Emma Lazarus's poetic tribute 'The New Colossus', inscribed in bronze inside the pedestal:

'Keep, ancient lands, your storied pomp!' cries she
With silent lips. 'Give me your tired, your poor,
Your huddled masses yearning to breathe free,
The wretched refuse of your teeming shore.
Send these, the homeless, tempest-tost to me,
I lift my lamp beside the golden door.'

That this sentiment was not always reflected in the reception given to immigrants cannot detract from the truth that more than twenty million of them sailed under the statue in the forty years following its construction, and were offered the chance, which most of them grabbed eagerly, of beginning life anew in America.

The statue was a gift from France, a nation never among the largest sources of immigrants but which sympathized with the American experiment. The sympathy took its most practical form in the military assistance given to George Washington by the Marquis de Lafayette, helping him recover from the early setbacks. A group of enterprising and enthusiastic Frenchmen including Bartholdi, a monumental sculptor, decided to present the statue to commemorate the centenary of the American Revolution, raising the money through an appeal to the French people. Getting the statue built and erected was a slow process. In 1876 its right arm, carrying the torch, was shipped to Philadelphia for a centennial exhibition and the following year came to New York, where it was exhibited in Madison Square Park for seven years. Though the statue had been completed, it proved hard to raise the money needed to furnish it with a base from skeptical Americans. This was finally obtained through a vigorous campaign by the *New York World,* then America's largest newspaper, owned by Joseph Pulitzer, himself an immigrant from Hungary and a fervent supporter of the statue. The campaign raised the necessary $100,000, eighty per cent of it in contributions of less than a dollar. In October 1886 the statue was unveiled in pouring rain by Bartholdi, in the presence of President Grover Cleveland, on Bedloe's Island, named for its first Dutch owner, Isaac Bedloo.

The base was designed by the architect Richard Morris Hunt, and although it is in no sense his masterwork it is appropriate that we should meet him thus early in our visit, because he exercised a profound influence on the architecture we shall be looking at in succeeding chapters. In the 1850s he became the first American student at the École des Beaux Arts in Paris. Returning to New York in 1858, at the age of thirty-one, he established a studio and took pupils, among them George Post, who was to design the New York Stock Exchange and other important commercial buildings. Hunt did much to establish the Beaux Arts neo-classical style as the idiom in which a rapidly burgeoning America expressed itself; his specialty was private houses, the most famous of them the elaborate mansion he concocted for the Vanderbilts on Fifth Avenue, now demolished. His best surviving work in New York is the stately Fifth Avenue front of the Metropolitan Museum of Art. He was one of the architects of the 1893 Columbia Exposition in Chicago, which confirmed the ascendancy of the Beaux Arts style — a fine vindication of his life's work just two years before his death.

In 1972 the **American Museum of Immigration** was opened around the Statue of Liberty's base. It is one of those museums which uses audio-visual displays to illustrate the history of immigration, from the Dutch and onwards, and to convey something of the experience of being an immigrant. The thorough presentation includes some explanation of the misfortunes and persecution in Europe which drove the millions to seek refuge here, as well as specific displays illustrating the culture of the groups of immigrants and maps depicting where in America they settled and how they got there. It does not stop at 1921, when the introduction of a quota system stemmed the immigrant flood, but goes up to the present day, when new Americans come from Asia as much as from Europe.

Apart from seeing the museum, visitors can climb inside the statue to its crown and peer over the harbor. An elevator takes you to the top of the pedestal, which itself commands some fine views, and then you must walk up a narrow staircase to the top. I have never been there when there was not a long and slow line waiting to do the second climb, and I suggest that if you are determined to do it you take an early boat out — say 9 a.m. — on a weekday. (The staircase inside the arm, leading to the gallery on top of the torch, has been closed since 1916. And the whole statue will close for some months in 1984 for renovation.)

The Museum of Immigration gives a full account of conditions on **Ellis Island**, the main clearing house for immigrants between 1892 and 1924. The island, named after an eighteenth-century farmer who owned it, is a half-mile north of the Statue of Liberty. Its low red-brick and stucco buildings, in a late Victorian institutional style with four tall towers crowned by curious white domes, are visible from many points in the harbor.

However much you read or hear about Ellis Island, nothing can substitute for the experience of actually wandering through the buildings which introduced America to millions of people. Clean-limbed young guides from the National Parks Service meet the ferry boats and take visitors on a tour of the cavernous halls and corridors, giving a scrupulously objective account of what happened to the immigrants.

The place was invariably crowded and bewildering. New arrivals, most speaking no English and many dressed in peasant clothes from their native countries, dragged their bundles of possessions from line to line as they faced relays of overworked and often short-tempered officials. They were checked for poor health (their eyelids lifted with buttonhooks in the search for signs of trachoma), asked to show the money with which they could support themselves, questioned about any relatives they had in America and where they were going to stay. It was dubbed by the immigrants 'the Isle of Tears' and there were quantities of those, as friends and relatives were sought in the confusion, as officials raised difficulties serious enough to have the immigrants detained overnight, as corrupt money changers swindled them out of their meagre savings and a they were fed for the first time with unfamiliar, sometimes unpalatable American food.

The following first-hand account of conditions, a letter signed by a hundred detained immigrants, mostly Russian Jews, was printed in 1909 in the *Jewish Daily Forward*, the leading Yiddish newspaper. Many of the detainees were deserters from the Russian army or political refugees, threatened with repatriation because they did not have the $25 which the authorities insisted was the minimum means an immigrant must possess:

> It is impossible [they wrote] to describe all that is taking place here, but we want to convey at least a little of it. We are packed into a room where there is space for 200 people, but they have crammed in about a thousand. They don't let us out into the yard for a little fresh air. We lie about on the floor in the spittle and filth. We're wearing the same shirts for three or four weeks, because we don't have our baggage with us. Everyone goes around dejected and cries and wails. Women with little babies, who have come to their husbands, are being detained. Who can stand this suffering?[2]

The letter added that many of the detainees would jump into the harbor rather than board a ship for home.

Yet despite all the heart-rending stories, eighty per cent of immigrants were cleared through Ellis Island in three or four hours and in the end only two per cent were sent back to Europe. The remainder, with enormous relief, followed the passage signposted 'To New York', the remains of which are still at the Ellis Island jetty, crumbling into the water, to board the Manhattan ferry.

A few 'props' — luggage trolleys, doctors' cabinets, dirty crockery and broken desks — are scattered through the rooms of the building but they are mostly empty, paint peeling from the walls and ceilings, awaiting the restoration which will be undertaken if the Federal Government decide they can afford it.

Castle Clinton and P.T. Barnum

To round out your glimpse of the great immigration, when you leave the Ellis Island ferry at its Manhattan terminal in Battery Park walk a few yards north along the Battery promenade — so called because it was here that the cannons used to stand to repel invaders. The low round building, matching Castle Williams on Governor's Island, is **Castle Clinton.** Abandoned as a fort, this preceded Ellis Island as the immigrant clearing centre: then it had a roof and a number of outbuildings. Seven million immigrants were processed there before the flow became too heavy and the Ellis Island facility had to be built. Today Castle Clinton has been restored to something like its appearance when a fort, although in those days it stood off the shore, connected to the Battery by a low bridge. All around Manhattan's lower tip, the original shore line was more than two hundred yards back from where it is now. Space has always been at a premium there, and during the eighteenth and nineteenth centuries it was several times extended by landfill.

Before it became an immigration station Castle Clinton, then called Castle Garden, was New York's largest public arena and theatre. Its most notable occasion was the appearance in 1850 of Jenny Lind, 'the Swedish nightingale', whose visit was so successfully promoted by Phineas T. Barnum, the supreme showman, that tickets were bought for as much as $225. (As we tour the sights of New York I shall pause from time to time to offer thumbnail sketches of people significant in the city's development or who personify an aspect of its character. It is entirely appropriate that I should begin with Barnum, because showmanship, show business and individual acumen are vital parts of the mix that makes New York the city it is.) In 1851 an English visitor, John Delaware Lewis, wrote: 'Barnum is a representative man. He represents the enterprise and energy of his countrymen in the nineteenth century, as Washington represented their resistance to oppression in the century preceding.'[3]

Barnum was born in Connecticut in 1810, the descendant of an early New England settler. In 1835 he moved to New York, where he began a career as a promoter of curious and scarcely believable phenomena, for which the appetite of Americans seemed insatiable. In 1842 he bought the American Museum on the corner of Broadway and Ann Street. Because conventional theatres suffered under a scabrous reputation, 'lecture halls', attached to museums, would provide respectable cover for variety entertainment of the sort nowadays seen in circuses. Barnum scouted for fresh sensations to fill the museum and to perform at the lecture hall. He presented a troop of wild Indians; he exhibited the corpse of a 'mermaid'; most fabulous of all, he found a five-year-old boy in Connecticut who was only two feet high, switched his birthplace to England, doubled his age to make his size seem the more remarkable and changed his name to Colonel Tom Thumb. People queued to see him at the museum, on tours of eastern cities, and later in Europe.

His fame now established, Barnum sought other peaks to conquer and in 1849 he conceived the idea of bringing to America Jenny Lind, the Swedish soprano who had become the most celebrated singer in Europe. Throughout the 1840s entrepreneurs had brought European artists across the Atlantic to spread culture to a nation lacking much of its own. This was the most ambitious and expensive of such promotions. To lure Miss Lind Barnum had to put up $187,500 and deposit it in a European bank in advance.

Like most successful purveyors of popular entertainment and journalism, Barnum had a low opinion of the intellect and cultural tastes of the mass audience. 'There is,' he would say, 'a sucker born every minute.' To protect his investment he set out to promote Miss Lind's appearances as, in today's jargon, a 'media happening' rather than simply as a musical treat. The newspapers co-operated eagerly — after all, sensation was their business too. Tens of thousands of people turned out to welcome Jenny Lind's ship steaming into the harbor. She was garlanded and serenaded. The crowds followed her to her hotel on Lower Broadway, where they insisted she appear on the balcony. The correspondent for *The Times* of London analysed what motivated the enthusiasm: 'They cannot help being proud of their city, of their visitor, of themselves and of their singular good taste.'

Came the morning of the concert, 11 September 1850, and the press was aquiver with excitement, each newspaper trying to outdo the next in the extravagance of their speculation about the treat in store for the lucky seven thousand at Castle Garden. For a time it seemed as though Miss Lind would not be able to begin. As she stepped on to the stage, wearing white, facing a display of flowers spelling the message 'Welcome Sweet Warbler', the applause was tumultuous and nearly interminable. When it did subside Miss Lind was so nervous that her first notes were distinctly wobbly, but she survived that false start, as well as an attempt by water-borne invaders to break into the Castle Garden while she was singing.

The show was the anticipated huge success and Miss Lind's fame grew to legend. As for Barnum, he continued to thrill New Yorkers with fresh attractions at his museum until it burned down in 1865, was rebuilt, and burned down again three years later. He was elected to the Connecticut assembly but defeated for Congress in Washington. He became the first operator of the original Madison Square Garden arena — a converted railway terminal — and with James A. Bailey started the Barnum and Bailey circus, 'The Greatest Show on Earth', which years later merged with the Ringling Brothers circus and still visits New York every spring, at the new Madison Square Garden on Eighth Avenue and 32nd Street. He died at the age of eighty-one, but the spirited promotional techniques he perfected live on in countless over-excitable advertisements, in the press and on television, for films, shows, sports events and even clothes and food. They help oil the wheels of high finance, whose engine we shall examine as we walk through Wall Street in the next chapter.

3
The Financial District

MONEY IS THE THEME of this chapter so it is logical to start at the **New York Stock Exchange**, the hub of the capitalist world. The exchange, on Wall Street between New and Broad Streets, is a short step from any of the Wall Street subway stations. The visitors' gallery and a small explanatory exhibition area adjoining it are open during trading hours. Admission is free. The entrance is on the Broad Street side of the building, in the modern extension to the left of the formal pediment above the Roman columns designed by George Post in 1903. Post was a pupil of Richard Morris Hunt, the father of the American Beaux Arts style. Unlike his mentor, Post specialized in commercial buildings, giving them the dignity demanded by the entrepreneurs of the day. His most pleasing work is the red-brick headquarters of the Long Island Historical Association in Brooklyn Heights, and later in this walk we shall see his Cotton Exchange on Hanover Square.

Here at the Stock Exchange the figures on the pediment (reinforced in metal when the marble began to crumble) are an idealized tribute to American commerce and industry, the toil at the root of the profits which allow stock trading to prosper. They represent various kinds of industrial undertaking: the two crouching burrowers on the right are miners, and so on. In the middle, her arms reaching forward to spread her benign influence over all she surveys, is the allegorical figure of integrity. As we shall see, her arms have not always spread far enough. Throughout the years, integrity has from time to time been in notably short supply among some who have sought their fortune here.

Despite the introduction of computerization, the scene on the trading floor is generally one of unmitigated frenzy. Dealers rush from pillar to post, trying to get the crucial quarter of a cent advantage on the millions of dollars' worth of stocks they are bartering. It is unedifying and, towards the end of the afternoon, scruffy, as the brokers and their clothes get ruffled, their nerves frayed. Scraps of paper pile up on the floor around

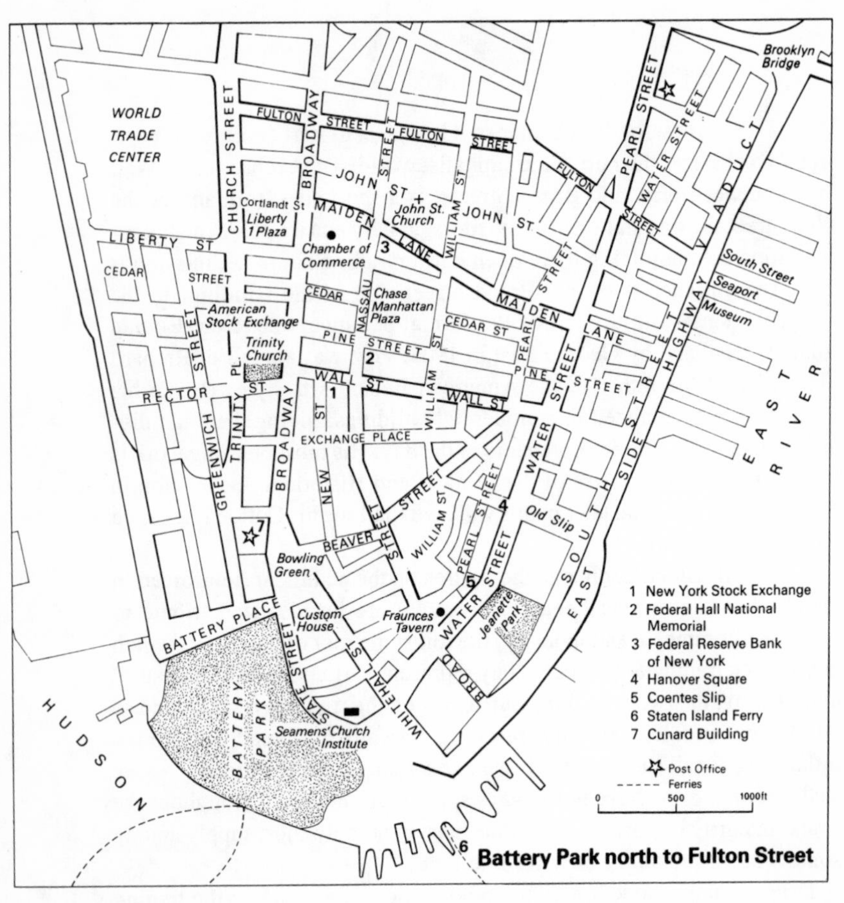
WORLD TRADE CENTER
CHURCH STREET
FULTON STREET
BROADWAY
JOHN ST
MAIDEN LANE
WILLIAM ST
Cortlandt St
Liberty 1 Plaza
LIBERTY ST
Chamber of Commerce
John St. Church
CEDAR
STREET
American Stock Exchange
Chase Manhattan Plaza
NASSAU
CEDAR ST
PINE STREET
Trinity Church
TRINITY PL.
RECTOR ST.
GREENWICH STREET
WALL ST
EXCHANGE PLACE
NEW ST
BEAVER STREET
Bowling Green
PEARL STREET
WATER STREET
Old Slip
FULTON
Brooklyn Bridge
South Street Seaport Museum
SOUTH STREET VIADUCT
EAST SIDE HIGHWAY
SOUTH STREET
EAST RIVER
BATTERY PLACE
Custom House
STATE STREET
Fraunces Tavern
WHITEHALL ST
BROAD
Jeanette Park
BATTERY PARK
Seamens' Church Institute
HUDSON
1 New York Stock Exchange
2 Federal Hall National Memorial
3 Federal Reserve Bank of New York
4 Hanover Square
5 Coentes Slip
6 Staten Island Ferry
7 Cunard Building
Post Office
Ferries
0
500
1000ft

Battery Park north to Fulton Street

them. It has the virtue of truth, an accurate portrayal of the way commerce is conducted. Success goes to the swiftest, the slickest and the most single-minded, the one best at cutting corners, catching influential eyes and striking deals.

Defenders of the system claim that big business and finance have been cleaned up since the rip-roaring days of the nineteenth and early twentieth centuries, when swindles, panics and collapses brought quick ruin to the unlucky or gullible, and instant wealth to the unscrupulous. Nowadays, they say, probity is the rule, the quality most generously rewarded. This, at least, seemed to be the intention of the stock dealers who formed the exchange in 1792 by signing the Buttonwood Agreement, named after the tree, long since disappeared, at the eastern end of Wall Street beneath which they used to sit to carry out their transactions.

Between then and now scores of entrepreneurs have been able to manipulate the system for their own profit, proving the truth of P. T. Barnum's dictum about suckers. Two of the most notorious swindlers were the ascetic Jay Gould and the playboy Jim Fisk. Gould began his manipulative career, and claimed his first victim, before he reached twenty-one. He went into partnership with one James Luepp in the ownership of a Pennsylvania tannery. Luepp was content to let Gould run things until, too late, he discovered him using the tannery's money for speculations on the stock market, all lost in the crash of 1857. Luepp, ruined, shot himself, but Gould went on to profit richly from the Civil War, when he was able to anticipate the rise and fall of the market by having the results of critical military engagements cabled to him before they were public knowledge.

It was then that he met Jim Fisk, a gregarious operator who had also made money from the war. The two decided that railways were going to be the basis of great fortunes and joined Daniel Drew — a comparatively inexpert crook, later one of their victims — on the board of the Erie Railroad. Never frightened of taking on the financial giants, the three engaged in a rough tussle for control of the railroad with the mighty 'Commodore' Cornelius Vanderbilt, a collector of railways trying to gain a monopoly of transport between the east coast and the midwest. The Erie, which went as far as Buffalo, was a rival route to Vanderbilt's New York Central. They inflicted a rare defeat on the Commodore by issuing ten million dollars' of Erie bonds which the eager Vanderbilt kept buying, while the price dropped. Vanderbilt spent eight million dollars on the bonds until, realizing he was being taken in, he had one of his tame judges issue a warrant against Fisk, Gould and Drew. Drew eventually made a separate peace with Vanderbilt, whereupon Fisk and Gould punished their former partner by engaging in a stock manipulation against him. This provoked Drew to say of Gould: 'His touch is death', while the defeated Vanderbilt paid the enormous compliment of naming him 'the smartest man in America'.

In 1869 Gould and Fisk began buying gold, trying to corner the whole American market. As they bought, the price rose, but their ultimate success depended on whether President Ulysses Grant and his Treasury Secretary would authorize the release of new government gold. If they did so while Fisk and Gould kept their holdings, the value would fall and they would sustain losses. The two buccaneers worked to prevent this by bribing Treasury officials. As the conviction spread that Grant would not authorize the release of government gold, the price soared. Finally Grant did release the gold. Naturally, Gould was able to learn of the plan in advance, unloading his holdings as the price was still rising. When it fell, Gould had made another fortune and in the crash of 'Black Friday' thousands of small speculators were destroyed. One of his victims, James Keene, called him 'the worst man on earth since the beginning of the Christian era'.[4] When Gould died in 1892, aged fifty-six, *The New York Times* wrote: 'Jay Gould was an operator pure and simple, although he was as far as possible from pure and as far as possible from simple.'

The last big stock market panic, the great crash of October 1929, was caused not by the manipulation of any cunning entrepreneur but by a fit of collective greed, incaution and unwisdom. In the expansive boom days of the early 1920s, Wall Street came to be seen as a route to certain riches. Speculators could buy stocks on margin, which means they would have to put up only a small amount of the required money, borrowing the rest (often from the brokers themselves), using the stocks as security. So long as the market kept rising it worked a treat: investors could pay off the loan interest with dividends and see the capital value of their stocks appreciate. When prices fell, though, they had to find more money to make up for the drop in value of the collateral. This meant they had to sell their stocks at a loss, until panic set in and prices dropped disastrously. Thousands saw their fortunes vanish in days. In his sardonic book *The Great Crash 1929*[5] Professor John Kenneth Galbraith delivers his judgment on those who would maintain that the Stock Exchange is a repository of financial responsibility:

> Wall Street, in these matters, is like a lovely and accomplished woman who must wear black cotton stockings, heavy woollen underwear, and parade her knowledge as a cook because, unhappily, her supreme accomplishment is as a harlot.

There have been market booms and slumps since 1929, but nothing on the same scale. Defenders of the system say a recurrence is impossible because the Federal Reserve Board now has the power to fix margin rates, to say how large a proportion (up to a hundred per cent) of the price of their stocks investors must put up as cash. The Securities and Exchange Commission was created in the 1930s as an extra regulator. All the same, Galbraith would find his colorful simile well borne out were he today to repair to the visitors' gallery of the Stock Exchange, where none of this scandalous history is retailed. Instead, we get an informative but self-righteous account of how the market works, of its contribution to the American economy and way of life. I cannot truly recommend that you bother to spend the fifteen minutes to sit through the film at the 'Experience Theater', where two winsome co-hosts explain capitalism in terms that might seem excessively folksy even to a class of ten-year-olds. I should have preferred a racy account of Gould and the other swindlers, the panics, the crashes and the booms. The souvenir shop sells ties and headscarves with bulls and bears on them, ashtrays printed with stock lists, and money clips.

Now back to Wall Street. This marks the line of the wooden stockade the Dutch built at the northern border of their settlement. Wall Street now is a dark, narrow gulley between tall skyscrapers, most of them grimy and dull, respectable fronts for sometimes suspect enterprises. Look west to where the black spire of Trinity Church stands framed between the tall buildings, symbolizing poignantly the admirable facility with which man is able to reconcile the demands of God and Mammon. To the east, the street rather fizzles out in some dull modern skyscrapers. Look at the people, sharp businessmen and lawyers, rushing to catch something or other, their secretaries carrying emergency supplies of coffee and cake in brown paper bags. Outside the Stock Exchange messengers loaf, in their breaks from duty, discussing what? The bull market in copper futures or the latest baseball scores?

The building on Wall Street that stands out from the rest, for its incompatibility as much as its architectural quality, is the **Federal Hall National Memorial**, across from the Stock Exchange. Squat and ungainly in its present-day context, the Doric columns in front indicate its origin in the heyday of the Greek Revival movement. Built in 1842 as the Customs House, it was later used as the headquarters of the Federal Reserve Bank. A statue of George Washington dominates the steps leading to the entrance, sharing them on fine days with office workers and itinerants taking advantage of one of the few places to sit down in the immediate vicinity.

The exhibits inside relate chiefly to the history of the previous building on the site. A city hall was put there in 1699, the scene of several anti-British demonstrations before the Revolution. It was remodelled as Federal Hall in 1788, when it was thought that New York would be the federal capital. George Washington took his oath of office as America's first president on the balcony on 30 April 1789. After the British sailed away from Staten Island Washington hoped he would be able to resume life as a farmer at Mount Vernon, Virginia. 'I am not only retired from all public employments,' he wrote in a letter in 1784, 'but I am retiring within myself.' Yet in the next few years, as the need for a new form of government to cement the victorious nation became apparent, Washington was sucked into the constitutional discussion. As America's most prominent — indeed almost its only — national hero, it was natural that his support for, and eventually his participation in, the new constitutional initiative should be sought. In 1787 he went to the constitutional convention in Philadelphia and was chosen its president. The new constitution allowed for an elected national president. In succeeding months, as it was gradually and in some cases painfully being ratified by the states, people came to accept that Washington would be the first to hold the office.

In April of 1789 he rode from Mount Vernon to New York for his inauguration, a ride which took him eight days, because at every town and village on the route large crowds turned out to fete him. Thousands lined Murray's Wharf, at the east end of Wall Street, to greet him as he stood in the specially made ceremonial barge bringing him to the jetty from Elizabeth Town in New Jersey. A vivid contemporary account of his arrival is given in the letter written by Dr. James Cogswell and published in the *Historical Magazine* of August 1860:

> The general's barge had an awning hung round with red morene curtains, festooned. It was attended with the New Haven and Rhode Island packets and a number of boats and barges decorated in the most beautiful manner. From the Battery to the Coffee House, where the General landed, the ships, docks and houses were crowded with people as thick as they could stand. The guns of the Battery were fired as soon as the General passed, and all the people upon the Battery gave three huzzas. The cheers were continued along the Battery unto the place of landing, as the barge passed . . . The successive motion of the hats from the Battery to the Coffee House, was like the rolling motion of the sea, or a field of grain waving with the wind when the sun is frequently intercepted with a cloud. A pair of elegant stairs, with the sides covered and carpeted, were erected to land the General safe upon the dock. Immediately upon his landing, thirteen guns were fired from the dock, and the whole city rung with repeated huzzas.[6]

Washington, dressed in blue, took part in a parade along the downtown streets, where he was cheered to the echo and sometimes wept with emotion. A week later, still larger crowds gathered outside Federal Hall to watch the swearing-in ceremony on the balcony, where again for a few minutes emotion overcame the first president. This time he wore brown. In today's Federal Hall is a suit which, according to its descriptive label, 'persistent family tradition holds' was the one he wore. The stone on which he stood, as well as a portion of the balcony railing, may also be seen there, along with illuminated models of that original building. They show that it was less pretentious than the present one and in some respects more fitting. When the federal government moved to Philadelphia in 1790, before settling in to the new capital in Washington, the historic old Federal Hall was allowed to fall into disrepair and was pulled down. The museum includes a display of Washington memorabilia and an upstairs room which tells the story of John Peter Zenger, a newspaper publisher whose acquittal on a libel charge was an important blow for press freedom in colonial America: partly as a result of it a free press was enshrined in the first amendment to the constitution. At two on Sundays in the summer and at five-thirty on Tuesdays in the winter, free concerts of chamber music are held in the hall.

Other individual buildings to visit in Wall Street relate to its financial function. Emerging from Federal Hall by the front entrance, turn left towards the East River and cross the road to **No 55 Wall Street**, now Citibank, built in 1842 to replace the Merchants' Exchange destroyed in the fire of 1835 which razed much of the city center. The 1842 building was topped by a dome above the lower row of Ionic columns. In 1907 McKim, Mead and White replaced the dome with a second row of columns, this time Corinthian, to raise it to a height commensurate with the dignity of the bank then occupying it. The double row of columns are replicated inside, although here both layers are Corinthian. This is the first of many grandiloquent bank interiors we shall see on our peregrinations. Its finery includes a large tapestry of Belgian settlers arriving in Manhattan in 1623 and calling it Novum Belgium, a name which happily (at least for song writers) never stuck.

No 23 Wall Street, across Broad Street from the Stock Exchange, is the headquarters of the Morgan Guaranty Trust. The scars on its outside walls date from 1920, when thirty-three people were killed in an explosion; those who planned it, presumably opponents of capitalism as personified in the Morgan family, were never caught. It was one of several symbolic violent assaults on the nerve centers of high finance in the street's history. Inside, the large lobby has been renovated in the style of a hotel ballroom, but even this pales in comparison with **No 1 Wall Street**, the Irving Trust Building on the corner of Broadway, whose Art Deco entrance hall in red and gold mosaics is so overwhelming that it is remarkable how the clerks and secretaries working in it keep their minds on their jobs. Across the street, the tower at No 14 accommodates the only high-altitude restaurant with a Wall Street address. La Tour d'Or is on the thirty-first floor, just below the gold pyramid which caps the building. You have to change into a special elevator at the twenty-ninth. The food is French and quite pricey, eaten in a series of dining-rooms with pretty views of the harbor and the East River, through the tops of the surrounding skyscrapers.

Across Broadway, **Trinity Church** is the third on this site. The first was erected in 1698 but, like so many structures of its time, it fell victim to fire, in 1776. This fire, which destroyed about a third of the city, occurred only a week after the British had driven out the American army:

New York, the largest city in the States, is still run from its 1811 headquarters. City Hall is open to the public; its staircase, gallery and council chambers provide one of New York's finest interiors.

Trinity Church, designed in 1846 by Richard Upjohn, still commands the eye, despite its overbearing neighbors. Upjohn's stained glass window, behind the altar, was one of the first to be installed in America.

Howe, the British commander, believed it to be the work of rebel sympathizers. The church remained in ruins throughout the war until being replaced in 1790. The second came to a less common end, being damaged beyond repair by heavy snow in 1839.

The present one went up in 1846 and has survived natural and unnatural disasters since. Though it was built before its surrounding skyscrapers, the architect, Richard Upjohn, seems to have anticipated the shape of things to come. Viewed from Wall Street, the church looks impossibly slender and fragile, as though squeezed to a thin point by its overbearing neighbours. Upjohn, born in Dorset in 1802, emigrated to Boston when he was twenty-seven and worked as a draughtsman. He was summoned to New York to supervise repairs on the old church and, when it was declared irreparable, was commissioned to design the new one. It was so well liked that it established him as a fashionable church architect and made Gothic the dominant idiom for American churches for almost the rest of the century. Upjohn established the American Institute of Architects in 1857 and was its president until 1876.

Inside the church, the sweep of the tall central arches is reminiscent, on a small scale, of the great Gothic cathedrals of Europe. The large stained glass window behind the altar, also by Upjohn, was one of the first to be installed in America. (Note that the altar is at the west end, a quite frequent phenomenon in Manhattan churches, symptomatic of the early Protestants' disregard for ritual observances and of the fact that most churches had to fit in with the existing street geography, practicality taking precedence over canon law.) The bronze doors, depicting biblical scenes and moments from Manhattan's history, were installed in 1898 in memory of John Jacob Astor III. Bits of eighteenth-century tombstones are in a monument room in the north-west corner and in the shaded graveyard outside, a cool summer retreat for office workers. Its largest memorial, in the style of the Scott monument in Edinburgh, commemorates the unknown martyrs imprisoned by the British during the Revolution and buried here anonymously. There are memorials to William Bradford, New York's first printer; Robert Fulton, the inventor of the steamship; and Alexander Hamilton, the first Secretary of the Treasury.

Hamilton was one of the most important and attractive figures in the city's early history. He came to New York from his native Nevis, in the Caribbean, in 1774, two years before the Revolution, and quickly made a name for himself as a forceful anti-British pamphleteer. A young man approaching twenty, he enlisted in Washington's army and distinguished himself in early battles. Washington noticed him, made him his confidential secretary and appointed him to a field commander for the successful Yorktown campaign of 1781. The following year he qualified as a lawyer and in 1783, when the British evacuated New York, he opened a law office at 57 Wall Street. A year after that he was a founder of the Bank of New York, one of the institutions which helped the fledgling country set up an ultimately sound financial system. In 1789 he became Secretary of the Treasury, presiding over the tricky business of transferring states' debts to the federal government. When speculators began trading in these new government issues, the New York securities market was born. Hamilton resigned in 1795 because of persistent attacks by political opponents, notably Thomas Jefferson, and in 1798 he was made Inspector-General of the army.

By this time his long and ultimately fatal enmity with Aaron Burr had begun. The two were roughly the same age, both had served creditably in the war and both had set up as lawyers as soon as it was over. Their first open breach had come in 1791 when Burr beat Hamilton's father-in-law for a seat in the United States Senate. A few years later Burr established the Bank of Manhattan Company as a rival to the Bank of New York: he did it surreptitiously, setting it up first as a water supply company. In 1800 Burr tied with Jefferson in electoral votes for the presidency. Hamilton disliked them both but had his allies support Jefferson when the election was turned over to Congress. Burr became vice-president and four years later ran for governor of New York. Hamilton openly opposed him in a bitter letter-writing campaign, provoking Burr to challenge him to a duel on the other side of the Hudson in Weehawken, New Jersey. Hamilton was hit and died from his wounds. Burr, disgraced, went adventuring in the west and abroad, until he returned to New York in 1812, though he never re-entered public life. In 1833, at the age of seventy-seven, he married Mrs Stephen Jumel, a widow, only to have her divorce him three years later. Their house in Upper New York, the Morris-Jumel mansion, still stands and is open for visits, as is Hamilton Grange not far away.

Trinity is proud of its choir, which performs at the Sunday service at 11:15. On Tuesdays at 12:45 there are short instrumental concerts. Leaving the churchyard into Trinity Place, at its west end, note the small cherub's head over the center gate. It is from Wren's church of St

Mary-le-Bow in London, destroyed by bombs in 1941. The cherub was rescued and presented to Trinity in 1964.

The unfussy Art Deco front across Trinity Place, No. 78, belongs to the **American Stock Exchange**, the junior of the two exchanges, established in 1921 to deal in stocks of companies not important enough to be listed by the New York Stock Exchange. Until then, trading in these securities had taken place in the street and through open office windows: this is recreated at the head of the escalator inside. It was originally known as the Curb Exchange in deference to that history but it was decided that the name lacked dignity. Like its larger sister it has a visitors' gallery, an explanatory exhibition and an audio-visual show that ends dramatically when the screen rolls up to reveal the trading floor behind it.

Walk north up Trinity Place and turn right into Cortland Street, opposite the southern end of the World Trade Center on the left. At No 22 is the headquarters of the *Wall Street Journal* and of its parent company, Dow Jones. In 1882 Charles Dow and Edward Jones, two young men from Providence, Rhode Island, saw that what stock market speculators needed was reliable and timely information about prices, trends and business developments which could affect share values. They started a financial news bulletin, updated hourly, distributed by teleprinter. Seven years later they collated all this into a daily paper, the *Wall Street Journal*, now the largest-selling daily in the country. Though it still concentrates remorselessly on business matters, it regularly contains a handful of articles of more general interest, written with style and sometimes with wit. In 1897 Dow Jones had the idea of monitoring the daily performance of a small number of key shares and stocks as a guide to the state of the market. Today the Dow Jones index is widely quoted and analyzed, its daily rise and fall reported in newspapers, television and radio news bulletins, almost as a religious observance. It has been emulated in most major capitalist countries.

Turn right into Broadway and stop at the corner of Liberty Street, as good a place as any to ponder in its various manifestations the skyscraper, that distinctly American architectural form which has become a symbol of the soaring ambition that infects American commerce. We shall see many good and bad examples in this and succeeding chapters. Skyscrapers originated in Chicago a hundred years ago (the word 'skyscraper' was first used to denote the topmost sail of square-rigged clipper ships). In the mid-1880s the introduction of a building method based on the construction of steel cages to support the weight meant that the height of a building was, in theory, unlimited, save by the speed and efficiency of lifts. The old method, where the weight was supported by masonry walls, meant that to construct a building of any size the walls had to be immensely thick. The tallest building in the world, for a dozen years after it was built in 1873, was the New York *Tribune* office on Park Row, with eleven storeys and a tower.

New York took a decade and more to realize the possibilities of the new construction method. Anything from Chicago, the brash second city of the union, was regarded with suspicion. In 1908, on the site of **One Liberty Plaza** where we are now standing, Ernest Flagg showed how traditional decorative styles could be adapted to the new form with his extraordinary Singer Building and Tower, its lobby a symphony in marble and bronze, fussy columns forming arches reaching up to end in uniform round skylights. In 1970 the United States Steel Company pulled it down for their present monotonous block, an insensitive act which goaded the city finally to legislate to preserve what historic buildings remained.

The Singer Building's elegance and restraint were a result of the good taste and civic responsibility of the architect and the owners. When it was built, no zoning restrictions curbed the worst excesses of greedy landowners, seeking to exploit their sites for the maximum return. An example of a less public-spirited work, so gargantuan as to persuade the city to exert some control over what the builders were doing, is a block south, the **Equitable Building** across Broadway between Pine and Cedar Streets. From our vantage point on Liberty Street we can see this dour, inelegant hunk in all its overbearing solidity. In 1915, when its two thick towers were built to rise sheer from the street, the citizens began to fear that if many similar megaliths were constructed Lower Manhattan would become a darkened tunnel, where sunlight never penetrated. The first zoning ordinance was therefore enacted in 1916. By its terms, the floor space in a building could not be more than twelve times the area of the site. (The Equitable's is thirty times the area: look at the diagram of it above the building directory in the grandiose lobby to get an idea of its mass.) This restriction led to the 'setback' or wedding-cake style, buildings getting narrower as they grew higher, the hallmark of skyscraper architecture between the wars and best embodied in the Rockefeller Center. The ordinance stayed in effect until 1961 but scarcely succeeded in preventing the streets around Wall Street from becoming gloomy and forbidding.

The 1961 ordinance encouraged vertical slabs in the middle of spacious but often soulless plazas, whose area determines the building's permitted height. One Liberty Plaza is an example. The small square on the block to its south, across Liberty Street, was bought by U.S. Steel together with the old Singer site, so that its open space would form part of the calculations of how high the tower could rise. Across Broadway is the Marine Midland Bank at No 140. Its chief interest is the large red cube outside, balancing on one of its corners. This is a characteristically jokey piece by the sculptor Iasamu Noguchi, whose anarchic inventiveness suits New York well. Although of Japanese parentage, he was born in Los Angeles in 1904 and studied under Brancusi in Paris in the 1920s. Apart from these apparently gravity-defying works, he became known for his surrealist stage sets for Martha Graham's modern dance company, and he designed a number of innovative playgrounds for children, so fanciful that nobody could ever be persuaded to build them. We shall see more of his work as we move up through the city.

Before plunging into Liberty Street, glance back across Broadway at the building south of US Steel's plaza. The US Realty Building, at No 115, is one of the early skyscrapers that fared better than the Singer Tower. Together with 55 Liberty Street, **Liberty Towers**, on our left as we head east, is an example of careful and imaginative terra cotta detailing. In 1979 Liberty Towers avoided Singer's fate by being converted into expensive apartments. Next to it, at No 65, the 1901 **Chamber of Commerce Building**, with its stately Beaux Arts front, gives a feeling of what filled these streets before the skyscrapers. On the south-east corner of Liberty and Nassau Streets the sixty-storey **Chase Manhattan Building** overawes the pale Dubuffet sculpture nestling awkwardly in a corner of its bleak plaza. It went up in 1961, the first big office tower to be built in the financial district after the Second World War. The bank's chief executive officer, David Rockefeller, was a driving force behind the building, seen at the time as a gesture of faith in Lower Manhattan. His family has exerted a profound influence on the look of modern New York but this is a less successful piece of planning than his father's Rockefeller Center on Fifth Avenue. Although the plaza provides visual relief from the dark and crowded streets around it, nothing much happens there except small-scale drug traffic. It has deliberately been cut off from its surroundings by a high wall which at some points seems nearly impenetrable, as though defending itself from the tawdriness beyond.

North, across Liberty Street, the impressive bulk of the **Federal Reserve Bank of New York** bears down on you, a fortress of a different kind. Its walls faced with limestone slabs, the iron grilles shielding its windows, and the castellated tower, all bolster its impregnable aspect. The architects, Edward York and Phillip Sawyer, alumni of McKim, Mead and White, went into partnership in 1889. Like George Post, they specialized in the design of large office buildings, banks in particular, on which they let their considerable inventiveness run riot. (In later chapters we shall see two of their most extravagant works, the Bowery Savings Bank on 42nd Street and the Central Savings Bank at 73rd Street and Broadway.) The Federal Reserve is dour by contrast, the architects presumably feeling that solidity was the quality needing to be emphasized here. Free tours must be arranged in advance. It is worth the effort if your imagination is fired by seeing billions of dollars worth of gold stashed in vaults hewn from Manhattan bedrock, five floors below the street. The gold belongs to foreign countries, which settle their accounts by having it moved from one vault to another. During the fifty-minute tour, visitors also see thousands of dollar bills being checked for forgeries.

This is the largest of the twelve regional banks in the Federal Reserve system, created by Act of Congress in 1913 to stabilize the banking industry and the supply of money. It is not a national bank in the sense of being government-owned: its stock is divided among the country's leading banks. Members can borrow from the reserve, a facility which has served to avert disastrous financial panic. The Federal Reserve banks trade in government securities and fix the discount rate, helping control economic trends. They issue currency, as well as overseeing the destruction of currency bills when they are worn out.

The bank is wedge-shaped, its narrower end pointing west. Just beyond it, forming the point of its V, is a small triangular plaza named after Louise Nevelson, the sculptor whose works it contains. There are four of them, in a group Mrs Nevelson called 'Shadows and Flags', all in her distinctive collage style and her favourite color, black. 'I fell in love with black,' she said in an interview with *Time* magazine. 'It contained all color . . . Black is the most aristocratic color of all, the only aristocratic color. For me this is the ultimate.' Not until she was over forty, in 1941, did Mrs Nevelson have her first one-woman show, and her reputation was not truly secured until her late sixties. She had come to the United States with her family from Kiev when she was five, moving to New York when she married Charles Nevelson, a shipowner, in 1920. The marriage ended after eleven years but she stayed in the place she had come to love as the 'city of collage'. The author of the *Time* article, Robert Hughes, finds the set of four pieces, placed here in 1978, 'big, imposing and mannered'. He adds: 'This kind of post-constructivist sculpture-in-the-round is not her forte at all.' If you stand at the very point of the V and look back towards the biggest piece, its long crossed poles imposed against the sturdy end wall of the Federal Reserve Bank, it looks mighty incongruous. Other examples of her work in New York are in the concourse of the World Trade Center, the junction of Park Avenue and 92nd Street and the Jewish Museum on Fifth Avenue.

Just north, 100 William Street is the downtown location for buying cheap theatre tickets. Continue north and turn left for the **John Street Methodist Church.** Philip Embury, an Irish follower of John Wesley, founded American Methodism in 1766 and built a church on the site the following year. It was rebuilt on a grander scale in 1818 but had to be pulled down twenty-three years later when the street was widened. The present church, a plain balconied rectangle, cool and sparsely adorned, dates from 1841 but contains fitments from the 1818 building, including the pews and brass light brackets. It also boasts Embury's original pulpit and a clock given by Wesley in 1768, which is still working.

Leaving the church turn left, then left again into **Nassau Street**, the cheap and cheerful lunch-hour shopping center for workers in the financial district. The shops sell clothing, shoes and jewelry and there are plenty of snack bars for pizza, hamburgers and ice cream. On a fine day the scene is sociable. You might come across an itinerant musician playing the violin or even the bagpipes. Fast operators turn cardboard boxes on end and set up games of 'Three-card monte' or 'Find the Lady', the old street swindle. They seem to find ready victims among the Wall Street stock dealers, whose own business is, after all, based on fostering in their clients the optimistic belief that they have the knack of striking it lucky. You may want to stay for a bit, browsing.

When you have finished, turn east on Pine Street (between Wall and Liberty Streets), intersecting the Chase Manhattan Plaza on your left and the back entrance of the Federal Hall on your right. Cross William Street, admire the extravagant façade of 56-58 Pine Street on your left and head for the Art Deco skyscraper beyond it, the **American International Building** at No 70. This is a good 1932 example of the wedding-cake style and one of the tallest skyscrapers in the financial district, its pencil-thin tower culminating in a Gothic crown. Seeing how hard it is to get a proper view of it from the narrow street, the architect has thoughtfully placed a model over the main doors. Go into the lobby and drink in the rich decorative detail, notably the elaborate metalwork on the doors of the elevators. This building was an early example of what the *AIA Guide* calls 'addressmanship'. For years after it was built its owners insisted on calling it 60 Wall Street because it had an extension across the road whose entrance was on that more recognizable and glamorous thoroughfare, although the main body has always been on Pine.

There is another example a bit farther east, across Water Street, where 88 Pine Street, I.M. Pei's symphony in white, has been named **One Wall Street Plaza**, although it is a block from Wall Street. The trend is deliberately provocative to taxi-drivers and postmen: moreover the pay-off, the resulting increase in prestige, is surely entirely illusory. Do not let this quibble distract us from Pei's work, the most successful of the row of office warrens built in the 1960s and 1970s along the east side of **Water Street.** This one, finished in 1974, has wide window spaces suggestive of the early Chicago skyscrapers. It helped build Pei's reputation to the point where he was awarded the commission for the extension to the National Gallery in Washington and then for the massive New York Convention Center due to go up shortly at the east end of 34th Street. Pei was born in China in 1917 and attended the Massachusetts Institute of Technology when he was eighteen. He stayed in the Boston area to teach at Harvard until he formed his own architectural firm in 1955, specializing in modern shopping centers and commercial buildings with clean, functional lines.

To our right, farther south, are some of the less pleasing buildings in the Water Street development. This controversial row of office towers began in the early 1960s, when the city's movers and shakers began to worry about the future of Lower Manhattan as a commercial center: companies were taking their headquarters uptown, to 42nd Street and beyond, partly because, in the crowded canyons round Wall Street, there was precious little room to expand. There were fears and threats that corporations would leave the city altogether and go upstate, or to New Jersey or even Texas. Some did.

So the Water Street development was devised. Until then the street was lined with blocks of low nineteenth-century buildings, many of them warehouses and artists' lofts, a welcome contrast to the tall skyscrapers. Few remain except the South Street museum area to the north and the Fraunces Tavern block which we shall be seeing in a moment. Critics of the development believe that the arid new towers were a poor trade-off for the destruction of the historic waterfront. They are occupied mostly by large financial institutions — American Express and the major banks — and though their decorative styles differ, they have a forbidding aspect in common. They are all set into ground-level plazas, which became fashionable after the acclaim won by Mies van der Rohe's Seagram Building uptown on Park Avenue. When Seagram was built, though, it stood out in a crowded avenue. The effect of plazas *en masse*, as in Water Street, is deadly. They are dotted with fountains and random modern sculptures, but few shops or other facilities encourage crowds to throng them.

In the middle and late 1970s the pendulum swung again and there was office space to spare in the financial district. The solution this time was less radical. Developers began to turn old commercial buildings, even tall office towers, into living accommodation — not primitive lofts for artists but expensive co-operatively-owned apartments with all modern comforts. Failing that, they would find other useful functions for them. Turn right out of Pine Street into Water Street, across Wall Street, and left into **Old Slip**, where the charming former police station, a Beaux Arts jewel box built in 1909, has been taken over by the Whitney Museum of American Art as the downtown annex to their main museum at Madison Avenue and 75th Street. (The 1930s building just north is the **United States Assay Building**, where gold is melted into bars.)

Cross Water Street again and walk into **Hanover Square**. The old Cotton Exchange, No 3 on the west side, has been converted into apartments since the exchange was moved to the World Trade Center. The trading hall used to be on the top, marked by the row of Ionic columns. The effect of this and a few other conversions in the nearby streets has been to bring an element of residential life into this area for the first time in many years. **Delmonico's**, south of the old Cotton Exchange, lasted for nearly a century and a half as a fashionable downtown restaurant before succumbing to conversion in 1978. To its left is one of the city's best proportioned and preserved mansions, **India House,** an

Italianate brownstone completed in 1854, now a private club. Brownstone is a pinkish sandstone quarried in New Jersey and Connecticut which gave its name to the terraced houses built in the second half of the nineteenth century all over the city.

Leave the square on **Pearl Street**, passing left of India House. When the Dutch came this street marked the limit of dry land, and was named thus for the glistening oyster shells and mother-of-pearl along the shore. **Coenties Slip**, which we pass on our left, was then an inlet where boats tied up. When the land was extended through filling the slip grew bigger too. You can follow its shape in **Jeannette Park**, now a charmless brick plaza, its nautical associations obliterated by the road traffic which separates it from the East River.

Just past Coenties Slip, on our left, is the **Fraunces Tavern** block, with the tavern itself on the corner of Broad Street. It is a reconstruction of the inn on this site where George Washington gave an emotional farewell speech to his officers on 4 December, 1783, after the British had finally sailed away and the war was won. It was a scene of great passion, heightened, as described earlier, by Washington's determination to fade from public life now that the new country was safely launched. Colonel Benjamin Tallmadge, one of the officers present, wrote a moving account. After drinking a toast, Washington invited all the officers to shake him by the hand.

> General Knox, being nearest to him, turned to the Commander-in-Chief, who, suffused in tears, was incapable of utterance but grasped his hand; then they embraced each other in silence. In the same affectionate manner, every officer in the room marched up to, kissed and parted with his General-in-Chief. Such a scene of sorrow and weeping I had never before witnessed and I hope I may never be called upon to witness again. . . . The simple thought that we were then about to part from the man who had conducted us through a long and bloody war, and under whose conduct the glory and independence of our country had been achieved, and that we should see his face no more in this world, seemed to me utterly insupportable.[7]

The building which was to become the Fraunces Tavern was put up on a landfill plot in 1715 as a private residence. Fifty years later it had become the Queen's Head Tavern, owned by Samuel Fraunces, a West Indian. It suffered three fires and a number of consequent structural alterations in the nineteenth century, and by the 1890s had grown from its original three storeys to five. In 1904 it was bought by the Sons of the Revolution, a group devoted to the preservation of revolutionary mementoes, who asked William Merserau, an architect, to rebuild it as it was in Washington's day. The trouble was that there were no contemporary documents to work from, so Merserau's reconstruction is conjectural. The result is handsome enough, and the two upstairs rooms have been turned into a museum. On the second floor is the long room, furnished as a tavern dining-room, as it was when Washington said his tearful goodbye. Across the passage the Clinton Room, with some elaborate nineteenth-century scenic wallpaper, is named after George Clinton, the Governor of New York after the British evacuation. The ground floor is a restaurant, patronized more for its historical associations than for its food.

Leaving the tavern, turn left on to Pearl Street, cross Broad and Moore Streets, turn left into **Whitehall Street**, named satirically by the first British settlers because it led to the official residence of Governor Stuyvesant. Turn right into State Street. Where the street curves stands the façade of the **John Watson House**, a Federal mansion built around 1800 to the design of John McComb, one of the architects of City Hall. Federal architecture is essentially an outgrowth of the Georgian style in England. It flourished in America between 1790 and 1830 but in its later manifestations developed substantially more elaboration than was evident in its spare, disciplined origins. This early example avoids that. The Ionic columns in front curve with the street but the house behind them is L-shaped, making for an unusual balcony above the entrance. In the early nineteenth century it was one of a group of similarly grand houses by the harbor and as such it must have been mightily impressive. Today it looks uncomfortable, shouldering the black glass-fronted skyscraper on its right. The house, its interior severely modified, is now the rectory attached to the shrine of St Elizabeth Ann Seton, the founder of the Sisters of Charity, who lived on State Street.

Next door, at No 15, is the tall headquarters of the **Seamen's Church Institute.** You need not be a seaman to eat at the reasonably priced public cafeteria or to drink at the bar, surrounded by nautical memorabilia, with a view over Battery Park. Leaving, turn right to follow State Street north; the old **US Custom House** quickly comes up on your right (The original Fort Amsterdam was built by the Dutch on this site, which in those days abutted on to the harbor and dominated it.) One of the city's most imposing neo-classical buildings, a granite mass, the 1892 Custom House was the first New York commission for Cass Gilbert, whose later work — most notably the Woolworth Tower and the George Washington Bridge — did much to shape the city's personality. Unlike many of the fashionable American architects of the time Gilbert had not been trained at the Académie des Beaux Arts in Paris, yet he was among the most fervent followers of the imaginative neo-classicism which that school fostered. That is what Beaux Arts architecture in New York means, and the Custom House is a textbook example. The four marble sculpture groups at the front are by Daniel Chester French, known for his Lincoln Memorial in Washington. On each of the forty-four capitals is a head of Mercury, the god of commerce, and the heads above the windows represent 'the eight races of mankind'. The twelve statues just below the roof symbolize, sometimes a bit eccentrically, the world's main commercial centers. Notice the third from the right: originally on her shield labelled Germany, she was altered in 1917 for patriotic reasons to be the representative of Belgium.

The steps down from the main entrance lead on to **Bowling Green,** which must once have been used for bowls, though this is hard to envisage now. It was set aside as a public space in 1733. The functional iron fence was imported from England in 1771 and is unaltered save for the removal of the crowns which used to top the posts: they were torn off in 1776 in the bout of nationalist fervor which saw the toppling of King George III's statue from the center of the green. The statue was reputedly melted down to make 42,088 musket bullets (who counted?) for use against the British, and in its place now stands an apolitical fountain.

Bowling Green serves as a seal at its southern end for **Broadway**, a monumental street which has always been the city's central artery, no matter how it has grown and changed. Following the route of an old Indian trail, it meanders the entire length of the city and beyond, into upstate New York. On its way through Manhattan it cuts diagonally across the north-south avenues, forming squares (triangles, more precisely) which have become focal points for the city as it sprawls northwards: City Hall Park at Warren Street, Union Square at 14th Street, Madison Square at 23rd, Herald Square at 34th, Times Square at 42nd, Columbus Circle at 59th. At 72nd Street it straightens to head due north, passing Columbia University before traversing Harlem and the Bronx and turning into Route 9 in Westchester County. Most functions from which the city's vivacity springs have been centered on Broadway. Throughout the nineteenth century the shopping district leapfrogged along it: first down here by the Battery, then near City Hall, through the cast-iron district to Union Square and beyond, to 34th Street and the largest store in the world. The theatre district began at Park Place, just off Broadway near City Hall, moved north to Madison Square and is now north of Times Square. Garment manufacturing, the city's most important industry, started in the stretch of Broadway that is now SoHo and nas settled around Herald Square. The main newspapers have seldom been far away. It was along this lower section of Broadway, where we are now, that Charles Dickens, visiting in the 1840s, noted the prevalence of pigs, strolling the streets and acting as non-mechanical rubbish collectors. He turned them into an unpleasant metaphor for the city at large.

We shall end this chapter by dipping our toes into Broadway but, before that, cross State Street to look at the unassertive cream-colored booth at a corner of Battery Park. It looks, and is, commonplace, a simple entrance to a subway station; yet it is a registered landmark, one of the few remaining examples of the kiosks which stood above all the stations on the first subway line, built in 1904 and 1905. As the city grew these above-ground booths were found to be an impediment and they were gradually pulled down, leaving subway entrances to be marked by uninviting stone staircases. This booth managed to hold out until the city's conversion to the idea of preserving its heritage. Some twenty yards north of it is a tall flagpole with a relief map of the Dutch Fort Amsterdam at its base. It was presented by the people of Holland in 1926, to mark the 300th anniversary of Peter Minuit's purchase of Manhattan from the Indians, depicted on the other side.

From it, cross Battery Place and walk up Broadway, past the tall office buildings that used to be the headquarters of shipping companies when sea travel still held sway. One or two still have their gaudy booking halls, designed to give the intending voyager a taste of the magnificence he might meet on his journey, of moving into another world. Gaudiest of all is the old **Cunard** building at **25 Broadway**, on the left. It is now a post office and, although only half the great hall is accessible to the public and some of the postal paraphernalia is obtrusive, it is still possible to get the feeling of its once awesome splendor. The walls and the vast domed ceilings are decorated with colorful stylized maps of Cunard routes; the illustrations represent the spirit and culture of the countries shown, while the central ceiling decoration is on nautical themes, with sea gods emerging from clouds of spume. Dolphins and scallop shells circle the walls. The scale of the hall and the exuberance of its decoration are typical of the early twenties, when it was built. The stock market crash was still eight years in the future and the airplane did not yet look like becoming a competitor to the giant liners. The hall reflects the prevailing confidence that people were going to get richer and richer and would have limitless funds to spend on sailing around the globe; in another twenty years it had become a white elephant.

Its architects were John Carrère and Thomas Hastings, who met at the Academie des Beaux Arts in Paris; both went on to work for McKim, Mead and White until they formed a partnership in 1886. They specialized in works of neo-classical grandeur such as this and they were responsible for two New York landmarks: the plaza and the Pulitzer Fountain outside the Plaza Hotel at the south-east corner of Central Park, and the Public Library at 42nd Street and Fifth Avenue. They also designed the Triborough Bridge at the north end of the city, and the Senate and House of Representatives buildings in Washington.

Across the street, 26 Broadway was built in the same period with an interior scarcely less pretentious, if more restrained. This was originally the headquarters of Rockefeller's Standard Oil Corporation. The company, later to be broken up by trust-busting legislation, saw the need to put across a dignified image and the entrance hall is extravagantly lined with acres of cool marble, harking back to classical Greece. (The Cunard interior is generally classified as Italian Renaissance, though I suspect it would startle Michelangelo.) There are dozens of office buildings in Manhattan which boast lobbies of unimaginable lavishness, motivated by corporate aggrandizement. Nearly all are readily accessible to visitors during normal working hours, and are worth nosing into. They are the exotic flowers of which Wall Street, where we began this chapter, is the tough and sometimes grimy root.

4

South Street Seaport to World Trade Center

THERE HAD BEEN limitedly successful experiments with steam-propelled vessels in America and Britain in the last years of the eighteenth century but in 1807 Fulton's *Clermont,* puttering its ungainly thirty-two-hour way up the Hudson from New York to Albany, earned its reputation as the ship which first established the commercial viability of the technique. (*Clermont,* with its British engine, presaged the development of a later revolution in transport, the jet plane, where again it was the British who pioneered the technology but the Americans who made it pay.) Robert Fulton, born to an Irish family in Pennsylvania in 1765, began his adult life as a promising painter of miniatures. It was while studying art in England that he became interested in mechanics, especially in nautical engineering, doing some pioneering work on submarines before turning his attention to steamboats.

In 1814, a year before his death, he started a ferry service between Manhattan and Brooklyn. He chose as its Manhattan terminal a slip on South Street, recently created from landfill, about half a mile north of the Battery. So dominant did the ferry become in the life of the two boroughs (then still separate cities) that the roads leading to it on both sides were re-named Fulton Street. Brooklyn's Fulton Street remains a principal commercial artery but Fulton Street in Manhattan declined in importance as the city center moved uptown and as Brooklyn Bridge, opened in 1883, largely superseded the ferry.

Today, the old ferry terminal on the Manhattan side is the site of New York's main fish market. Though now supplied with its fish by road, insomniacs visiting it before dawn will find it as bustling, smelly and full of life as when the fishermen would unload their catch straight from the boats. Joseph Mitchell, a writer for the *New Yorker,* described it thus in 1952:

> I usually arrive around 5:30, and take a walk through the two huge open-fronted market sheds, the Old Market and the New Market,

Liberty Street/Maiden Lane north to Worth Street

whose fronts rest on South Street and whose backs rest on piles in the East River. At that time, a little while before the trading begins, the stands in the shed are heaped high and spilling over with 40 to 60 kinds of finfish and shellfish from the East Coast, the West Coast, the Gulf Coast, and half a dozen foreign countries. The smoky riverbank dawn, the racket the fishmongers make, the seaweedy smell and the sight of this plentifulness always gives me a feeling of well-being, and sometimes they elate me. I wander among the stands for an hour or so. Then I go into a cheerful market restaurant named Sloppy Louie's and eat a big, inexpensive, invigorating breakfast — a kippered herring and scrambled eggs, or a shad-roe omelet, or split sea scallops and bacon, or some other breakfast speciality of the place

We shall get to Sloppy Louie's ourselves in a while, but first I want to introduce you to something which was not there in Mitchell's time. The junction of South Street and Fulton Street is now the hub of the most extensive attempt to recall New York's nineteenth-century history. Work on the **South Street Seaport Museum** began in 1967 and has progressed steadily, though slowly, since. The aim is to create a display area for old ships of the type which used to berth along South Street, and to restore the blocks of waterfront warehouses and shops as an historic district.

The South Street piers used to accommodate the sailing packets and clippers taking goods and passengers across the Atlantic to Europe and around Cape Horn to California and the Orient. The first regularly scheduled transatlantic passenger and cargo service was started here by the Black Ball Line in 1818. First once and soon twice a month, its sailing packets would set out for Liverpool, a voyage of seventeen days if they were lucky, with the westward journey taking at least a week longer. As trade grew, so other British and American shipping lines entered what was to become for more than a hundred years a fiercely competitive market.

Contemporary drawings and early photographs show a lively and crowded harborside, dominated by wooden masts and rigging, bowsprits poking over the street, the dockside laden with merchandise of all kinds. Along South Street were the saloons and hostels catering to the seamen, and on Fulton Street the shops to catch the trade to and from the ferry. In the late nineteenth century, as ocean-going ships grew larger, the city's main harbor moved to the deeper waters of the Hudson on Manhattan's west side. South Street took on the aspect of a backwater.

To conjure an image of the street in its heyday now requires a considerable exercise of the imagination, for the ugly elevated East Side Highway runs above it, following the line of the shore, visually separating the piers from the buildings which served them. The visitor could start at the **New York State Maritime Museum Visitors' Center** in the Schermerhorn Row block on Fulton Street, between Front and South Streets (walk east from any of the Fulton Street subway stations). Here are displays explaining the history of South Street and of the restoration project. Schermerhorn Row is named for Peter Schermerhorn, a shipowner and ships' chandler, descended from a Dutch family which arrived in New York in the middle of the seventeenth century. He bought the space in 1793 as a water lot and had it filled. The buildings he erected in 1811 are the ones which stand there today, originally warehouses at ground level with counting houses on the floors above. Nobody can call them pretty but they are authentically old, perhaps reason enough for New Yorkers to prize them.

Pier 15, opposite the end of John Street, is where the ships open to the public are moored, set up as museums of the heyday of sail; the *Peking* was one of the last great sailing ships built. All the exhibition ships, which include the old Ambrose lightship, can be visited for a single entrance fee. The pier is occasionally used for open-air folk concerts and children's story-telling, and is also the boarding point for three-hour trips round the harbor in the 1885 schooner *Pioneer*. (For reservations and prices, phone 669-9400.)

On the east side of the Schermerhorn Row block, fronting on South Street, are two historic fish restaurants. Sloppy Louie's, once the dining-room of the Fulton Ferry Hotel, tries to maintain the atmosphere of an old seamen's cafe which Joseph Mitchell prized. Its plain mahogany tables for six are lined up on either side of the central aisle. The fish cannot fail to be fresh but it is not especially cheap: I do not mean to imply that prices are excessive, but they might surprise diners who judge a place by its decor. The bouillabaisse is good, spicy and scarlet, and so is the clam chowder (Manhattan clam chowder is red; the New England variety is white and creamier). Sloppy Louie's closes at eight, so it is really more practical for lunch than dinner; and it does not serve alcohol, though it is permissible to bring in wine or beer.

Sweet's is the other famous old restaurant in the same block. The dining-room, which has kept much of its period character, is up a flight of stairs, its entrance on Fulton Street. This is another staple seafood place but one degree more comfortable and dearer. You can get beer and wine here: a cheap California Chablis goes well with fish on warm evenings — dress coolly because it is not air-conditioned. Last dinner serving is at 8:30 pm and tables may not be reserved in advance. Both restaurants closed for refurbishment in 1982 but were due to reopen in 1983. In the Fulton Market Building north of Fulton Street (not the fish market, which is hard by the East River) are some popular snack bars, patronized chiefly by office workers from the financial district.

Two blocks north, at the corner of South Street and **Peck's Slip,** Meyer's Hotel was built in 1873 in handsome red brick, and is the last survivor of the hostelries which once catered to the seafaring traffic. Now merely a bar, and a seedy one at that, its huge dark wood interior with patterned mirrors enhances the Victorian flavor. You will not be able to miss the pleasing trompe-l'oeil on the wall of an electricity sub-station on the north side of Peck's Slip, in which the artist, Richard Haas, has cut an imaginary arcade through the wall, offering an out-of-scale peep at Brooklyn Bridge nestling beneath the real bridge pier just behind it. Haas has done a few of these murals around the city, enhancing its gaiety. The bollards at the side of the cobbled street, where you might expect parking meters instead, signify that this was once a working slip, where boats moored.

The shops in the South Street area have a maritime theme. Captain Hook's Marine Antique and Sea Shells shop is on Schermerhorn Row. It is a fascinating jumble of brass, cheap souvenirs and thousands of shells. Across the road are shops selling nautical modelling kits, books, prints and toys. The most handsome shop fronts are a set of dignified Greek Revival façades, carefully restored, along **Water Street**, two blocks west of South Street, between Fulton and Beekman Streets. At No 211, Bowne and Co. are stationers and printers whose customers can see hand presses working, and buy stationery printed on them. Next door, the beautiful cast-iron façade fronts the Seaport Gallery and its exhibits of American art. Across Water Street a reconstructed lighthouse marks the boundary of the seaport area, which we are now leaving.

Before heading farther inland, look at the ground floor of 127 John

Street, a skyscraper at the corner of Water Street, whose designers have made a determined effort to bring back something of the district's nineteenth-century ambiance, albeit in a consciously twentieth-century fashion. Multi-colored public seats are set in inward-facing groups, for companionability, and there are intricate balconies and awnings, linked by ladders, which children can explore. Even the phone boxes have been given fanciful decorative treatment, and a remarkable giant digital clock keeps accurate time once you have worked out how to read it. Entrance into the building itself is through a square corrugated iron tunnel, lit with multi-colored neon, a welcome piece of cheeky showmanship.

Walk west on John Street, then turn right up Gold Street, passing the big South Street Towers residential complex on your right. Go left up Spruce Street, between the Beekman Downtown Hospital and Pace University, to reach the triangular junction of Park Row and Nassau Street. This was once called Printing House Square, where the city's main newspapers were published during most of the nineteenth century. A statue of Horace Greeley, the founder of the *Tribune* and the most celebrated of New York's owner-editors, stands — sits, rather — in the park nearby, east of City Hall.

Born in 1811 on a farm in New Hampshire, Greeley came to New York at twenty to make a career in printing and publishing. His first publishing venture was a weekly magazine, the original *New Yorker*. When he launched the *Tribune* in 1841 he wrote some two columns of persuasive editorials every day. His political stance was roughly Liberal Republican, but he embraced some causes which were for those days downright radical. He was in favor of equality for women, against slavery and capital punishment. He supported the struggles of workers for better conditions and established a trade union for the *Tribune*'s printers. For a time, Karl Marx contributed a weekly column to the paper. Yet Greeley was essentially a rigorous exponent of traditional American philosophy. 'The darkest day in any man's life,' he wrote, 'is that on which he first fancies that there is some easier way of gaining a dollar than by squarely earning it' — a maxim which, as we saw in the last chapter, was in New York honored as much in the breach as in the observance. He had a genius for the attention-grabbing phrase, and coined the still-quoted exhortation to youth to venture into the developing parts of the nation: 'Go west, young man.'

His success as an editor was not quite duplicated when he ventured into politics. Though winning the Liberal and Democratic nominations for President in 1872, he was beaten in the November election by Ulysses S. Grant, a general in the Civil War. Greeley's strange appearance, exploited to the full by the cartoonists of the day, may have contributed to his defeat. To judge from contemporary accounts, the statue flatters him. He was tall and plump, nearly bald on top but with a wispy growth of white hair between his chin and throat, as though someone had removed his hair and replaced it upside down. His face was a dramatic shade of pink, with small blue eyes framed in exaggeratedly large spectacles. By the time of the election he was ailing and he died a few weeks afterwards, before he could have taken office had he won. In 1924 the *Tribune* was merged with its long-standing rival, the *Herald*. The joint paper expired in 1966, the name surviving only in the *International Herald Tribune*, still published in Paris.

The *Tribune*'s old Printing House Square headquarters have also disappeared, replaced by the new Pace University campus. Only the building on the corner of Park Row and Spruce Street (also occupied by Pace) recalls the area's days as the center of newspaper publishing. This is the former home of *The New York Times*. The lower five storeys were built in 1858 and the building was made higher as the newspaper grew bigger, the last expansion coming in 1905. When even that became cramped, the paper moved to its famous skyscraper in Times Square, a block away from its present site on West 43rd Street. Park Row was, in the eighteenth century, a fashionable residential street and the city's early theatre district. Its junction with Broadway was a key traffic intersection, where the Albany Post Road, which followed the route of Broadway, split from the Boston Post Road, which went up the Bowery into Third Avenue.

City Hall Park, a well-maintained open space with blossom trees and a pleasing fountain, marks that fork in the road. From pre-revolutionary days it was the scene of political gatherings, occasionally riotous, and today one of its statues nicely captures the old colony's rebellious spirit. Nathan Hale, an early American martyr, stands half-way up the park along its Broadway front, his shirt unbuttoned romantically, looking like an especially dashing juvenile lead in pantomime. He was hanged by the British in 1776, at the age of twenty-one, after he had infiltrated their lines during the Battle of Long Island to spy for Washington's army. Before his death he delivered his magnificently defiant last words: 'I only regret that I have but one life to lose for my country.' Less than a hundred years later this brand of uncomplicated heroism was to seem a far cry from the viciousness rampant in the city, which culminated here in the brutal Draft Riots of 1863, during the Civil War. For three days the white poor, chiefly Irish, demonstrated angrily and violently against the pernicious operation of conscription: men were selected for the army by ballot but the wealthy would buy their way out of the obligation. The protestors lynched some Blacks, whom they blamed both for the war and for their depressed condition. They came to City Hall Park with the avowed aim of seizing Greeley, whose *Tribune* favored the draft law. One story has it that the panic-stricken editor escaped their vengeance by hiding under a tablecloth at a local restaurant. Unable to find him, the rioters invaded the newspaper's office, smashed windows and furniture and started fires until evicted by the police in a bloody struggle.

Nowadays the park's primary function is to allow office workers to catch some midday sunshine, and it provides the finishing point for the triumphant tickertape parades along Broadway which mark notable civic or national events. Thus, when the New York Yankees or Mets win the baseball World Series, thousands gather here to fete and cheer their heroes and to watch the mayor greet them at City Hall itself, at the north end of the park. The first parade was for Charles Lindbergh, the aviator, in 1927, and the biggest (they are judged by the weight of rubbish collected when they are over) in celebration of the victory over Japan in 1945: it made 5,438 tons. There will never be as big a one again because the old telegraph machines which reported stock prices and financial news on tickertape have been superseded by computer terminals, resembling television screens. When the American hostages returned in January 1981, after spending fourteen and a half months of detention in Iran, hundreds of miles of tape for their parade had to be trucked in from companies which kept old supplies, and handed out to workers in offices along the route.

For many, **City Hall** is the finest neo-classical Federal building in New York. It represents a happy blossoming of the 'auld alliance', the work of Joseph Mangin, a Frenchman who became a citizen of New York in 1795, and John McComb, a Scot, whose family had been in New York since the early eighteenth century. He and Mangin, who worked for the city, entered a competition for the design of City Hall in 1802 and won the $350 prize, although the parsimonious city fathers later asked them for a scaled-down version which, after many delays, was finished ten years later. McComb was appointed supervisor of the works at a fee of $6 a day. Two other long-lasting buildings by McComb we have seen already: the John Watson house near the Staten Island Ferry, and Castle Clinton nearby. Mangin's other remaining building is the first St Patrick's Cathedral on Mott Street, in what is now Little Italy.

While City Hall's exterior had decidedly French detailing, the interior style could almost be that of a grand English country house. By 1956 its marble and sandstone walls were crumbling, so they were re-faced with durable limestone and granite. City Hall is open to the public although, typically, there is no sign outside which informs visitors of the fact, and to get in you might have to struggle past a clutch of cameramen and reporters interviewing councillors — or even the mayor himself. Inside, a dramatic circular marble staircase leads to a gallery with wrought-iron balustrades. At its edge, slender Corinthian columns support the domed roof, decorated with rosettes inside panels and culminating in a skylight. This is a copy of McComb's original dome, which was destroyed in 1858 during a fireworks display celebrating the laying of the first Atlantic cable. At the top of the stairs, the Governor's Room is a finely proportioned rectangle at the front of the building, furnished with good eighteenth- and nineteenth-century furniture and paintings of prominent New Yorkers. There is a writing-table used by George Washington between 1789 and 1790, during the brief period in which New York was the federal capital, and two unusual settees, their feet joined by an odd bulbous rail, which some attribute to Duncan Phyfe, one of the most reputable early American furniture designers. The son of a Scotsman named Fife, he was born in Albany in upstate New York and moved to the city when he was twenty-one, in 1789, to open a joinery shop. He began building furniture in the Sheraton style, generally well ornamented. Soon he changed his name to the more distinguished Phyfe and in 1795 moved from his shop in Broad Street to larger premises, which he extended as the popularity of his furniture grew. He was much imitated and his original work fetches a high price today.

When the City Council or the Board of Estimate is in session, visitors are generally admitted to the other rooms on this floor. In the Board of Estimate's airy and attractive chamber in the west wing, the board sit on a raised dais with columns, matched by a similar dais at the other end. Beyond is the small committee-room, domed and with a circle of columns around the edge. Across the landing, in the east wing, the more grandiose council chamber dates from the merger of New York's five constituent boroughs in 1898 and is unmistakably Victorian. The dark wood furnishings and window frames, together with the gilt cornices and balcony rails, make for a heaviness which contrasts with the earlier rooms opposite. The ceiling painting, done in 1903, self-importantly symbolizes New York receiving the tributes of the nation. I suspect no intentional irony here, though it is a fact that New York is generally, for one reason or another, in bad odor with the rest of the country, regarded — unjustly — as a sink of fecklessness and depravity.

The monumental buildings north and north-east of City Hall, forming the **Civic Center**, come nowhere near equalling the style of the hall itself. Built to symbolize civic grandeur, they reek instead of pomposity. Across Chambers Street, now looking suitably abashed, grimy and careworn, is the old **Criminal Court Building**, a monument to the disgrace of the notorious 'Boss' Tweed in 1871. Tweed was the man who gave Tammany Hall its bad name as he and his friends in the ruling Democratic Party, known as the Tweed Ring, conspired to carve up contracts for civic projects and make extortionate profits from them. The building of the criminal court was one such project. The city paid $12 million for a building which should not have cost more than $3 million. It is not a bad piece of work in itself, in the Palladian style with a central well. But for years it could not overcome the scandalous circumstances of its birth and now stands, blackened and crumbling, awaiting projected renovation. Until a few years ago it was scheduled for demolition but it is now a registered landmark.

William Marcy Tweed was born in 1823 on the Lower East Side of New York, to a middle-class Presbyterian family with its origins in Scotland. He climbed from the bottom rung of the Democratic Party machine as a member of one of the volunteer fire companies which then played a vital role in getting out the vote in elections. By the time he was twenty-one he was an alderman, and soon manoeuvred himself into the pivotal position of chairman of the party's state central committee. He packed Tammany Hall, the party's seat of power, with his own men, the Tweed Ring. Helped by a compliant mayor, 'Boss' Tweed quickly established a tightly controlled and corrupt party machine, exerting a vice-like grip on the city's government and finances which proved tremendously difficult to pry loose. In this, he set a pattern which has been followed in other large American cities. He was as ruthless and unscrupulous as Jay Gould, except that Tweed took his chances with the public's money rather than that of gullible private businessmen.

It was majestically simple. By buying off anyone in a position to thwart his schemes, by extorting fees from businessmen for performing routine services and by collecting handsome commissions from contractors who wanted the business of a fast expanding city of a million people, Tweed and his friends were able to siphon an estimated $160 million into their own pockets. He kept his control over the electoral process by organizing the registration of many thousands of aliens and by developing an effective welfare system at ward level, where local party officials would attend to the grievances of their supporters.

The city was a heavy advertiser in the press, and this for a time discouraged the newspapers from exposing corruption. Finally a clerk in a city office handed some documents to *The New York Times*, strongly suggestive of chicanery. The newspaper's publisher, George Jones, was said to have refused a bribe of half a million dollars to refrain from publishing the documents, and they duly appeared. But the man most often credited with destroying the Tweed Ring is Thomas Nast, a cartoonist for *Harper's Weekly*. His cruel portrayals of the grossly corpulent Tweed and his henchmen aroused public scorn. (Nast was also the inventor of the donkey as a symbol of the Democratic Party and the elephant for the Republicans.) A committee of seventy public men was established in 1871 to investigate the corruption and, in its report, described the Tweed Ring as 'a handful of cunning and resolute robbers'. Theodore Roosevelt, in a charming little history of New York published in 1893, called Tweed 'a coarse, jovial, able man, utterly without scruple of any kind'. After several years in and out of prison and the courts and an abortive flight to Spain Tweed, although never convicted of a crime, died in 1878 in Ludlow Street jail — ironically a prison built during his term as commissioner of public works. To this day, scandals reminiscent of the Tweed Ring still bubble to the surface in New York — allegations of payoffs to city officials to ignore faults in new equipment, suggestions of corruption in awarding new contracts and the like.

Across the road, the Surrogate's Court and Hall of Records, on the north side of Chambers Street, pleases some by the very ostentation of its interpretation of the French Beaux Arts style. Its architects, in 1911, seem to have believed that their creation would be judged by the sheer weight of decoration they managed to apply to the exterior. Inside, it is brown and gloomy, combining the atmosphere of a dungeon with the trappings of a palace: marble columns and stairs, ceiling paintings in the Egyptian style. All this for the essentially humble function of storing city records and settling disputes over wills and probate.

East of this is McKim, Mead and White's **Municipal Building**. Most of New York's public buildings date, like this one, from the early years of the century, when neo-classicism was in style for the dignity and authority it suggested. In truth, New Yorkers have seldom had much respect for the people they elect to govern them, but they felt then that they should at least be able to respect the buildings in which they governed. McKim, Mead and White were the most fashionable firm of architects in this idiom for a score of years, designing a prodigious seven hundred and fifty buildings. We shall see dozens of them on our progress through the city. Charles McKim studied at the École des Beaux Arts in Paris and returned to America in 1870 to join the office of the establishment architect, Henry Hobson Richardson. He went into partnership with William Mead, whose role in the firm was chiefly that of manager and construction supervisor. In 1879 they were joined by Stanford White, who had also worked for Richardson, specializing in the interior details of his buildings — always his strong point. McKim was the more sober of the creative pair, designing solid, dignified buildings harking back to classical Greece and Rome. White was a fast and enthusiastic worker, preferring the extravagant fripperies of the European Renaissance. Among their happiest collaborations were the Villard Houses on Madison Avenue, now incorporated into the lower floors of the Helmsley Palace hotel, and Penn Station, demolished in the 1960s, which was based on the Roman baths of Caracalla. They did not design many skyscrapers and this Municipal Building dates from 1914, when both were dead but their tradition was continued by former assistants. It is much admired but I find it blighted by the windswept desolation of its ground-level entrances, straddling the cavernous Brooklyn Bridge subway station. Nor is it enhanced by the gaunt (but also well thought of) police headquarters erected behind it in 1973, guarded by an intimidating modern sculpture.

Down the hill to the north, **Foley Square** stands on the site of a large pond, filled in at the start of the nineteenth century. Here the federal and county court houses look askance at each other, facing into the square from the east: classical monuments to the majesty of the law. The farther

Cass Gilbert's Woolworth Building, a Gothic skyscraper, with the twin towers of the World Trade Center behind it. The Woolworth lobby is one of the most arresting in the city.

Chinatown: a favourite strolling place for the New Yorkers and visitors alike, it has dozens of food shops, gift shops and restaurants.

of the two, the **County Court House**, was designed in 1912 but not completed until 1927. This is a hexagonal building with a row of Corinthian columns at the front, a resplendent interior and a pompous motto (a quirk of the period) beneath the roof: 'The true administration of justice is the firmest pillar of good government.' South of this, the **US Court House** was built in 1936, the last work of Cass Gilbert. I doubt whether this curious building is the one for which he would want to be remembered. The massive columned base is fitting enough, but he has stuck a skyscraper on top, scarcely related to the rest.

Luckily, Gilbert's finest work is only a few minutes' walk away, back past City Hall and across its park. In the **Woolworth Tower**, on the corner of Broadway and Park Place, he showed how to marry traditional Gothic architecture to the form of the modern skyscraper. The Gothic style was selected by Frank Woolworth, the 'five-and-dime' store magnate for whom it was built; he had seen London's Houses of Parliament and noted how well the form was suited to soaring structures of the kind he desired to commemorate his success, one of the classic 'poor boy made good' tales of American business. Born in New York State in 1852, he worked as a junior clerk in several local shops until he read of one selling only goods which cost five cents. The concept attracted him and, helped by his employer, he opened a shop of that kind in Utica, New York. It failed but he tried again in Lancaster, Pennsylvania, where the idea caught on. Soon he added ten-cent items to the range and the familiar red and gold shopfronts began appearing in several Eastern cities. By 1901 he was rich enough to own a mansion on Fifth Avenue but, a man of unashamed vanity, he wanted to build something which would unequivocally symbolize his business acumen.

Because the style of the Woolworth Tower derived from European cathedrals, it was quickly dubbed the 'cathedral of commerce'. Opened in 1913, its height of 792 feet made it the tallest building in the world until 1930, when it was outreached by the Chrysler Building on 42nd Street and later by the Empire State Building on 34th Street. The elaborate gargoyles, flying buttresses and traceries adorn an essentially functional design: if you replaced the decorative terra cotta with steel and glass, you would have something approaching a finely balanced skyscraper of the second half of this century. The carving and tiling above the entrance are especially delicate and inviting: accept the invitation, for here is one office lobby you really must not miss. The glittering mosaic ceiling, an exotic aviary in blue, green and gold, is exquisitely worked by craftsmen, many of whom came to work here almost as soon as they stepped off the immigrant ships from Italy. Much of the gilding is in pure gold leaf and every detail is sumptuous, even down to the brass mail-boxes.

Above the staircase, carved figures portray items sold in the Woolworth shops. Do not overlook in the corners of the lobby ceiling the funny caricatures of men who played a role in the building's creation. Gilbert, the architect, holds a model of the tower in his hand and Woolworth is counting out his money (he paid for the whole thing in cash, as his customers were required to do in his shops). These appealing little carvings illustrate the enthusiasm and self-confidence which were hallmarks of the success, not just of Woolworth, but of other entrepreneurs throughout the city's commercial history.

A few yards north, on the other side of Broadway, the undistinguished squarish building on the corner of Chambers Street was, when it opened in 1846, the first fully fledged department store in the United States. Its founder, A. T. Stewart, was as much a pioneer in the carriage trade end of retailing as Woolworth was in its cheaper reaches. The clock on the west wall is evidence of the building's later role as headquarters of the *Sun,* one of New York's many defunct newspapers.

Back south, at the corner of Vesey Street, is an architectural delight from another era. Built in 1776, **St Paul's Chapel** is New York's only public building to survive from before the revolution. Thomas McBean, its architect, was a Scottish pupil of James Gibbs, who built St Martin-in-the-Fields in London, and there is an affinity between the two churches. As McBean designed it, St Paul's was a plain Georgian hall in the local brownstone, unadorned with the present spire and portico, which were added thirty years later. Inside, it is orderly, airy and uncluttered, though the color scheme, in garish pastel shades of pink and blue with sparkling gold highlights, is a bit assertive, discouraging repose. One of the two box-like enclosures bounded by three-foot wooden walls is the pew where George Washington used to sit when he attended the church regularly after his inauguration, until the seat of government moved to Philadelphia the following year. His first action after taking his oath of office was to lead his cabinet to St Paul's for worship; but they might not recognize it today, because at the time of the addition of the spire and portico the interior was modified by Major Pierre L'Enfant, the French architect who served in the continental army and who drew the master plan for Washington DC. In St Paul's his most distinctive work is the flamboyant altar and the decoration surrounding it, a vigorous interpretation of the tablets of the law handed down at Mount Sinai.

St Paul's remains a chapel of Trinity Church, though it has outlived two older churches on the Trinity site. When it went up on the corner of Vesey Street (named for William Vesey, Trinity's first rector), there were fields around it, one of them sloping down to the Hudson River lapping against Greenwich Street at a point now roughly in the middle of the World Trade Center site. The fields were part of Queen Anne's Farm, which occupied many acres of Manhattan's Lower West Side and which was granted in its entirety to Trinity. Much of that gift of land has been sold but the church still owns some, assuring the survival and prosperity of Trinity and its chapels.

Now walk west down **Vesey Street**. No 14, the New York County Lawyer's Association, is a well-proportioned Georgian mansion, another late work of the prolific Cass Gilbert, less ambitious and much more pleasing than the Federal Court House. No 20, two doors away, is the old *Evening Post* building, dating from 1905, one of New York's very few examples of the Art Nouveau style. Look up to the top floors, adorned with crouching and now rather deformed limestone figures.

The **New York Telephone Building**, sometimes called the Barclay-Vesey building, occupies the block between Barclay, Washington, Vesey and West Streets. Built in 1926, it has always been highly regarded by architects. Outside the building is embellished with lavish carvings of leaves, vines and wild animals, a bit reminiscent of the work of Grinling Gibbons. The theme is continued on the richly colored murals and ceilings inside, which include some designs with American Indian motifs. The telephone company is from time to time the target of bomb threats and is a little paranoid about security, so if you go into the lobby you will probably be challenged by a guard to state your business. It is worth risking that small embarrassment, because it is one of the most handsome interiors in the city. The sheltered arcade along Vesey Street is a rare amenity in New York. It was once the busy terminal of one of the ferries to New Jersey and near to the extinct Washington Market, prized for its fresh produce; but nowadays it is seldom used.

In the latter part of this walk you have seen, in the Telephone Building and the Woolworth Tower, two of New York's finest examples of the still young art of designing skyscrapers. But much of your perambulation will have been dominated by the two gigantic towers now just to your south which represent, at least in their engineering aspects, the very latest development of the form. The twin towers of the **World Trade Center** are the second tallest buildings in the world, exceeded only by the Sears tower in Chicago. Built between 1966 and 1976, the 1,350 feet, hundred and ten storey towers were among the first skyscrapers to abandon the steel frame construction which had been the only technique used since the end of the nineteenth century. In one sense they revert to older building methods in that most of their weight is borne on their walls, though the walls are made of modern high-strength steel rather than of old-fashioned brick or stone. The central elevator shafts share the task of bearing the load and the absence of steel supports means that the floor space is free of interruption, ideal for airy open-plan offices.

The towers, with the three lower buildings surrounding them, were built by the New York and New Jersey Port Authority, a joint body established by the states to administer the harbor and the area's three airports. The object was to provide a single prestige location for the international commerce conducted in the city and most of the Center's tenants are involved in enterprises related, if sometimes a bit tenuously, to that theme.

The best way to approach the Center is from the east, where Trinity Place broadens and becomes Church Street. From here you have access to the large white plaza, which can lay claim to being the windiest spot in New York. The gust whooshes in from the south-west, the towers forming a tunnel which concentrates its force. The new hotel on the south-west corner may encourage greater use of the plaza for the recreational purposes for which it was presumably intended. Its fountain and modern sculptures must have looked monumental in the studio but are inevitably dwarfed by their surroundings.

Go into any of the Center's main buildings and down one floor on the escalator for access to the retail heart of the complex, directly underneath the plaza. Here are some useful shops, entrances to several subway lines and to the PATH (Port Authority Trans-Hudson) commuter trains to New Jersey. Nearly a dozen restaurants serve varied fare of remarkably consistent quality. For the visitor in a tearing hurry, a booth offers hot soup and a roll. There are delicatessen counters and snack bars, a vegetarian section (Nature's Pantry) and some specialty cafés grouped under the name of The Big Kitchen, spelled out in giant letters resting on the floor, all with ledges at a suitable height for balancing your tray and eating. The most elaborate of the basement restaurants — though by no means overpriced — is the Market Diner, with pretty decor suggestive of a Victorian saloon. Here you can choose between quite imaginative dishes — rough patés, home-made pies, fish and the like, freshly made. The restaurants are all busy at lunch time but service is efficient.

The public catering in the World Trade Center is centrally controlled, including the Windows on the World, the prestige restaurant on the 107th floor. This is an establishment of high class and high price, though many of the dishes seem to rely too heavily on those all-purpose machines which grind food and make it into a bland purée. If you want to enjoy the view without committing yourself to the time and expense of eating a meal at Windows of the World, you can have a drink at the bar or pop into the Hors d'Oeuvrerie next door, where you drink and nibble, paying individually for whatever you fancy.

At the top of the other tower is the observation deck. Be careful to avoid excessively misty or windy days for your visit: mist will spoil the view, and if there is a high wind the outdoor observation platform will be closed, leaving visitors to peer through the windows of the floor below. Not only that, but in a high wind the towers sway alarmingly.

There are intriguing views from the observation deck in all directions. To the south is a panorama of the entrance to the harbor and the Verrazano Narrows Bridge. East is Brooklyn, linked by the Brooklyn, Manhattan and Williamsburg bridges. The dockyards of Hoboken are off to the west, with the rest of America beyond. The northern view is the most thrilling. The big midtown skyscrapers are bunched in the distance, the avenues pointing straight towards them, leading the eye along. Between them and the skyscrapers of Lower Manhattan, at whose summit you now stand, is a valley of lower structures, the stretch through which the heart of the city drifted in the nineteenth century before the start of the craze for towers pointing into the sky. You have to look down at a sharp angle to see the target of our next excursion. This is ethnic Manhattan — Chinatown, Little Italy, the Lower East Side — where we shall search for the immigrant roots of New York's people and for the sight and smell of exotic foods. For today, though, take the express elevator to the foot of the tower and catch a subway train home.

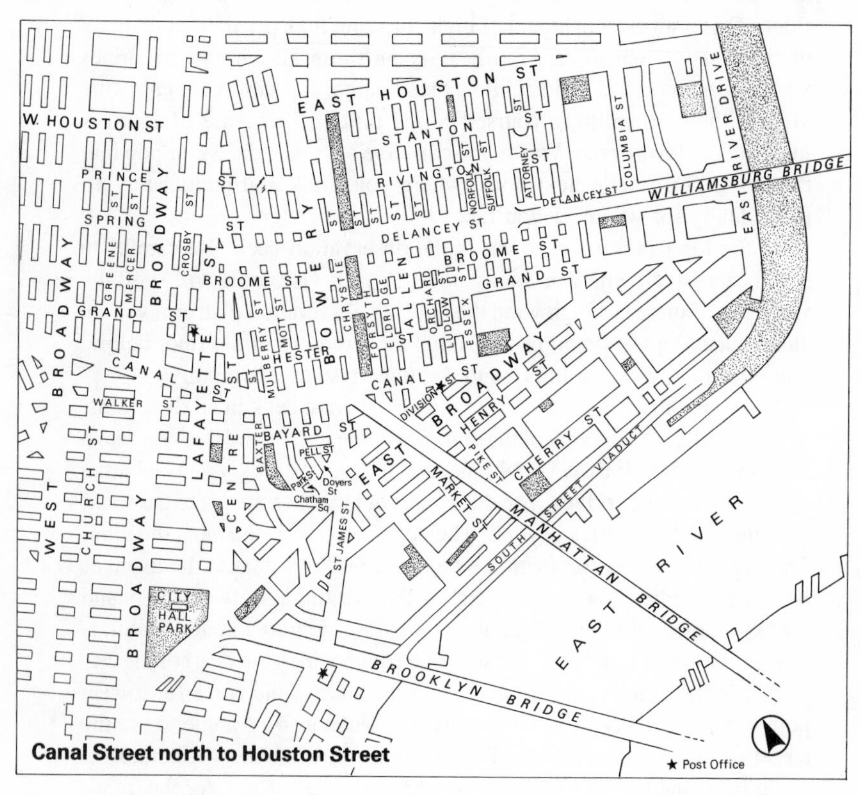

Canal Street north to Houston Street

5
Ethnic New York

VISITORS TO A STRANGE CITY want, above all, to discover its essence. The truly dedicated tourist soon tires of the palpable pleasures of the museums, theatres and restaurants. He has come to find what kind of town New York really is but, sadly, he customarily has only a few days in which to do it. That is why friends beg to be told just where, in a short time, they can locate the elusive quality which sets New York apart from other cities. As often as not, my reply is: 'Go to the Lower East Side. Go on a Sunday. Have lunch there. Walk around the streets.'

The area just north of Lower Manhattan, between Houston Street and Brooklyn Bridge, is ethnic New York. There are, it is true, many other sections of the city which have become the preserve of distinct national communities; but during the mass immigration of the late nineteenth and early twentieth centuries, this is where most of them came, dividing themselves into three groups — Italian, Jewish and Chinese — and to that flood of immigrants New York owes much of its present character. The abundant literature of the Lower East Side teems with tales of men and women who came there as children with their parents through Ellis Island, driven from their European homelands by persecution or poverty, only to find conditions of sometimes greater hardship. Nonetheless, many fought their way out of the slums to wealth and even fame. The tenements built for the immigrants are still standing, some streets barely altered in essence from their appearance in photographs taken seventy and eighty years ago.

Take the F train (Sixth Avenue line) to the corner of Delancey and Essex Streets. On the east side of the junction is the **Essex Street covered market**, dreary from the outside but lively and full of interest once you get in. Wandering around the stalls is a quick way of getting to know the ethnic mix of the area. The traditional Jewish fare abounds: pumpernickel bread, poppyseed cake, bagels and bialys — these last two are chewy rolls, delicious with smoked salmon (lox) and cream cheese. Puerto

Rican delicacies cater to the new wave of immigrants who, in the last twenty years or so, have moved into the tenements vacated by Jewish families heading for more salubrious apartments uptown, in Brooklyn or Queens, or for houses in the suburbs. There are Caribbean vegetables — apio, yula, yams and plantains — as well as a sprinkling of Chinese and Korean foods.

Walk a couple of blocks west down **Delancey Street**, a broad highway often choked with traffic from Williamsburg Bridge, lined with cheap clothing stores, shoe shops, instant opticians and fast food restaurants. In the eighteenth century this area was owned by James Delancey who remained loyal to the losing side in the revolution and had his lands confiscated as a result. **Orchard Street**, two blocks west of Essex Street, ran through his orchard. During the heyday of the Lower East Side it was one of the chief shopping streets. Hard bargains would be driven for food, clothing and furniture with the shopkeepers and pushcart peddlers whose carts lined the cobbles. The founders of some of New York's smartest shops and department stores began their commercial careers as peddlers on the Lower East Side.

Orchard Street has kept something of its old character. The pushcarts are gone, but to replace them the shops have spilled out on to the street, selling from outdoor racks and tables. The dark tenements remain and so do the hand-painted shop signs, though some today are in Spanish. Orchard Street merchants sell mainly clothes, of all types and quality, as well as shoes, hats, belts and a few toys and novelty goods. The merchants will still offer you a deal: 50 cents off if you buy three sets of underwear instead of one, an extra pair of socks thrown in with a half-dozen. The narrow shops quite patently have not been modernized for years. Go on a Sunday, when it is full of bustle and when Orchard Street between Houston and Delancey Streets becomes a pedestrian precinct. It is far from the slick, super-efficient retailing which we think of as typically American.

The tenements, in the years surrounding the turn of the century, housed the notorious sweatshops which fed New York's burgeoning clothing industry. The manufacturers had their own cutters to cut the pieces and pass them to outside contractors for finishing and pressing. The contractors would either have their own workrooms in which their employees, mainly young women, finished the work, or they would subcontract to others who would have it done in their homes, aided by friends or relatives who were paid according to how many garments they completed. The name 'sweatshop' was merited by the necessity of keeping a stove hot at all times to heat the flatirons used for pressing. Children were commonly employed, and the working day would stretch from dawn to nightfall.

An affecting description of life inside one of the tenements which doubled as workrooms comes in *The Time That Was Then*, by Harry Roskolenko, who was born on the Lower East Side to parents who had emigrated from the Ukraine.

> They were upstairs and downstairs; up five, six and seven flights — in flats which looked like warehouses, hardly places to sleep and to live. Small children, aged five, were already experts with the needle. They sewed buttons. They carried cloaks. They tied up cloaks. They threaded needles. They heard their tortured parents bemoan America's greatness. For this they had left Europe?[8]

And Roskolenko quotes from a contemporary newspaper account of the view from the elevated railway which used to run down the lower part of Second Avenue:

> Men and women bending over machines or ironing clothes at the window, most of them half naked. The road is like a big gangway to an endless work room with vast multitudes forever laboring. Morning, noon or night — it makes no difference. The scene is always the same.

A series of strikes in the garment industry during the first decade of the twentieth century resulted in higher wages and improved conditions. The subcontracting of work to tenement sweatshops was outlawed. More reforms followed one of the Lower East Side's greatest tragedies, the Triangle Shirtwaist Factory fire of 1911. The factory was on the top three floors of a ten-story building at the corner of Washington Place and Greene Street, a block east of Washington Square. Some six hundred workers, mainly young women, were preparing to leave for home when a fire engulfed all three floors. Many of the exit doors to the emergency stairs were locked — common in such factories during working hours — and a hundred and forty-six workers were killed, many leaping to their death from the high windows. The public outcry resulted in the enforcement of much stricter safety standards in factories. In the 1930s and 1940s the clothing factories moved uptown, to between 34th and 42nd Streets on the West Side, the present garment district.

Clothing manufacture was the chief but not the only industry of the Lower East Side. Cigar-making was another which gave employment to the new immigrants and also gave rise to complaints by workers about the conditions. Samuel Gompers was born in London in 1850, the son of a Dutch-born cigar-maker who moved to New York in 1863. He followed his father's trade and became an important union organizer in the industry and later in the American labor movement, which drew some of its most important early strength from the immigrant workers of the Lower East Side. Gompers rose to become the first President of the American Federation of Labor, a post he held until his death in 1924. In his autobiography he describes his Lower East Side home, at the corner of Houston and Attorney Streets:

> Father began making cigars at home and I helped him. Our house was just opposite a slaughter house. All day long we would see the animals being driven into the . . . pens and would hear the turmoil and the cries of the animals. The neighborhood was filled with the penetrating, sickening odor. The suffering of the animals and the nauseating odor made it physically impossible for me to eat meat for many months.

A block west of Orchard Street is **Allen Street**, once known for its Greek, Turkish and Arabian cafes (and for the belly dancers who would perform, scarcely restrained by modesty, in the clubs and cabarets on the upper floors). Now it is ramshackle, notable only for the dozens of small tie shops which line its east side between Delancey and Houston Streets. This is the place to come for ties, many made up on the premises in the small workrooms behind the shops. Prices are keen and the salesmanship enthusiastic. Many are family concerns and on entering you may interrupt some good-natured (at least I assume it to be good-natured) banter between the husband and wife who run the place. They will continue arguing while you riffle through the selection of ties, though they will pause long enough to encourage you to close a deal by offering discounts for bulk buys, like the sock salesmen of Orchard Street, and rolling their eyes in disbelief at the prices at which they are prepared to part with the goods.

Exploring the local streets, notice how the shops of merchants selling the same categories of goods cluster together. Where Orchard Street meets Grand Street you find ladies' underwear, while jewelry is centered on Canal Street between Allen and Forsyth Streets. Where Eldridge Street joins Hester Street are the few remaining suppliers of Jewish religious paraphernalia. Grand Street has a section for furnishing fabrics and bed linen between Allen and Forsyth Streets. A clutch of pickle shops nests on Essex Street between Grand and Hester Streets.

By now you may be ready for sustenance. Most of the cafes and food shops are on East Houston Street. Of the half dozen delicatessens in the row, the best known is Katz's, on the corner of Ludlow Street, established in 1889. Service is cafeteria-style: you take a ticket when you enter and the server scribbles the cost of the food on it. Sandwich cutters stand behind the long counter, awaiting your choice. Hot pastrami with rye bread is traditional central European Jewish fare which has become, by adoption, a New York specialty. Pastrami is beef marinated in salt and spices and then smoked. The cutter will chop off a morsel for you to taste while he is stuffing the sandwich to what is a positively indecent thickness. He will give you a pickled cucumber which might be a bit sharp for unaccustomed palates, and you will be invited to smother the meat with mustard. It is a juicy delight but if you don't want to risk it you can have the more straightforward corned beef. Cold sandwich fillings include chopped liver or a variety of pressed meats and salamis. During the Second World War, Katz's became known for the slogan they coined to promote their service for despatching food parcels to the troops: 'Send a salami to your boy in the army.'

For more uncommon fare, turn the corner back into Essex Street and make for Bernstein-on-Essex, between Rivington and Stanton Streets, which claims to be the world's first Kosher Chinese restaurant — a claim which, as far as I know, is not disputed, though there are now several in New York. On the Chinese menu, sweet-and-sour beef replaces sweet-and-sour pork, and there are other ethnic compromises. They also serve non-Chinese Kosher dishes — their pastrami is said by the cognoscenti to be among the finest in the city — and it is probably best to stick to these, saving essays into Chinese cuisine until Chinatown is reached later in this chapter. Bernstein's is a busy restaurant, and you may have to wait if you go for Sunday lunch, but it is worth the trouble, because it has a cosy Jewish family atmosphere, complete with wisecracking waiters. As a rule, the senior waiters are Jewish and their helpers Chinese.

A few yards farther east on Delancey, between Norfolk and Suffolk

Streets, not far from the foot of Williamsburg Bridge, is Ratner's Dairy Restaurant. Because the Jewish faith forbids drinking milk with meat, restaurants are divided into dairy, which serve no meat, and those like Bernstein's, which serve no milk. Ratner's is large and popular, with world-weary waiters serving excellent fish, blintzes (pancakes filled with sweet cottage or cream cheeses) and cheesecake. Just north of it, on Rivington Street near the junction with Norfolk Street, is an unlikely diversion, the only wine-making plant in New York City. Schapiro's have been making wine here, for both religious and lay enjoyment, since 1899. On Sundays, between twelve and five, you can join what is grandly called a 'tour', but in reality is a quick look at one or two of the one hundred and ten giant vats in the cellars which run beneath the whole block. Afterwards, in the tasting-room, you sample some of the twenty-six varieties, which include wine made from plums, elderberries and honey as well as from New York State grapes. Much of it is on the sweet side, but the tour is free and companionable and does not take much time. On the walls of the tasting-room are some marvellous photographs of the Lower East Side at the turn of the century, which alone would justify the visit.

Those hungering for a still more authentic and adventurous ethnic experience will have to detour half a dozen blocks south along Essex Street to the south-east corner of East Broadway. The Garden Cafeteria is as unprepossessing inside as out — a dull chrome and plastic snack bar, cramped and often crowded with impatient customers. The serving method is the same as at Katz's; the servers at the self-service counter are not too meticulous about their appearance and are impatient with people who do not know what to choose from the array of blintzes, fried and boiled fish, often watery vegetables and items broadly resembling egg rolls. Soups — especially borscht — are popular and good value. First-timers can reduce the culture gap by sitting at one of the waiter-assisted tables, but then they will miss mingling with the Yiddish-speaking regulars, who give the impression of being fresh from the immigrant boats. The building next door used to be the headquarters of the *Daily Forward,* the city's main Yiddish newspaper, and although the paper has now moved uptown the cafeteria still seems to be a haunt of Jewish intellectuals, rich in culture if not in worldly goods. Once when we went there our gentle neighbor asked if we were going to finish all the bread we were allotted with our meal, and when we said no she parcelled it neatly in a paper napkin and packed it in her handbag without compromising her dignity.

This detour, as I say, is for adventurous gastronomes. If you take it you need not return north along Essex Street to pick up my main itinerary, but can instead head west along Canal Street and turn right into the Bowery. Those who did not take the detour will walk west along East Houston Street and turn left into the Bowery.

The Bowery shares the character of the derelicts who lie dirty, drunk and often insensible in its doorways and on its pavements; you guess that they must have seen better days but it's precious hard to envisage them. The Bowery's best times were in the second half of the nineteenth century, when it was lined with restaurants, hotels, theatres, music halls and bars. Even then it had a raffish quality until, as happens, the raffishness degenerated into vice and squalor, helped on its way by the noisy overhead railway that used to run down the middle, showering a hot coal or two on unwary pedestrians below. Many buildings remain from the golden days. At street level they are now dull shops, wholesale suppliers of lighting, kitchen equipment and the like. One or two are soup kitchens. But look above the ground floor and, with imagination, you can guess which were once theatres and music halls. A few old hotels have their names picked out in relief on the front, ineradicably. As for the Bowery bums, they will do you no harm. Those who are not completely insensible may ask you for money but will merely shrug in resignation if you refuse. Most will simply stare through you, knowing that you are in passage and will be gone before long, leaving them to it — and it to them.

An early victim of the Bowery curse was Stephen Foster, one of the best writers of early American popular songs. He was born in Pittsburgh in 1826 and in his twenties wrote such still-popular melodies as 'O, Susanna', 'The Old Folks at Home', 'Camptown Races', 'My Old Kentucky Home' and 'Jeannie with the Light Brown Hair'. In 1860 he abandoned his family in Pennsylvania and came to the Bowery, where his songs were being performed in the minstrel shows. He rented a room in a cheap hotel on the corner of Bayard Street, hoping for inspiration, but instead developed an undetermined fever and a gargantuan taste for drink. One day in 1864 he fell and cut his throat on a washing bowl, dying a few days later at the age of thirty-eight.

Yet if the Bowery saw the ruin of one great song writer, it gave a start to another. Irving Berlin was born Israel Baline in Siberia in 1888. When he was four his parents brought him to New York, where they lived on Cherry Street. His father, a synagogue cantor, died when Berlin was eight, so after just two years of school he left to support his mother by selling newspapers, and began to supplement his income by singing popular songs on the corners of the Bowery. He was offered part-time assignments in the taverns as a singing waiter, a phenomenon of the time: at intervals between serving at the tables the waiters would burst into song, to add to the general merriment, and if the customers were pleased they would offer tips. At the ripe age of sixteen, Berlin became a full-time singing waiter at the Pelham Cafe in Chinatown, also known as Nigger Mike's — a beer hall with a brothel upstairs. He began experimenting on the piano, and collaborated with the house pianist to compose his first published lyric, 'Marie from Sunny Italy'. Berlin's early songs included several with ethnic themes: 'Oh, How that German Could Love' was another. 'Alexander's Ragtime Band' established his reputation in 1911. He left the Lower East Side to become a pioneer, first of the Broadway musical and then of its Hollywood counterpart, and he was always touchingly grateful to the country which fostered success stories such as his. His song 'God Bless America' is a sentimental tribute which is played on patriotic occasions almost as often as the national anthem. Of his early years, he said: 'Everybody ought to have a Lower East Side in their life.'

Be that as it may, the present-day visitor will not want to linger too long in the Bowery. One block will suffice for the time being: we shall return at the end of this chapter. For now, turn west into Prince Street. The Gothic church between Mott and Mulberry Streets, on the north side behind a high brick wall, is old St Patrick's Cathedral. The original building here, the first Catholic cathedral in New York, was put up in 1809 to the design of Joseph Mangin, the architect of City Hall. After a fire in the 1860s it was largely rebuilt, but the cathedral itself moved uptown to its new building on Fifth Avenue. The handsome Federal hall opposite the old cathedral, on the south side of Prince Street, is its associated convent and school, built in 1828.

Across Mulberry Street we enter another ethnic area, **Little Italy**, although the first manifestation of it that catches our eye and nose is a shop selling live chickens, catering to the adjacent Chinese. The Italians were the largest national group of immigrants between 1880 and 1925 but many quickly abandoned the Lower East Side, as the Jews had done, to establish enclaves in Queens, Staten Island and New Jersey. Little Italy is today (vide the chicken shop) a victim of encroachment by the Chinese from the south and the artists of SoHo from the west. All the same, a definable and lively Italian district remains, particularly on Mulberry Street which, for a couple of weeks in September, becomes Via San Gennaro for that Saint's festival and is filled with sideshows and stalls selling Italian food and drink.

There are a dozen or so good-looking Italian restaurants, each with its devotees, the best offering an attractive old-fashioned European atmosphere with polished wood, white tablecloths and napkins. Interspersed among them are tempting pastry shops and ice cream parlors. The Cafe Roma, near the junction of Mulberry and Broome Streets, has its own adjoining bakery, into which the curious may peer, watching the baking of robust pastries. If you arrive here at about tea-time, venture into the small cafe, with its narrow marble-topped tables, to sample a pastry or, if it is a hot day, one of the Italian versions of ice cream soda, a lemon water ice in a drink flavored with almond, cherry, grenadine or tamarind. On Grand Street, between Mulberry and Mott Streets, is Ferrara's, a larger and more famous confectionery shop, worth going into for a look at the intricately iced cakes and elaborate sweets.

Most shops and restaurants are on the ground floor of old tenement buildings, forbidding edifices in spite of the elegant wrought iron fire escapes which adorn some. A few yards down Mulberry Street, on the right, Paolocci's, one of the oldest and most reputable of the restaurants in the area, occupies a small Federal town house built in 1816, with the characteristic dormers still on the roof. Farther down still, on the corner of Hester Street, is Umberto's Clam House, an Italian fish restaurant with modern decor which is notorious for a reason which it does not relish and which has nothing whatever to do with the food. On 7 April 1972, at about twenty past five in the morning, Joe 'Crazy Joey' Gallo, reputed to be a leader of organized crime, was shot dead at Umberto's as he was rounding off a night on the town with his wife and step-daughter celebrating his forty-third birthday. The killing was part of the continuing vendetta between rival factions of the New York Mafia competing for the control of particular criminal undertakings in specific areas of the city.

Italian Americans resent, with some justification, being identified with the Mafia. They point out that people with Italian surnames have no monopoly on crime in America. Yet the Mafia certainly exists and is surely the best-documented secret society in the world. The newspapers carry detailed reports of the strength of the parties in the gangland rivalries — largely based on briefings from the Federal Bureau of Investigation. They endow the gangsters with cute pet names, though whether these are actually used by their partners in crime or invented by the FBI is a moot question. Thus, apart from Crazy Joey, we have 'Kid Blast', 'Tony Ducks', 'Fat Tony', 'Matty the Horse', 'Jimmy Nap', 'Cockeyed Ben', 'Gentleman John' and many others. The enterprises over which these colorful-sounding gentlemen fight and die include illegal gambling (all gambling is illegal in New York except state-run race courses, betting shops and lotteries), prostitution, drugs and many quasi-respectable undertakings such as rubbish collection, pizza parlors and restaurant laundries, whose markets are 'protected' by unorthodox and illegal methods. The technique is to use threats of violence to ensure that small businesses patronize Mafia-controlled suppliers.

The chain of events which led to Gallo's death began during the summer of 1971 at an Italian American rally at Columbus Circle, outside Central Park. It was a protest meeting organized by Joe Colombo to complain that he and fellow Italian Americans were being stigmatized as gangsters by the FBI. Gallo, said to have been a rival of Colombo's for dominance in the Brooklyn Mafia, had been released from prison only a few weeks earlier. At the rally Colombo was shot in the neck by a black assailant who was himself shot dead on the spot. Colombo lived for a few years but was never able to resume an active life. His relatives and colleagues were convinced that Gallo had master-minded the shooting, and his death at Umberto's was said to be their revenge. 'Public executions' of that sort are a traditional way of settling scores in the Mafia. Gallo used to boast to friends that he had been involved in one of the most notorious of them — the killing of Albert Anastasia as he was having a shave in the barber's shop of the Park Sheraton Hotel on Sixth Avenue — in an earlier round of the factional squabble that was to result in his own death. For lower grade gangsters, more routine disposal methods are used. From time to time their bodies are found in the trunks of parked cars, or at the bottom of rivers, weighed down with concrete. To be fair to Umberto's Clam House, it has to be said that it is a decent seafood place, with conveniently long opening hours, where many thousands have eaten non-fatally since the Gallo shooting.

We are now close to Canal Street and Chinatown, but before we plunge into yet another ethnic bustle this might be the time for a stroll round the quieter streets of **SoHo**, a few blocks west. The name has nothing to do with London's Soho, but was devised because it lies south (So) of Houston Street (Ho). In the second half of the nineteenth century this stretch of Broadway housed fashionable department stores, hotels and restaurants. In the streets behind were more stores as well as warehouses supplying the shops in the main street. When the stores moved uptown, the buildings were devoted to light manufacturing until, in the 1960s, artists came to take an interest in their high ceilings and large windows as suitable spots for studios. They started to drift here, and a few opened galleries on the ground floor. Soon, living in a SoHo loft became the smart thing (not just for artists but for anyone who wanted to be in the swim). Rents climbed, and it is now as expensive to live here as in the more traditional residential areas of Greenwich Village and uptown. Some artists meanwhile have moved south, to the area known as Tribeca (triangle below Canal) and some to Brooklyn and Queens.

Architecturally, SoHo's most interesting features are its buildings with cast-iron façades. Though there had been experiments in Britain with cast-iron buildings from 1830, they never became popular on a large scale until introduced in America. The pioneers in New York were Daniel Badger and James Bogardus, who quarrelled over which was the true originator. Badger erected a building with a cast-iron front in Boston in 1842 but the first with a complete iron structure was built to Bogardus's design in New York in 1850. The advantage of cast iron was that it obviated the need for massive stone pillars to support tall buildings. The same weight could be carried on slender iron columns, allowing daintier designs and more window space — important in the new department stores. The elaborate Italianate decoration popular at the time could be much more easily reproduced in cast iron than in stone, where each piece had to be carved separately. The typical early cast-iron façades contained row upon row of arched windows separated by thin columns extravagantly and identically embellished with leaves, scrolls and curlicues, seeking the effect of a Venetian palazzo. In later years a more sober style became the fashion. One of the claims the designers made for the buildings was that they were fireproof, but experience proved that this was not the case and they went out of fashion in the 1890s when the introduction of steel-cage construction led to the beginning of true skyscrapers.

As you walk west down Grand Street from Little Italy, the pretentious but now abandoned pile on your right between Baxter and Center Streets is the old police headquarters. Cross Crosby Street and approach Broadway. The white store which fills the whole block on your right is a good example of the cast-iron style, except for the modernized ground floor. It was built in 1879 as a fashionable lace and linen shop; you can still see the outlines of the old display windows on Grand Street and envisage the fashionable Victorian textiles displayed therein. One or two of the old bishop's crook iron lamp-posts survive on Broadway to help the fantasy along. Turn right up Broadway to the corner of Broome Street for the **Haughwout Building,** assembled by Daniel Badger in 1857 as an emporium of fine glass and china, and boasting the most striking, as well as one of the oldest, of the city's surviving cast-iron façades, though painting it black has made it too sombre. It was the first New York shop to install a passenger elevator.

Farther north, on the opposite side of the road, the **Singer Building** (No. 561) was designed in 1907 by Ernest Flagg, one of the most original of the turn-of-the-century architects, whose better-known building for Singer on Lower Broadway was unforgivably razed. The delicate iron tracery on the front of this one is charming and unique. Flagg was born in Brooklyn, the son of the rector of Grace Church in Manhattan. He graduated from the Ecole des Beaux Arts in 1888, when he was thirty-one, and three years later opened an office in Manhattan, which he was to maintain for fifty years. His other outstanding building in the city is Scribner's bookshop on Fifth Avenue, much farther uptown.

Turn west off Broadway into Prince Street and take the second turning on the left. This is **Greene Street**, lined with characteristic cast-iron buildings, some still used as warehouses and others as loft residences. You can pick out the latter by their distinguishing badge — potted plants curling round the fire escapes. You are now in SoHo proper and may wander round the art galleries as your taste dictates. A few health food and cheese shops, jazz lofts and restaurants have sprung up here to cater for the new breed of resident. As you continue south down Greene Street you may care to know that, before it was taken over by warehouses it was notorious in the nineteenth century for commerce of a different kind in some of the city's best-known brothels. Now it chastely crosses **Canal Street**, a joy for bargain-hunters in new and second-hand clothing, electronic equipment, hardware, kitchen things and almost everything you can imagine. Turn left on Canal Street and left again into Mercer

Street for a detour into the **Museum of Holography**, a small but intriguing display of this new three-dimensional art form. Children, standing on milk crates to see the exhibits at the proper level, find it especially exciting and may urge purchase of some of the simpler holographs on sale.

Where Canal Street forms a fork with Walker Street, coming in on its right, is the beginning of **Chinatown**. You can tell when you are there by the stalls selling unmistakably Chinese vegetables and fruit on the right-hand pavement of Canal Street. This area of town was settled by the Irish in the middle of the nineteenth century, then by the Italians and finally by the Chinese, who came in the 1870s and 1880s to escape the violence directed against them on the West Coast. In 1880 there were barely a thousand Chinese living here; by the turn of the century the figure was up to ten thousand and there are now thirty-five thousand Chinese on the Lower East Side. Since the mid-1960s their colony expanded, following the repeal of legislation discriminating against Chinese immigrants, until it now spreads north over what was part of Little Italy and east into some former Jewish areas. In the early part of this century, visitors were apprehensive about venturing into Chinatown because of the widely publicized violence of the Tong Wars — the Chinese equivalent of Mafia vendettas. Now it is one of the more benign parts of the city: gang warfare still emerges fatally from time to time, but it is internecine and scarcely a hazard to the casual visitor.

The original Chinatown occupies a small but fascinating few blocks south of Canal Street between Center Street and the Bowery: dozens of food shops, gift shops and, above all, restaurants. The familiar Cantonese cuisine still predominates but many New Yorkers prefer the spicier Hunan or Szechuan style and there are a growing number of establishments reflecting that taste. It would be invidious to make specific recommendations — obviously I cannot have eaten in them all — but *The New York Times* singles out among the Cantonese restaurants the Yun Luck Rice Shoppe in **Doyers Street**, a crooked alley between Pell Street and the Bowery. Like some of its neighbors it makes do with a positively spartan decor and serves large portions of tasty food at outstandingly low prices. The whole fish in sweet-and-sour or gingery sauce is excellent. Next to it, the Num Wah serves only dim sum, a succession of *hors d'oeuvre*-type dishes brought round on trays. You take the ones you want and your bill is always reasonable, calculated by the number of empty dishes on your table at the end. It is a good way of sampling many varied dishes and avoiding the commitment of choosing from a menu. The room itself is small, inelegant and invariably crowded. The Szechuan Taste on Chatham Square is more comfortable and has a reputation among lovers of Hunan cooking. At 22 Mott Street the Peking Duck House keeps a supply of that famous delicacy ready to serve: elsewhere you normally need to order it twenty-four hours in advance to allow for the complex preparation. At Foo Joy on Division Street, enthusiasts recommend the pork chops in red sauce with scallions (spring onions). The Silver Palace on the Bowery, near Canal Street, has fine food with an authentic festive atmosphere and winking dragons. A useful general rule in choosing a restaurant here is to go to one patronized chiefly by Chinese, although you might want to avoid those that do not supply menus in English — an indication that they do not really welcome non-Chinese customers.

For a snack in mid-stroll, the Original Chinatown Ice Cream Factory on Bayard Street sells ices in flavors you will not find at the Baskin Robbins parlor a few doors down: red bean, ginger, mango, green tea, and so on. The retail food shops are engrossing. There is a spectacular display of fresh fish at Wing Woh Lung at 50 Mott Street, and it is fascinating to wander round Kam Man Food Products at 200 Canal Street, where you will see salted duck eggs, eels and live lobsters, and where glazed ducks hang temptingly in the window. No 8 Mott Street, the site of the first recorded Chinese shop in New York, is now a small museum which will not take up much of your time but which contains exhibits explaining Chinese culture. The display of fruit and vegetables will enable you to identify the mysterious shapes you have seen in the shops.

In the Chinatown areas of other large cities — San Francisco is the best example — attempts have been made to reproduce, in an Americanized form, China's distinctive architecture. There is not much of that here, though the Chinese Merchants' Association Building on the south-west corner of Canal and Mott Streets is a successful example. Among the buildings which pre-date the Chinese influx is the Church of the Transfiguration at the corner of Mott and Park Streets, on the right, built in 1801 along pleasingly straightforward Georgian lines. (A similar church, dating from 1817, showing the influence of the Gothic revival in its pointed windows, is at the corner of Market and Henry Streets, a block or so east of where this chapter will leave you on Chatham Square.)

The oldest surviving dwelling in New York is on the Bowery at the corner of Pell Street, a very early Federal house dating from the 1780s. The exterior has been well enough restored, but inside it is a busy and squalid betting parlour (the Chinese are enthusiastic gamblers). Olliffe's Apothecary has been at No 6 the Bowery, a few doors down, since 1805. The interior has been modified since but, under its Chinese ownership, it keeps an old-time atmosphere, with nineteenth-century drug jars lining some of its shelves. In **Chatham Square**, at the foot of the Bowery, a statue of Confucius claims the area for the Chinese, and Confucius Plaza, a modern red-brick apartment complex alongside the square, has only Chinese residents: watch for the Chinese telephone kiosks.

Among the houses pulled down to make way for the tall apartments was that in which Stephen Foster had his fatal mishap. We have now, as I promised, returned to the Bowery. The southernmost extremity of the notorious street ran into an area called the Five Points and had a more alarming reputation even than the street itself. In his *American Notes*, Charles Dickens describes a visit there in 1842:

> These narrow ways, diverging to the right and left, and reeking everywhere with dirt and filth. Such lives as are led here bear the same fruits here as elsewhere. The coarse and bloated faces at the doors have counterparts at home, and all the wide world over. Debauchery has made the very houses prematurely old. See how the rotten beams are tumbling down, and how the patched and broken windows seem to scowl dimly, like eyes that have been hurt in drunken frays . . . So far, nearly every house is a low tavern . . . all that is loathsome, drooping and decayed is here.

The Five Points may no longer exist but the spirit of the Bowery is not much altered. While making notes for this book I stood on a bench in an unwelcoming, litter-choked concrete park off Chatham Square to peer into the seventeenth-century Jewish cemetery at the corner of St James Place, locked and overgrown with weeds. A young man listening to a radio and drinking from a can in a brown paper bag saw me making notes and said: 'They ought to clean up this place. You can write that down.' But New York does not usually clean up after itself. When it has done with a place, when the gay life has come and gone and depleted its resources, it is discarded and abandoned to its fate while the parade moves uptown. In the next chapter we shall see, in Greenwich Village, a triumphant exception to that rule.

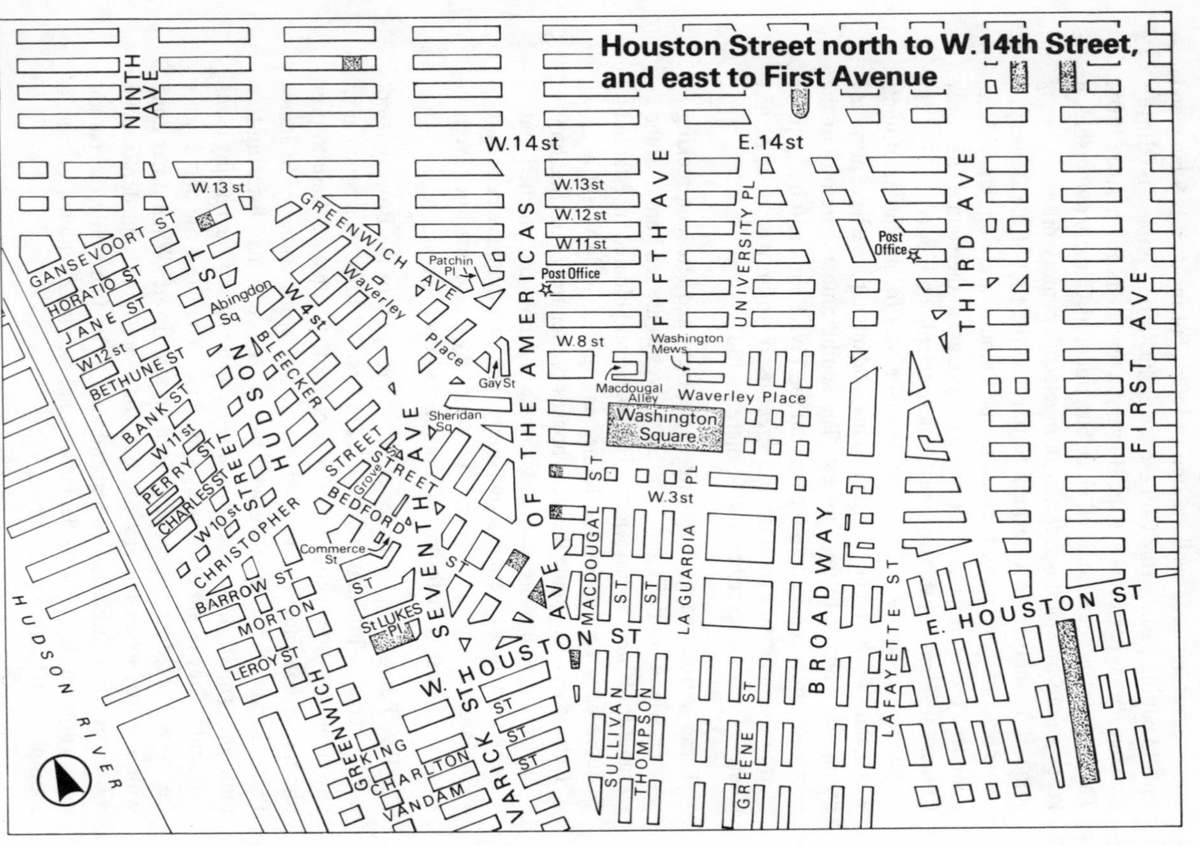

Houston Street north to W. 14th Street, and east to First Avenue
NINTH AVE
W. 14 st
E. 14 st
W. 13 st
W. 13 st
W. 12 st
W. 11 st
W. 8 st
W. 3 st
GANSEVOORT ST
HORATIO ST
JANE ST
W 12 st
BETHUNE ST
BANK ST
W 11 st
PERRY ST
CHARLES ST
W 10 st
CHRISTOPHER STREET
BARROW ST
MORTON
LEROY ST
GREENWICH
KING
CHARLTON
VANDAM
VARICK ST
W. HOUSTON ST
HUDSON ST
Abingdon Sq
W 4 st
BLEECKER STREET
Grove St
BEDFORD
Commerce St
ST
St LUKES PL
SEVENTH AVE
GREENWICH AVE
Waverley Place
Patchin Pl
Gay St
Sheridan Sq
AVE OF THE AMERICAS
Post Office
FIFTH AVE
Washington Mews
Macdougal Alley
Waverley Place
Washington Square
MACDOUGAL ST
ST
SULLIVAN ST
THOMPSON ST
LAGUARDIA PL
GREENE ST
UNIVERSITY PL
BROADWAY
LAFAYETTE ST
Post Office
THIRD AVE
E. HOUSTON ST
FIRST AVE
HUDSON RIVER

6
Greenwich Village

ITS NAME makes Greenwich Village sound the most attractive part of New York and in many respects it is. It is more than a hundred and fifty years since the term 'village' was technically appropriate to the district, once a large tobacco plantation. Since then it has, physically at least, become part of the metropolis, even if spiritually it has managed to keep its distance. The biggest early influx of residents came in 1822 as a consequence of a yellow fever epidemic in the city to the south. Everyone living south of City Hall was ordered to leave home, so they came to the Village and erected temporary wooden shanties. The banks followed their customers north and set up shop in what has ever since been called Bank Street. When the epidemic subsided, some refugees stayed to build permanent houses. The name Greenwich was bestowed by one Captain Peters, a British colonist who thought the settlement resembled Greenwich in south-east London — though apart from its situation beside a broad and beautiful river, the similarity is today elusive.

Although my suggested itinerary can be completed in a day, spend longer if you have time. More than any other part of the city, the Village rewards the browser who has time to poke around in the bookshops, the craft and antique shops. Stop for a half-hour in an Italian coffee-house or a quaint bar with mementoes of the literary and artistic figures of the 1920s and 1930s, who gave the place its Bohemian reputation. While you will want to see the grand old terraced houses by day, save at least one night to explore the streets south and west of Washington Square, which come alive after dark.

For your daytime tour, find your way to the Spring Street subway stop on the Eighth Avenue line. There is a station exit on **Vandam Street**, which, with its neighbors **Charlton** and **King Streets,** form an enclave of Federal-style terraced houses dating from the 1820s. Some have been pulled down or altered but as a whole they form a group now unequalled in New York in the style which once dominated Lower Manhattan. The

Federal style as expressed in these houses is more rectangular and fussier — so fussy indeed that it provoked, by way of reaction, the severe Greek Revival style in the 1830s. The large Federal doorways typically have thin fluted columns on either side, flanked by narrow ornamental windows, a decorative fanlight above. Steps with wrought-iron railings lead up from the street — and a few still have their original iron urns guarding the entrance. Plain but distinctive lintels adorn the large front windows, while a pair of dormer windows jut out from the roof above the second floor, though these have in some cases been obliterated to make way for an extra full storey. The bricks are laid in the 'Flemish bond' pattern — one long side (stretcher) and one short side (header) alternating.

Walk west along Vandam Street, turn right into Greenwich, and right again into Charlton. The houses at 37 and 39 Charlton Street are fine examples of the Federal form in something close to its original conception and you will find others as you walk along these three unusually wide streets. Where Charlton Street meets the Avenue of the Americas, turn left and left again into King Street. These streets occupy the site of **Richmond Hill**, which served as George Washington's New York headquarters during the revolution and which John Adams, the Vice-President, used as his home in the brief time that New York was the federal capital. A few years later it was acquired by the tempestuous Aaron Burr. The house was sold in the 1820s to John Jacob Astor, one of the first of New York's truly home-grown millionaires, who was interested more in the estate surrounding it than in the building itself, which no longer stands.

Astor, born in 1763 in the German town of Waldorf, came to New York in his teens and built a lucrative business in fur trading, pioneering the valuable Chinese market. A clever investor, he had the vision to foresee the northward spread of New York and bought up huge tracts of land in what is now midtown Manhattan but was then effectively a wilderness. Having acquired the Richmond Hill estate from Burr he built on it the houses which now stand on Charlton, King and Vandam Streets. For a while Astor maintained a residence at one of his new houses, 43 King Street. He had a reputation, only slightly deserved, for being ruthless in the foreclosure of mortgages and was never a popular man, even after leaving $400,000 for the establishment of the city's first public library after his death in 1848. His estate was said to have been worth some $20,000,000 and the *New York Herald* reflected popular sentiment when it suggested that, since it was the hard work of New Yorkers which had made his holdings appreciate in value to so great an extent, he should have left at least half his money to the city. 'Instead of this,' said the editorial, 'he has only left less than half a million for a public library. He has exhibited, at best, but the ingenious powers of a self-invented money-making machine . . . without turning it to any permanent benefit to that community from whose industry he obtained half the amount of his fortune.' His wealth remained in the family, forming the basis for the social advance of succeeding generations of Astors in the United States and Britain.

Of the men who loom large in the history of New York, few were regarded in their time as heroes in a city which is more comfortable with villains to abuse than with great men to admire. Even those to whom, for a time, it is persuaded to pay homage fall from grace more often than not. That is what happened to the next character we are to meet, the dandy Jimmy Walker, sometimes called Beau James, mayor of New York from 1926 until he resigned under the pressure of a financial scandal in 1932. He was born in 1881 in Leroy Street, three blocks north of King Street. His father, a carpenter who had come from Ireland to escape the potato famine, moved the family in 1886 to St Luke's Place, a comfortable row of Federal houses which today stand nearly intact, their façades camouflaged with wisteria, opposite a children's playground named after Walker. From King Street, walk north up Varick Street for three blocks and then turn left into **St Luke's Place.** Walker's house, No 6, may be identified quickly by the pair of lamps at the entrance, a traditional way of marking the New York mayor's residence.

He had begun his professional life as a song writer, an occupation that fitted well with the happy-go-lucky style that was to be his trade mark. His only real hit was called, prophetically, 'Will You Love Me in December as You Do in May?' To many, Walker's irreverent wit, his ebullient spirit, his taste for alcohol, sharp clothes, night life and the company of pretty actresses, were symbolic of New York in the jazz age. His address, in Bohemian Greenwich Village, reinforced the sybaritic image inherent in his nickname. But soon, as the Depression began to get a grip on America, his extravagant social life became increasingly unsuitable. Newspapers criticized his lack of application to the post to which he had been elected, and finally the whiff of scandal began to permeate City Hall. It was a tale familiar in American cities — undercover payments for the award of contracts, the exchange of favours and the like — and although no crime was proved, Walker resigned in 1932. He never returned to elected office though he did retain a hold on the affection of New Yorkers nostalgic for the heady excitement of the twenties. He died in 1946.

From St Luke's Place, walk north on Hudson Street to **Morton Street** and turn right. Morton Street is not long but contains, in its stately old houses and apartment buildings, many of the attributes of a typical Greenwich Village neighborhood. Look for the Federal doorway on No 59, much admired for its original detailing. On the other side of the street is a characteristic nineteenth-century apartment house in brownstone. The early low apartment buildings in the Village all exude a strong European influence. Though we nowadays associate apartment buildings with America, the concept was originally a European one. Behind 44 Morton Street is an alley leading to a patch of secluded gardens. If the gate is unlocked go and look at them — you will be surprised at their rusticity in such a crowded part of the city.

Just before you reach Seventh Avenue, turn left into **Bedford Street**. Nos 64 and 66 have kept their dormers as well as their keystone lintels, which do not often survive. No 75½, built in 1873 on the site of an alley between its neighbours, is the narrowest house in the village, only 9 ft 6 in across. The poet Edna St Vincent Millay lived here in 1923 and 1924. She is associated with several Village houses, cafes and theatres and in the 1920s came, with her two sisters, to be regarded as personifying the free-spirited Bohemian life. Next to it, the Isaac-Hendricks house at No 77 is the oldest in the Village, built in 1799 but the victim of numerous alterations since. A brick façade has been put over most of the original wood, and the dormers have been incorporated into an extra storey.

Turning right into **Commerce Street**, two comparatively unspoiled groups of two-storey Federal houses on the right are separated by an apartment house. Across the road, near the corner of Seventh Avenue is No 11, for a time the home of the author Washington Irving. His *Knickerbocker History of New York,* a parody published in 1809, was hailed by one English critic as the first truly original work of literature produced in the former colonies. A satire on pedantry and false scholarship, it purported to have been written by one Diedrich Knickerbocker, an old Dutch colonist. Because of its success, the word 'Knickerbocker' became a term for New Yorkers of Dutch ancestry and was extended as an affectionate nickname for the city as a whole. There is a Knickerbocker Savings Bank and the professional basketball team, the New York Knicks. Irving's *Rip Van Winkle* and *The Legend of Sleepy Hollow* have become international classics.

Back along Commerce Street, crossing Bedford Street again, you come to the Cherry Lane Theatre, which Miss Millay helped to establish in a former brewery — one of the first of the little theatres which were later to be grouped under the collective title 'Off Broadway'. Follow the block around to the right and back along Barrow Street into Bedford Street. Turn left and hunt for the forbidding door of No 86, with metal grilles covering its window. Only a sign outside announcing the acceptability of certain credit cards, plus its liquor licence, give a clue that behind the door is a large, ill-lit bar and restaurant, a fascinating throwback to Prohibition and the 1920s. It is Chumley's, an authentic old speak-easy in something like its original form, even down to the back alley to Barrow Street that allowed customers to enter discreetly and slip away in the event of a police raid. Greenwich Village, with its reputation for anti-authoritarianism, was a good place to come for a drink in the twenties. The first bar-owner convicted of breaking the prohibition law, after it came into force in 1919, was Barney Gallant, owner of the Greenwich Village Inn on Sheridan Square. He was imprisoned and became an instant hero. When the much-flouted law was repealed in 1933, many regretted the loss of the risk and romance which used to go with finding a drink. Certainly the illegal liquor importers and the speak-easy owners regretted the loss of their impressive profits.

Turn left from Bedford into Grove Street and enter a passage between Nos 10 and 12. You are in **Grove Court**, a leafy yard where birds sing, in front of a terrace built in the 1850s to house the Irish laborers who were flocking to America (and once dubbed 'Ale Alley' to celebrate one of their notable peculiarities). The tidy red-brick terrace adorned with white shutters makes a splendid picture, and across the yard are the wooden backs of the old houses at 6, 8 and 10 Grove Street.

Turn right on Hudson Street, past Public School 3 on your right, to **Christopher Street**, the social center of New York's large and assertive community of homosexuals. The movement for 'Gay Rights' in the 1960s and 1970s had its roots here, and because of it there is now little stigma attached to homosexuality. The street certainly evinces no sense of shame, boasting several shops specializing in fancy leather gear, cake shops called the Erotic Baker and Kiss My Cookie and, farther on, the Oscar Wilde Memorial Bookshop. You need not be homosexual to walk the street and enjoy its relaxed ambiance. Nobody will make you feel uncomfortable and there are many shops of universal appeal to enjoy: the Li-Lac Chocolate Shop at No 120 and McNulty's Tea and Coffee Co at No 109 are long-established period pieces. The street is graced by several good modern restaurants and by St John's Evangelical Lutheran Church, a handsome Federal building of 1821, with a pretty octagonal tower.

Homosexuals are an important but in no sense a pervasive element in the mix of Village people. Students and faculty members from New York University dominate the streets around Washington Square, providing two more characteristic ingredients — youth and learning. In the West Village, where we are now, the population is older, more settled, though they may still like to be thought of as retaining a streak of Bohemianism. The best way of meeting them, if you are lucky enough, is at a block party. This New York phenomenon of fairly recent growth flourishes in the summer in the streets of the Upper East and West Sides, in Brooklyn and here in the Village. Residents will band together to organize the urban equivalent of a garden fete. The street is closed to traffic and booths are erected for the sale of books, snacks, balloons, handicrafts, ice cream, drinks and the like. Musicians and clowns stroll through the crowd. Games and side-shows for children and grown-ups foster a cheerful and neighborly mood. Look around on the lamp posts and bulletin boards (many supermarkets have these at their entrance) for announcements of block parties or street fairs and try to drop in on one. It is the best way of encountering New Yorkers off duty.

At the convergence of Christopher Street, Seventh Avenue and four other streets is **Sheridan Square**, named not for the Irish playwright but for Philip Sheridan, the Civil War general who succeeded General Sherman as commander-in-chief of the US army in 1883, holding the position until his death in 1888. It is a compressed and ramshackle triangle, with a small, apologetic seating area in the middle peopled chiefly by down-and-outs who failed to make it to the Bowery. On the north side, down a flight of stairs at 59 Christopher Street, is the **Lion's Head Tavern**, popular with journalists and other minor literary figures (usually distin-

Right:
The Cooper Union Foundation Building houses a school of art and science; in its Great Hall in 1860 Abraham Lincoln delivered his famous 'right makes might' address.

Below:
Washington Square was previously a paupers' burial place, an execution site and a parade ground before being turned into a public park in 1828, with some of the city's most fashionable houses built round it. The arch, opposite the entrance to Fifth Avenue, was built to celebrate the centenary of George Washington becoming President.

Gramercy Park, built on reclaimed swamp land in 1831, is reminiscent of some of London's streets and squares, and has some of the most attractive and graceful residential architecture in New York.

guishable from the 'bums' on the square by being more expensively dressed). It sells Bass and Guinness on draught.

On the other side of Christopher Street, at its junction with Waverly Place, stands the Northern Dispensary, an imposing triangular building in red brick that has been a Village landmark since it was established in 1827 — northern because at that time it represented the northern limit of civilized habitation. Edgar Allan Poe, who lived in the Village for a while, is reputed to have been one of the early beneficiaries of the free medical treatment which the institution bestowed — and still does — upon those who cannot afford to pay. The most shameful event in Sheridan Square's history occurred in 1863, during the Draft Riots. This was where the mob brought the blacks, the scapegoats for their wrath, for lynching. Gay Street, a turning off Christopher Street a little farther east and on the right, was at that time a tiny black ghetto, and it was from there that the angry protestors dragged their victims. Nowadays Gay Street is a pretty little street containing several Federal houses in something like their original condition, complete with shutters.

Christopher Street ends when you get to the Avenue of the Americas — a thoroughfare which was much less confusing when named plain old Sixth Avenue. The triangular plot of ground on this corner, now a tranquil flower garden voluntarily and well maintained by residents, used to be occupied by a more raucous institution — the Women's House of Detention, demolished in 1974. To walk past it was nightmarish. The air would be filled with the shrieks of the inmates — not shouting because of mistreatment but simply to converse with friends in the street below. Beyond it is the old **Jefferson Market courthouse**, now a branch of the city's public library. The red brick structure, built in 1876 in a highly fanciful Victorian Gothic style, is admired by the moulders of architectural opinion — partly, I fancy, due to their jubilation at its being converted in 1967 to a new civic use instead of being razed to the ground. Everyone to his taste: mine does not extend to over-elaborate Disneyland castles of this sort. The circular balcony half-way up the tower, incidentally, was a look-out point for fire-watchers.

Turn left by the courthouse into West 10th Street, then immediately right into **Patchin Place**, a narrow cul-de-sac lined with low apartments built in 1848 to house Basque waiters from the Brevoort, a renowned European-style hotel on lower Fifth Avenue. In the 1920s and 30s Patchin

Place became a fashionable address for writers. E. E. Cummings lived here for nearly forty years until his death in 1962. Other residents have included John Masefield, Theodore Dreiser, Eugene O'Neill and John Reed, whose *Ten Days That Shook the World*, a vivid description of the Russian Revolution, remains a model of reporting and the inspiration for the movie, *Reds*. At right angles to Patchin Place is Milligan Place, a similar, smaller enclave built a few years later, which has its entrance on the Avenue of the Americas, four shops up. Both are peaceful havens except when it is playtime at the school immediately at their back.

Cross the Avenue of the Americas and start walking south, passing (or, if you cannot resist it, entering) Balducci's, the famous Village delicatessen and grocery shop. Alongside it is Bigelow's, an historic chemist's shop which displays in its windows, from time to time, items from its little museum of pharmacy: old Delftware drug jars, historic prescriptions. Notice, when you go inside, the Victorian wood shop fitments and the ceiling mouldings with their 'B' motif. Bigelow's was established in 1832 but this building dates from later in the century. Before we turn left into 8th Street, look at the plaques on the lamp posts in the Avenue, with coats-of-arms from the Latin American countries. These are repeated along its whole length and are a help in establishing which avenue you are on if you get lost.

West 8th is the Village's liveliest shopping street. In the last decade it has taken on a razzmatazz character to meet the demands of the tourist trade. Here are bookshops catering both to visitors and to students from nearby New York University, a couple of ice cream parlours and shops selling T-shirts, shoes, art materials, posters, jeans and souvenirs. The street is at its most lively after dark.

To your right you are getting some tantalizing glimpses of Washington Square, which we shall explore later. For the present, press on to the lower reaches of Fifth Avenue, the first turning on the left. A mile or so uptown this will become the most glittering of all the city's streets but this lower stretch, once lined with the mansions of the newly rich industrialists of the mid-nineteenth century, is an unassuming avenue of offices, shops and apartment houses interrupted by the occasional place of worship. It is towards two of these that I want to direct your attention, both built in the 1840s, textbook examples of different aspects of the Gothic Revival.

The **Church of the Ascension**, on the north-west corner of the junction of 10th Street, was designed by Richard Upjohn, also responsible for Trinity Church at the end of Wall Street. This is a restrained interpretation of the Gothic form with — fairly unusual in this country — a tower instead of a spire. The soaring interior was redesigned in 1889 and is dominated by John La Farge's altar piece, 'The Ascension of Our Lord'. La Farge, one of the most respected American artists of the nineteenth century, painted his first church mural for Richard Morris Hunt in Boston and thereafter became something of a specialist in the form, basing his style on the Venetian tradition. He was fascinated by the problems of light and became an American pioneer in stained glass: some of the windows here are his, illuminated after dark. Next to it along 10th Street, the parish house was one of the first homes in New York to be built from brownstone. North along Fifth Avenue, between 11th and 12th Streets, is the much more elaborate **First Presbyterian Church**. Where Upjohn's windows, cornices, pinnacles and parapet were studiedly plain — perhaps in recognition of the Puritan roots of the American churches — the architect here, Joseph Wells, has followed more extravagant English Gothic models. The body of the building is said to derive from the Church of St Saviour in Bath and the tower from that of Magdalen College, Oxford. Inside (you have to go through the school entrance on 12th Street) the flattish shallow vault of the ceiling lacks the majesty of Upjohn's arches.

Across the road at 47 Fifth Avenue is the only survivor of the nineteenth-century mansions still in its original state. Now the **Salmagundi Club** for artists, it was built in 1854 for Irad Hawley, a Pennsylvania coal baron. It is open in the afternoons most days, when you can see the baroque double parlor, the two parts separated by a group of four highly decorated marble columns. In the front part is a marble fireplace adorned with carvings of women in Victorian dress, and the rooms are furnished in something like the opulent style to which Hawley would have been accustomed. Just north, on the south-east corner of 13th Street, the Lone Star Cafe is known for its Texas hoe-down music and hot chili.

Cross Fifth Avenue and head down **West 11th Street**. A row of fine Greek Revival houses on your left is broken by a modern intruder, No 18, its ground floor window sticking out at an angle, symbolic of its uneasy relation with its neighbors. The reason for this involves a slice of social history recalling the political turmoil of the late 1960s and early

1970s. In March 1970 the old row house on the site was destroyed by an explosion in which three people were killed. The victims were members of the Weathermen, a radical group who were using the basement of the house as a bomb manufactory. In 1981 one of the suspects, Kathy Boudin, was captured during an attempted bank robbery, after eleven years on the run. The gap in the row was filled with an experimental modern building rather than with a replica of the old one, and it does not look altogether outrageous: at any rate it makes less of an eyesore than some other liberties taken with the old houses, one or two of which we are passing as we walk west along 11th Street. Look at No 154, where the window has been taken right down to the full depth of the ground floor, reaching the pavement. It must let in more light but adds nothing to the appeal of the street.

Nor, I fear, does the low white building which you see on the right as you come into the complicated six-sided junction of 11th Street with Greenwich and Seventh Avenues. This was built as the headquarters of the seamen's union, which could explain why the double row of round windows near the top have the look of portholes. Now it is an annex of St. Vincent's Hospital. It was in the older part of the hospital, on the other side of Seventh Avenue, that the Welsh poet Dylan Thomas died in November 1953 after collapsing at the Chelsea Hotel on West 23rd Street. The hospital is not many blocks from the **White Horse Tavern**, on the south-west corner of 11th and Hudson Streets, where Thomas would spend hour after hour drinking and talking with his friends and a coterie of hangers-on who went hoping to be dazzled by his boisterous rhetoric — no different really from the stargazers who now flock to Elaine's on the Upper East Side, begging first to be allowed in and then just to be in the same room as one or two famous faces from the literary and show business establishments. In Thomas's case, many of his old drinking 'friends' crowded St Vincent's waiting-room during his long-drawn-out death, rendering it as unedifying as much of his late life. The cause of his collapse was alcohol poisoning; he boasted just before passing out that he had drunk eighteen whiskies at the White Horse that evening, though he may have been exaggerating. Until Thomas came to patronize it this bar was frequented by sailors from the ships which then still docked in that part of the Hudson. It is scruffy — not a bit like Elaine's — surviving mainly on the poet's memory. The side-room is lined with Thomas mementoes — articles, photographs and programs of his plays and readings.

Farther north up Hudson Street, where it crosses Gansevoort Street, is New York's meat market. There is no need to investigate it unless you have a passion for the sight of raw meat or the sound of heavy trucks racing their engines. If you enjoy thick steaks, though, go to one of the restaurants near the market which specialize in them. The Old Homestead, on the corner of West 14th Street and Ninth Avenue, is the oldest, recognizable from a distance by the large figure of a bull dominating the entrance. For years it has been serving magnificent roast beef and steaks, cooked to a turn, in much larger hunks than I can imagine anyone chomping their way through; but you are allowed to take what is left home in a bag (tactfully labelled a doggie bag).

From the White Horse, walk along the south edge of Abingdon Square (really another triangle) and turn right down **Bleecker Street**. This is among the most villagey streets in the Village, with antique and second-hand clothing shops, cramped restaurants, a launderette whose window serves as a community bulletin board and, farther down, a clutch of Italian food shops. It was once a predominantly Italian neighborhood and the site of one of the city's most active street markets, until Mayor LaGuardia banned the pushcarts in the 1930s for reasons of hygiene and good order. You will want to spend time poking about the shops before the street takes you across the Avenue of the Americas for the third and last time in this chapter, passing on the right the Little Red School House, an early progressive school established in the 1920s. This end of Bleecker Street is more lively at night than in daytime, with its theatres, movies, cabarets, jazz clubs and a bar or two. Jazz clubs appear and disappear with great rapidity. If you are interested it is best to check what is currently on offer in the *Village Voice*, the *New Yorker* or *New York* magazine, rather than just dropping in somewhere on spec. The Village Gate on Bleecker Street is the best known of the cabarets, usually harbouring big name musicians and singers and sometimes a satirical revue. The junction of Bleecker and Macdougal Streets has long been one of the focal points of the Village. The San Remo restaurant, once a popular meeting place for its coterie of writers and for that reason prolifically documented, used to stand on the north-west corner of the junction. It is now a Chinese restaurant.

Turn left into **Macdougal Street**, a companionable jumble of Village haunts. The Minetta Tavern on the left, at No 113, is stuffed with pictures of local characters, old and new. At No 119 is the Caffe Reggio, one of the old-established coffee houses that the Bohemians might recognize, a charming relic of 1927 with its abundance of dark wood. Across the road, the red brick house carrying the numbers 130 and 132 was, somewhat earlier, the home of Louisa May Alcott, the author of *Little Women*. Back on the west side of the street, the houses between 127 and 131 are well-used examples of the Federal style, worth remarking for having been built for the ubiquitous Aaron Burr. Just past them, No 133 is the present home of the Provincetown Players, a pioneer experimental theatre which has always been close to its present location. Named after the Massachusetts resort to which 1920s Villagers were wont to migrate in summer, the theatre premiered the plays of Eugene O'Neill (Paul Robeson played the Emperor Jones here) and later of Edward Albee.

We have now reached the corner of **Washington Square**, a place with so much activity in and around it that I shall offer you only a loose itinerary for this area. First turn right and walk a few steps along Washington Square South, keeping to the right-hand side of the road. Between Sullivan and Thompson Streets is the **Judson Memorial Church**, a fussy Romanesque building designed in 1892 by McKim, Mead and White. Of that firm's surviving buildings it may be the closest in spirit to White's long-vanished Madison Square Garden. The tower is now a student dormitory. In the church hall you can see more La Farge stained glass.

Turn away from the square for one block, south down Thompson Street, and watch for the chess shop just south of the junction with West 3rd Street. It has tables for indoor play but most addicts prefer, if the weather is good, to play out of doors. As we turn back east along West 3rd Street to get to where they play, we pass the second chess emporium on the corner of Sullivan Street, where we turn right, back towards the square. The chess tables are in its south-west corner. The players, of all ages and classes, have a streak of exhibitionism so they will not resent your watching. If a crowd gathers around one table it may mean that the players are involved in a high speed game, with only seconds allowed for each move — a dazzling and bewildering display of quick thinking. I am unsure why there are so many keen chess players in the city: I suppose

Russian immigrants were chiefly responsible — in a polyglot city a game where players do not have to speak the same language has obvious merits.

Washington Square was once a potter's field, a burial ground for unidentified paupers. It became a site for executions and then a parade ground before it was turned into a public park in 1828. The northern side is dominated by an arch, opposite the entrance to Fifth Avenue, built by Stanford White in 1892 to celebrate the centenary of George Washington becoming President. White had earlier built a temporary wooden arch but it was so popular that he was persuaded by local residents to put it in a permanent form. It remains a valued city landmark, adorned by statues depicting Washington as soldier and statesman.

Much of the square is paved but it has some pretty trees, a fountain and some statues, making it a retreat, if seldom a quiet one, from the crowded streets that surround it. At weekends it is alive with spontaneous activity. Solo instrumentalists try to attract knots of listeners and earn a few dollars; teenagers glide on roller skates, sometimes to disco music from their portable cassette players; freelance clowns and jugglers cater to the children who come primarily to use the adventure playgrounds at the north-east and west sides of the square. Occasionally someone will try to create a version of Speakers' Corner in London by launching into a passionate political speech; I have seen a group of old age pensioners giving a display of stately dancing and rhythmic movement. The square's habitués learned long ago not to be surprised by anything. When I asked a visitor once whether he had enjoyed it he replied, a bit puzzled: 'Yes, but why is the arch wrapped in burlap?' It turned out to be the work of a performance artist, no doubt making an important statement about the arch, about burlap and about Sunday afternoon in Washington Square.

Of the buildings which surround the square, many are owned or leased by New York University (the main campus is in the south-east corner) and used for accommodation, refectories, offices and the like. They include the stately early-nineteenth-century terraces at the northern edge, which provided the setting for an early Henry James novel, a witty comedy of manners which he named after the square and which was later dramatized and filmed as *The Heiress*. Though published in 1881, James set the novel in the 1840s and picked up his local color from visits he used to make to his grandmother, who lived at No 19, describing the 'solid and honorable dwellings' surrounding the square. The unity of the terraces has been broken by the intrusion of more modern structures, but part of that look remains. Some see it as the bit of New York most resembling a London square. The houses have always kept strong literary associations. Here and in the surrounding streets, hostesses such as Mabel Dodge installed their salons in the early years of the century. The growing community of artists and writers would meet there until, in the less formal 1920s, they moved out into more public gathering places: the coffee shops and restaurants. Look closely at 20 Washington Square on the north side, west of Fifth Avenue. When built in 1828 this was a five-storey country house, surrounded by green fields, until the adjacent terraced houses were put up about five years later. Some years after that the drive on the left was covered with an extension to the house, and you can see the break in pattern between the old and the new bricks.

Behind the old houses facing into the square are **Washington Mews** and **Macdougal Alley**, which used to give access to their stables and carriage houses. These low buildings have been modified but in some it is still possible to trace the outline of the large double doors for the carriages. Now they are, for the most part, dinky, desirable and expensive residences. Some were once used as artists' studios. Gertrude Vanderbilt Whitney, the sculptor who founded the Whitney Museum of American Art, had a studio in Macdougal Alley. She was an originator of the Washington Square Art Exhibition which occupies the pavements round the square for two weeks in the spring and autumn each year, showing off the work of varied local artists who, to judge from the uneven quality of their work, have little in common but their enthusiasm.

Going south again down Macdougal Street, at the corner of Waverley Place, the Earle Hotel tries hard to slow the downhill slide that afflicts most of New York's hostelries of its age remaining in business. In its better days it was where P G. Wodehouse used to stay on his American visits when, with Guy Bolton, he was writing witty dialogue and lyrics for light musicals. Dylan Thomas once stayed here too, but found the Chelsea more to his liking.

This has been a long haul and it may be time to take advantage of your return to Macdougal Street by taking your ease in one of the old cafes. There are, however, three optional extras in the vicinity of Washington Square which I ought to mention briefly for the benefit of those with limitless energy and special interests. On the corner of Washington Place and Greene Street, east of the square, a plaque posted by the International

Ladies Garment Workers Union marks the building whose top three floors were destroyed in the tragic Triangle fire of 1911. South of the square, near the corner of Bleecker Street and La Guardia Place in the Silver Towers housing estate, is a large stone sculpture, a copy of Picasso's 'Portrait of Sylvette'. Finally, enthusiasts of industrial architecture will not want to miss the only New York building designed by Louis Sullivan, the leading light of the Chicago School and a pioneer of skyscraper design. He coined the maxim: 'form follows function'. His 1898 **Bayard Building** at No 65 Bleecker Street, between Broadway and Lafayette Street, is a marvelous confection of spindly columns, accentuating the narrow building's verticality, ending in a splendid arched cornice whose exquisite detailed stonework is continued down the façade. It has little in common with the neo-classicism which was in vogue at the time but the fact that Sullivan was never asked — or never agreed — to design any more New York buildings is probably due to civic chauvinism rather than to any specific objection to his work. New Yorkers would not want to admit that a lad from out of town could put up better buildings than anyone they could find in their own city. And to prove no ill will, the Metropolitan Museum uptown now has a fine staircase from Sullivan's Chicago Stock Exchange Building in a position of honor in its American wing.

3rd Street north to 34th Street
HERALD SQUARE
W34st
General Post Office
Madison Sq. Gdn.
Penn Station
W29st
W28st
W24st
W23st
W20st
W18st
W16st
W14st
W12st
W11st
W10st
W9st
W8st
W3st
E23st
E14st
E8st
E9st
E7st
ELEVENTH AVENUE
TENTH AVENUE
NINTH AVENUE
EIGHTH AVENUE
SEVENTH AVENUE
AVENUE OF THE AMERICAS (SIXTH)
BROADWAY
FIFTH AVENUE
MADISON AVENUE
PARK AVENUE SOUTH
LEXINGTON AVENUE
THIRD AVENUE
SECOND AVENUE
FIRST AVENUE
F.D.ROOSEVELT DRIVE
MADISON SQUARE
Gramercy Park
PETER COOPER VILLAGE
STUYVESANT TOWN
STUYVESANT SQUARE
UNION SQUARE
IRVING PLACE
Chelsea Sq.
GREENWICH AVE
W4st
BLEECKER ST
CHRISTOPHER STREET
GREENWICH STREET
HUDSON
SEVENTH AVE
BLEECKER STREET
Waverly Pl
Washington Square Park
FOURTH AVE
ASTOR PL
COOPER SQ
Stuyvesant St
ST MARKS PL
LAFAYETTE STREET
Great Jones St
E. HOUSTON STREET
BOWERY
HUDSON
HIGHWAY
N
Post Office
Hospital

7
The Ghosts Around Union Square

WHEN NEW YORK's main shopping center headed uptown from the stretch of Broadway that now separates SoHo from Little Italy, it came to rest for a score of years and more around **Union Square**, the junction of Broadway and 14th Street. At the turn of the century most of the big stores were between 8th and 23rd Streets, on Fifth and Sixth Avenues and Broadway, a district of which the square makes a natural focal point. By chance, it was at that period that the subways were planned and built: this explains why so many subway lines converge under the square and why 14th Street, now by no means a main strategic artery, is served by one of the few crosstown lines.

Only one clue remains to remind us of the square's commercial history: May's, a serviceable low-priced department store looking into the square from the south. Until a few years ago Klein's kept it company, glowering from a group of converted row houses on the south-east corner, but even that once-famous bargain center expired, leaving its ugly quarters empty, awaiting demolition or renewal (which, it must be hoped, will not be long delayed). The surviving small shops on 14th Street have a makeshift, temporary look about them; they sell cheap clothes and utensils, rock-bottom quality at rock-bottom prices.

On the west side, notice a pair of dainty early skyscrapers, pencil-thin, just north of 16th Street. Apart from those, the square itself is in a condition comparable with that of Klein's crumbling hulk. Once a smart residential area, then a popular center for political demonstrations of a normally radical persuasion, it is now another haven for the city's always substantial population of drifters. To see the drifters, just climb a few feet — the ground level was raised for the construction of the subway station. It is worth the physical and mental effort only if you wish to admire the statuary which gives a hint of those former better days. The vigorous figure of Washington on horseback, facing south, dates from 1856. Lincoln dominates the north. On the grass at the east side is an 1876 statue of Lafayette by Frederic Bartholdi, responsible later for the Statue of Liberty. The Art Deco monument created in 1926 for the 150th anniversary of independence may once have been splendid but is now heavily defaced. It is a convenient base for the drug dealers who operate with shameless openness.

The square's single rural attribute is the presence of squirrels. Surprised that they could thrive on such a paltry patch of green, I inquired from the administrator of Central Park Zoo how they got there. Squirrels can and do survive in the city, he assured me, so long as they have a few trees and an ample supply of food — in this case the remains of sandwiches. Once a colony is established they seldom move, although the occasional squirrel has been seen scooting up the avenues late at night, seeking fresh pastures.

Fourteenth Street used to be known for its theatres, concert halls and restaurants. Of the latter, only one clings to life — Lüchow's large and elaborate dining emporium at 110 East 14th Street, panelled in dark mahogany, serving huge portions of a Germanic persuasion, accompanied by a group of musicians in fancy dress playing thigh-slapping oompah-oompah tunes.

Plans for rehabilitating the Union Square area flit occasionally across the pages of *The New York Times*, but until one is actually put into effect I would suggest now beating a hasty retreat, continuing north up **Broadway**. Here are some marvellous relics from the days when this was the shopping area colloquially known as 'Ladies' Mile'. Ignore the ground floors, which have for the most part been altered time and again since the stores, snake-like, abandoned their skins in the early years of this century and moved uptown to still roomier premises north of 34th Street. Look up to the stately, inviting façades and extend them in your mind's eye to the ground, as they would have appeared then, their windows framing mannequins in long dresses, with women in similar creations peering through from the pavement. On the south-west corner of 19th Street, crowned by an immense Parisian mansard roof stretching for two storeys, is the old home of Arnold Constable, a store which, throughout its life, vied with Lord and Taylor as the place where rich women shopped for clothing and fabrics. Lord and Taylor was then one block to the north, on the south-west corner of 20th Street, in a still more sumptuous cast-iron palace, the remains of which now moulder for lack of care. It was notable for being sliced off at the street corner to provide a triangular breathing space. In 1914 both shops moved up Fifth Avenue.

Turn right up **East 20th Street** to where, on the right, a Stars and Stripes flag flutters from a recess between two tall commercial buildings. The flag juts from a forbidding brownstone house, a reconstruction of the place where President Theodore Roosevelt was born in 1858 and lived until he was fifteen. Then, the streets crossing this stretch of Broadway were lined with the solid residences of merchants, but by 1900 they had been given over to commerce and the original birthplace torn down. A few years later a group of Roosevelt enthusiasts had a replica built which is now run by the National Parks Service as a museum and contains some of the original furniture. It is well maintained and one of the few Victorian interiors on display in New York. The museum houses various Roosevelt memorabilia including a stuffed lion, a bear skin, a beaver skin rug and some stags' heads — trophies from his hunting days.

The Roosevelts were among the original settlers in New York, coming from Holland in 1649. Theodore was a large man in every respect, of immense energy and a talent which ranged widely: he was a successful historian, naturalist, hunter and military commander, as well as politician. Briefly Governor of New York, he became Vice-President of the United States in 1900, and President a year later on the assassination of President McKinley. Immensely popular, he easily won a fresh term in 1904 but declined to be nominated four years later, setting off instead on a long scientific expedition to Africa. Though he subsequently re-entered politics and formed his own party, he never won elective office again and died in 1919. If you have a half hour to spare, the obliging young ladies of the National Parks Service will show you a film of Roosevelt's life, and if that whets your appetite his country house on Long Island, Sagamore Hill, is open to the public and makes a pleasant day's excursion.

For the present, continue east down 20th Street, across Park Avenue and into **Gramercy Park,** a name said to derive from the Dutch *crommessie fly,* meaning a crooked stream. New York does not have many residential squares of this kind. This one has survived since 1831. The well-kept park in the middle has avoided the depradations of most other green spaces because it is kept locked, with keys given only to those who live around the square or who stay at the Gramercy Park Hotel, an otherwise unremarkable hostelry at the west corner of Lexington Avenue.

The prettiest of the houses on the square are Nos 3 and 4 Gramercy Park West, built in 1846 and prized for their extravagant cast-iron porches and porticos, a hint of New Orleans.

On the south side, the large and too heavily ornamented brownstone at No 15 was two houses knocked into one for Samuel John Tilden, Governor of New York from 1874–6 and an unsuccessful presidential candidate. It is now the National Arts Club. No 16 was bought in 1886 by Edwin Booth, the actor (whose statue stands in the square) as a club for members of his profession, The Players.

On the east side of the square are two elderly apartment houses. No 34, with its remarkable well forming a set-back entrance, was built in 1883, one of the city's earliest multiple dwellings. Next door, the extravagant neo-Gothic confection in white terra-cotta is some twenty years younger. Though neither is a beauty, they are full of the atmosphere of the period and, unlike most of their contemporaries, will probably be preserved, part of the Gramercy Park historic district.

Walk west along the north side of the park, which becomes East 21st Street; turn right into Park Avenue South. On your right, between 21st and 22nd Streets, is the **Calvary Episcopal Church**, designed in 1846 by James Renwick Jr. It warrants a look chiefly for purposes of comparison with his justly more admired Grace Church, south of Union Square, which we shall get to at the end of this walk. Turn left up 23rd Street to **Madison Square,** a small patch of park which has managed to stay reasonably pleasant without resorting to Gramercy Park's device of locking itself up. It has not gone to seed like Union Square or, farther uptown, Bryant Park, probably because the streets surrounding it have kept their dignity. At the south-west corner of the park, the **Flatiron Building** is a quirkish early skyscraper which visitors find appealing, a suitable landmark for the junction of Fifth Avenue and Broadway, New York's most famous streets. Its shape, to which it owes its graphic name, derives from the wedge-shaped plot it fills. When finished in 1902 it was the wonder of the town, one of the very first New York buildings to employ the steel-frame method of construction. This permits its slender shape, which would never have stood up had it been built in the old way, with load-bearing walls. When it was opened, people were said to be nervous of going to the observation platform at the top (long closed), fearful that an unexpected gust of wind might bring the whole thing tumbling down. It has survived, though, and pleases the eye today partly because of the faintly undulating surface of its walls, like ripples on a calm lake. The ugly ground-floor protuberance at, as it were, the thin end of the wedge, was added later and was once known as the cow-catcher, after the device on the front of trains.

Madison Avenue begins on the east side of the square. The **Metropolitan Life Tower** at No 1 was the tallest office building in the world from 1909, when it went up, until the Woolworth Building outreached it four years later. In 1962 the original office block alongside it was razed and replaced and, while the structure of the tower was kept for old time's sake, it was stripped of its rich ornamentation, giving it a starkly antiseptic look. The gold dome was preserved, glistening from a distance when the sun strikes it at the right angle. The enormous clocks on each side, 26½ ft in diameter, have hands that weigh half a ton. The annex one block north was built in 1932 and is joined to the original tower by a bridge over 24th Street.

Continuing north, the classical building on the next corner, which would look at home in London's St James's, is the **Appellate Division** of the New York State Supreme Court, built in 1900 and self-conscious about its high moral purpose. Sculptures inside and out represent Wisdom, Peace, Force, Justice and, in case you miss the allegorical point, some are captioned in Latin. Worthy maxims are engraved into the external fabric: 'Every law not based on wisdom is a menace to the state' and so on. The lobby, entered from 23rd Street, is lined with murals, rich both in color and in further allegory: as we saw in Foley Square, court houses inspire the prosiest excesses in architects. The brown glass skyscraper next door is on the site of the old Jerome mansion, the childhood home of Jennie Jerome, Sir Winston Churchill's mother.

Still following Madison Avenue north, the next monumental structure is the headquarters of the **New York Life Insurance Company,** a 1928 work of Cass Gilbert, designer of the Woolworth Tower and the Bowling Green Customs House. This is undistinguished Gothic Revival, with a golden pinnacle presumably put there so as not to be outshone by the Metropolitan Life a few doors down. Indeed, it is notable chiefly for what was pulled down to make way for it, and for its associations with Gilbert's predecessor as the doyen of New York architects. Stanford White was the third partner in McKim, Mead and White and the best known, both for his professional skills and for being a pillar of the fast social set that revolved around Broadway.

On this site, the terminus of the New York and Harlem railroad until the city banned trains south of 42nd Street, White designed the original Madison Square Garden. (In fact it was the second building of that name: the first was the converted railway depot, for a while the base of P. T. Barnum's enterprises.) For thirty-five years after its construction in 1890, White's Garden was a famed area for prize fights, circuses, concerts and displays of every kind. John L. Sullivan's fights drew huge crowds of opulently clad patrons until they were stopped by the police, boxing then being illegal in New York. The complex, in the (somewhat imaginative) style of the Spanish Renaissance, included a theatre, a restaurant, a roof garden and a tower crowned with a revolving statue of the goddess Diana, in a state of undress which caused short-lived outrage.

In June 1906, when he was fifty-two, White was shot and killed in the roof garden of Madison Square Garden while watching the opening performance of a new revue. His murderer was Harry Thaw, the eccentric heir to a Pittsburgh fortune; he had recently married Evelyn Nesbit, a showgirl from the hit *Floradora* ('Tell me, pretty maiden, are there any more at home like you?') who had been White's mistress five years earlier, when she was sixteen. The trial and the newspaper reporting that surrounded it drew a lurid picture of Broadway society: there were tales of orgies lasting for several days and nights, of showgirls popping from pie dishes, of champagne supper parties at which the female participants would find gold coins under their plates, of White's 'love nest' adorned with a red velvet swing in which his guests would display themselves for his delight. Thaw was acquitted on grounds of insanity, and spent much of the rest of his life in mental institutions until he died in 1947. Miss Nesbit later resumed her show business career in films and sordid speak-easies in Atlantic City: she became a heroin addict and worked for a while in a brothel in Panama City. Yet she lived until 1966, by which time Madison Square Garden had long since moved to 50th Street and Eighth Avenue, from whence it would move again in 1968 to its present location at 32nd Street. New York is a city whose people, however abused, customarily survive longer than its buildings.

For some years around the turn of the century, Madison Square Garden marked the southern end of the Broadway theatre district, the original Great White Way, which then stretched only as far north as the old Metropolitan Opera House on 41st Street. Now the theatres have vaulted across Times Square and into the side streets off Broadway between 43rd and 55th Streets. One pleasant left-over from the theatrical days of this lower section is the **Episcopal Church of the Transfiguration,** on 29th Street between Madison and Fifth Avenues. For more than a hundred years this has been a favourite place for weddings, christenings and funerals of people in show business, who know it affectionately as the 'Little Church Around the Corner'. Its littleness, in terms of height, is its most charming feature. When the church authorities in 1848 were seeking a style they decided on the fashionable Gothic but displayed heroic restraint in not going for the usual mini-cathedral with a soaring spire, choosing instead this modest 'cottage Gothic', in red brick and set back from the street, with the path to the entrance leading from a roofed gate through an area of shrubs.

The atmosphere of a country church is maintained inside where, although there is in fact a great deal of room, the low ceiling, supported by carved wooden pillars and beams, makes for an intimate and unassertive atmosphere of unusual repose. The most obvious theatrical memento is a stained glass window in the south transept, by John La Farge, of Edwin Booth as Hamlet. If you study the other memorial plaques you might recognize other names from Broadway's past.

Leaving the lych-gate, turn right, then left down Fifth Avenue and take the first right again. Look down Fifth Avenue for a tremendous view of the Flatiron Building as you cross the road. We are still in the realm of show business here, for West 28th Street was the original **Tin Pan Alley,** the home in the early years of the century of the music publishers who sold songs to vaudeville artists and the producers of musicals. Their offices were in converted terraced houses, most of which have gone; but on the north side of the street, near its junction with the Avenue of the Americas, half a dozen of them survive with the original steps leading up to their entrances, though their façades are now painted an alarming shade of green. When the music people were here, pedestrians would hear a random medley of songs drifting from the windows as the house musicians, or pluggers, would try to interest buyers. In 1914, when he was sixteen years old, the composer George Gershwin — like Irving Berlin, the son of Lower East Side immigrants — worked as a song plugger for Remick's, at No 45. Today the song publishers have moved, along with the theatres, farther up the Great White Way.

Those green houses are now occupied by flower wholesalers and it is just here that the drab street suddenly undergoes one of those transformations characteristic of New York. Where 28th Street would once assault the ear, today your nose will give you the first hint of change. Not even its best friends, among whom I count myself, would say that New York is a fragrant city. Yet here, on the Avenue of the Americas, we enter a two-block oasis of cut flowers and potted plants. Their scent comes from the shops and warehouses where flowers are being boxed, bundled and made into corsages, mostly for the wholesale trade, although a few of them will sell you an individual bunch. The pavements outside are a jungle of plants, some in effect fully fledged trees. Business has boomed since the 1970s when it became the fashion to use them to decorate Manhattan homes and offices. (The size of your office plant, together with the depth of pile on your carpet, is a reliable guide to executive status.)

As you approach Seventh Avenue, still on 28th Street, the section ends as abruptly as it began, and clothing holds the center of the stage. The street sign for Seventh Avenue has another sign reading 'Fashion Avenue' posted beneath it. This is the southern end of the garment district, the home of New York's rag trade, which we explore in the next chapter.

For the time being, turn left away from the garment dealers, to 23rd Street, and turn right. Half way along the block between Seventh and Eighth Avenues is the **Chelsea Hotel,** a red-brick survivor from 1884, its inspiriting cast-iron balconies enlivening a street much in need of it. Originally one of the city's earliest co-operative apartment houses, it has been a hotel since 1905 and has traditionally catered to visitors connected with the arts, in the broadest sense of that term. Plaques outside commemorate Dylan Thomas, Brendan Behan and Thomas Wolfe, all of whom lived or stayed there. More recently, it was notorious as the place where, in 1978, Sid Vicious of the British punk rock group the Sex Pistols, stabbed his girlfriend to death; a few months later he died of a drug overdose. The lobby has a fine carved fireplace and serves as a gallery for modern paintings and sculptures.

Chelsea, the district for which the hotel is named, is two long blocks further west, and since you are to walk far in this chapter I shall not suggest that you go there. Its chief characteristics are the rows of mid-nineteenth century houses on West 20th, 21st and 22nd Streets, between Eighth and Tenth Avenues, but these do not vary greatly from houses of the same age which we have already seen in Greenwich Village. Chelsea's name derives from the estate, named after the London district, that belonged to Clement Clarke Moore (he wrote ''Twas the Night Before Christmas') which used to occupy the area. Chelsea Square, which he laid out, is now the **General Theological Seminary,** Gothic ivy-covered buildings surrounding a peaceful garden.

Go there another day perhaps; but now we shall head back along 23rd Street to the **Avenue of the Americas** to turn right on to another street of husks of turn-of-the-century department stores. From the grandeur of the structures and their air of permanence, the store owners must have believed that here at last, after their meanderings from the foot of Manhattan, they would find a final home, but it was not to be. Within a few years they had all either closed down or uprooted themselves again. The first ones we are looking at here are on the west side of the street, and you get the best perspective by viewing them across the road, from the east side.

The grimy cast-iron monolith which all but fills the block between 22nd and 23rd Streets was the Ehrich Bros Dry Goods Store, famous for bargains. On the next block down the old Adams Dry Goods Store has lasted better than most: you can still see the initials ADG woven into the façade, along with the date of construction (1900), and the ground floor is recognizable as a shopfront. It reminds me a little of Selfridge's in London's Oxford Street, which it predates by a few years. Selfridge's lives, though, while the Adams store went out of business only fifteen years after it was built. A few years earlier it had merged with the older Hugh O'Neill store, on the next block, between 20th and 21st Streets, whose name is still easily legible on the pediment; they faded away together. Between 19th and 20th Streets is the Simpson Crawford Dry Goods Store, also from 1900. And on the next block south is an earlier (1876) store built for B. Altman.

At 19th Street you should cross over to the west side of the Avenue of the Americas to see, back on its east side, the most gigantic of all the old stores, Siegel-Cooper and Company, which opened here in 1896. Imagine going through those immense columns at the front and, once inside, being confronted with a fountain surrounding an awesome replica of Daniel Chester French's monumental sculpture, 'The Republic'. It quickly became a favorite rendezvous for shoppers, but the store went out of business in less than twenty years, and served as a military hospital in the first World War; the fountain-statue is now at the Forest Lawn Cemetery near Los Angeles.

Cross the avenue again and walk down 18th Street alongside Siegel-Cooper, where you will get a better idea of its size and will also spot its monogram in cameos over the side entrance. Back on **Fifth Avenue** on the corner of 18th Street, is the original **Barnes and Noble** bookshop, now a chain-store with shops across the city. Here it has two shops, one on each side of the avenue. On the east side is a comprehensive store selling chiefly textbooks to students from the downtown universities; opposite is the bargain center, where current best-sellers are discounted by as much as twenty per cent, and other special lines of new and second-hand books are much cheaper. There is a classical record shop next door: records are good value in New York. If you are now in a buying mood, this stretch of Fifth Avenue contains a number of ready-made clothing stores, some at ground level but more on the upper floors of the office and warehouse buildings. You might find something cheap that you like, although my own experience on the single occasion I tried shopping here was not encouraging. Entering the room packed with row after row of fine suits, I told the salesman I would like something inexpensive. He studied me for a second or two and said: 'I am afraid we have nothing inexpensive in *your* size' — proof that the hard sell is less pervasive here than some think. If yours is a sleeker, more conventional shape, by all means try your luck.

You are unlikely to have left Barnes and Noble empty-handed, but if you do there are plenty of bookshops left before the end of our walk: New York is a marvelous city for the bookish. Go east down 17th Street, through a cluster of costume jewelry dealers, to the north-west corner of Union Square, then head south along its east side. Cross 14th Street and continue south down **Broadway,** along the left-hand side of May's department store. The Strand bookshop, at the corner of 12th Street and Broadway, boasts 'millions' of books on eight miles of shelves in their ground floor and basement and I would not challenge them to prove it. As well as second-hand books, the Strand deals in review copies and publishers' overstock at below the published price. Daytons, across 12th Street, has a large selection of new and old records, many out of print. For current releases at low prices, find a convenient branch of a chain-store such as Sam Goody or King Karol.

The plain beige nineteenth-century building at the south-west corner of Broadway and 11th Street used to be the Hotel St Denis. When it was converted to offices in 1917 the ornamentation on its façade was stripped away, but for sixty years after it opened in 1848 the St Denis was the smart place to stay in New York, playing host to presidents, wealthy businessmen and theatrical superstars. Abraham Lincoln and Sarah Bernhardt are two very different immortals among its recorded guests and Alexander Graham Bell gave an early demonstration here in 1877 of his invention, the telephone. On the north side of 11th Street, opposite, notice the 1868 cast-iron store, well converted to residential use, though with a jarring extra floor on top.

The majestic English Gothic Revival structure opposite is **Grace Church**, built between 1843 and 1846, the work of James Renwick, later to design St Patrick's Cathedral on Fifth Avenue. His career as a church architect began when his charming plan for Grace Church won a competition established by the church authorities. Some judges believe he never bettered it, although his largest work, St Patrick's, is better known.

Because Broadway bends north-east here, the thin spire of Grace Church, with its delicate ornamentation, dominates the view uptown from Lower Manhattan. The rectory and surrounding buildings are in a compatible style, somewhat reminiscent of London's Royal Courts of Justice. Inside the church, the tall columns support a vaulted ceiling faithful to the best medieval originals. In the lunch hour on Thursdays a public organ recital is held here, but the church's claim to a place in New York history rests on a less decorous event. In 1863 the showman P. T. Barnum persuaded the rector to allow the church to be used for the wedding of General Tom Thumb, the midget who was the main attraction of Barnum's museum and freak show. Excited crowds pressed to get close to the diminutive couple, and invitations to the ceremony were ferociously sought by high society. Although the bride and groom were naturally anxious that good taste be preserved, the wedding, thanks to Barnum, turned into a rowdy street event bordering on chaos.

Going south down Broadway, turn left into 9th Street. At Fourth Avenue the two bookshops on the north-east corner are all that remains of Booksellers' Row, once a thriving street of second-hand bookshops. Continuing along 9th Street, the Pageant Book Shop at No 109 has moved from the avenue itself and has some nice old prints: easy-to-carry souvenirs. Cross Third Avenue and bear left into **Stuyvesant Street**, at an angle to the main grid, along the line of the original driveway from the Bowery to Peter Stuyvesant's farmhouse. The oldest building in the street is No 21 on the left, spacious and wide-fronted, built around 1800 as a country house and occupied for years by one of Stuyvesant's descendants. East of it, and on the other side of the triangle in 10th Street, are brick and brownstone terraces, put up in the 1850s in what was the garden of No 21.

The church of **St Mark's-in-the-Bowery** stands at the corner of Second Avenue and 10th Street, on the site of an earlier chapel alongside Peter Stuyvesant's farm. Stuyvesant and his descendants are buried in the churchyard. It was built in 1799 as a plain Georgian church, had its steeple added in 1828 and a cast-iron porch in 1854; surprisingly, the overall effect is harmonious. The church, especially the interior, was badly damaged by fire in 1978, during a restoration, but it is being restored afresh. To its left, a toddlers' playground is landscaped with bizarre brick humps. It also contains a bust of Daniel Tomkins, a former Vice-President.

Turn right into **Second Avenue** and look at a couple of charming buildings from the late years of the last century, appealing examples of small-scale decorative Victorian institutional architecture. The white building on the right between 9th Street and St Mark's Place is a clinic built in the 1880s. It has been less well preserved than its neighbor, the red-brick **Ottendorfer Library**, built in 1884 to serve the German community which then dominated this district. The first lending library built for the purpose in New York, it was originally privately funded and is named after the benefactor; now it is a branch of the New York Public Library. Outside, on the terra-cotta façade, open books, globes and contemplative owls signify the building's purpose, and the German inscription confirms it. The interior is exquisite, barely altered in a hundred years, with lovely two-tiered iron bookcases in the rear. This stretch of Second Avenue was once known for its abundance of Yiddish theatres serving the Jewish immigrants on the Lower East Side. The apartment houses, with their decorative fire escapes on both sides of the avenue were, like the library and clinic, built in the 1880s for the German immigrants. A few still are theatres.

At St Mark's Place, determined literary researchers may turn left to see the quiet terraced house at No 77, near First Avenue, where the poet W. H. Auden lived on the third floor from 1953 until 1972, a year before his death. From the same building the Russian Communist periodical *Novy Mir* used to be published. Leon Trotsky, during his brief stay in New York in 1917, just before the Russian Revolution, was among its most illustrious contributors; he would come down from his apartment in the Bronx, probably using the elevated railway. No plaques mark either historic occupancy and some will not find it worth the detour. Those who do, rejoin us at Second Avenue where we now point west along the section of St Mark's Place that has become the social center of the East Village, as Macdougal Street is of Greenwich Village proper.

The East Village has always been lower on the scale than its western neighbor, lacking its hint of rustic charm. In the 1950s and 1960s its rundown tenements became a literary outpost of Greenwich Village, where rents had become too steep for the new 'Beat Generation' of poets and writers. Allen Ginsberg, Jack Kerouac and William Burroughs were in the vanguard of the literati who roosted below 14th Street, between First and Third Avenues.

St Mark's Place is the haunt of street people, a mix of artists, students, hustlers and transients who congregate on the pavements to exchange gossip or, as you may detect from their drawn and sometimes dazed appearance, to engage in illicit drug transactions. The shops here reflect their variety of interests. The well-stocked paperback shop at No 13 has a large section on drugs, another on radical politics and another on avant-garde literature. The second-hand clothes shops specialize in old military uniforms or whatever happens to be the trend. There is a cheap hotel, an ice cream parlor called 'Scooped Again', a hairdresser ('Heads and Tales') and a couple of tiny theatres which would qualify as Off Off Off Broadway, if such a category existed. The East Village is a late-rising community: many of the shops do not open until after lunch.

Where St Mark's Street joins Third Avenue is **Cooper Square**, dominated by the solid, brown Cooper Union, a school of art and science founded in 1859 by Peter Cooper, an industrialist who made his fortune producing such varied innovations as iron girders, an early steam train and a strong and reliable glue. The Union building, restored in 1970, was the first in New York to use Cooper's iron beams as a means of support. Originally it had shops on the ground floor along its Third and Fourth Avenue sides, which explains the iron-framed windows with pleasing circular tops interrupted by unusual iron lamp brackets. The two top storeys were added later in the nineteenth century.

The Cooper Union played a dramatic role in history when Abraham Lincoln spoke there in February 1860, as he was starting to consider offering himself as a presidential candidate. In spite of heavy snow, fifteen hundred people crammed into the lecture hall to hear the awkwardly dressed and, at first, diffident country hick. In warming to his theme — an attack on the southern states on the issue of slavery — he coined a phrase which has not died: 'Let us stand by our duty fearlessly and effectively . . . Let us have faith that right makes might and in that faith let us, to the end, dare to do our duty as we understand it.' He was cheered to the echo and the momentum of that meeting swept him to the presidency.

Turn left into the square and left again opposite Peter Cooper's tall statue, into East 7th Street. A little way down on your left is **McSorley's Old Ale House,** enshrined in American folk literature by Joseph Mitchell as McSorley's Wonderful Saloon, established in 1854 and scarcely altered — at least in spirit — since. A 1964 drawing by Paul Hogarth in *Brendan Behan's New York*[10] captures the essence of the place, a brown and gloomy dust trap with sawdust on the floor, yellowing photographs and newspaper clippings on the walls, a pot-bellied stove and an ancient refrigerator panelled in dark wood. Behan wrote about it: 'If you are interested in seeing a wonderful saloon which has not changed in the century . . . in good ale and raw onions, and in the fact that you can leave your wife outside with excellent excuse, because she is not allowed in, then this is the place.' A few years later McSorley's was forced to change with the times when a New York City ordinance compelled the admission of women, though it did not give in without a well-publicized struggle. Several young women, chiefly students from the Cooper Union, are now to be seen enjoying its ambience, but it's no good their ordering wine or spirits; if they try, they will be told uncompromisingly: 'Ale or porter or Guinness' — for that's all, apart from biscuits and cheese and raw onions, that McSorley's sells.

Before turning back into Cooper Square, notice the **St George Ukrainian Catholic Church** across the road from McSorley's, at the corner of Taras Shevchenko Place. You will already have seen other Ukrainian shops and institutions in this area, for the community has managed to keep its identity despite invasions by other groups. The Ukrainian Restaurant on Second Avenue between St Mark's Place and 9th Street, opposite the Ottendorfer Library, offers unassuming but tasty home cooking in the peasant style and is remarkably good value.

Back at Cooper Square, turn left, then right into East 4th Street, where two excellent early nineteenth-century houses have survived in unlikely surroundings; both are on the right of the street. The first, No 37, is the younger of the pair, built in 1844, but the less well restored. The bulky columns supporting the porch label it as pure Greek Revival. Together with the better-kept No 29, a Federal house twelve years its senior, it illustrates the swift switch between the two styles. The hideous garage between them was once three smaller town houses and if you can ignore its blighted appearance you may be able to imagine, with a bit of effort, what the street looked like in the mid-nineteenth century.

No 29, **the Old Merchant's House**, is in fact one of the very few that remains intact, inside and out, from the Federal period, and has recently been reopened as a museum. The old merchant was Seabury Tredwell, who bought the house in 1835. His descendants, three spinsters, lived in it until the last of them died there in 1933, aged ninety-three. She had lived for years as a recluse, hoarding her family's treasures, and it was this deliberate withdrawal from the upward and northward mobility prevalent in the city throughout her lifetime which preserved the house as a unique nineteenth-century relic. It still contains the furniture it had when built — heavy mahogany Victoriana matching the high mahogany doors in the main rooms, functional if lacking in delicacy. The interior has been carefully restored, with new carpets and curtains woven to the original patterns, and it provides the most authentic glimpse available of life in New York in the period when this was its most fashionable residential center.

Turn right into **Lafayette Street**, to look at two buildings, not as old or as dainty as the Old Merchant's House, but nearly as interesting architecturally. The plain and sturdy red-brick warehouse on the north-east corner of 4th Street was built in 1885 as the headquarters of the De Vinne press — one of the massive structures that just predated the introduction of steel-frame construction. A bit farther south, on the north-west corner of Great Jones Street, the smaller but more ambitiously decorated pile, four squat columns bearing much of its weight, was designed by Henry Hardenbergh, who was to go on to create two of New York's best-known landmarks, the magnificent Plaza Hotel at the south-east corner of Central Park, and the Dakota apartment house on 72nd Street and Central Park West. In this earlier frolic he seems overly obsessed with prettiness, trying too hard, slapping on every decorative device he can think of.

Turning back north on Lafayette Street, on the left before its junction with Astor Place, are the delicate, crumbling columns of **Colonnade**

Row. This curious and now decrepit terrace, with pillars stretching from the balcony to the roof, is all that is left of a row of nine houses built in 1831. Five were destroyed to make way for the warehouse which adjoins them to the south: what remains was originally split into four dwellings. As soon as it was built the row became the most fashionable place to live in New York. The houses had thirty-foot gardens in front, meaning that the street was a narrow, quiet cul-de-sac, blocked off where Great Jones Street now crosses it. The ubiquitous John Jacob Astor, who owned the property on which the houses were built, once lived in one, as did Washington Irving, who liked to move every year or two to keep up with shifting fashions. The roof of the house on the far right has retained the original fringe of stylized honeysuckle leaves which once topped the whole row.

Opposite is the forbidding Italianate brownstone and red-brick palazzo built in the 1850s as the Astor Library, established with the Astor bequest on which the *New York Herald* had poured so much scorn. It was the city's first major research library open to the public, although its restricted opening hours, coinciding with most people's working day, made it of limited use to New Yorkers. In 1911 it merged with two other private foundations to form the New York Public Library at Fifth Avenue and 42nd Street. For twenty-four years from 1921 the Lafayette Street building housed the Hebrew Immigrant Aid Society, affording help and shelter to millions of Jewish refugees coming to America. Now it is the **Public Theater,** the headquarters of Joseph Papp's New York Shakespeare Festival, one of the city's most lively cultural institutions. Papp, born to Jewish immigrant parents in Brooklyn, is a gifted director and impresario who pioneered free performances of Shakespeare in Central Park in the summer. Among successful shows which originated at the Public Theater before moving to Broadway are the musicals *Hair* and *A Chorus Line*, as well as serious plays by young American writers. The interior of the building has been ingeniously converted into a handsome lobby and seven auditoriums. Seeing a show at the Public Theater should be an unmissable part of a New York visit. After six in the evening you can get any unsold tickets at a reduced price, but do not bank on anything being available: better to book by phone.

The success of the Public Theater has done something to obliterate the shame which attaches to theatrical history in this part of New York. The city has always been earnest about show business, but never has its enthusiasm resulted in a tragedy comparable to that on 10 May 1849, when thirty-four people were killed in a riot outside the Astor Place Opera House, between Broadway and Lafayette Street. There existed a long-simmering rivalry between an American actor, Edwin Forrest, and an English one, William Macready, making a farewell performance at the opera house in *Macbeth,* before returning to England after an American tour. Macready had accused Forrest of hissing at one of his performances and Forrest in turn blamed Macready for his having received a hostile reception from an English audience four years earlier. It became a *cause célèbre* which ignited latent anti-British sentiments: the New York populace, naturally enough, took Forrest's part — they thought British artistes looked down their noses at them. A mob was organized to stone the opera house as Macready left, with the aim of capturing him. The militia were summoned and fired into the crowd when they refused to disperse, causing many injuries and the thirty-four deaths. Macready escaped in disguise. Fortunately the beneficial interchange between stars of the London and New York stages was not long disrupted by the incident.

The Public Theater is as good a place as any to leave you. After the show, you can catch the East Side subway at Astor Place.

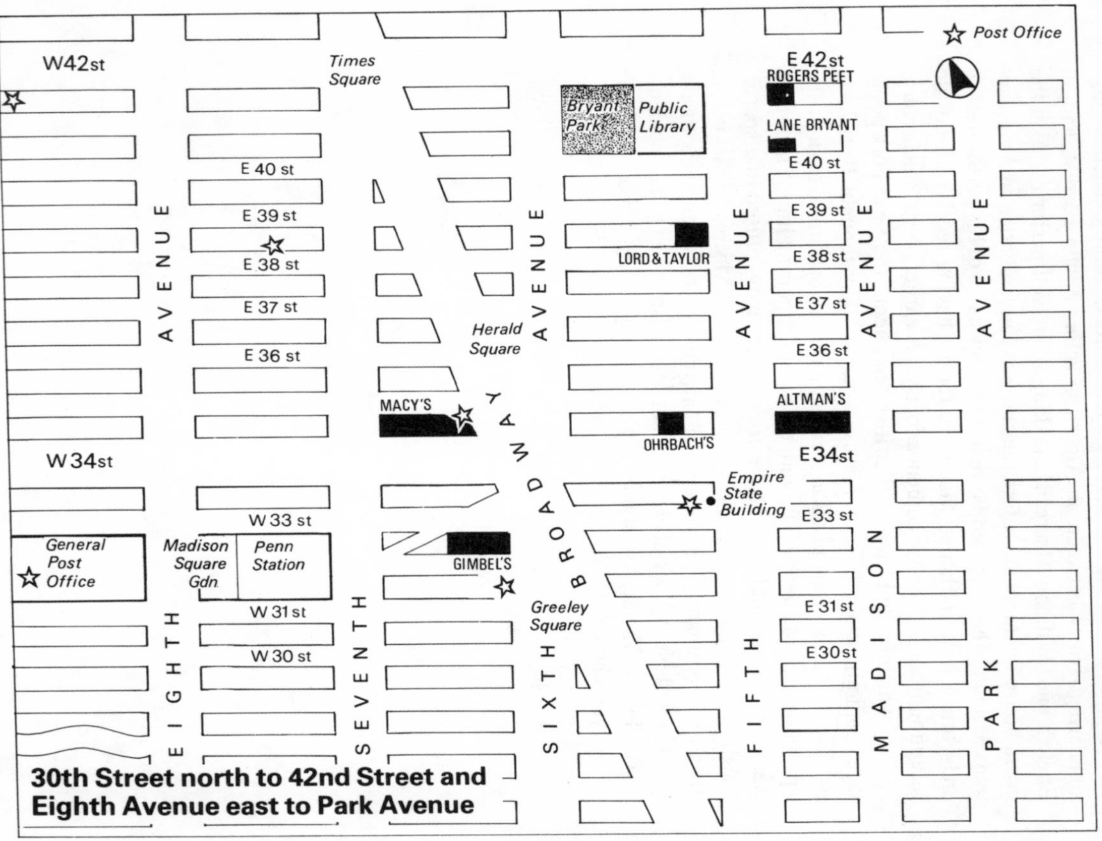

30th Street north to 42nd Street and Eighth Avenue east to Park Avenue

8
The Garment District and the Department Stores

WALK SOUTH down Seventh Avenue from Times Square. On the corner of 39th Street you come across a glass-walled information booth proclaiming New York City 'The Fashion Capital of the World', a self-confident assumption that marks the beginning of the garment district. Although you could scarcely tell from the dreary rows of pre-war skyscrapers which contain its warehouses, factories and showrooms, this is, in economic terms, the mainspring of New York. The clothing industry is the city's largest employer, dealing in goods worth some $12,000 billion a year at wholesale prices: three-quarters of all the ladies' and children's garments made in the United States are manufactured here. The industry developed in the nineteenth century because of the city's strategic position. Raw cotton from the south was shipped to the East River piers; the finished goods, made on newly invented machines, could be taken to the heartlands via the Hudson and the Erie Canal. The mass immigration provided an ample supply of suitable labor; although the industry moved from the Lower East Side and SoHo between the wars, it is still predominantly Jewish.

The showrooms do not sell to retail buyers but a short walk amongst them will provide an impression of tremendous energy. Trucks are double parked in the side streets loading goods and unloading machinery. Racks of clothes and trollies piled with bolts of cloth are forever being wheeled across roads and pavements, into and out of buildings, claiming right of way over the crawling cars and buses and certainly over the put-upon pedestrians. Small-time toilers make deliveries as best they can, struggling with large suitcases — or perhaps they are designers touting their works to the manufacturers. From nine to five all is bustle approaching chaos.

To savor the atmosphere further, slip into Dubrow's cafeteria between

37th and 38th Streets on the east side of the Avenue, for a coffee and Danish pastry. The emphasis is on Jewish delicatessen-style food, but eggs and bacon are available for non-believers. It is a large, cheap and cheerful self-service establishment where dealers go to chew on large cigars and to make deals or swap gossip. By seating yourself cleverly you are almost certain to hear something fascinating, couched in the kind of dialogue that Damon Runyon persuaded us was real New Yorkese: 'So I says to him: "Are you kidding? For that price? For that price I could get it at Bloomingdale's," I says to him. And he says, "I'll tell you what I'll do, Mort" . . . and then he says: "You're killing me, you know that, Mort?" and I says: "So I have to make a living, or don't I?" '

Farther down Seventh Avenue Macy's department store looms on the left but we shall not go inside yet. Instead, cross over and turn right up West 33rd Street, devoting your attention to the glass office tower on your left and the connected circular building west of it, together occupying the whole block between Seventh and Eighth Avenues. This is the present resting place of the itinerant **Madison Square Garden** complex which, in addition to a large indoor stadium, a smaller auditorium called the Felt Forum and their supporting bars and steak houses, includes the booking hall and platforms of **Pennsylvania Station,** the terminus for trains from Washington, the West, the South and Long Island.

New Yorkers still lament the passing of the old Penn station, which this undistinguished piece of modern architecture replaced here in 1968. *The New York Times* called its destruction a monumental act of vandalism, adding: 'We will probably be judged not by the monuments we build but by those we have destroyed.' Built in 1910, the old terminus was entered through a row of Doric columns, balanced by the Corinthian columns of the central Post Office building which went up a few years later and still remains on the other side of Eighth Avenue. People used to admire the interior more than the pretentious façade. A towering glass and steel concourse rose above platforms that are now entombed underground. I never saw the old station, so I cannot say whether it is one of those buildings more appealing in retrospect than in real life.

The Post Office now looks a bit out of place across from all that modernity, but its chief architectural problem springs from its very conception — the front just goes on too long. It is overpowering in the worst way. Who wants to climb all those steps and go into such a grand place just to buy a stamp? One theory is that it had to be built that wide to accommodate the inscription above the columns: 'Neither snow nor rain nor heat nor gloom of night stays these couriers from the swift completion of their appointed rounds.' My son spent some of his formative years on the Eighth Avenue bus and that was almost the first set of words he learned by heart.

Go back east down 30th Street and pause at No 257, at the Eighth Avenue end. It is one of two or three hand-made cigar shops in this area, catering to the demands of the garment manufacturers. Cigar-rolling is a nimble process and by displaying his workmen in the window the proprietor hopes to lure you in to buy. If you like cigars you could do worse, for they are not over-priced.

As you approach Seventh Avenue again, you can notice from the showroom windows that this is the fur section of the garment district, rather less frenzied. On the left, about half way down, **St John the Baptist Church** provides a rare refuge from the commerce of the street. Brownstone Gothic, dating from 1872, it is a well-balanced work in two senses: it has a pleasing formal symmetry and it strikes a happy medium between the over-elaborate and the austere, set off to advantage by the mansard-roofed red brick church hall next door. Inside, its qualities are sustained: the marble pillars, the pale green and lemon color scheme combine for a cool, airy effect.

At Seventh Avenue, turn left. The Statler Hotel on the right was built in 1918 and was famous for the big bands that played in its ballroom between the wars. Now elderly by the short-term standards of New York hotels, it struggles to keep a modicum of gentility in an area which is no longer one of the most desirable, and remains notable chiefly for its phone number — 736-5000. Before the phone company abolished letters, this read as PEnnsylvania 6-5000, the title of a Glenn Miller tune written to celebrate the hotel's standing with big-band enthusiasts.

Now we come to **Macy's,** the world's largest store and one of its most famous. The bald statistics are that it has two million square feet of selling space for some four hundred thousand items. Before I attempt the impossible — guiding you through its monstrous departments — it would be appropriate to give some statistics about Mr Macy himself who was, on the face of it, an unlikely person to have his name perpetrated, in large letters, in the annals of commerce.

Rowland Hussey Macy was born on Nantucket Island, off Massachusetts, in 1822. At fifteen he joined the crew of a whaler on a four-year voyage. Returning to dry land in 1841, he was employed in a few shops in Boston, and several times tried to set up his own. His early misadventures would have deterred all but the most dogged. He went to California to sell goods to the gold rush pioneers, but his business failed. Returning to Massachusetts, he opened a cloth and clothing shop in Haverhill, where he pioneered the ideas of low fixed prices, heavy advertising and cash on the barrelhead which were to be the foundation of his later success. Fixed prices were the exception rather than the rule in America before the Civil War — the custom was for shoppers to bargain with the salespeople, so that the sharpest of them, or those friendliest with the proprietor, would get the best deals. Macy's policy was one price for all, and insisting on full cash payment, he declined to give credit to anyone. But Haverhill, with a population of only nine thousand, was too small a town to support such revolutionary and costly sales promotion, and Macy went bankrupt in 1855.

After a couple of years of land speculation in Wisconsin, he decided to go back into retailing, this time in the country's most populous city, New York. He rented a shop on Sixth Avenue, as it was then, near the junction with 14th Street, selling fancy trimmings and finishings for ladies' clothes, and in 1858 launched himself on the metropolis with attention-grabbing advertising which matched in volume that of Arnold Constable, Lord and Taylor, and A. T. Stewart, then the giants among New York retailers, whose stores were much farther downtown. Within a few years, partly to offset trade fluctuations caused by the war, he began to introduce other goods and to expand into surrounding properties. By 1869 he had twelve distinct departments and by 1877 he had twenty-two, including a china, glass and crockery section sub-contracted to two Bavarian-born brothers, Isidor and Nathan Straus. In 1877, Macy died in Paris. The store's ownership passed to some of his former colleagues until, in 1888, the Straus brothers were admitted as partners and soon took a controlling interest. It was a vibrant partnership. Isidor was a sober, hard-headed businessman while Nathan was more flamboyant, with a flair for publicity and philanthropy. (In 1912, in a rare burst of extravagance, Isidor decided to travel home from Europe on the *Titanic*. He and his wife died when the ship went down.)

By 1902 Macy's had outgrown its 14th Street premises. The city's central shopping section, which had been some way south when Rowland Macy first opened, had overtaken the store and was moving up to 23rd

Street. Isidor's sons, Jesse and Percy, were now in the business and they assumed. correctly, that retailing would continue its northward drift: thus the firm acquired its dominant site on 34th Street and Broadway. The eastern half of the present Macy's is the original 1902 store, with the huge selling area on the ground floor broken only by the structural columns and escalator shafts. The building right on the corner of Broadway was bought by a rival and never incorporated into Macy's: today it is a hot dog bar propping up a large Macy's advertisement. The main, almost ceremonial, entrance to the store is on 34th Street, close to the Broadway corner, and is dominated by four caryatids, coyly holding hands in pairs. The turn-of-the-century lettering etched into the stone and the matching clusters of five lamps on each side combine for a nice sense of period. What's more, the venerable clock amidst it all actually works.

Macy's strength has been to change its marketing approach with the shifting styles of the city. Low prices are now a less important ingredient of their selling strategy than they have ever been — they're not going to undersell the large-volume discount merchants who keep limited ranges of goods and pare their overheads by eliminating fancy decor and all but the most rudimentary personal service. In the early 1970s Macy's decided not to compete on that level but to move instead up-market, seeking the smart and wealthy young New Yorkers, whose aspirations were then realized by Bloomingdale's on the Upper East Side. The best symbol of Macy's decisive switch is in the basement, which used to be devoted to bargains but has been transformed into The Cellar, a series of alcoves resembling individual shops for the sale of fashionable kitchen furniture, utensils, gadgets and food. The best fancy food department in the city, The Cellar bursts with cheeses, smoked fish, cooked meat, home-made pasta, exotic fruit and vegetables, magnificently fragrant cakes and bread, as well as canned and packaged food from all over the world, including caviar at hundreds of dollars a pound. As a place to look and sniff, it is rivalled only by Zabar's on the Upper West Side and Balducci's in Greenwich Village.

We are going to visit several department stores during this chapter, but serious shopping is best left to a separate expedition towards the end of your stay. Macy's chief competitor on this section of Broadway is **Gimbel's,** which branched out from Milwaukee and Philadelphia in 1909, to set up shop two blocks south. The store, now British-owned, has its adherents, but finds it hard to promote a clear image in the shadow of its giant rival. Men's clothing is one of its strengths, and there is a large stamp and coin department for collectors.

Outside, the intersection of Broadway and Sixth Avenue forms two triangular 'squares', both connected with the newspaper industry. **Greeley Square,** the more southerly, celebrates the founder of the *Tribune*. The statue here represents him slightly younger than the one near City Hall, though still with that curious growth of hair around his larynx, and sitting in a less grand armchair. He gazes north at **Herald Square,** the former site of his great rival, James Gordon Bennett's *Herald*. In 1893, Stanford White built the *Herald* a low headquarters resembling a Venetian palazzo, in which the printing presses were installed behind the ground-floor windows, to be inspected by passers-by strolling under the dainty arcade which White wrapped around the building. In the 1920s it was demolished to make way for the nondescript offices there now. All that remains is the statue of Minerva and the bell ringers which used to tower above the twin clocks on the building's north face, the ringers beating out the hours. The statuary has been kept here as a memorial to Bennett, who may well be amused by the thought that a city which detested him for much of his life should want to pay tribute to him after his death.

Bennett studied to be a priest in his native Scotland before coming to America and taking up journalism. Establishing the *Herald* in 1835, he turned it into the most successful of the one-cent papers. It was unusual in that its prime purpose was not the advocacy of a political line but the dissemination of brightly written news on an unusually wide range of topics. Bennett made a start at investigative journalism, exposing and denouncing corruption in government. When he extended this technique to reporting on financial affairs — his was the first popular paper to report on them regularly — he became greatly disliked in the business community, one or two members of which would set about him with their canes if they saw him in the street; a parcel bomb was delivered to him but did not explode. He made himself still less popular with the prudish city establishment by campaigning for more candor in the published discussion of bodily functions and intimate apparel. In one editorial he caused an outcry by writing: 'Petticoats — petticoats — petticoats. There, you fastidious fools, vent your mawkishness on that.' He was shunned and denounced for weeks, and the *Herald's* circulation duly soared.

Bennett also saw the importance of foreign news and was a pioneer in the use of the newly invented telegraph for its transmission. But it was his son, James Gordon Bennett Jr , who, when he became editor of the *Herald,* was responsible for its greatest scoop — the despatch of Henry Stanley to search for the explorer Livingstone in Africa. On 3 November 1871, Stanley found his quarry beside Lake Tanganyika. 'Dr Livingstone, I presume,' he said, and telegraphed news of the encounter back to New York. He did not, however, get the editorial plaudits he was entitled to expect. The younger Bennett was vain and unpredictable, and grew jealous of the fame which the adventure had brought to Stanley and not to him, whose idea it was. The Bennetts' lasting contribution to journalism was to establish the overseas edition of the *Herald* in Paris (where James junior was born); it is now the *International Herald Tribune*.

Walk east down **31st Street,** unusually full of architectural interest if you keep your eyes up. First look at the exaggerated gingerbread mansard on the south-east corner of Broadway, on a complex called Clark apartments. Next to it, the former Hadson Hotel is now part of the same apartment building: notice the heavy ornamentation on the top floor. Further east, on the north side of the street, No 31 is a good red-brick Deco. A few doors along, No 19 is yet another monument to journalism, the headquarters of the original *Life* magazine, once a humorous periodical on the lines of Britain's *Punch*. The attractive little building, with distinct European overtones, was designed in 1894 by Carrère and Hastings, architects of the Cunard Building and the Public Library on 42nd Street. The name 'Life' is picked out in iron on the balconies and a back-to-back 'L' design with the words 'wit' and 'humor' remains in the stonework over the door. In 1936 the magazine's title was bought by Henry Luce of *Time,* who used it for his new weekly pioneer of photojournalism (now monthly). It is a happy surprise to find the building with most of its ornament intact, despite its present role as an unprepossessing hotel. Across the street again, near its junction with Fifth Avenue, is another surprise, the Wolcott apartment building, a red-brick palace with pretty balconies, a bit like the Chelsea Hotel on West 23rd Street. The ostentatious decorative details include a pair of heads, near the top of the building, which look as though they belong to Aztec gods.

Turn left on Fifth Avenue. At 34th Street you reach the entrance to the **Empire State Building**, since its completion in 1931 an instantly recognizable symbol of the city. Like most very tall buildings, its base is the worst place to see it from: there are splendid views of it from nearly all parts but this. Many connoisseurs of Art Deco skyscrapers now prefer the Chrysler Building on 42nd Street, built a year earlier, whose short reign as the world's tallest building the Empire State ended. Chrysler is certainly more frivolous and spectacular, especially at its crown. The Empire State, although it too boasts some fine Deco details, exudes more solid dignity overall; it seems to mean real business.

Since the middle of the nineteenth century, the block of Fifth Avenue between 33rd and 34th Streets has been a prime location. Two grandsons of John Jacob Astor built mansions there and in the more northerly of them Mrs. William Astor, a member of the Schermerhorn family from the old Dutch 'aristocracy', entertained the city's social leaders with fabulous extravagance. In 1890 William Waldorf Astor, who had inherited the other house, converted it into a hotel, the Waldorf, which opened in 1893. His aunt, Mrs. William Astor, found it inconvenient to live and entertain next to so much bustle: four years later she moved farther up Fifth Avenue and had her house demolished to make room for the Astoria Hotel. The two were linked as the Waldorf-Astoria and became the smartest address in town until the block was bought in 1929 for the erection of the world's tallest building. Prophetically, the old Waldorf-Astoria closed its doors only six months before the stock market crash which bankrupted many of the old customers who had attended its nostalgic closing party. Two years later the owners opened a new Waldorf-Astoria on Park Avenue at 50th Street, where it remains.

The syndicate which built the Empire State was headed by Alfred Smith, a former governor of New York and a gifted showman. Largely due to the Depression, it took nearly ten years to rent all the two million square feet of office space. The mooring mast on the top, fancifully supposed to be for airships, was never used as such, though it proved a useful anchor for the gorilla King Kong when he climbed the building in the memorable 1933 film. The worst day in the building's history was 28 July 1945, when a Navy bomber crashed into its 79th floor in fog, the resulting fire killing eleven people in the office as well as the pilot and his two crew members.

The hundred and two floors are 1,250 feet high. For nearly forty years it was the highest building in the world; it is now outreached by the World Trade Center and by giants in Chicago and Toronto. The Empire State Building is open to visitors and is not a sight many want to miss, so at

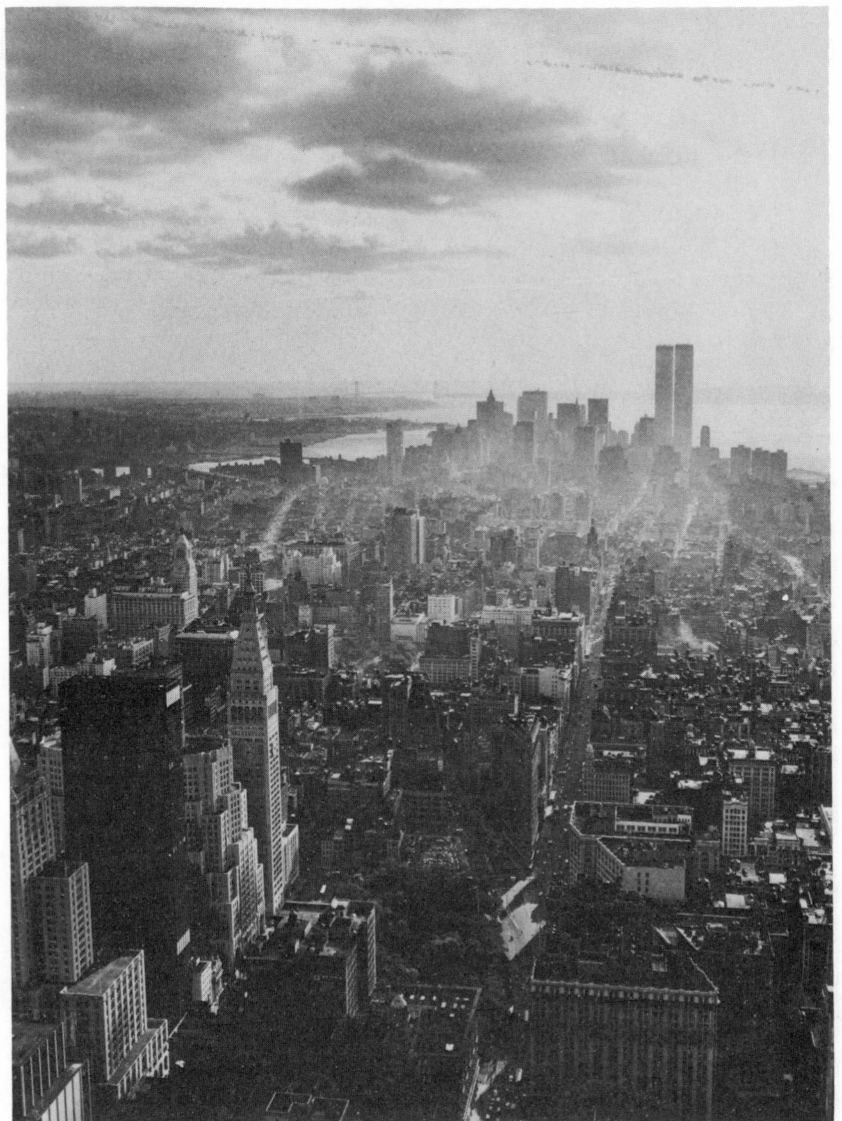

In the centre of this view across the south of Manhattan is the Flatiron Building, so named for its distinctive shape; it was one of the very first New York buildings to employ steel-frame construction. Its corner site is where Fifth Avenue and Broadway converge at Madison Square.

Left:
New York was chosen as host city for the United Nations in 1946 and the UN Center has become one of the most recognizable landmarks in the world.

The lake in Central Park. In the centre background, behind Calvert Vaux's bridge, is the Dakota apartment building. When built in 1884, it was described as so far outside the city center that it might as well be in the Dakota Territory.

weekends and during holidays there is often quite a wait for the trip to the top: you have to use three separate elevators to reach the 102nd floor observatory and the last of them can take only a handful of passengers. If you are short of time, the view from the 86th floor observation deck is scarcely inferior.

Looking south, you get a fine idea of the angled streets of Greenwich Village and see clearly where the Albany and Boston Post roads diverged at City Hall Park, as well as the junction of Broadway and the Bowery at Union Square. It is not worth the price of admission to the top if the visibility, indicated on a board in the ticket office, is less than two miles, but it costs nothing to go into the marvellous grey and brown marble lobby on the ground floor, where illuminated panels along the 34th Street side illustrate the seven wonders of the world and offer the interesting statistic that if you piled all seven one on top of the other, they would not reach the Empire State Building's top. For those who like to be amazed by such things, a small hall by the ticket office in the basement contains the Guinness world record exhibition, including life-sized models of the tallest and fattest people. The illumination of the building's spire and upper portion change color on special occasions: white for Easter, green for St Patrick's Day; red, white and blue for elections and patriotic holidays, and blue and white if the New York Yankees have performed some specially memorable baseball feat.

Diagonally opposite, on the north-east corner of Fifth Avenue and 34th Street, is a monument of less height but greater age, the Altman department store. **Altman's** is near the carriage trade end of the spectrum (in the days when the rich spent their summers on Long Island, the store would base a fleet of wagons there to deliver ordered goods, picking them up from trains) but there are other shops, such as Lord and Taylor or Bloomingdale's, which might claim social precedence.

I have always found Altman's one of the most comfortable of the New York stores to shop in, less frenetic than its competitors to the west and north. It has good ranges of china, glass, domestic linens and furnishing fabrics, and a substantial art gallery on the eighth floor: this is an indication of the enthusiasm of its founder, Benjamin Altman, a connoisseur who bequeathed his impressive collection, including a clutch of Rembrandts and much fine porcelain, to the Metropolitan Museum of Art. The store's building, a restrained Renaissance palace, also suggests a man of sensibility. Part of the restraint may be because when it was built, in 1906, this stretch of Fifth Avenue, except for the Waldorf Hotel, was still lined with the mansions of the rich, and Altman did not want to arouse their anger — or lose their patronage — by building anything garish. It is said that he was persuaded to leave the firm's name off the façade by J.P. Morgan, the financier, who lived only a few blocks away and deplored the commercialization of the district. It is not recorded what Morgan thought of the dolphin fountain by the entrance. I like it.

In a few years other stores had followed Altman's lead north and the mansions were being pulled down to make way for them. Some of the shopkeepers were less conservative than Altman: look at the terra-cotta façade, mixing Middle Eastern and oriental motifs, elaborate to the point of decadence, on No 409 on the north-east corner of 37th Street. Its ground floor is now an ugly branch of Citibank. On the south-east corner is the colonnaded mansion Stanford White designed for Tiffany's, the jewelers. In 1940 Tiffany's moved north again to the corner of 57th Street but Altman's stayed put and so did **Lord and Taylor,** the city's oldest surviving merchants, who moved up from the cast-iron building near Union Square in 1914 to their present location at Fifth Avenue and 38th Street. Lord and Taylor are noted for high quality men's and women's fashions. The stately building, beneath its broad green cornice, is the only one around here, except Altman's, whose ground floor exterior remains as the architect drew it. I am fond of the ground floor inside as well, the counters arranged between mirrored columns, and panels beneath a prettily curving ceiling with decorated mouldings. At Christmas, New Yorkers queue on the pavements outside for a glimpse of their window displays, featuring electric moving models.

Lord and Taylor is a monument to the art of marrying cleverly. Samuel Lord came from Yorkshire in England, where he worked in James Taylor's iron foundry. In 1824, when he was twenty-one, he married the boss's daughter and came to seek his fortune in America. Arriving in New York, he borrowed $1,000 from his wife's uncle and opened a drapery shop in the Bowery. The following year he took his wife's cousin, George Washington Taylor, as a partner and enlarged the store. Taylor returned to England in 1852, his fortune made, but Lord stayed on to see the store grow in fame and size.

For years Arnold Constable, another smart clothes store, rivalled Lord and Taylor, and the pair followed each other uptown from one fashionable location to the next. A few years ago the rivalry ceased when Arnold Constable went out of business: their old shop on the south-east corner of 40th Street and Fifth Avenue is now the Mid-Manhattan branch of the New York Public Library, separate from the Central Reference Library in the Beaux Arts building on 42nd Street. Lane Bryant, across 40th Street, specializes in — and can indeed claim to have invented — maternity clothes and outsizes. When Lane Bryant, a lately widowed Lithuanian immigrant, began the business in the early 1900s, the newspapers were at first too prudish to accept her advertisements. Back on the west side of the avenue, note the abandoned store of S. Kress & Co., with its stylish 'Aztec Deco' front and little diagrams illustrating the type of goods 'five and dime' stores sell. It closed in 1977.

We are getting dangerously close to 42nd Street, the subject of the next chapter, so turn south again and east down 37th Street, approaching the Murray Hill district, to pause for a little history. The area is named after Robert Murray who, in the eighteenth century, owned a farm where Park Avenue now meets 37th Street. An abiding legend has it that Murray's wife saved George Washington's army from capture by the British on 15 September 1776. General Howe had landed his troops at Kips Bay, where 34th Street runs down to the East River, and marched them as far as the Murray farm. There, it is said, Mrs Murray proffered tea and perhaps even some sympathy, luring Howe to dally while Washington's troops were able to retreat to Harlem Heights. Had Howe acted more expeditiously he might have trapped 3,500 of Washington's men in Lower Manhattan; but within two months the British had control of New York anyway, and kept it until the end of the war.

As we approach Madison Avenue down 37th Street we enter the part of town once dominated by the financiers J.P. Morgan, father and son, still the home of the library of rare books that the elder Morgan amassed. The first bit of the Morgan empire we see is the sturdy brownstone mansion on the south-east corner of Madison Avenue and 37th Street, once the home of J. P. Morgan Jr , now the office of the Lutheran Church in America. (Lutherans do not mind visitors going to see the brownstone during working hours; though furnished as an office, details from its residential days remain.) It was built in 1852, one of three similar houses on the eastern side of the avenue: J.P. Morgan Sr lived in one, on the corner of 36th Street, and bought this one for his son in 1904 — the third, which stood between them, was pulled down to provide a garden. The original residence of Morgan senior was destroyed to make way for an extension to his library in 1926.

The entrance to the **Morgan Library** is on 36th Street, east of the avenue. The low, classical earlier building, its façade reflecting the richness of the material within, was created by Charles McKim in 1906 to house the collection of rare books on which the crusty and taciturn financier had spent part of his wealth. The buildings are open as a museum. You enter through the new wing and walk along the connecting corridor, past the gift shop, to the west room of the older building, Morgan's study. Like many wealthy men of his day, Morgan was attracted to medieval and Renaissance art; on his trips to Europe he would buy what took his fancy. The study is stuffed with it, dominated by a carved wooden ceiling of the Italian Renaissance and a fifteenth-century Florentine fireplace surmounted by a pair of painted wood candelabra. The windows contain fifteenth-century Swiss stained-glass panels and the walls are hung with deep burgundy damask. Morgan's desk and chair were carved for the room to McKim's design, but apart from them the only contemporary artifacts are portraits of Morgan père et fils, interspersed with fifteenth-century Italian works.

Just a year after it was built, Morgan's library served as the gorgeous stage setting for a heart-stopping financial melodrama which kept a worldwide audience on the edge of their seats throughout its fortnight's run. The 1907 panic began with the bankruptcy of a prominent investor who controlled several financial institutions. This aroused fears for the solvency of a number of banks, and lines began to form outside their downtown offices, as frightened depositors sought to rescue their savings. Even banks which were basically sound had difficulty raising the huge amounts of cash they needed, since because of the prevailing uncertainty they were unable to realize their assets.

Morgan, by then seventy, was America's leading investment banker, as much by dint of his dominant, almost tyrannical, personality as of his controlling interests in many companies, notably US Steel. Appreciating that the panic, unless stemmed, would cause the collapse of the country's financial system, he summoned the chief bankers and businessmen of Wall Street to a succession of meetings in his library, lasting until the small hours of morning after morning. He persuaded them to put up cash to bail the shaky banks out of their immediate crisis, but it was like shoring up a sand castle with the tide coming in. At one stage during the fortnight New York City was threatened with one of its periodic bouts of bankruptcy and could not raise money: Morgan scribbled a promissory note for $30 million — at six per cent interest — on his library notepaper.

The crisis continued. While the bankers sat beneath Morgan's Renaissance ceiling, surrounded by his rare books and medieval artifacts, agonizing over the need to raise millions, the real victims of the panic were still lining up all day in the autumn chill to withdraw their modest savings from banks. Finally Morgan persuaded — some say bullied — the others to agree to put up enough money to save the banks, and the panic ended, like all good cliff-hangers, in the early hours of the morning, when the agreement was announced to waiting reporters. The panic was an important factor in the creation of the Federal Reserve system and federal insurance of depositors' savings, and soon stricter rules were imposed on the conduct of savings institutions.

The worried bankers would have entered the study through the curved formal lobby, looking up to a domed skylight in the center of the richly decorated ceiling. The seats, the floors and the classical pillars are fashioned from contrasting types of marble, while the walls between the pillars are mosaic panels. Not all the negotiations took place in the study: some were in the library itself, with another carved fireplace, a painted ceiling and a large tapestry on the eastern wall. The three tiers of bookcases, with access galleries in front of them, appear to sink unobtrusively into the walls, dominated by the size and elaboration of their environment. The entrances to the upper tiers are cleverly concealed behind the bookshelves.

Today, the library serves as an exhibition hall for some of the highlights of Morgan's manuscript collection, notably three copies of the world's first printed book, the Gutenberg Bible. Specialized exhibitions of parts of the collection, as well as other exhibits of a literary nature, are held in the display room in the new wing. Near it is the reading room where scholars can consult the collections, whose strengths include important autograph manuscripts — over ten thousand of them — of leading eighteenth- and nineteenth-century writers, along with autographed first editions of later works; musical manuscripts, notably Gilbert and Sullivan; early children's books; and some five thousand old master drawings, including a group of Rembrandt etchings. Pierpont Morgan's son, J.P. Morgan, also a banker and collector, ceded control of the library to a board of trustees in 1924 and provided it with an endowment for its maintenance.

Back south down **Madison Avenue,** No 211 was the carriage house for Pierpont Morgan's old residence on the site of the library extension. If you have time (and if you are not drawn down the hill back to Altman's rear entrance) the surrounding streets are worth exploring for their remaining Beaux Arts mini-palaces and their superior brownstones. By a happy chance, the few blocks around the Morgan Library have remained an oasis of elegant living, resisting commercial encroachment from all sides. Your nearest subway is at 33rd Street and Park Avenue, and on your way to it you might want to look at a few good Art Deco skyscrapers on the avenue. These are small compared with the Empire State Building but they will get you in the mood for the little feast of Deco we shall enjoy on 42nd Street in the next chapter.

9
42nd Street

THERE IS scarcely anything you cannot do on 42nd Street. It is Main Street, New York, with something for everyone: the one street, I would guess, which no serious tourist, from the beginning of the century, can have omitted from the itinerary. You can stay on 42nd Street in one of the city's most expensive or in some of its shoddiest hotels. You can catch a train, an inter-city bus or a sightseeing boat and buy tickets for most airlines. You can eat at one of the best restaurants, gain access to America's third largest reference library, visit films and shows ranging from the sombre to the salacious. You can buy fine fresh food at the street's western end and bargains from peddlers near Grand Central Terminal. There are two outdoor parks and an indoor garden. The two main morning newspapers have their offices here (allowing a one-block license in the case of *The New York Times*) and you can buy papers from all over the country and abroad. Finally, where the street meets the East River, stands the headquarters of the world. That is where we begin.

In neither the administrative nor the spiritual sense is the **United Nations Center** truly a part of New York, yet it has had such a profoundly beneficial effect on the city's life and culture since 1952 when its building was completed, that it is hard to conceive of what things were like before its appearance. The streets off First Avenue, from 42nd up into the 50s, are now crammed with marvelous little restaurants of all nationalities and price ranges, catering to the eclectic tastes of delegates from member nations, which currently number more than one-hundred and fifty and which increase steadily as more and ever smaller territories become independent. Because they cater partly to nationals of the countries whose dishes they serve, these restaurants are often more authentic than those in other parts of town, making fewer concessions to American tastes, and some of the best French, Chinese and Indian restaurants are to be found in this area (until the UN came, there was hardly anywhere in New York to get proper Indian food).

37th Street north to 57th Street

The relation between the UN and its host city is not always smooth. From time to time, especially in the autumn when heads of governments come to town for the General Assembly, citizens complain about the traffic jams and about the number of extra police needed. If the visitor is controversial, like Cuba's President Castro, who came in 1979, security precautions are more stringent and the complaints more bitter. Every year or so there is a press outcry about the number of unpaid parking fines which delegates, exploiting their diplomatic immunity, accumulate. In turn, the diplomats bemoan the difficulty of parking and moving about the city and about crime. At times of greatest frustration, they press for the headquarters to be moved elsewhere. Essentially, though, I think New Yorkers are proud to have the UN here and appreciate the consequent broadening of their horizons — even if, being New Yorkers, they will not admit to being impressed by anything. While some delegates, fuming as their limousines take a half-hour to cover ten blocks, may feel they would be happier in Vienna, Geneva or Nairobi, most appreciate the advantages of a city where the UN is just one element in the cultural mix rather than dominating it, as it would almost anywhere else.

The headquarters complex was designed by an international team of architects and the result is entirely appropriate: a building of dignity with no individual quirks. The main office tower is a thin glass wafer, unusually wide on its long side and only seventy-two feet thick on its short one. The curves of the low General Assembly Building, with its curious brown helmet, are a carefully considered contrast, as well as providing a dramatic backdrop to the flags of member nations following the bend at the front. It looks what it is, a home for a thriving, stateless bureaucracy. The land on which it stands, donated by the Rockefellers, used to be an area of small light industries and slaughter-houses. It was called Turtle Bay because, many years before then, it was inhabited by turtles.

The public entrance is at the northern end of the complex, in a large lobby housing occasional exhibitions. Tours, conducted by multi-lingual guides, take place frequently every day and last about an hour, though in the summer you might have to wait a while before being allotted a place on one. It will take you into the General Assembly Hall, the Security Council and the two other original council halls, all donated by member nations and all stylish examples of the design fashions of the 1950s. Tourists enjoy most the humbler-scaled national offerings scattered through the building: rugs, tapestries, mosaics, paintings and sculpture.

Turkey's gift was a copper-cast copy of the world's first identifiable peace treaty, hacked out on stone; China's is among the most spectacular, an intricate marble carving representing the construction of a railway bridge over a ravine; Britain contributed the most prominent work of art — the monumental sculpture by Barbara Hepworth in the courtyard outside the entrance to the Secretariat; a Chagall stained-glass window, symbolizing man's struggle for peace, is in the entrance lobby, on the right as you go in.

Below the lobby shops sell gifts from member countries, UN publications and souvenirs; there's a coffee shop and a post office selling the UN's own stamps. Tickets to Assembly or Council meetings are available at the information desk in the lobby, but the odds are against your catching anything fascinating should you decide to drop in on a debate. In seven years of reporting United Nations affairs, I can hardly remember a time when what actually went on in the chamber made news, as opposed to the intricate diplomacy in the corridors around it. The fact that old hands still talk nostalgically about the time Nikita Khrushchev of the Soviet Union banged the podium with his shoe reveals how little of real excitement takes place.

A better way to catch the flavor of the UN is to eat in the delegates' dining-room, on the third floor of the General Assembly Building. This is open to the public for lunch — just pick up a pass at the visitors' information desk — and it is not usually necessary to reserve a table. The food is of superior cafeteria standard, always including at least one national specialty of a member nation; most of your fellow-diners will be UN delegates. The service is cheerful and motherly. If you get a table near the window you'll enjoy a pleasant view over the East River.

As UN membership has grown, even the thirty-nine-floor office block has proved too small and overflow offices are now located in several nearby buildings, including the sparkling green glass tower, with cutaway corners and pitched canopies, on the other side of First Avenue. Put up in 1976 it houses the UN Plaza Hotel, a luxury establishment popular with officials on government expense accounts. Below the lobby level is a top-class restaurant and bar, where mirrored alcoves provide endless vistas. They are serious about maintaining the tone: it is the only place in New York from which I have been evicted for not wearing a jacket — on a Sunday to boot.

Rather than plunge straight into 42nd Street, under the bleak bridge that carries Tudor City Place across the road, climb the steps at the back of **Ralph Bunche Park** straight across from the Secretariat Building. The tall metal sculpture is a memorial to Bunche, a black American prominent in the UN's Middle East peace-keeping efforts in the 1950s. This small open space is a favorite spot for demonstrations, often by exiles against an official visiting from their native country. From the top of the stairs you get one of the best views of the UN. If you want to savor it longer you can eat at La Bibliothèque, the pricey restaurant at the top with a glass-covered terrace. To the south, Tudor City was built in the 1920s as a self-contained community of apartment dwellers with a kind of village green in the center. The architecture is a free interpretation of the Tudor style, expressed chiefly in the stonework surrounding the doors and windows and in the turrets on the roofs, scarcely visible from ground level.

Walk west, away from the Ralph Bunche steps. Before you get to Second Avenue enter, on your left, the back door of the **Ford Foundation,** the modern building immediately past No 330. You will know it is the right one when you get there because of the extraordinary indoor garden at its core. Many New York offices have displays of plants in their lobbies — or atriums, as it is now obligatory to call them — but none is as ambitious nor as successful as this full-scale semi-tropical shrubbery, a particularly cozy retreat on a cold winter's day.

From the entrance on 43rd Street follow the zigzag path through the garden and down several flights of steps to emerge on 42nd Street. Continue west, across Second Avenue, and you are opposite the *Daily News* Building, mostly dating from 1930 and of architectural importance as the city's first major skyscraper to abandon all hint of Gothic and reveal itself as unabashedly modern. Its architect was Raymond Hood, the most visionary designer of early skyscrapers, who had been apprenticed early to R. A. Cram, best known for his strictly literal Gothic churches. A graduate from the École des Beaux Arts in 1911, Hood rose to prominence when he won the competition for designing the Chicago Tribune Building in 1921. In that he was still following Cass Gilbert in adapting Gothic patterns to the new tall buildings, and there are traces of Gothic in the superb American Radiator Building which we will see later in this walk. With the *Daily News* Building he broke away and went further still with the McGraw-Hill Building at the other end of 42nd Street. His last work was on Rockefeller Center, whose shape he masterminded; he died in 1934. Here at the *Daily News* Building look at the Art Deco frieze over the main entrance then edge into the lobby to see the giant globe, with astounding astronomic facts revealed in captions beneath it: 'If the sun were the size of this globe and placed here, then comparatively the world would be the size of a walnut and located at the entrance to Grand Central Terminal.' The *News*, a tabloid newspaper, has the largest circulation in the city.

On the same side of the street, at the corner of Third Avenue, is a surviving Horn and Hardart automat, one of the early fast food enterprises which I have regarded as typical since I marvelled at them in Hollywood comedies of the 1940s and 50s. Was it Doris Day who put her money into the slot by the plate-sized window and exchanged badinage with a face peering through it? The slots and windows are still there, though mainly nowadays for dispensing cold sandwiches. More substantial meals are to be had from a conventional self-service counter.

As soon as you cross Third Avenue you notice the change of pace. This is the heart of the midtown office area, where the scurrying never stops from eight in the morning to seven at night. As the day begins, pale-faced commuters step from the subway entrances and trot to the coffee shops. They come out bearing dainty brown paper bags containing a warm drink in a styrofoam cup and something doughy to nibble, to sustain them in the early part of the day. They disappear through the revolving doors of the skyscrapers and into the elevators. Anyone really anxious for an insight into the day-to-day life and concerns of a New York commuter might follow them in and spend some time travelling up and down with them until stopped by a suspicious janitor. You would hear intriguing snatches of conversation about wives, families, lovers, food, money, weekend activities, entertainment: everything on the mind of men and women starting their working day. A while later, back on the street, the merchants appear, selling handbags, sweaters, watches, toys and, if the weather is suitable, umbrellas, all from cardboard boxes which they gather up swiftly should a representative of the law decide they do not have a proper license to trade. In the evening the film is played in reverse. The mood is more festive as the toilers pour out of the elevators, talking excitedly now of the small triumphs or setbacks of their working day. The resourceful street vendors are selling flowers: people buy them to celebrate their survival of another day of corporate in-fighting. Soon the rhythm subsides and all that are left are the out-of-towners from nearby hotels, walking the streets watchfully, averting their gaze from the sad transients nesting in the vicinity of Grand Central Station.

The Mobil Building, dating from the mid-1950s, takes up the south side of the street between Third and Lexington Avenues, exuding a botched, boxy modernity with its embossed steel panels and the heavy silver crescent over the entrance. Across Lexington Avenue, still on the south side, is the 1929 Chanin Building, elaborately faced in terra-cotta with whirls of stylized leaves, flowers and curls. Next door, the overblown entrance to the Bowery Savings Bank leads into what could be the city's most elaborate commercial interior. Built in 1923, it relies for its effect on extravagance in the Renaissance style rather than on any Deco gimmicks. The floor is inlaid with mosaics and each of the Corinthian columns supporting the arches round the walls is fashioned from a different kind of marble.

Now that you have caught the mood for opulent interiors, cross 42nd Street and return to the corner of Lexington Avenue. The **Chrysler Building**'s angular lobby, faced with red and brown marble, was fashioned seven years after the Bowery Savings Bank and, though very different, is no less stunning. At the beginning of the 1970s Art Deco returned to popularity and this building became a symbol of the style, one of the best liked in the city as well as the most easily recognizable from a distance. Its stainless steel pinnacle, based on the design of the radiator cap on the 1930 Chrysler car, and the fanciful metal spurs jutting from the corners, so perfectly represent the fantasy inherent in Deco that the building was chosen as the model for the castle of the magical city of Oz in the film *The Wiz*, made in the mid-1970s. It is now as well known as (and sometimes confused with) the spire of the Empire State Building. In the lobby, study the lovely brown doors of the elevators, patterned like Tiffany glass. The red and brown ceiling paintings show the builders at work, all wearing hats.

Crossing Lexington Avenue for a second time, we reach the Grand Hyatt Hotel, until a few years ago the Commodore, one of three monster hotels grouped round Grand Central Station. For years before it closed in 1977 this had ranked below its neighbors, the Biltmore and the

Roosevelt: it was essentially a travelling salesmen's hotel and lost its point as fewer and fewer salesmen arrived by train. Then the Hyatt chain, operators of flashy modern hotels in city centers, took it over and, instead of pulling it down and starting again, sheathed the old masonry front in glass to provide the illusion of modernity. The result is not pleasing: glass buildings should soar. This is too dumpy but one happy consequence is that the heroic sculpture group above the front of Grand Central Station is reflected in the glass on the west side. The old hotel lobby is similarly sheathed now in modern materials, its deep settees and cushioned benches in brown, the chain's house color. Peter De Bello's sculpture 'Bronze Tracery', seventy-seven feet long, hangs from the ceiling. The greenhouse-style bar suspended over the pavement was a nice idea except for the grim view it commands of the day-long traffic jams on 42nd Street. If you slip in for a drink be warned that a standard cocktail (or short) is pretty expensive.

Whatever you think of the hotel as such, it is a shame they could not have incorporated the old name into the new, for it was an apposite memorial to 'Commodore' Cornelius Vanderbilt, one of America's railway pioneers, who built the first station on the site. He was born in 1794 to a Dutch family that had settled on Staten Island in 1640, and at first he worked on his father's ferry to Manhattan. Soon he had a boat of his own and, discovering a talent for the cut-throat competitive tactics which then characterized the New York shipping business, he acquired more until he had a small fleet, operating up the Hudson and in Long Island Sound. With the arrival of steam his fortunes grew fast and by 1840 he was a millionaire. At first he bought shares in railways because they complemented his steam ships — combining land and water travel could knock hours off the journey times of boats alone — and he was seventy before he began to take a serious interest in running railways. In 1864 he sold most of his ships and bought controlling interests in three lines that ran into New York. The terminal was then at Madison Square. Because of the noise, dirt and danger the council barred steam engines south of 23rd Street: carriages were unhooked from the engines and drawn by horses to the City Hall area. As the city spread north, so did the cordon sanitaire and in 1871 the terminal was re-sited at its present spot on 42nd Street, the trains chugging noisily and dirtily north through open cuts up Fourth Avenue, renamed Park Avenue in 1888.

When Vanderbilt died in 1877, aged eighty-three, he left over a hundred million dollars, more than any American had previously amassed. The bulk of it went to his son William, though only after a spectacular law suit in which the other children tried to gain a larger share. When William himself died, only eight years later, he had doubled his inheritance. He had also coined a phrase that was to be regarded by their enemies as the motto of the 'robber barons'. Having decided to discontinue a fast train between New York and Chicago, he was asked by a reporter whether he saw his first duty to the public or his stockholders. 'The public be damned,' he replied. He and his descendants were known for their free spending, their yachts, racehorses and their opulent houses on Fifth Avenue, all now razed. Today, when ownership of a railway is a sure route to bankruptcy rather than instant riches, the New York Central and the other lines to the city are run by State or Federal bodies. The Vanderbilts, their fortunes substantially reduced, have moved to other things. The best known now is Gloria Vanderbilt, the 'poor little rich girl' of the 1930s, victim of a cruel and much publicized fight for her custody. Today she is a fashion designer who has given her name to a popular line of jeans. The Commodore, whose career was founded on the speed with which he spotted new trends, would have approved.

The present **Grand Central Terminal** was built in 1903 to cope with increasing rail traffic. This Beaux Arts building, a fittingly heroic departure and arrival point for trans-continental trips lasting several days, is from time to time threatened with the fate of Penn Station. Developers would like to knock off the upper part, so prodigal in its use of space, and replace it with something modern and cost-efficient. Conservation groups have managed to stave off the threat, though they could not prevent the erection of the Pan Am Building just north of it in 1963, dwarfing the vista of the station and its rococo companion, the New York Central Building (now carefully restored as the Helmsley Building). Walter Gropius, a founder of the Bauhaus in Germany, was the principal architect of the Pan Am Building. He had been designing forward-looking buildings in his native Prussia even before the First World War and his work on the second Bauhaus school at Dessau is revered by present-day architects. In 1934 he fled from Germany (Goebbels had described the Bauhaus as 'cultural Bolshevism') and soon settled at Harvard; he was eighty when the Pan Am Building was finished. It does not have the purity of his earlier work, yet though it is the fashion to decry it I admire its rugged strength and distinctive lines, best seen from the north, down Park Avenue. The helicopter pad on top was closed in 1977 following a fatal accident.

Go inside the station to admire its enormous concourse, the ceiling representing a medieval astronomy chart, with lights pinpointing the stars. The circular information booth in the middle with the four-sided brass clock on top used to be the only encumbrances in an otherwise open area, but clutter has since crept in. Now, at the Merrill Lynch booth just alongside, computer terminals give instant quotations for any stock on the market and a broker is on hand in case you get the urge to dabble. To each his own investment medium: just to the right of the concourse entrance, other speculators line up at the former ticket windows converted, in 1971, into the city's first legal off-track betting parlor. Now there are scores of betting shops run by the OTB (Off Track Betting), a state agency; but I am still fond of this one as an example of resourceful adaptation of surplus facilities for new purposes.

The station's downstairs concourse is in more pristine condition and I find it more appealing, in particular the wooden destination boards alongside the platform entrances. They exude a faintly clerical air, as though announcing hymn numbers rather than trains. The Oyster Bar at the lower level is a cheerful station restaurant, invariably busy. The oyster or clam stews are creamy and delicately flavored; prices are high but by no means outrageous and there is a good cheap Californian white carafe wine. The noisy dining-room, under its curved ceiling lined with criss-cross yellow tiles, is the one place in the station which comes close to duplicating the bustle and excitement of the railways' boom years. If you feel adventurous, go up the stairs in the south-west corner of the station, through an entrance marked 'Traffic Club of New York'. There take the elevator or stairs to the fourth floor and walk through a narrow glass-lined passage on the western end of the concourse. Though the windows are dirty, they afford a fine bird's-eye view of station activity. Every Wednesday at noon a free tour of the station leaves the Chemical Bank's Commuter Express counter at the east end of the concourse: a good idea if it fits your schedule.

Our next call is at another Beaux Arts monument from the same period, the **New York Public Library** on the corner of 42nd Street and Fifth Avenue, formerly a favorite site for physical recreation before turning to its present intellectual role in 1911. In 1842, when it was beyond the limits of the settled part of town, the Croton Reservoir was built here.

Though primarily a functional water storage depot, its high, unadorned sloping walls had a promenade on top, a popular spot for weekend walks: the promenaders, looking south, would get an unobstructed view of the whole city. In 1899 the reservoir was removed to make way for a building to house the city's three main private libraries — the Astor, the Lenox and the Tilden — which were to be merged into a public research library. It is now one of the half-dozen most complete research libraries in the world.

The British Library in London is proud, in a perverse kind of way, of having been the place where Karl Marx did research for his seminal work *Das Kapital*. The New York Public Library, a younger institution, could, but for understandable reasons does not, make a similar if lesser boast with regard to Leon Trotsky, who worked here occasionally during his brief stay in America before the 1917 Russian revolution. The record is detailed. Arriving with his wife Natalia on the Spanish steamer *Monserrat* on 3 January, Trotsky was met by the Communist Bukharin, whose first recorded words to the newcomers were to tell of a marvellous library open in the evenings; he insisted on rushing Trotsky over to the new library at the earliest opportunity. If he came today he would be less impressed. In the city's periodic economy drives the opening hours have been progressively shortened and only by dint of corporate philanthropy can it run to a single late night — Tuesdays until nine. On Thursdays and Sundays it is closed all day. These hours change quite often, as various sources of money become available or dry up.

Outside, the broad front steps are flanked by stone lions. Sculptures alongside the entrance depict truth and beauty, and above are philosophy, romance, religion, poetry, drama and history. At the top of the steps, the elaborate entrance lobby is a confection of crisp, clean-cut marble, its square pillars supporting romanesque arches. Here, at the desk on the left, you may join a tour, led by pleasant volunteers; they are free and last an hour (no reservation necessary). If you prefer to guide yourself, go up the corridor on the right of the main information desk and peer into the Map Room, looking up at its ornamental panelled ceiling. (Most of the individual rooms house specialized book collections and you are not supposed to go in unless you have business there, but nobody minds if you poke your head in for a look.) Where the corridor turns left, take the elevator to the third floor, the main business level. Walking back towards the center of the building, an Exhibition Room on your left holds changing displays of historic manuscripts. On the walls hang portraits, several of George Washington. Gilbert Stuart's often reproduced full-length study of the first president dominates the far wall, and a little to its right is an intriguing curiosity, a portrait of the Marquis de Lafayette in old age, done by Samuel Morse, the pioneer of the telegraph system.

Back in the corridor is a fine print showing New York in 1855, with the Croton Reservoir in the foreground and next to it the short-lived Crystal Palace, occupying what is now Bryant Park. The view was taken from the Latting Observatory, a wooden tower on the north side of 42nd Street which burned down a year after this view was drawn. We are now in the main third-floor lobby, an elaborate tribute to learning, with murals that represent the history of the written word from Moses and the tablets of the law to the linotype machine, while on the ceiling Prometheus steals fire from heaven. This leads into the main Catalogue Room, No 315, where readers discover the books they want and put in their requests. The books are delivered, sometimes in a matter of minutes, to one of the two reading-rooms beyond. These are really one colossal room, covering nearly the whole width of the building, divided by the book counters in the middle.

Along the corridors are prints, paintings and display cases, holding material on themes which change from time to time. There are more of them on the floor below, where also hangs a vital piece of New York history in the shape of the map, drawn up in 1811 by the city commissioners, which introduced the grid system for Manhattan's streets. The pattern has been adhered to with remarkable accuracy, except that nobody had by then thought of Central Park, and the only open space on the map is a large parade ground which would have had as its center what is now Washington Square. On this second floor is the Trustees' Room, which you can see only if you take the guided tour. It is of immense richness, its walls panelled with Philippine teak and walnut, pink marble door frames, a carved marble chimney-piece, finely inlaid tables and a couple of large Tiffany vases. Four seventeenth-century tapestries depict America, Asia, Africa and Europe. You need special permission to enter the Manuscript Room, containing among its treasures a Gutenberg bible and a hand-written copy of George Washington's farewell address. Another restricted room contains a collection of books and artifacts relating to tobacco. Back on the ground floor, the south corridor leads to the Periodicals Room and its international collection of magazines. On the wall of the corridor hangs a print of the Triumphal Arch, a highly intricate work made up of a hundred ninety-two woodcuts done by Albrecht Durer between 1515 and 1518 to honour the Emperor Maximilian I.

When we can manage to tear ourselves away from the library, we shall take a short rest from 42nd Street; but coming down its steps, take time to admire the broad backs of the eight tortoises who bear the weight of the flagpoles on either side, four to each. Walk south and turn right up **West 40th Street,** at the mansarded palace that was once the shop of Knox the hatters but is now occupied by a bank. This stretch of 40th Street used to be lined with men's clubs and a few of their buildings remain. No 20, with a Dutch gable, was the New York Club, and No 32, now converted into apartments, the Engineering Club. The jewel of a skyscraper at No 40, with its unusual black and gold color scheme, is an early work of Raymond Hood, built in 1924 for the American Radiator Company. He was at that time still using Gothic detail — look at the delicate bronze window-frames on the lower floors and the mysterious allegorical figures above them. This was the first skyscraper in New York to be declared a protected landmark, an honor it gained only as late as 1974.

On the north side of the street, behind the library, **Bryant Park** was until recently one of the city's least appetizing open spaces. The park is named in honor of William Cullen Bryant, a nineteenth-century poet, editor of the *New York Post* and one of the prime movers in the establishment of Central Park. Its site, just a few steps from the main Times Square sin section, makes it a natural base for drug peddlers, who have held on despite the latest and so far successful bid at upgrading it to a pleasant midtown park. In trying to rescue this kind of open space from the demi-monde, style is all-important: once you attract enough respectable citizens to outnumber the rogues and addicts, you can reclaim it for the real world. This has been achieved partly by colorful seasonal flower plantings at the north end alongside 42nd Street, and by installing some second-hand bookstalls in the north-west corner. During the lunch hour in summer, bands play (free) popular music concerts beneath the library wall, making life bright for passers-by, if difficult for students in the reading-rooms above. On the north side of 42nd Street, the Grace Building, a 1974 skyscraper, slopes outwards towards ground level for no easily explicable reason other than the surprising effect.

West of Bryant Park runs the Avenue of the Americas. In the days when an elevated railway ran down it Sixth Avenue, as it then was known, was a watershed between the respectable and the raffish part of the city. West of the avenue, all was vice and honky-tonk; though you might venture gingerly as far as Broadway for the theatre or the opera, you would, if you wanted to maintain your sober reputation, hurry back east afterwards. The avenue itself was lined with bars, occupying the ground floors of low row houses, and although many have now been pulled down to make room for skyscrapers, you will spot a few of the old four-and-five-storey buildings. The elevated railway has long since been replaced by the Sixth Avenue subway, but the character of the area has changed little: between here and Eighth Avenue, 42nd Street is lined with peep shows, pornographic cinemas and book shops, 'dating rooms' and the like. You will find it more pleasant to make another detour here, so ignore 42nd Street and carry on north up the avenue.

At 44th Street step a few paces east to the **Algonquin Hotel,** an old literary haunt much favored by British visitors, especially writers of a romantic bent. In the 1920s it was known for being the venue of the Round Table lunch club of literati, mainly contributors to the *New Yorker,* which has its offices nearby. Harold Ross, founding editor of that most civilized and entertaining of magazines, was a regular here, as were the humorists Robert Benchley and Dorothy Parker. That the *New Yorker* has managed to keep its style of ruminative good humor while remaining a vehicle for some of the most vital modern writing is a miracle of publishing and good management. The Algonquin hasn't changed much either since those days, with its comfortable lobby, its oak-panelled dining-room and its cramped bar just to the right of the entrance. The bedrooms are on the small side compared with newer and grander hotels but this does not matter to its band of *aficionados*. It is a pleasant and convenient spot for supper after the theatre, with an imaginative cold buffet.

Now we go back west, across the Avenue of the Americas, and a block north, using 45th Street as our route to Broadway. On the right, the **Lyceum** is an appropriate monument to mark our entry into the theatre district, since it is New York's oldest theatre still used as such (though it often stands empty because Broadway producers have lately taken against theatres lying east of Times Square). Built in 1903, its pretentious columns, elaborate stucco and wavy canopy are fine examples of the freedom from restraint which theatre designers of that time felt they could enjoy. It is a registered landmark and rightly so — they don't build them like this any more. When such theatres are pulled down for office buildings, the new ones which developers grudgingly provide as replacements are often stuffed into the basement, their entrances so unobtrusive that they are hard to locate.

When you reach Broadway you are at the north end of **Times Square.** This was Longacre Square until Adolph Ochs moved *The New York Times* here from its Park Row headquarters in 1905, erecting a twenty-four storey Gothic skyscraper on the triangular plot where Broadway collides with Seventh Avenue and calling it **No 1 Times Square.** Topped by an awkward-looking narrow tower it was, though readily identifiable, no architectural masterwork. Soon the paper wanted more space and built a large annex on 43rd Street, west of Broadway. (This is not, by the way, the building with the stubby clock and globe on top: that is the Paramount Building; *The New York Times* is next door.)

The New York Times was founded in 1851 and, though conscientious and moderately successful, was not, in its early years, able to match the flair of Horace Greeley's *Tribune* or James Gordon Bennett's *Herald*. Its most important contribution to the city's well-being had been the unmasking of 'Boss' Tweed in 1871, but by the 1890s it had declined into a ponderous sheet of little distinction and dwindling appeal. In 1896, with its circulation down to nine thousand, it was bought by Adolph Ochs, an enterprising publisher who had worked in newspapers since he was eleven and who had built up the *Chattanooga Times* in Tennessee from virtually nothing into one of the most respected newspapers in the South. In the first issue of the *New York Times* under his ownership he summarized his credo in words which the paper still tries to honor: 'To give the news impartially, without fear or favor, regardless of any party, sect or interest involved.' It is still owned by Ochs's heirs, the Sulzbergers, and its success has been built around a literal (and, moreover, a literate) interpretation of that philosophy. While other papers burned themselves out competing ever more fiercely with sensational stunts to increase their circulation, the *Times* soberly but energetically set out to make itself a complete organ of reliable and timely information: 'All the news that's fit to print.' Within twenty years Ochs had built an unmatched news-gathering machine. Its reward was to survive in a competitive market while nearly all its rivals gradually died off. Today the paper's strengths are the same as the ones Ochs initiated: comprehensive coverage of world and local events written with style and cool detachment and with an understanding of its readers' concerns, making few concessions to the sensational. Though typographically it looks old-fashioned, it has kept up editorially with changing styles, and has important and profitable sections devoted to entertainment and domestic consumption. In any list of the half-dozen best newspapers in the world, *The New York Times* must be included.

In 1960 the paper sold the Times Square tower and centralized on 43rd Street. The tower's new owners kept the frame but stripped away the Gothic face and replaced it with unappealing white marble. On the ground floor, Hotaling's is the place to buy foreign and out-of-town newspapers and magazines: London papers, for example, may be there on the afternoon of publication. On the eighth floor, the Songwriters' Hall of Fame (admission free) is a small temple to idolatry, containing such objects of worship as Elvis Presley's guitar pick, a cane and top hat used by Fred Astaire (the cane a gift of Cole Porter), Johnny Mercer's typewriter, Ted Lewis's clarinet, Victor Herbert's desk and Jimmy Durante's hat. A slide-show traces the history of American songwriting, while among the displays of sheet music is a collection of songs about New York, some of which are illustrated with drawings of the Times Tower before it was modernized. It was in those days that the tradition was established of celebrating New Year's Eve in Times Square, with many choruses of 'Auld Lang Syne' and the expected Bacchanalian excess. A lighted ball still drops to the ground from here at midnight every 31 December. There is a piano bar on the fifteenth floor and a restaurant, both with dramatic views.

Some ten years before Ochs was to invest Longacre Square with its new name, it was already beginning to assume its character as a magnet for show business and restaurants which, in their relentless leapfrogging up Broadway, reached 42nd Street in the 1890s. The pioneer of theatre development here was Oscar Hammerstein I, the grandfather of the Broadway lyricist who collaborated so prolifically with Richard Rodgers fifty years later. A cigar-maker from Germany, Hammerstein opened his first theatre in 1880 in Harlem, and in 1892 started an opera house on 34th Street. In 1895 he brought an ambitious entertainment complex, the Olympia, to Broadway between 44th and 45th Streets on the east side — a site today notable chiefly for the colossal billboard standing on a set of dingy, low buildings. The Olympia consisted of a music hall, concert hall and theatre, with a roof garden and a cafe. Yet, like that of much else on Broadway, its life was short. By 1898 it was clear that the Olympia was uneconomic, so Hammerstein closed it. Undaunted, the following year he opened the Victoria Theater on 42nd Street and Seventh Avenue, and the Republic next to it with a roof garden spanning the two. The shells of these still stand on the north-west corner of the junction, though scarcely resembling their original form. One of the few buildings which does still look somewhat as it did at the start of the century is that on the south-east corner of 42nd Street and Broadway, the old Knickerbocker Hotel. Enrico Caruso, the tenor, and George M. Cohan, the father of the Broadway musical, were two of the many stars who lived or stayed in this 1902 mansard-roofed palace, now converted into offices.

Just across the road was the magnificent Café de l'Opera, where two thousand waiters served lobster and champagne to twenty thousand diners nightly, on pink tablecloths which stood out from the black marble columns and blue and gold decor. Here you could spend up to $14 on a slap-up dinner for two, but the more discerning would slip a few blocks north to Rector's — smaller but no less opulent — where, said the gourmets, the cooking was more careful. In 1899 Charles Rector and his son George came from Chicago to open their restaurant in a low yellow-fronted building on the east side of Broadway between 43rd and 44th Streets, where now stands the National Cinema and a brown glass office tower. For a short and glamorous period Rector's was paramount among the 'lobster palaces' frequented by the new theatrical aristocracy, with a Russian string orchestra, mirrors from floor to ceiling, thick red carpeting, green and gold ornamentation and waiters in full evening dress. It had one of the city's earliest revolving doors, and for a time people would clutter the entrance by simply whisking themselves round the full circle.

Rector's most prominent patron, in every sense of the adjective, was Diamond Jim Brady, who would dine there with his close friend, the actress Lillian Russell. A man of gargantuan girth and appetites, glistening with jewels, Brady would, according to contemporary chroniclers, gorge himself on plate after plate of oysters, then a lobster or two to keep him going until the main course, a lavish helping of steak, game or roast meat. Miss Russell could not keep up fork for fork but was no mean trencherwoman, and she would allow herself a glass or two of champagne to help the digestion. Brady, probably because he was a saloon-keeper's son who saw the harm drink could do, stayed teetotal all his life, but that did not stop George Rector calling him 'the best twenty-five customers we had'.

Brady deserves a place in any book about New York, not simply for the feats of conspicuous consumption on which he chose to spend his money, but because of how his money was earned. He was among the first to perfect the technique of social salesmanship which later became an accepted way of doing business, pioneering the expense account lunch, not to mention the expense account dinner and the expense account visit to a night club afterwards. Starting work as a hotel bellboy when he was eleven, Brady moved into railways at fifteen as a baggage clerk at Grand Central Station. Three years later he was promoted into a clerical position senior enough for him to make contact with influential people in the industry. At twenty-three he became a salesman for a firm of railway equipment manufacturers and soon, combining his expansive, glad-handing personality with some powerfully impressive technical expertise, he became the best known salesman in the land. His diamonds — and by the time he died he had a considerable collection — were bought and worn as a calculated part of the flamboyant, free-spending image which he saw as an important tool of his trade. Thus, when Brady became known as a substantial pillar of lobster-palace society, it was partly because he very much enjoyed the life and partly because he was doing his job. Lillian Russell may have been the most striking of his companions but as often as not he would instead be entertaining the visiting president of a mid-western railway, softening him up for the next sales trip. In later years Brady would hold court in Rector's, dispensing largesse to needy acquaintances and sponging strangers.

Rector's short history parallelled that of Times Square. Its reputation began to change from the fashionable to the raffish, then to the scandalous. It became a place where a man's female companion would be assumed to be his mistress rather than his wife — a reputation which in the end hastened its demise. Like many of the old lobster palaces, it closed just after the First World War, a victim of prohibition: nobody was going to take his amour for an intimate, sinful, after-theatre supper, and toast her with a milk shake. Nowadays Times Square still can't really offer fine food and high life. Sardi's, at 234 West 44th Street, is the best-known of the theatrical restaurants, where you may still see a stage celebrity dining before or after the show; but you are more likely to see other tourists. Most who go there do so because it is a famous institution, with old playbills and theatrical sketches lining the walls, exuding the odor of Broadway. The food is all right, though a bit overpriced.

The area's numerous other places to eat change hands so rapidly that it is hazardous to make specific recommendations. Many are oriental — Indian, Chinese or Vietnamese — and if a menu looks appealing I would not discourage you from experimenting, although there are probably better examples of these cuisines elsewhere in town. Of the longer-lasting institutions, Mamma Leone's at 239 West 48th Street is a large place with a calculated, madcap exuberance, catering chiefly to tourists. The food is Italian and heavy, with portions of impossible size, and the prices are fairly high. There is jolly music and waiters who sing from time to time. I know of no native New Yorkers who would dream of going there — they hate to risk being thought of as hicks and would not admit to liking such nonsense — but that's a snobbish attitude: you might find Mamma Leone's fun if you are in the mood.

The theatres of the Broadway district were for the most part built in the early years of the century. Some have kept their frontages but many have been almost entirely subsumed by the surrounding architectural squalor. Wandering around, you will find a few of the old frontages pleasing. I am fond of the Art Deco mosaics on the **Shubert** on 44th Street, opposite the strange modern skyscraper with wings on top which replaced the Astor Hotel. The **Lyric** on 43rd Street has some good terra-cotta work and was, like the **New Apollo** a bit farther west, recently reclaimed for the legitimate theatre after years as a movie house. This runs against a trend which has seen a steady decline in the number of theatres around Times Square, from eighty-five in the 1920s to less than half that number now.

When you have had enough of the Times Square area continue west along 42nd Street. The impressive rows of movie marquees on either side survive from the 1940s and 1950s, when this was the place in New York to see a film. The general seediness of the street, with drug peddlers and pimps lurking in doorways, engaging in their business without trying too hard to be discreet, may lead to the initial presumption that the movies now show nothing but pornography; closer inspection will show this to be true of only about half of them. One or two, though altered outside, have kept the interior decoration from their days as straight theatres. The **New Amsterdam,** on the southern side of 42nd Street, was the first home of the Ziegfeld Follies, until Florenz Ziegfeld had his own theatre built on 54th Street in the 1920s. Slip into the lobby and admire the elaboration of the doors to the lifts which used to take patrons to the roof garden, and the wall panels just below the ceiling, depicting heroic scenes from Shakespeare. Outside again, continue walking on this side and look across the street to discern, above the flashy modern cinema entrances, the remnants of several neo-Georgian and Art Deco theatre façades. Notice the back entrance to the Carter Hotel, a fine example of Deco detailing. The Apollo, its main entrance now on 43rd Street, was once the home of Minsky's burlesque, which scandalized the town at a time when it was more easily scandalized. The tone of 42nd Street does not improve as you head west. Its corner with Eighth Avenue can fairly be called the single most squalid spot in town, though it does not lack competition. Eighth Avenue between 40th Street and Central Park is dubbed by police the Minnesota Strip because at nights it is lined with prostitutes who are often runaways from the Midwest. Why Minnesota? I once heard a police chief explain that girls from that cold part of the country were better equipped to patrol the streets on the frostiest New York nights. On the west side of Eighth Avenue, between 40th and 42nd Streets, what looks like a giant 'Erector set' (Meccano) structure is the busy **Port Authority Bus Terminal,** where long-distance buses leave and arrive, from Minnesota and elsewhere. Conditions at the terminal have improved since it was enlarged in 1979 and bus travel is worth considering as an inexpensive and comfortable alternative to the plane or the train.

Still going west up 42nd Street you pass, on the left, the former McGraw-Hill Building, designed by Raymond Hood just after his work on the *Daily News* Building. Where the newspaper office features vertical stripes, here Hood chose to accentuate the horizontal, and did so in a wild shade of green. Nonetheless, the building is highly regarded by architectural critics and in 1979 was designated a city landmark. In his guidebook *The City Observed*, Paul Goldberger wrote: 'There is no other building in New York with so impeccable a modernist pedigree that is also so much fun to look at.'[12]

Have your fun and move on to **Ninth Avenue.** This is our last stop, so you can spend as much time as you like among the fresh food shops along the avenue which stretch for several blocks north and south of 42nd Street, a gastronomic United Nations. Here are butchers and fishmongers, delicatessen stores and greengrocers, many of which stay open most of the night. The food shops came into being as the market for Hell's Kitchen, a large and violent slum area that stretched from Broadway down to the Hudson River. In the years when Broadway glittered most brightly, these streets just a block away contained some of the city's most disgraceful housing. The remnants of the slums still exist, though matters have been improved by Manhattan Plaza, a red-brick tower between Ninth and Tenth Avenues originally intended as luxury apartments. When those who could afford the asking price decided they did not want to live in so lively a district, the apartments were turned into subsidized accommodation for people in the performing arts. At the same time some warehouses on 42nd Street, also between Ninth and Tenth Avenues were converted into experimental theatres. The newcomers have revived the Ninth Avenue shops, which would have proved less and less viable had the population decreased any further. Every year, on a weekend in May, the avenue is closed to traffic between 34th and 57th Steets and becomes the Ninth Avenue Food Festival. The shops and restaurants spill out on to the pavement and stalls sell multi-national snacks. Ethnic entertainment — singing and dancing — fills the outdoor stages built at strategic crossroads. It is a true New York event, combining two of the city's chief preoccupations: exotic food and show business. If you don't hit the right weekend, go anyway to admire the fruit, squeeze the bread and catch the whiff of salami. Buy a picnic, perhaps, and take it to Central Park, a short ride by the Eighth Avenue bus or subway. After the stew of 42nd Street, you deserve a bucolic break.

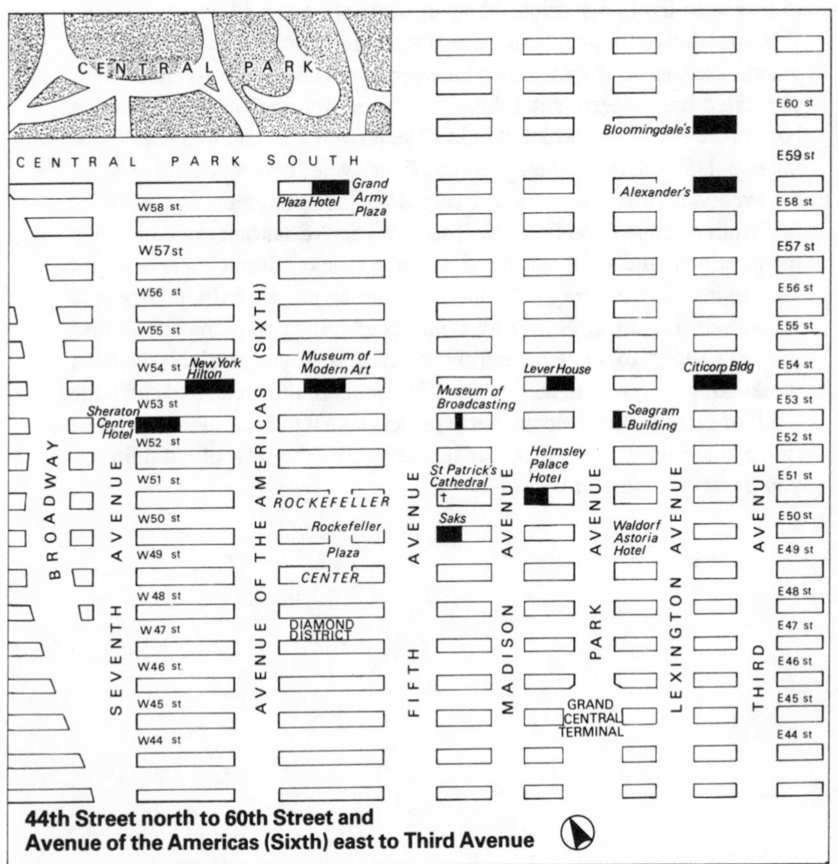

44th Street north to 60th Street and Avenue of the Americas (Sixth) east to Third Avenue

10

Fifth Avenue

IN A WALK in which we shall penetrate New York's most glittering shopping area it is fitting that we should start at **Brooks Brothers,** on the 44th Street corner of Madison Avenue, where it has spawned a small clutch of men's clothing shops, though none with its lustre. Traditionally the clothier for bankers, advertising people and the Ivy League alumni, Brooks Brothers' chief claim to a place in the sartorial record books is as the inventor of the shirt with the button-down collar, which in the 1960s became a badge of the Establishment (matching, as the Establishment's opponents would jest, their buttoned-down minds). In the lunch hour you can spot the Ivy Leaguers bustling in from their college clubs nearby: they're a shade taller, healthier, more muscular and look less hounded than your run-of-the-pack New Yorker. They can often be seen wearing tweeds with loafers, sporting a squash racket tucked neatly under the arm, as they call in for a little shopping.

Brooks Brothers flourishes by selling its high-quality and high-priced clothing in an atmosphere which it believes to be English but which I find more intimidating than anything London has to offer. It depends, naturally, on what intimidates you. What intimidates me are the hearty salesmen approaching as soon as I get out of the elevator — no flashy escalators here — asking what I'm looking for and what my size is. There are people who clearly love such attention and who spend cordial lunch hours feeling the quality of the cloth and exchanging pleasantries with their friendly salesman.

From Brooks Brothers walk a block west to Fifth Avenue, along 45th Street. Pause at No 11, on the right, where J & R Cigars makes the hard-to-test claim that it is the world's largest cigar store. No doubt New York is a more hygienic city since the fashion for round-the-clock cigar-munching went out after the Second World War, but it has lost a part of its flavor. Even if you do not need or like cigars, go inside for the mellow aroma and the sight of piles of cigar-boxes stacked on the tables behind hand-written price signs. The owner, Lew Rothman, is an exuberant, wise-cracking man who could have been invented by Damon Runyon, as could many of his regular customers, thoughtfully sniffing at the stock.

Reaching Fifth Avenue, we are not quite in its finest shopping zone but in the short fallow stretch between the splendors of Lord and Taylor farther down and Saks farther up. Here the fast-buck shops predominate, purveyors of electronic marvels and Persian carpets, maybe both in the same emporium, who come and go at a bewildering rate, often using the cheap last few years of a lease. Here also are opticians, shoe shops, airline offices, a bank or two: nothing to detain us during the two-block walk to 47th Street, where suddenly we are in the diamond district, the block of West 47th Street between Fifth Avenue and the Avenue of the Americas. There is no clear reason why it should be precisely here, but here it is, a single street crammed with dealers in precious stones and metals. Whenever the diamond district gets into the news, for a spectacular theft or the murder of a dealer, the newspapers talk about the secrecy characteristic of the trade. What strikes the outsider is the very opposite, the panache with which the multi-million dollar business is carried on.

Much of the jewelry business is in the hands of Hasidic Jews, with their beards, black hats and dark overcoats, who carry out transactions in the street. Even indoors, the commerce is open to public scrutiny. If you walk through one of the arcades, mostly on the north side of the street, you will see jewelers testing and assessing merchandise brought in by clients, repairing and replacing settings and cajoling customers to buy. Should you deal here? Only if you are absolutely confident of your ability to judge authenticity and value. But you need have no compunction about making a less weighty purchase of a pastrami sandwich at Deli City, on the north side of the street near the Fifth Avenue end.

On the same side cut through the Plaza Arcade to 48th Street and turn back into Fifth Avenue, passing — or browsing through — a cluster of bookshops between here and 57th Street. The branch of Barnes and Noble between 48th and 49th Streets offers bestsellers at a discount and a huge selection of inexpensive remainders in the basement. Upstairs a large section is devoted to board games, and there is also a record department. Four blocks north is the New York branch of B. Dalton, a national chain, with a greater range of titles and a book ordering facility. On the east side of the avenue, by 49th Street, is Scribner's, another old-timer (established 1846) whose spindly black and gold shopfront by Ernest Flagg harks back to the street's earlier elegance. Not far away are two branches of Doubleday's which, like Scribner's, has its own publishing imprint but sells books of all publishers.

Walking north on the avenue, we get our first close-up look at Rockefeller Center, a most ambitious and successful piece of urban planning. We are not going to explore its marvels yet, but you can stop and appreciate how its grey, well-balanced towers give a solid and dignified character to the street without overwhelming it: a masterpiece of subtlety. To do so you will be standing approximately outside Saks, on the east side between 49th and 50th Streets, a clothes store which since the 1920s has contributed to the avenue's high reputation as a shopping area.

One block north, **St Patrick's Cathedral** is the city's main Roman Catholic place of worship. It replaced the old cathedral in Little Italy in 1879, though it was started twenty years earlier and not completely finished until twenty-seven years later. This is New York's major building by James Renwick, though many prefer the exuberance of his earlier work on Grace Church downtown. This is a solid Gothic granite pile, said to have been modelled on Cologne Cathedral; yet St Patrick's looks decidedly puny surrounded by skyscrapers — any European medieval cathedral dominates the landscape for miles. Inside you do not notice this disproportion. The soaring Gothic arches exude an authentic majesty and the richly colored stained glass actually benefits from the cathedral's hemmed-in location: the light filters in sparsely, affording a delicate luminosity. In the side chapels modern tableaux and sculptures are mixed with more traditional works. A gift stall sells Catholic devotional objects.

Cross over 51st Street and turn right. On your left, only a few yards from Fifth Avenue, go through the glass doors into **Olympic Place,** a public thoroughfare at the foot of an office and apartment building built in 1976 to take advantage of the zoning law which allowed developers to put extra floors in their buildings if they supplied a pleasant public space as a trade-off. The scheme worked in the Citicorp Center, which we will see a couple of blocks east, but here the atrium is insufficiently assertive. Go inside, though, to sit on the iron chairs and relax for a few minutes in front of the indoor waterfall. In the same block, on the south-east corner of 52nd Street, Cartier's the jewelers have their showroom in one of the avenue's few remaining grand mansions, built in 1905.

Turn right and go east along 52nd Street, then right again into Madison Avenue, a street which became synonymous with advertising when the pioneers of this new craft settled here between the two world wars. It is still used as a code name for the industry, now grown into a dominant cultural and commercial influence on the city's life. As it expanded it couldn't be contained in a single avenue and the offices of its practitioners have spread over the whole midtown area. As a result many smart shops that used to be on this stretch of Madison have moved uptown, to be replaced by dull commercial buildings. It is almost the only avenue which has continued the leap-frogging tradition of New York commerce: the clothing boutiques, the art and antique shops are now to be found way up in the 70s and 80s.

For now, head back south to the Helmsley Palace Hotel, on the east side of the avenue between 51st and 50th Streets. The business part of the hotel is a modern, brown, fifty-one storey tower; but as part of the terms for acquiring the property from the Catholic archdiocese the developers were obliged to incorporate into it the **Villard Houses,** a group of distinctive Italianate brownstones built around a courtyard by McKim, Mead and White in 1884 for Henry Villard, a newspaper proprietor and railway magnate. It is good that a few of the stately homes on Madison and Fifth Avenues should have survived but they look incongruous supporting the glass box containing the hotel. Inside, though, the designers have done a fine job in restoring the most handsome rooms of the old houses. The hotel lobby is dominated by a massive chandelier and behind it, at the head of two curving staircases, a reddish marble fireplace designed by Augustus St Gaudens and removed from one of the adjacent rooms; its detail is marvelous, down to the dolphin fountains on each side. Turn right into the Gold Room, designed by Stanford White as the Music Room of an Italian Renaissance palace, with a minstrels' gallery. Tea is served here if you come at the right time of day, an afternoon refuge from the teeming shops on Fifth Avenue. At other times you can sit and have a drink or coffee and pastries. The old Dining Room, panelled with inlaid walnut, runs off the Gold Room and is now a bar. A standard short drink will be expensive but for the price you can look at the ceiling paintings, the ornamental doors and, if you can see them in the soft darkness, the Latin mottoes on the frieze. This room leads out into the lobby of one of the old houses, its mosaic ceilings and floors and colonnaded staircase giving an effect of such richness that it is hard to

The Empire State building, forever associated with King Kong. At night its upper thirty storeys are illuminated except during the migration season, as the birds might be disoriented by the lights and fly into it. To the left can be seen the Art Deco Chrysler Building.

Left:
The Beaux Art building of Grand Central Terminal. Over the entrance is Jules-Alexis Coutan's group 'Transportation', of Hercules, Mercury and Minerva; below is a statue of 'Commodore' Cornelius Vanderbilt, who had had built the previous station on this site.

Below:
Channel Gardens in the Rockefeller Center, with Valerie Clarebout's herald angels, and the giant Christmas tree outside the RCA Building.

imagine it ever serving as the foyer of a private home. At the far end a door leads into the Madison Room, a cocktail lounge, again by Stanford White. The green marble pillars, gilt capitals and sconces and romantic wall paintings continue the impression of impossible luxury. Back in the mosaic foyer, climb the stairs to see two more restored rooms, the Library over the bar, filled with patently fake book covers, and the Drawing Room over the Madison Room. These two are hired for private meetings and functions but if they happen not to be in use you can take a quick look. Don't miss the lovely St Gaudens zodiac clock on the left of the stairs.

There is a nice New York story surrounding the opening of the Helmsley Palace in the autumn of 1980. The developer, Harry Helmsley, had not at first wanted to marry his name with that of the hotel, believing that The Palace, the name by which it was known before it opened, would be simpler and more dignified. But people wanting to make reservations for the opening weeks would look up The Palace in the telephone directory and find when they rang that they weren't talking to a haven of luxury but to a small hotel on the Bowery which had been there for years and was, not to put too fine a point on it, a flophouse; its average price per room a fraction of the $100 or so now prevailing at the Madison Avenue establishment. When the proprietors of the new hotel asked those of the old if they would mind changing their name, they said yes, they would mind quite a lot, since they had after all been there first. So the new hotel had to switch.

To the north of the Villard Houses is the **Urban Center of the Municipal Art Society,** a pressure group working for the retention of New York landmarks. Sometimes they have a small exhibition, and always a selection of good literature about the city.

Go east down 50th Street, alongside the hotel, until you get to Park Avenue. Here you can look south at the squashed octagon of the **Pan Am Building,** acting as a backdrop for the rococo **Helmsley Building** (the same Helmsley) built in 1929 as the headquarters of the New York Central Railroad. Ever since the Pan Am Building was completed in 1963 people have complained that it destroys the vista south down Park Avenue and obliterates the charms of the older building in front of it, whose colonnaded crown bulges out above the modest (by present standards) stem. I didn't know Park Avenue in its pre-Pan Am Building days and I find something impressively astounding about the view, which changes character the farther north you proceed. In the late 1970s the

Helmsley Building was restored by being given a fresh coat of gold leaf and some powerful floodlighting, enabling the crown to assert itself more powerfully against its dominating neighbor. I think the two buildings together form one of the most distinctive panoramas in New York.

Park is wider than the other avenues because it covers the railway tracks leading north from Grand Central. Originally the trains ran through uncovered cuts in the road, with access from one side to the other by bridges following the line of the crosstown streets. When electricity came the cuts were covered and for a few years Park Avenue deserved its name. The proportion of road to greenery was roughly the reverse of what it is today: wide expanses of grass ran from the buildings to a central footpath dotted with public seating. In 1927 the pressure of traffic made it necessary to turn it into a conventional two-way avenue, with a strip of grass down the middle to remind pedestrians of their surrendered primacy. The old and formerly rustic apartment buildings became less desirable as the motor-car took over and they were gradually replaced, below 60th Street, with tall glass office towers, though along this stretch retail shops are banned. The flowers and shrubs in the central strip are kept in reasonable order, bearing in mind their hostile environment.

Cross the avenue and enter the lobby of the **Waldorf-Astoria,** which moved here from its old site in 1931 to make way for the Empire State Building. As soon as it reopened it regained its status as a fashionable address — both the hotel itself and the forty-two storey tower of service apartments alongside it. The Duke of Windsor had an apartment here and today so have many world statesmen and diplomats, though some of the latter now prefer the UN Plaza Hotel. The Waldorf exterior is a good example of Deco architecture, with lacework Gothic caps on its towers only visible properly from a few streets away; lit at night they look like twin space ships on a launching pad. Once inside, it's harder to pinpoint the exact style: it used to be Deco, too, and still has Art Nouveau panels on the elevators; but when Deco faded from fashion in the 1950s a version of French Empire replaced it, which would seem hopelessly overdone — except that the lobby is so large and so perpetually busy that you don't have to notice; at the Lexington Avenue end it takes on a Moorish aspect to fit with the Mediterranean-style restaurant and the Peacock Alley night club. The bronze clock in the middle of the east lobby is worth a second look; made by the Goldsmiths' Company in London in 1893, it was brought here from the old Waldorf. Its eight panels portray seven presidents and Queen Victoria, with sporting scenes chiefly below the presidents and the Forth Bridge beneath the queen.

You can walk right through the lobby and down an escalator into Lexington Avenue but we don't want to because there are still things to see on Park. One block north of the hotel, between 50th and 51st Streets, is **St Bartholomew's Church.** This also moved here from downtown, in 1919, some years earlier than the Waldorf. The low, extravagant Romanesque entrance was transplanted from the older, short-lived church in Madison Square, designed by McKim, Mead and White only seventeen years earlier. This explains why it differs from the Byzantine main body of the church, with its fanciful bulbous domes colorfully tiled outside and lined with mosaic inside. The interior of the main dome is a remarkable criss-cross patterning of beams, colored like crazy patchwork. Covering the west wall of the church (which seats fourteen hundred worshippers) is the tremendous organ loft: the instrument is said to be the largest in New York and the fourth largest in the Western Hemisphere. St Bartholomew's choir, once under the direction of Leopold Stokowski, is a city institution much in demand at Christmas. It gives concerts at the church most Sundays at four, and there are also Sunday tours of the building.

The tall tower rising to the east is the General Electric Building on Lexington Avenue. While this harmonizes better with the church than might be expected, the buildings on Park Avenue on either side do bear down quite menacingly, showing as with St Patrick's that a church survives in a crowded commercial area at its peril and to an extent under sufferance. In London, Paris or Rome you could organize a quick if selective tour of the city's highlights and scarcely set foot outside a place of worship, while in New York just the opposite is true. To hammer home the point, from time to time plans are divulged to pull down St Bart's, provoking anguished protests.

Park Avenue between 52nd and 54th Streets attracts serious students of modern architecture, who station themselves outside the now anachronistic Italian Renaissance **Racquet and Tennis Club** (a 1918 work of McKim, Mead and White) to gaze across the avenue at the Seagram Building and across 53rd Street to Lever House. To discuss them chronologically, **Lever House** was put up in 1952, the city's first glass-encased office tower, and as such, you might think it has much to answer for: but you cannot make a building take responsibility for shoddy and unfeeling imitations (there are several near it on Park Avenue itself) and Lever House remains remarkable and innovative. Before it was built there was a general belief, except among the hypermodernists of the Bauhaus school, that buildings ought to be single, solid masses faced with masonry. Skidmore, Owings and Merrill, the architects of Lever House, broke with that tradition. Moreover, instead of a single block, the building is formed from two slabs, one horizontal, resting on stilts, and the other pointing upwards at right angles to it. The result is remarkably light and graceful, and in 1952 must have looked sensational among the rugged stone apartment houses which were then its neighbors. Passers-by are lured into the concourse under the stilts by displays of art in the lobby, but this is one part of the building which has never worked well, because it's mostly shaded from the sun and lacks seats. (It is additionally blighted by an overly pious message from the founder, the soap magnate William Hesketh Lever, about his mission to promote cleanliness, health and freedom from drudgery.)

The **Seagram Building,** across the avenue and a block to the south, was erected in 1958 for the firm of liquor distillers and importers that had established its fortune during Prohibition; many regard it still as the finest of New York's skyscrapers. Its chief architect was Ludwig Mies van der Rohe, the German apostle of functionalism and modernism; he was assisted by Philip Johnson, now the Grand Old Man of American architecture. Van der Rohe was a follower of Walter Gropius, succeeding him in 1930 as head of the Bauhaus, that fount of modern architecture. In 1933 he closed it as a protest against the Nazis and soon afterwards left Germany for Chicago, where he was director of the architecture school of the Illinois Institute of Technology for twenty years. His method was based on visible construction, illustrating the techniques of modern building. Unlike Louis Sullivan, he saw form as a consequence of structure rather than of function.

A spare, sleek building in brown glass and bronze (oiled annually to keep it from going green), the Seagram model was readily embraced by less visionary architects as a means of putting up modern-looking buildings on the cheap. In the next few years New York suffered from a nasty rash of brown skyscrapers, none built with the care or quality of this one. Another innovation of the Seagram design was to set the slender tower in a plaza instead of having the ground floors fill out the block to the pavement line. This resolves the difficulty encountered by previous skyscrapers, of being mostly invisible from street level, and again it was copied in many other buildings along the avenue, turning it, for pedestrians, into a series of miniature parks instead of a proper street. Though there is no public seating on this plaza either (Mies van der Rohe saw it as a visual rather than a practical feature) on warm summer days hundreds of young people perch on the low wall surrounding it, passing the time and enjoying the fountain.

The contradiction between the visual and practical is evident in the two restaurants alongside the building. The Four Seasons, entered through the Seagram lobby or from 52nd Street, is stunning to look at, the interior designed by Philip Johnson and containing a stage backdrop painted by Picasso. The food is fine too but expensive. On 53rd Street is the more functional La Brasserie, with average French-style food at moderate prices, served twenty-four hours a day — a useful place to know for onion soup after a night on the town.

A block east, on 53rd Street between Lexington and Third Avenues, stands a skyscraper which, twenty years after Seagram, had a similarly revolutionary effect on the cityscape. Earlier in this walk we saw, in the Olympic Towers Building, an example of a cursory and unenthusiastic compliance with the 1971 zoning code allowing a trade-off of ground floor amenities for extra office space. Here, at the **Citicorp Center**, built as the headquarters of a leading bank, the outdoor piazza and the indoor public areas, beginning in the basement and stretching up three floors, are an enjoyable and useful facility. At the basement level are a number of international specialty restaurants, ranging from the leisurely and elegant to fast-food purveyors for office workers, who can buy their kebabs in pita and eat them at tables jammed around the square shrubbery in the center of the atrium. More greenery tumbles over the balconies for several stories around this large daylit well. The main street level is a jumble of small shops, mainly connected with food, the theme running through all three floors. The Third Avenue side of the ground floor, with the balcony above, is Conran's, the New York outpost of Habitat, British purveyors of modern kitchen equipment, furniture and fabrics. At the north-west corner, St Peter's Church, tacked on to the skyscraper, replaced a nineteenth-century Gothic church on the site. Jazz services are to be heard here on some Sundays — you can wander on to the balcony and listen for a few minutes — and the church hall next door doubles as a theatre.

The building itself is innovative. The idiosyncratic sloping roof, facing south, turned it into an instantly recognizable part of the Manhattan skyline as soon as it went up. The original intention was for the building's electricity to be produced by solar panels built into this slope, but the technology was unequal to the concept and conventional electricity sources are used. Like the World Trade Center towers, it is supported not on a steel frame but on steel-bearing walls and the elevator shaft, all poised on the massive columns seen best from the Lexington Avenue side. Its white façade, copied in several later skyscrapers, gives the building a sense of lightness.

If you feel like a snack or a drink at this point cut away two blocks north to P.J. Clarke's, on the north-east corner of Third Avenue and 55th Street, a block north of the ungainly post office. Lurking in the shadow of a modern office tower, this original Edwardian saloon with Irish overtones is nearly always bulging with noisy crowds who spill out on to the pavement on warm days. Keep away from it (and all other Irish bars) on St Patrick's Day, unless you enjoy a mêlée. On your way back west, stop to look at the **Central Synagogue** on the south-west corner of 55th Street and Lexington Avenue. Its twin spherical cupolas signal that the style is neo-Moorish, but other details reflect the eclectic Gothic taste in vogue when it was built in the 1870s.

Crossing Park Avenue, we reach Madison again and come face to face with Philip Johnson's spectacular new granite-clad skyscraper for America's largest company, the communications conglomerate AT&T. The most dramatic aspect of this first post-modern skyscraper, deliberately harking back to the early years of the form, are the towering lobby and distinctive breakfront pediment at the top, giving it the aspect of some gargantuan tallboy.

Head south to 53rd Street, turn right and cross Park and Madison Avenues. On the right, just before 53rd Street meets Fifth Avenue, is the attractive pocket-sized **Paley Park,** much enjoyed by office workers in their lunch hour. Though only the width and depth of a single town house, it provides a retreat, rare in this area, from the crowded pavements. The waterfall not only looks stunning but also blanks out some of the city's noise. It is named after its donor, William Paley, the radio pioneer and long-time chairman of the Columbia Broadcasting System. Paley was also the founder of the institution next door, the **Museum of Broadcasting** at One East 53rd Street, one of the city's newest museums. You can spend an engrossing hour or so watching old television programs or listening to historic radio broadcasts: ask if any of the twenty-three viewing booths is free, and select a program from the catalogue, a representative selection of American broadcasting from its inception to the present day. The museum shows films from its archives in viewing rooms on the ground and second floors.

After crossing Fifth Avenue, stop for a brief look inside **St Thomas's Church** on your right. This is late (1914) French Gothic revival in Kentucky limestone, fairly routine though sparsely ornamented outside, presumably because of the narrowness of the plot. (It has no transepts for the same reason.) Inside it is dominated by the spectacularly carved reredos on the west wall and by a quantity of stained glass, mostly English. Farther along 53rd Street, about half way up the block, is the **Museum of Modern Art,** one of the city's cultural landmarks which must be on the itinerary of even the most fleeting visitor.

In *Palaces for the People*, Nathaniel Burt writes:

> Art-loving tourists to New York City go as a matter of course to the Metropolitan and the Frick, but these museums aren't specifically 'New York'. They derive from European precedents — the Louvre and the Wallace Collection in London. The museums art-loving tourists visit that are very specifically 'New York' are those three sisters of modernism, the Museum of Modern Art (1929), the Whitney Museum of American Art (1930) and the Solomon R. Guggenheim Museum (1937).[13]

Though New York is now indisputably among the most fertile cities for the creation, exhibition and sale of modern works of art, it took longer for the modern movement to be accepted here than in Europe: its first big show, at the New York Armory in 1913, provoked rage and incomprehension from some critics.

Three women were the guiding spirits behind creation of MOMA: Mrs Abby Rockefeller, wife of John D. Rockefeller Jr ; Miss Lillie Bliss, a wealthy heiress; and Mrs Cornelius Sullivan. Although Rockefeller had no taste for modern art, his wife persuaded him to give the land for the museum. At its founding in 1929, MOMA was the first museum in the city to have on permanent display works by the major impressionists. Many of the best older paintings, especially the Impressionists, are from

Miss Bliss's bequest. MOMA opened in 1939 after ten years of camping out in temporary accommodation.

Since 1939 the museum has been extended and embellished three times: the earliest building, appropriately unfussy in glass and marble, near the center of the present frontage, was designed by Philip Goodwin and Edward Stone, early exponents of modernism; the idiom emerged in the 1930s and became known as the International Style — a soubriquet given it early in the decade at one of the museum's own exhibitions of architecture. In 1951 and 1964 Philip Johnson designed compatible extensions east and west. Cesar Pelli, dean of the Yale School of Architecture, was responsible for co-ordinating the design of the most recent westward extension, where a tall apartment tower has been built on top of new gallery space; it is due to be completed in 1983. The Argentinian-born Pelli worked for Eero Saarinen from 1954 until 1964, when he branched out on his own in Los Angeles, designing high tech skyscrapers based on the theories of Mies van der Rohe. He moved east in 1976 and this is his first New York work. When it's finished there will be roughly double the former space to show the museum's collections, offering a more cogent account of the development of modern art in the last hundred years than you are likely to encounter anywhere else. On the ground floor, the garden hall will give access to the galleries and to the renovated sculpture garden: this has long been one of the prized assets of the museum, with works by Moore, Rodin, Matisse, Picasso and others in as bucolic a setting as may be expected in the heart of a midtown block. The museum's new public restaurant will offer views across it.

The ground-floor galleries are for temporary exhibitions. The permanent collection is arranged in chronological sequence on the upper floors, beginning with the Impressionists and post-Impressionists. Cezanne is especially well represented. Two versions of Monet's water lilies, one done on three canvases arranged at angles round a corner, are a highlight of this section. Two of Henri (le douanier) Rousseau's spectacular naive jungle canvases have long been favorites with visitors and postcard buyers. The first Picasso appears in one of the early galleries and his works stretch through the central (in the chronological sense) section of the display, as is only proper, since they span a large segment of the modern movement and Picasso was an enthusiast for the museum. His first cubist work, 'Les Demoiselles d'Avignon', is here; so, for many years, was his emotive mural 'Guernica', on long-term loan until his heirs could agree to its return to Spain. Matisse and the Fauvists are followed by Klee, Kandinksy and Modigliani. As we proceed, we move closer to the present day, from Dada surrealism and abstract expressionism to the solid squares and shapes of the New York school of the 1950s and 1960s.

Separate sections of the new display space are planned for photography, design, architecture, prints and illustrated books: the free guide available at the entrance will direct you to them. The shops by the main entrance have some excellent cards, posters, books and unusual gifts; rare and classic old films are shown in the cinema.

Opposite the museum the **Donnell Library Center** has one of the world's largest collections of children's books on the second floor, with a pleasant reading room open in the afternoon. Farther west, on the north side of the street, the **Museum of American Folk Art** occupies at present only one floor of a terraced house, which means that it can only mount exhibitions of specific aspects — weather vanes, quilts and the like — but it is hoped to extend the premises before long so that a permanent display can be housed. American folk art is primitive but, deservedly, it has its devotees who have pushed prices up at the Madison Avenue auction rooms to a level which the makers of these crude objects in the eighteenth and nineteenth centuries would have found laughable. Across the street, the **Museum of Contemporary Crafts** brings the story up to date, again with a changing exhibition.

On the corner of 53rd Street and the Avenue of the Americas, the black glass headquarters of CBS, the television network, stands forbiddingly in a sunken plaza. It is the only skyscraper designed by Eero Saarinen, whose best New York work is the marvellous TWA Terminal at Kennedy Airport: like a jet plane, it has wings and soars — I often choose that airline just because it will allow me to leave from it. The **CBS Building** is a complete contrast, rooted to the spot like a thirty-inch screen television set. Saarinen was the son of a Finnish architect who settled in America in 1923. He won much praise for Dulles Airport, near Washington, but his design for the chancery of the United States embassy in Grosvenor Square, London, is not universally admired. His other New York building is the Vivien Beaumont Theater at the Lincoln Center. CBS is one of the office towers which rose in the 1960s along this stretch of the avenue, formerly lined with low row houses whose ground floors accommodated bars with lurid reputations. The 21 Club, in 52nd Street between here and Fifth Avenue, is a remnant of that time, though now a highly respectable haunt of the city's elite, decorated on the outside with miniature jockeys in what I suppose were once the racing colors of its famous patrons. Another memory from between the wars is the sign 'Swing Street', placed on the corner of 52nd Street and recalling the clubs where that kind of music was in vogue.

The skyscrapers along the Avenue of the Americas south of here are of the same vintage as the CBS Building. Starting from the New York Hilton, they are the postwar fringe of the **Rockefeller Center,** though these arid glass monsters have so little in common with the imaginative pre-war architecture on the other side of the avenue that it is conceptually misleading to lump them together. On the lower concourse of the McGraw-Hill Building, between 49th and 48th Streets, a mock-up of a subway car leads into the **New York Experience Theater,** a multi-media show depicting a day in the life of the metropolis. It lasts fifty minutes and if you can spare the time it will give you something of the city's flavor.

On the opposite side of the avenue, the first part of the original Rockefeller Center we see is **Radio City Music Hall,** a colossal theatre seating six thousand, one of the city's finest examples of Art Deco interior design. For years the entertainment there comprised a family film and a stage show, featuring the Rockettes dance troupe, but in 1979 the film was abolished and the stage show expanded. If spectacular revues are not to your taste there will probably be other entertainments on and off Broadway which you would prefer to see, but you should still try to look inside the music hall. The best way of doing that without seeing the show is to go on the guided tour of Rockefeller Center which leaves every half hour or so from an office in the lobby of the RCA Building, the skyscraper at the heart of the complex. This is worth doing in any case, since it gives you access to one of the well-kept roof gardens on the Fifth Avenue side and includes a visit to the observation platform at the top of the RCA Building. If you just want to see the music hall without going on the tour of the rest of the center it will cost you more, but you will see more backstage secrets.

How did the Rockefeller family rise to a position of such dominance that New York is dotted with landmarks that would not be there but for their perspicacity or generosity? They include the Chase Manhattan Plaza downtown, the United Nations, the Museum of Modern Art, the Lincoln Center, the Rockefeller Center and the Cloisters. (To those could be added the re-creation of a colonial town at Williamsburg, Virginia, and a substantial Rockefeller donation to the restoration of Rheims Cathedral and the Palace of Versailles in France.)

John D. Rockefeller was the son of an itinerant quack doctor in upstate New York. In the 1850s the family moved to Cleveland, Ohio which, in the next decade, became the center of the emerging oil industry. In 1862 Rockefeller, aged only twenty-three, became a partner in an oil refinery. By being the most ruthless practitioner of the cut-throat competitive tactics prevailing in the oil industry, he raised his Standard Oil Company to dominate the market. His reputation was fearsome: one of the most effective methods of eliminating competition was to pressure the railways into offering rebates on freight charges to the largest shippers. The penalty for refusing to co-operate, or for giving similar rebates to competitors, was a switch of patronage to a competing railway — and competition among the railways was as fierce as it was among oil refiners. Sometimes Standard Oil would demand and receive rebates on oil shipped by its rivals — a medieval form of exacting tribute. By 1879 Standard owned ninety-five per cent of the refining capacity in the United States, and in that same year all Rockefeller's associated companies were grouped together as a trust which embarked on a policy of buying up oil production facilities as well as refineries. At that time oil was used chiefly for heating and lubrication, but the introduction of the automobile fuelled a swift expansion of the market and of Rockefeller's fortunes. In 1898 there were only eight hundred automobiles in America; by 1911 the number had risen to 618,000.

Rockefeller's public image, largely justified, was that of an unfeeling, profit-crazed ogre who drove weak competitors to the wall in his greed to expand his empire. There was public outcry for action and the government responded by launching the historic anti-trust case against Standard Oil. In 1911 the Supreme Court ruled that the company must be separated into smaller units. Chief Justice White outlined the reason for the verdict:

> We think no disinterested mind can survey the period in question without being inevitably driven to the conclusion that the very genius for commercial development and organization, which it would seem was manifested from the beginning, soon begot an interest and purpose to exclude others . . . from their right to trade and thus accomplish the mastery which was the end in view.

The *New York Times* put it less judiciously:

> No further disclosures were needed for a complete exhibition of tne greed, injustice and oppression that are a part of the Standard Oil Company's stock in trade.

Yet the break-up of the trust failed to check Rockefeller; in fact his fortune was increased by swapping shares in the trust for stocks in the new component companies. An increasing amount of the money was being given to philanthropic works, and by simply living to the age of ninety-eight he was able to soften his image, though, as President Theodore Roosevelt said, 'No amount of charities in spending such fortunes can compensate for the misconduct in acquiring them.'

Rockefeller's son, John D. Rockefeller Jr, was responsible for the family's most spectacular and lasting good works, including most of the building projects. He was a modest and conscientious man: the heir to a multi-million dollar fortune, he did not, after all, need to employ suspect methods. Rockefeller Center began in 1929 as a scheme to provide a glamorous new home for the Metropolitan Opera, bursting the seams of its old headquarters on Broadway at 39th Street. The opera house was to be the centerpiece of a cultural and commercial complex containing theatres, shops, restaurants and some office space to provide enough revenue to keep it functioning. The land chosen belonged to Columbia University. In 1801 the Elgin Botanic Gardens had been established here but towards the end of the century Columbia built streets of terraced houses to rent. Rockefeller agreed to lease the land for $3.3 million a year, to pull down the houses and build the center.

Scarcely had he made the deal than the stock market crashed and the Metropolitan Opera Company, fearing both a reduction in charitable donations and the inability to sell their old opera house in a depressed property market, pulled out of the scheme. Rockefeller, left with this valuable parcel of land, decided to demolish the houses anyway and go ahead with the project, shifting the emphasis to commercial rather than cultural amenities. It meant that he would have to foot the bill for the whole construction, estimated at $200 million, and finding tenants for the offices was at first a problem in the uncertain financial climate; but his son Nelson, who was to become Vice-President of the United States in the 1970s, applied himself to the task with characteristic vigor. The emerging entertainment industry of radio provided the tenant for the sixty-nine story central skyscraper, still occupied by the Radio Corporation of America and its affiliate the National Broadcasting Company, which has its New York television studios here. This is what inspired the nickname Radio City, once applied to the whole complex but now confined to the music hall.

Overseas companies were encouraged to move in by giving global designations to some of the buildings surrounding the RCA Building: there is the International Building, the Italian Building, the British Empire Building and the Maison Française, these last two separated by a pedestrian retreat which soon, naturally enough, came to be called **Channel Gardens.** For most of the year this is planted with seasonal shrubs and flowers around pools and fountains, and in December it is adorned with a flock of magnificent wire herald angels, trumpets raised to the sky, which from the Fifth Avenue end seem to frame the giant Christmas tree outside the RCA Building. The Gardens, lined chiefly by tourist offices, lead to the sunken plaza at the foot of the RCA Building, which is a skating rink in winter and an open air cafe in summer. At its eastern edge, below where the Christmas tree is sited, the bronze statue of Prometheus thrusts his flaming brand as though he were trying to set the whole complex alight. To stand on the edge of the plaza, under the massed flags of all the nations, and look down at the winter skaters carving elegant patterns, gets as close as any other single experience to characterizing the best of New York — its style, its energy, its elegant modernity. The price for this rather splendid concept is a heavy dose of self-righteousness, some would say cant: as you stand facing the gold figure of Prometheus, the Rockefeller creed is spelled out in gold letters on a black marble slab. Nobody would quarrel with the lofty sentiment, but it looks prim.

The architects of the center were initially headed by Raymond Hood whose work on 42nd Street we saw in the last chapter. He died before this project was completed and the leading role was assumed by Wallace Harrison, later to co-ordinate the design teams for both the United Nations and the Lincoln Center. Between them, Hood and Harrison created a highly functional urban village, redolent of the 1930s. The chief practical attraction is the care taken over amenities for the casual visitor. Inside, below ground level, a complex of arcades lined with shops and restaurants leads you straight into the Sixth Avenue subway.

Nelson Rockefeller inherited a taste for modern art from his mother and saw to it that the center was liberally dotted with representative works. Atlas stands outside the International Building on Fifth Avenue, bearing a stripped-down world on his shoulders. Outside the Associated Press Building, north of RCA, is Noguchi's interpretation of 'News' — telephone, notepad and typewriter. A few years later and he would have had to include a video computer terminal. At the front of the RCA Building, the Thor-like figure of Wisdom ('Wisdom and knowledge shall be the stability of thy times' — yet more moral uplift) casts electronic thunderbolts at those who dare to enter. The lobby inside is adorned with 'American Progress', a heroic mural by José M. Sert, portraying muscle-bound men building the nation through the sweat of their brows. The mural was the result of the most publicized row during the center's construction. Nelson Rockefeller originally commissioned one from Diego Rivera, the Mexican socialist painter, but when it was nearly finished it emerged that one of the identifiable heroes of the composition was Lenin. Rockefeller, an ardent capitalist after all, thought this unsuitable and tried to persuade the artist to remove it. He would not. At the opening ceremony the mural was coyly hidden behind a tarpaulin. A few months later it was destroyed and Sert engaged to provide this anodyne replacement. You will have to go to the Palace of Fine Arts in Mexico City to see a copy which Rivera made of his original. I suspect it was not just Lenin but the uncompromising socialist message of the work as a whole that made Rockefeller judge it unacceptable. A shame, because it is patently of far greater quality.

Of the eating places in Rockefeller Center, the most spectacular and expensive are the Rainbow Grill and the Rainbow Room at the top of the RCA Building, both with dancing and entertainment as well as the view and decent food. If you want the view without the food you can go up just for a drink. For the view from the very bottom, have a snack in summer at the open-air tables on the plaza.

Leave Rockefeller Center on the Fifth Avenue side, because we still have the rest of the avenue to explore, the ten blocks north to the corner of Central Park. Less than a hundred years ago this was a stretch of the most lavish — some would say grotesque — houses in the world, the fanciful Renaissance palaces put up by the Vanderbilts, the Goulds, the Dodges and the Rockefellers themselves. Now they have been replaced by grey commercial buildings, their limestone façades lending a deceptive air of permanence — deceptive because they will as like as not suffer the fate of their predecessors. Some are already doing so, giving way to gaunt palaces of glass. On the north-west corner of 54th Street is a survivor, the stately University Club, designed by Charles McKim in 1899. McKim, Mead and White had a virtual monopoly on the major men's clubs that sprang up in that period. Because their members constitute the city elite, they have stood up to the razers and developers and now form a valuable repository of turn-of-the-century Beaux Arts architecture. This is among the most effective. If you know somebody who can invite you inside, accept with enthusiasm, for the dining-room and especially the library are gems of the extravagant interior decoration thought proper in that expansive era.

On the other side of the avenue, a block north, the St Regis Hotel is a good place to stay if you can afford it, combining Edwardian ambiance with a first-rate location. The Old King Cole Room at street level has a sprightly mural once famous with Broadway actors when it decorated the Knickerbocker Hotel on Times Square. Back on the west side of the street, the Rizzoli bookshop boasts one of the avenue's most spectacular shopfronts (it used to belong to Cartier the jeweler, now in a converted mansion over the road). Rizzoli's specializes in art books and keeps overseas newspapers and periodicals. Another block up, on the east side, the old Bonwit Teller fashion store has been pulled down but the shop has returned to the replacement building.

Tiffany's, next door, is New York's most famous jeweler, and has been since not long after Charles Tiffany and his partner John Young opened their first shop near City Hall in 1837. They began as dealers in stationery and fancy goods, and after a few years added cheap jewelry to their line, but a buying trip by Young to Paris in 1848 laid the foundation of the firm's reputation. He arrived just as Louis Philippe was being overthrown and the aristocracy were in desperate need of ready cash to make provision for flight. Trading his cash for their jewels, Young returned to New York with a sensational collection of fine things which became the talk of the town. At about the same time Charles Tiffany began a lucrative business in commemorative silver. As his reputation as a jeweler increased, he came to be offered most of the precious gems reaching the market. The wives of the newly rich business, industrial and railway tycoons snapped them up eagerly, competing for the most glittering. One of the finest, a yellow diamond found in South Africa in 1877 and named after Tiffany, is displayed in the shop.

Tiffany also came to be a household name for a distinctive style of colored and patterned glass, often made into lamp shades or vases. It was named after Charles Tiffany's son, Louis Comfort Tiffany, a fairly successful painter before he took up domestic design and joined the firm as design director. He was a sought-after interior decorator, creating schemes of great richness: one of his commissions was for the White House in Washington. His well-defined Art Nouveau mosaic concepts influenced much contemporary design, even down to the patterned tiles on the stations of the elevated railway and subway systems, and many churches in the New York area have windows of Tiffany stained glass. His own house on Long Island held some of his most attractive work until it was destroyed by fire in the 1950s. (A loggia was rescued and is in the American Wing at the Metropolitan Museum.) If you are tempted to buy a prestige gift at Tiffany's, not everything will run you a bill of three figures or more. Even if you dare not venture in, the discreet jewel-box windows are an attraction in themselves. The clock over the door, borne on the shoulders of Atlas, came from Tiffany's second shop, on Broadway in the cast-iron district.

Zigzagging across the road again, you come to Bergdorf Goodman, an expensive retailer of ladies' high fashion; back on the east side, there is FAO Schwarz, the city's best known toyshop. Its windows are a delight and it is marvelous for browsing with children. The Plaza Hotel, on the corner of Central Park, is a suitable place to finish our look at the best New York has to offer. This quintessentially Edwardian hotel, designed by Henry Hardenbergh in 1907 in the French Renaissance idiom, is my favorite building in the city, so spendidly different from anything else because of the accident of its site. Set back behind its plaza with the park on one side, it avoids being jostled by overbearing newer neighbors and stands as an entity, redolent of the grand hotels of Europe. Even the black glass monster just south of it helps out with a cunning reflection from the proper angle. The Plaza used to be known for its lavish suites where the rich camped out while their Fifth Avenue palaces were being constructed. Unlike other hotels of its vintage it managed successfully to modify to the demands of the modern traveller. Have a drink at the Oak Bar or simply stroll by the fountain and General Sherman's statue outside.

Facing the Plaza on 58th Street is the unobtrusive Wyndham Hotel, a favorite with theatre people who do not want the limelight. Lord and Lady Olivier, Donald O'Connor, Henry and Jane Fonda, Lena Horne, Tennessee Williams have all appeared in the impressive guest register: stargazers might like to loiter outside. Across Fifth Avenue, the Pierre and the Sherry Netherland offer 1920s versions of elegance. Around the corner in West 59th Street you can take your chance in a carriage pulled by one of the scrawny and peculiarly adorned horses. It will cost more than you expect but it's a romantic way to see Central Park. Those who want to explore the park more conventionally, on foot, must wait until the next chapter.

55th Street north to 110th Street
Hospital
Post Office
Cathedral Parkway
CENTRAL PARK NORTH
F D Roosevelt Circle
Frawley Circle
Block House
Harlem Lake
106st.
Frederick Douglass Park
The Pool
The Loch
West Drive
Transverse
South Meadow
East Drive
Reservoir
96st
96st.
86 st
86st.
THE GREAT LAWN
Metropolitan Museum of Art
82 st.
Delacorte Theater
Great Obelisk
Shakespeare Gdn
Belvedere Lake
79 st.
Museum of Natural History
Whitney Museum of American Art
The Lake
Dakota Building
72 st
72st.
Bandstand
Bowling
Playground
The Sheep Meadow
The Mall
Children's Zoo
Lincoln Center
Wollman rink
Fordham University
The Pond
62st.
59st
57 st.
Columbus Circle
CENTRAL PARK SOUTH
CENTRAL PARK
CENTRAL PARK WEST
AVENUE
COLUMBUS
BROADWAY
EIGHTH AVE
SEVENTH
SIXTH
FIFTH AVENUE
MADISON AVENUE
PARK AVENUE
LEXINGTON AVENUE
THIRD AVENUE
SECOND AVENUE
FIRST AVENUE
YORK AVENUE
SUTTON PLACE
Sutton Sq
QUEENSBOROUGH BRIDGE
FRANKLIN D ROOSEVELT DRIVE (EAST RIVER DRIVE)
FOOTBRIDGE
WARD'S ISLAND PARK
HARLEM RIVER
MILL ROCK PARK
HELL GATE
Gracie Mansion
CARL SCHURZ PARK
WEST CHANNEL
ROOSEVELT ISLAND
EAST RIVER

11
Sutton Place and Central Park

THERE IS NO SUBWAY STATION convenient to Sutton Place and only one bus route, but usually plenty of taxis, a clue to its standing as New York's most exclusive residential address. When the Circle Line boat cruises past it, the guide reels off a list of the famous people who live or have lived in its solid apartment buildings and town houses. The East River Drive, which blights much of the eastern shoreline of Manhattan, here passes through a tunnel beneath the apartments and gardens looking out over the river. You won't be allowed inside the houses, unless you are an acquaintance of the likes of the Secretary-General of the United Nations, who lives in the neo-Georgian No 3, but nobody will stop you wandering outside. Although the newer apartment buildings are little different from those elsewhere on the Upper East Side, and you may see similar town houses in many crosstown streets, Sutton Place exudes an air of quality.

This chapter is going to take you through Central Park, so you will have to pick a fine day for it. Why not, then, start as you mean to go on, with an al fresco breakfast in one of the small public plazas overlooking the river which seal the east end of the cross streets from 55th to 58th? Buy, perhaps, bagels and cream cheese (and smoked salmon if you can afford it) from one of the delicatessens on First or Second Avenue and head east down 57th Street, whose plaza is the prettiest, with its curious statue of a boar and smaller wildlife. Queensborough Bridge, functional but not overwhelmingly ugly, stretches over to Queens on your left and Williamsburg Bridge is away in the distance on your right. Opposite is Goldwater Hospital on Roosevelt Island and, south of it, an abandoned Victorian isolation hospital. If you are lucky the water jet at the southern tip of the island will be playing for you. Watch the river traffic — small tankers, a few pleasure boats, barges filled with cement or garbage — cutting between New York harbor and Long Island Sound.

After breakfast go back to the junction of 57th Street and Sutton Place.

To your south, the red brick apartment houses are not much to look at from outside, but are of superior quality behind the façades: the older grey buildings nearer 57th Street are less mistakable reflections of the comfort to be found inside. Co-operatively owned by the residents, these buildings are occasionally the focus of well publicized scandals when an indignant prospective owner, perhaps connected with show business, is refused the right to buy into the building because the high society residents fear orgiastic scenes and invasions by noisy party-givers. The disgraced President Nixon was rejected on a different pretext: the owners felt he would be a security risk, a possible target. The small cluster of town houses on the east side of Sutton Place between 57th and 58th Streets are again not lavish but redolent of class. Go east down 58th Street (called Sutton Square) and see **Riverview Terrace,** the lovely enclave of brownstones on your left, facing a short private driveway and looking out over the river. There can be few prettier places to live in the city and none more expensive.

Pass beneath Queensborough Bridge, whose dank caverns have from time to time been spoken of as the site of future antiques, crafts and produce markets, though as yet no start has been made on the scheme and the space is partly filled by an outrageous beige balloon covering tennis courts. Beyond the bridge the street becomes York Avenue and slides a notch or two down the social scale with its box-like apartments mostly filled with the young people who congregate at the singles bars scattered along First and Second Avenues between 60th and 90th Streets. Turn left up 61st Street. The pleasing eighteenth-century stone building on your right, between York and First Avenues, is the **Abigail Adams Smith House,** although Mrs Smith, the daughter of President John Adams, never actually lived here. It was the stable of Mount Vernon, an estate which her husband, William Smith, began building in the last decade of the eighteenth century but never finished. In the nineteenth century the stable was converted into the Mount Vernon Hotel and later still into a private home. In 1924 it was bought by the Colonial Dames of America as their headquarters; they restored and furnished it in eighteenth- and nineteenth-century styles and it is now open as a museum. It is one of the most agreeable houses in New York and, together with its small formal garden, is certainly worth half an hour of your time.

The best overall view of its exterior is to be had from the aerial tramway (cable car) connecting Manhattan with **Roosevelt Island,** the slender strip of land in the East River between Manhattan and Queens. The tram station is on Second Avenue between 59th and 60th Streets and the journey of four minutes in each direction will repay the $1.50 return fare in the unusual view it affords of Manhattan's East Side. It is claimed to be the only aerial tramway in the world used for regular daily commuting: most of the island's six thousand residents travel on it to and from work every day. It runs every fifteen minutes except in the rush hour, when it doubles its frequency, and it operates from 6 a.m. until 2 a.m., extending to 3:30 a.m. on Saturday and Sunday.

If you just want to see the view, you can go straight there and back, but Roosevelt Island itself is pleasant enough if you have a spare half-day and the weather is fine. A red bus (free) meets the tram and takes you north up Main Street, which runs between the chunky blocks of flats built in the 1970s as state-financed mixed-income homes. You may prefer to walk: if so, keep to the west side of the island and enjoy the view of Manhattan and the river. Main Street, with its unusual brick surface and glass-covered arcade running along one side, is practical and pleasing. The Church of the Good Shepherd, refreshingly unadorned nineteenth-century red brick Gothic, has been retained as the centerpiece of the community, and it harmonizes well.

In the eighteenth century the whole island was a farm, named Blackwell's Island after the owner; the original wooden farmhouse, carefully restored when the new buildings went up, stands at the southern end of Main Street, and there are plans to turn it into a museum. Later the island was acquired by the city as a site for a prison, a poorhouse, a lunatic asylum and hospitals: there still are hospitals at either end. In his *American Notes* Charles Dickens, who took a dedicated interest in prisons and institutions of that nature, describes being rowed here from Manhattan by convicts wearing their prison stripes. He was much taken with the grand staircase in the center of the lunatic asylum, calling it one of the finest in the United States. It now rots inside the octagonal ruin at the north end of the island, about a quarter of a mile beyond the supermarket. Mae West was one of the prison's celebrated inmates, after being arrested for giving a lewd performance in 1927. Farther north still, beyond the Bird S. Coler Hospital, a nicely landscaped park has been created, with the nineteenth-century lighthouse at its apex. No bridge connects Roosevelt Island with Manhattan, but there is a bridge to Queens.

Back at the Manhattan tram station, walk north up Second Avenue to 62nd Street and turn left. I'm taking you on this short detour because the block of 62nd Street between Second and Third Avenues gives you a vivid idea of what most of these cross streets were like at the turn of the century. In the middle of the block on the left is a group of high quality brownstones and around them terraced houses in a compatible style. This short block, known as **Treadwell Farm,** has been designated an historic district.

Cross Third Avenue and turn left back to 59th Street, where two of New York's most interesting and contrasted department stores occupy opposite sides of the street. **Bloomingdale's**, on the north side, was, in the late 1960s and 1970s, more successful than any of its rivals downtown in defining a sharp image as an emporium catering to the Young East Sider — in capitals because that's the name of one of its fashion departments. After a while Bloomingdale's moved from simply reflecting the tastes of the singles bar set to creating it. Its advertising invented the notion of 'Saturday people' — carefree, self-indulgent and in love, preferably with a partner they had met during a visit to the store, the focal point of their weekend. Everything is slick, shiny, knowing and of the moment. The non-Saturday person who is just visiting New York will be less jostled on a weekday.

When you come seriously to consider making purchases, **Alexander's** may be the better bet. Prices are low and if you happen to hit a good 'special offer' the value can be spectacular. Men's shirts are a good buy here. If you are coming from Europe, you will find bed linen is generally better value in America and this is one of the places you might look for that. Give yourself plenty of time for there are invariably long lines at the cash desks, which employ a laborious payment system; and don't plan on early morning shopping: like many New York department stores Alexander's doesn't open until ten, but stays open until nine most evenings, and from twelve to five on Sunday afternoons. Bloomingdale's has fewer late evenings and doesn't open on Sundays, except near Christmas. The popularity of the two stores has turned the corner of 59th Street and Third Avenue into one of the liveliest points of the city. Many movie theatres have opened here and on Second Avenue, their lines filling the pavement with musicians, street traders and fun.

Continue up 59th Street towards the park. On your left, between Lexington and Park Avenues, the Argosy Book Store is among the best organized second-hand book and print shops in the city. Cross Park Avenue at about the point where it changes from offices to apartments. North of here, stretching nearly forty blocks, is a ribbon of moderately tall apartment buildings, mostly erected between the wars after the railway tracks were covered over. They are close to the top of the New York social scale. Diplomats of just below the highest rank are the kind of people who live here: while ambassadors to the United Nations tend to live on or just off Fifth Avenue, their senior deputies live on Park.

Christie's, the London auction house, occupies one corner of Park Avenue and 59th Street, in the converted ballroom of the former Delmonico's hotel. Regine's, in the same building, is a fashionable night spot. Just beyond them on 59th is Kaplan's, another of the city's first-rate delicatessen cafes, a cheerful venue for a tasty hot sandwich or salad. At Madison Avenue make a detour and approach the park from 60th Street, where, on the right just before you get to Fifth Avenue, is another of Stanford White's clubs, the Metropolitan, built in 1893 under the auspices of J. P. Morgan, for himself and his friends who were too newly rich to be accepted in the older, snootier clubs downtown. Naturally, then, it had to be grander than the others, so White fitted in an oval drive for carriages, managing to create an effect of expansiveness without taking up too much space.

Across Fifth Avenue is the entrance to the park, but first you may want to browse through the shelves of the outdoor bookstalls operated by Barnes & Noble and the Strand. **Central Park** stretches north from here to 110th Street and west to Eighth Avenue, seven hundred and fifty acres of it. The first man-made park of anything like that size in an American city, it represents New York's most enlightened piece of planning. Coincidentally, the third quarter of the nineteenth century, when it was laid out, was a period of more than usually deep corruption in the city's civic politics and the project was often threatened by squalid political maneuvering. That it was completed in a form which makes it still a model big-city park is due almost entirely to the efforts of one man, Frederick Law Olmsted.

Olmsted was a restless soul who tried his hand at numerous occupations. In 1843, aged twenty-one, he went to sea for a year, then returned to spend three years as a farmer. In 1850 he visited England, whose civic parks impressed him greatly. Agitation for a park in New York had begun in the mid-1840s, led by William Cullen Bryant, the poet and editor of the

Evening Post, and supported powerfully by Washington Irving, America's most respected man of letters. As a result of the campaign the city decided in 1851 to buy the long, thin strip down the middle of Manhattan. A parks commission was established and work began on draining the area, then a wild and inhospitable marsh dotted with trees and boulders and the shacks of squatters who had nowhere else to live; they stoned the first workers who came to clear the site.

Olmsted had returned from England and begun a promising career as a writer. One of his articles, in a magazine called *The Horticulturalist*, lauded the city park in Birkenhead in the north of England. This put him in good standing with the park lobby and in 1857, when the commissioners were looking for a superintendent to oversee work on the new park, they approached him. He agreed to take the job. The following year the commissioners, dissatisfied with the original plans which had been prepared some years earlier, held an open competition for a new design. Olmsted teamed up with Calvert Vaux, an English-born architect, and submitted the scheme the commissioners selected in 1858 out of the thirty-five entries.Bearing in mind the difficulties encountered between design and completion, it is remarkably like Central Park as it appears today.

One of the stipulations of the commissioners was that the park should accommodate four crosstown roads. Olmsted and Vaux achieved this in an original way, cutting roads through in trenches invisible from ground level, with ornamental bridges carrying the park circulation above them. Even today, when the traffic is heavier than anything the two men could have envisaged, the device is very effective. Such engineering aspects of the design were the contribution of Olmsted; the architect Vaux made the detailed drawings for the bridges, fountains, shelters and other buildings.

The work began at a cracking pace. By July of 1858, only three months after the Olmsted-Vaux design had been accepted, about two and a half thousand workers had been employed. The following year, though, the administration cut the funds needed to keep the project going. Olmsted promptly resigned as the park's architect-in-chief, but the city refused to accept his resignation and granted more funds. Even before the park was opened in 1876 it was the object of envy of other cities, and soon Olmsted was being asked to submit designs elsewhere. He and Vaux collaborated again on Prospect Park in Brooklyn — still a separate city — and on Morningside and Riverside Parks in Manhattan. Olmsted laid out two university campuses in California — Stanford and Berkeley — as well as parks in Boston and Montreal, and Capitol Hill in Washington. In 1893 he designed the World Fair in Chicago, a project which was to have a profound influence on twentieth-century American architecture, creating a vogue for Classical and Renaissance revival styles.

Of the later hands which have embellished the park, the most controversial is that of Robert Moses, parks commissioner from 1935–60 and known for his devotion to large-scale road construction projects. He is responsible for much of the asphalt and concrete here — the children's playgrounds, sports facilities, ice rinks and baseball fields. These are much used and of obvious value, but some of the park's most devoted friends believe they compromise its rusticity and were not what Olmsted had in mind. August Heckscher, parks commissioner from 1967–72, wrote of Moses's philosophy: 'Rather than being liberated through contact with the gentler elements of sun and shade, trees and brooks, the city man was thought of as one to exercise on asphalt and play behind a chain-link fence.'

The popular metaphor for Central Park is that of a valve letting the steam escape from the pressure cooker city. On a hot summer Sunday, though, the reverse of that image is more appropriate: the park itself becomes the pressure cooker as people pour into it to celebrate their youth, their age, their bodies, their freedom and the pleasures of the senses. They come on bicycles, roller skates, or their sometimes unshod feet, bringing frisbees, dogs, cats, books, magazines, newspapers, chess sets, musical instruments, portable radios, things to eat, drink and smoke. People stroll, sit, lie, jog, hold hands, embrace, play games, push prams, dance, smile or simply watch others doing those things. It's not a place for quiet relaxation but rather for renewal, for affirmation of a common humanity. It is here, rather than on Wall Street or Fifth Avenue, that New York's character is most concisely expressed. Sunday in Central Park is a ritual act of thanksgiving for having survived a week in the inhuman city.

My trail through the park may sound complicated but taken at proper park-strolling speed it will lead you to most of the best-known sights and allow you to share its exuberance. Entering the park at the corner of Fifth Avenue and 60th Street, follow the footpath to the left of the road down to the pond. Stay on the bank of the pond until you cross Gapstow Bridge, then go right, down steps, and follow an inlet of water to the **Wollman**

Rink. In winter you may wish to stay and watch the skaters; in summer the rink is sometimes used for rock concerts and other popular manifestations. Skirt it on your right, passing as you do one of the first of the many rocky prominences which dot the landscape: these were not here when the land was in its wild state, but were brought in by Vaux and Olmsted to add interest. Climb the steps on the far side of the rink, ignoring the graffiti, and turn right at the top then almost immediately left up the hill. The red and yellow brick chess house containing indoor and outdoor tables with chess boards inlaid is up a few more steps: if you want to play you have to take your own chessmen along. If not, go down the steps and over to the grey stone building nearby, on the left, designed by Vaux and called **The Dairy** because it was originally a milk bar; now it has been well restored as the park's information center. Here you can see a short slide show, pick up a map and ask about events in the park. One of the maps is a guide to what is grandly called the 'Central Park National Recreation Trail', a longer walk than I'm going to take you on and ending at the very north, at 110th Street; by all means follow it if you have the time and energy.

From the Dairy turn right, pass under the bridge and you will soon hear, then see, the pretty Victorian **carousel**, well maintained inside a formidably grim brick shell. It offers a gentle ride for 30 cents and the traditional merry-go-round music should put a spring in your step and get you ready for the carnival atmosphere. Just to the west, you can watch games of softball in the spaces Robert Moses laid out for it. Take the path between the ball fields and the carousel, heading west. At the end of it, turn right and walk north on the path alongside Park Drive, to the Tavern on the Green. Its building was a sheep shelter when it went up in 1870 but frequent modifications have left it unrecognizable as such. An old-established restaurant, recently restored, it is quite expensive but pleasant for lunch, either on the outdoor terrace or inside.

The open space on the right is **Sheep's Meadow**, the venue for the open-air concerts by the Metropolitan Opera Company, the New York Philharmonic and the occasional big-name pop singer. On a fine evening people take picnics and spread themselves on the grass; if you want to get a spot where you can see and hear properly it's necessary to stake your claim many hours in advance. Continuing north on the footpath alongside the road, you pass, on the left, a bust of Mazzini, the Italian patriot, and beyond it one of several well-designed children's playgrounds, a boon for mothers and nannies (as a rule, it's mothers on the west side and nannies on the more prosperous east) who do not otherwise find much scope for exercising their infants in central Manhattan. Farther on, you will find bowling greens on your right. The path alongside them leads to a refreshment kiosk (not always open) and a place where you can rent roller skates. This was a popular craze as this book was being written — it was necessary to keep a sharp watch to avoid being struck by a speedy skater — but such fads are ephemeral.

Resisting skates (or not), stay on the path next to the main drive, cross the road at a pedestrian crossing by some traffic lights where a feeder road joins the main peripheral road, and bear left on a path which runs alongside the horse-riding track, parallel with Central Park West. Pass uphill through the first of two pergolas, in mid-May tumbling with wisteria. Before moving on to the other pergola, walk a few yards to the park entrance for a look at the **Dakota Building** on the north corner of 72nd Street and Central Park West. When this brooding apartment house was built in 1884, the cognoscenti said it was so far north that it might as well be in Dakota — hence its name. In those days the wealthy didn't live in apartments: the house along Fifth Avenue or its environs was the only socially acceptable dwelling. But the entrepreneurs behind the Dakota, who included Isaac Merritt Singer, founder of the sewing machine empire, could see that the legions of the rich were growing at a faster rate than the city could accommodate in the style which they had been led to expect. So they had Henry Hardenbergh — the architect responsible for both this and the Plaza Hotel — design a stretched version of a German Renaissance mansion, a gigantic Central Park West folly. With its lavishly proportioned rooms and its park views it became a smart address, popular with stars of the theatre and show business. Judy Garland, Roberta Flack, Leonard Bernstein, William Inge, Lauren Bacall are some of its twentieth-century inhabitants. Wander about outside, peek in at the carriage drive, admire the gods and dragons on the iron railings: the watchful guard at the gate won't let you in, unless you've been invited. On December 8, 1980, John Lennon, a founder of the Beatles, the Liverpool singing group of the 1960s, was shot and killed here by an obsessive fan to whom a few hours before he had given his autograph. For days afterwards, admirers brought flowers to the spot and kept a silent vigil.

Back inside the park, pass through the second pergola, north of the 72nd Street transverse road; this will lead you down some steps to a road.

Cross it at the traffic lights and walk down to **the lake**, where in summer people will be rowing boats. (These can be rented from the boathouse at the other side of the lake; we shall pass it later.) From almost anywhere on this side of the lake there are spectacular views of the city skyline to the south, and they get better as you follow the path alongside the lake, walking north. Take the right hand path at the fork to the **Ladies' Pavilion,** a pretty iron gazebo said to have been designed by Vaux as a bus shelter for the south-west corner of the park, by Columbus Circle. Recently restored and painted blue, it provides a picturesque foreground for photographs of the skyline.

Now go back to the main path between the water's edge and the road, and continue north. Cross over the concrete bridge for another version of the view from the Ladies' Pavilion, showing Hardenbergh's Plaza Hotel to fine effect against the black skyscraper behind it. Turn right and cross the wooden bridge, up the hill and, after about ten yards, right again up some steps. Yet another right turn takes you over a stone bridge crossing a path. Keep left of the lamp-post, descend some steps and turn left again, keeping the iron rail on your right. This part of the park is known as **the ramble,** a tangle of intersecting paths through a woodland area: because it is so secluded you must be a bit careful. The essential rule, as in most of New York's danger spots, is to make sure that there are always plenty of other people nearby. You won't want to come here at night or very early in the morning, but at the height of a summer weekend you'll be perfectly safe. It is one of the pleasantest parts of the park, so don't let apprehension keep you from it.

Turn left where the railing ends, pass between some rocks, and turn right by the seats. After twenty yards or so take a left fork and then bear right. Suddenly you are in a clearing, with a grassy patch on your left. Follow the path round to the left and look through the trees for a grey stone building with a tiled roof and green parapet, for which you should steer. As you get closer you will see that it is labelled as an insecticide storage house and also has public lavatories. Turn left by the building and, when you come to a four-way junction, turn right. Soon there are some steps to **Vista Rock**, on whose peak sits the Belvedere Tower, a dilapidated Gothic castle used as a meteorological observatory. North is the **Great Lawn**, the filled-in bed of an old reservoir, now dotted with baseball diamonds and an alternative to Sheep's Meadow and the Wollman Rink as a site for open-air concerts.

Descending the stairs on your left, you can pass by the **Delacorte Theater,** where free outdoor performances of Shakespeare are given during most summers: this is where Joseph Papp, creator of the Public Theater downtown, first claimed attention as an imaginative director and impresario. Some of the performances he initiated here, notably a rock version of *Two Gentlemen of Verona* in the early 1970s, and *The Pirates of Penzance* in the 1980s, went on to become successes on Broadway. As with all the city's free entertainment, you have to start lining up at the Delacorte Theater very early if you want to be sure of a seat and should telephone to discover when to start the vigil.

As you descend towards the theatre, look at the **Shakespeare Garden**, on an incline just to its south-west. Here you may detect, if you have the will and the patience, an example of every plant mentioned in the bard's works. Those who merely want an overall view of the garden can look upon it from a semi-circular platform on the way down from the Belvedere. Keeping the theatre superstructure on your right, notice the statues of Romeo and Juliet and Prospero and Miranda. Walk east on the path that runs along the south edge of the Great Lawn; when the path divides into three, take the center one crossing to the east side of the park. In spring you will enjoy the clump of flowering cherries to your left; watch for groups of uniformed children from the exclusive East Side schools when school is in session.

Soon, on your left, you will see the **obelisk,** Cleopatra's needle, behind the Metropolitan Museum. It was a gift from the Khedive of Egypt in 1880, one of a pair from Heliopolis, dating from about 1500 BC; its twin stands on the Embankment in London. You pass under one of Vaux's nicest bridges to find the new wing of the museum straight ahead; bear right between the museum and a playground, then turn right to pass over another bridge. Cedar Hill, the park's most popular dog run, is now on your right. Pass through a further road tunnel, keeping right at the first four-way junction, then take the middle path at the next. This brings you out beside the lively statue of Alice in Wonderland, portrayed with characters and quotations from Lewis Carroll's book on plaques around the edge. This, too, bears the name Delacorte and, since we shall meet him again before we leave the park, this is a good time to introduce this benefactor of New York's public spaces.

George Delacorte's philanthropy is of more recent vintage than that of Carnegie or the Rockefellers and differs in that it is unaccompanied by high moral strictures or uplifting sermons. He made his money from publishing pulp fiction — he founded Dell, a pioneer in this field and now a paperback publisher, in 1921. He had always given to charities but, after a conversation with a Parks Commissioner, decided he would like to put his money into things which would afford New Yorkers tangible and visible enjoyment. The open-air theatre was his first venture in Central Park, then the Alice statue (in memory of his wife), then the musical clock at the zoo which we shall come to later. Fountains give him particular pleasure: he funded one at Columbus Circle, one at City Hall Park, one at Bowling Green, and there are plans for one in Times Square; he is also responsible for the water jet in the East River, south of Roosevelt Island. The best kind of benefactor, Delacorte does not ask you to look at these wonders and praise him or his works: he simply hopes you will enjoy what he has put there.

Alice holds court at the north end of the **Conservatory Water,** the model boat pond, where on a good day you will see some magnificent vessels controlled for the most part by sophisticated radio devices deployed by enthusiasts on the banks. Peep through the grimy windows of the boat house on the left bank to see more models, and stop, perhaps, for refreshment at the Ice Cream Café next door. On the opposite bank is another statue enjoyed by children, Hans Christian Andersen with his waddling ugly duckling. Under it, in the summer, storytelling sessions are held. The path on its left leads to a snack bar and the rental office for boats on the big lake. Next to this is the bicycle renting station; if you want to explore all the park, including its northern reaches, renting a bike is not a bad idea.

Follow one of the paths back to the model boat pond and make for its south-east corner, a few yards south of the boat house. Climb a slope into an area for tree fanciers, where most trees are labelled, save those that have fallen victim to vandals or other predators. Go up some steps to the transverse road (the eastern end of the one we crossed by the Dakota Building) and turn right on to a path beside it, past one of the park's most pleasing statues, commemorating the Pilgrim Fathers. Cross the road and follow the sign 'Park Drive South', leading to another focal point, a plaza looking down to the right at the Bethesda Fountain and, again, the boating lake. On a fine summer Saturday this is where the roller-skaters, dope-smokers and radio-players congregate, cruising on their skates to the beat of their radios. Freelance clowns with painted faces, jugglers and magicians, dancers, musicians, men with monkeys on their shoulders, vendors of balloons and many kinds of refreshment will jostle you here and on the park mall, which leads from the bandstand behind you south towards the zoo. Before walking down the mall, though, find the steps behind the bandstand. They lead to another pergola, the largest and prettiest in the park, quite undetectable from ground level; venerable wisterias twine around it. Then go down the steps at the south end, follow the railing on to **the mall,** turning left before the statue of Samuel Morse — artist, engineer, polymath and inventor of the Morse code.

The southern end of the mall is flanked by two monuments to Scottish literature — statues of Sir Walter Scott and Robert Burns. Shakespeare and Columbus are just beyond them. Cross the road behind Shakespeare and turn right on to the path over a bridge, then sharp left between some picnic tables. This path takes you through a gate, down past the polar bear cage into **the zoo**, where this park tour ends. It is a small zoo but popular, I suppose partly because admission is free. It has lively monkeys, a huge brooding gorilla and some demonstrative sea lions in the pond at the center, surrounded by four blue bird cages. North-east of this central plaza is the animal clock, another of Mr Delacorte's donations. It plays tunes every quarter of an hour, sending an orchestra of small animals whirling about its face and making a suitable triumphal archway to the children's zoo, where a small admission charge is made. West of the sea lions is an ill-kept cafeteria and beer garden, not of a kind which would be recognized in Bavaria. Take refreshment here if you dare, then leave the park on to Fifth Avenue, up the path past the ivy-clad arsenal (now Parks Department offices) or back to the 59th Street entrance where you came in.

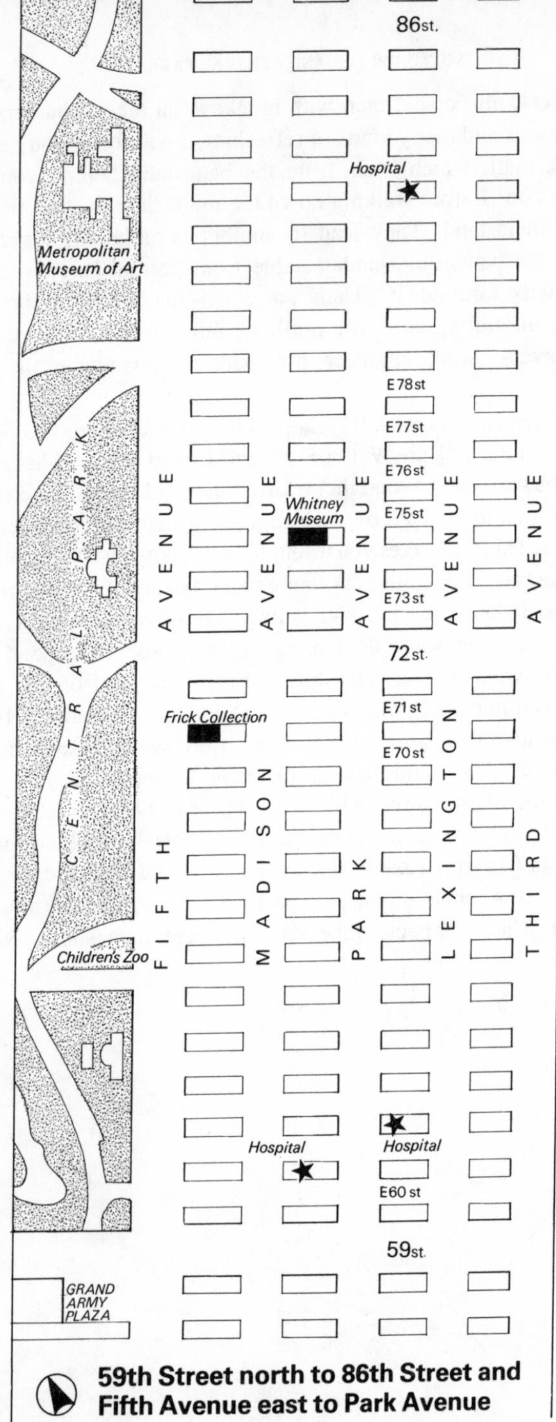

59th Street north to 86th Street and Fifth Avenue east to Park Avenue

12

Museum Mile

THE NEXT TWO CHAPTERS take us through the most important museums and art galleries in New York, which means some of the most important in the world. Museums present difficulties for a guide book organized into walks that are not supposed to take more than a day to complete: you could easily spend a day split between the Frick and the Whitney, the first two galleries on the route — and what a day of rich rewards and richer contrasts that would be; the Metropolitan is worth at least a day by itself, and even then you would be skimping. How long you devote to each, therefore, will be decided by your inclinations and the time at your disposal; but for the sake of order I simply shall link them in a continuous itinerary. **The Frick Collection** is at 70th Street and Fifth Avenue, overlooking the park; you get there on a Fifth or Madison Avenue bus. It is a favorite of many, partly because its treasures are arranged in the rooms of a real house and partly because it is small, easily absorbed at one visit. Debilitating gallery fatigue has little chance of overcoming you here: if it does, you can recuperate at leisure in the charming garden court at the center of the house, a glassed-in cloister with a fountain, flowers, Ionic columns and stone benches, and be imbued with uplifting calm by Jean Barbet's fifteenth-century bronze angel.

The house, one of the few survivors of the string of Beaux Arts mansions which used to line the avenue instead of today's grey apartment buildings, was built in 1914 for Henry Clay Frick by Carrère and Hastings, the architects of the Public Library on Fifth Avenue. Frick, a Pennsylvania accountant, made his millions producing coke, a vital ingredient in the manufacture of steel. In 1882, when Andrew Carnegie dominated the steel industry, he took Frick, then aged thirty-two, as a partner, partly to guarantee coke supplies and partly because he detected in him the ruthlessness which makes a successful industrialist. (By coincidence, Carnegie's Fifth Avenue mansion, twenty-one blocks north, has also survived and is also now a museum.) The two men were different in temperament and quarrelled constantly. Carnegie was expansive and generous, giving millions to charities and public projects both in his native Scotland and in America: Carnegie Hall is one of many. Frick was cold and tight-fisted, preferring to spend his money amassing works of art for his own enjoyment, though his will specified that they be put on public display after the death of his widow.

It's lucky for Frick's reputation that it now rests on this most alluring memorial, because in business he is best remembered for an incident that helped give the word 'steelmaster' its autocratic overtones. In April 1892, workers at the Homestead steel mill in Pennsylvania, enraged by a threatened pay cut, occupied the building and Frick sent three hundred private security guards to take it from them. For five days the men held out. Fourteen people died before state troops moved in, returning the mill to its owners and effectively destroying unions in the steel industry until the 1920s. Frick became an object of public disgrace and, two weeks later, the victim of an assassination attempt in his office. He survived that, though he had only five years more to enjoy the fruits of his acquisitiveness in their Fifth Avenue setting before he died in 1919. Still, for that brief period he was able to act out the fantasy he shared with those other American millionaires who had visited the grand houses of Europe and wished to emulate the refined and pampered style of the princes in their Italian palazzos, noblemen in their French chateaux and English gentlemen on their country estates. While the realities of late nineteenth- and early twentieth-century Europe made it increasingly hard for such establishments to be maintained, the American merchant princes, armed with almost inexhaustible untaxed bankrolls, injected a generous dose of hard cash into its declining social system and marched off with some of the gaudiest trappings of European culture. A breed of opportunistic middlemen was established to oil the wheels of this commerce, matchmakers between the European nobility in their discreetly reduced circumstances and the hot-breathed transatlantic suitors, eager to slake their passions on anything suggesting a bit of history and tagged with a reasonably plausible certificate of authenticity. In the circumstances it was not surprising that some of these brokers used dubious methods to bring the buyers and the sellers to mutual fulfillment. The most energetic and, later, the most notorious, was Joseph Duveen who, according to recent research, would send works of doubtful authorship or in a poor

Two of the best art collections in the world: the garden (designed by Russell Page) of the Frick Collection and (*below*) the Fifth Avenue façade of the Metropolitan Museum of Art, with its curiously uncut piles of masonry over the entablatures.

The Cloisters, in Fort Tryon Park, houses the Metropolitan Museum of Art's medieval collection. Several medieval European cloisters and chapels have been reconstructed here; amongst the treasures are the Unicorn Tapestries and the illuminated manuscript, the *Très Riches Heures du Duc de Berry*.

state of repair to a factory in Paris whence they would return as fully accredited Old Masters in near pristine condition. Frick may once or twice have been fobbed off with something of that dubious nature — most of the big collectors were — but they are not among the works now on display at the house. It is a gem of a collection.

In the **Entrance Hall,** below the grand staircase, a sampling of the riches hang among a suite of furniture made for Marie Antoinette. Two of the three Vermeers in the collection are here. His 'Officer and Laughing Girl' is relatively early: its extraordinary power derives from the way the officer dominates the canvas. Renoir's 'Mother and Children', in the alcove under the stairs, is appealing in a softer way, as is Corot's limpid landscape of Mortefontaine. The 1767 calendar clock, its tulipwood case by Lieutaud and bronze ornamentation by Caffieri, almost matches one in ebony on display at Versailles. The first of many Bouchers — Frick obviously enjoyed his ornate extravagances — is here, a 1743 portrait of Boucher's wife, reclining on a day bed in an untidy room. This is much more literal than his later pastoral works, eight of which we see next in the **Boucher Room**, west of the entrance hall. These panels depict the arts and sciences and were painted for Madame de Pompadour's chateau near Chartres in the 1750s; though over-sugary for today's taste, they are saved by a pinch of wit.

To reach the next set of Bouchers we must cross the **Dining Room** where we may be diverted by some fine examples of English portraiture by Gainsborough, Reynolds, Romney, Hogarth and Hoppner. In the adjoining vestibule, overlooking the terrace, is the charming and popular series, 'The Four Seasons', which Boucher again painted for Madame de Pompadour. The Wallace collection in London has a more erotic suite that he painted for her and Louis XV. Jean Honoré Fragonard, working a few years later for his patron, Madame du Barry, had less luck. She rejected his four works on 'The Progress of Love' that are to be seen in the **Fragonard Room**, next to the vestibule; it was nearly twenty years before he found a home for them, in his cousin's house at Grasse. There he painted seven smaller panels on the same theme, notably more wistful. Competition among American millionaires for the best was intense. In 1899 J. P. Morgan paid $310,000 for the panels. Fourteen years later, when he died, they were bought by a dealer from his estate and sold to Frick for $1,200,000.

The **Living Hall** was the focal point of the original house (the garden court and the buildings east of it were added in 1935 just before it opened as a museum) and contains the most concentrated collection of treasures. The furniture in this hall is a representative selection of the work of André-Charles Boulle, whose elaborate marquetry set the taste in European furniture from the late seventeenth century for more than a hundred years. Surely no group of five sixteenth-century portraits can better represent the period than the two Titians, two Holbeins and the El Greco on view here. The Titians are the early 'Portrait of a man in a red cap' and the later and more powerful 'Pietro Aretino'. The gravitas of El Greco's 'Saint Jerome', over the fireplace, contrasts with the serenity of Giovanni Bellini's 'St Francis in Ecstasy', showing the saint in a translucent allegorical landscape. Holbein's portraits of Sir Thomas More and a shifty Thomas Cromwell are magnificent character studies, though less well known than his jaunty rendering of Henry VIII, whom both men served. The More portrait was done during Holbein's first visit to England in 1527 and there is a miniature version of it at Lincoln's Inn in London.

In the **Library** are more English works from the eighteenth and nineteenth centuries, with Constable's captivating view of 'Salisbury Cathedral' and Turner's interesting treatment of 'Mortlake Terrace'. One of Gilbert Stuart's many portraits of George Washington hangs in a corner while Frick himself, white-bearded and more benign than one might expect, looks from above the fireplace at the low bookshelves, filled with leather-bound volumes of English literature. The **North Hall**, east of the Library, has Ingres' portrait of the Comtesse d'Haussonville and Monet's 'Vetheuil in Winter'.

The **West Gallery,** with its glass roof, was designed by Frick to show off the bulk of his collection. The four Rembrandts include a gloomy self-portrait, done in 1658, and 'The Polish Rider'. Four portraits by Franz Hals are executed with characteristic vigor, notably the one of a man whose paunch is bursting through his waistcoat. Another El Greco is here, as well as Velasquez's sly-looking Philip IV of Spain. Those who know van Dyck's work chiefly from his paintings of English royalty and nobility will be interested in the two portraits from his earlier Antwerp period, of Frans Snyders and his wife. There is another splendid Constable, 'The White Horse', while Turner's renderings of Cologne and Dieppe face each other across the sixteenth-century Tuscan walnut table. A collection of Limoges enamels is at the west end of this gallery and at the east end, the **Oval Room** is lined with the slender portraits of Whistler, suitably accompanied by Houdon's terra-cotta sculpture of Diana the Huntress. In the **East Gallery** are two more Gainsboroughs, two works by Goya, Aelbert Cuyp's 'Dordrecht', Claude Lorrain's 'Sermon on the Mount' and Van Dyck in a more familiar vein, with his portrait of the Earl of Derby and his family.

Leaving the Frick walk east down 70th to Madison Avenue and turn left. We have joined the avenue some ten blocks north of the start of its liveliest stretch, where the press of small antique shops, boutiques and fancy food emporiums places it among the city's most spirited and enjoyable thoroughfares. Wander back towards 60th Street if you want to do some extra browsing but our main route now takes us north.

Across the road, on the block between 71st and 72nd Streets and a few doors up from the ill-conceived brownstone church of St James (1884) is a fanciful townhouse built in 1898, when a Madison Avenue address was inferior on the social scale to one on Fifth Avenue by a few barely measurable degrees. Though the ground floor has been converted to shops, the sculptured figures above the balconies remain, as well as the rococo chimneys. Phillips, the smallest of the three London auctioneers who have opened branches in New York, have a small auction room on the second floor (their larger one is on 72nd Street by the East River). Walk a few steps west up 72nd Street to admire two more Beaux Arts town houses on the north side, dating from 1896 and 1899 and now joined as the Lycée Français. The next street up, 73rd, is a good example of what the crosstown streets linking these stretches of Fifth and Madison looked like sixty years ago — grandiose houses in different Beaux Arts styles jammed tight to each other, their architects refusing to be deterred from their ambitious schemes by limitations of space. Thus styles which evolved in Renaissance Europe, where the fine houses generally stood apart on their own land, have here been copied in a less suitable environment, with the result that the jumble of conflicting ornament is too much for the eye to take in. Yet if bewildering, it is certainly distinctive.

Continuing along Madison, we reach the next of our art galleries, the **Whitney Museum of American Art**, a scarcely missable, uncompromisingly modern (1966) granite-clad building on the corner of 75th Street, perversely top-heavy, its upper floors jutting progressively over the pavement. It is the work of Marcel Breuer, the Bauhaus architect whose most famous design was the tubular steel chair he devised in the late 1920s. He died in 1981. The original museum was founded in 1931 in Greenwich Village by Gertrude Vanderbilt Whitney who, as a patron of the arts, was almost the precise opposite of Frick, Morgan, Altman and the others who would lavish their riches on the famous and prestigious works of dead Europeans. Mrs Whitney, a great-granddaughter of Commodore Vanderbilt and wife of the heir to another fortune, had as much money as the rest but chose to spend it in support of living American artists amongst whom, as a sculptor of talent, she was to be counted.

Mrs Whitney is a pivotal figure in the history of New York, a link between the commercial adventurers of the mid-nineteenth century and today's cultural establishment. Born in 1875, she was the daughter of Cornelius Vanderbilt, the chief heir to his father William, who had inherited and enhanced the Commodore's fortune. Her childhood therefore was one of pampered privilege, spent in the colossal Vanderbilt mansion on Fifth Avenue between 57th and 58th Streets. In 1896 she married the well-connected Harry Whitney, whose father had been Secretary of the Navy and whose uncle, Oliver Payne, was a partner of John D. Rockefeller in Standard Oil. The marriage conformed to the prevailing norm in American high society at the turn of the century — in other words it was, behind a façade of respectability, racked with infidelities and barely submerged scandal. Dissatisfied with her lot, Gertrude, at the age of twenty-five, decided to take up sculpture seriously. Soon she began offering her patronage to promote the works of other artists and in 1913 moved to the studio in Macdougal Alley, between Washington Square and Eighth Street, which was to grow into the first Whitney Museum. By 1916, augmented by purchases of surrounding properties, she was holding her first small exhibitions of painting and sculpture. Gertrude's own career progressed in concert with her sponsorship of others, attracting attention for the oddity of a wealthy woman, who had opted to starve in a garret, being a successful artist. A critic in *Town Topics* wrote: 'That so frail a physique could have achieved so much, and in spite of the handicap of large wealth and strenuous social obligation, is a marvel.' No less an authority than Auguste Rodin wrote: 'Aristocratic and very rich, she works with the sincerity and fervor of a poor artist whose ideals are the only luxury.'

By 1931 the studio had been enlarged and converted into the country's first permanent gallery of American works. The museum moved uptown in 1954 and north again in 1966 to its present site, where it houses a permanent collection of more than six thousand paintings and sculptures. The full collection is not on show, but it is drawn on as the basis for the three or four specialized exhibitions in progress at any time. American art is by definition modern but the Whitney, reflecting Gertrude's taste, has generally been stronger on realism than on the abstract paintings which dominate the Museum of Modern Art, though naturally these are represented here too. One appealing item on permanent display, just inside the entrance, is Alexander Calder's circus with wire acrobats, clowns and performing animals.

Outside again, walking north up Madison Avenue, notice that almost every shop now is selling art and antiques. As bees around a honey-pot, they have homed in on the severe, boxy auction gallery of Sotheby Parke-Bernet between 76th and 77th Streets, an unhappy product of the 1950s school of brutalism. This largest of the New York auction houses was taken over by Sotheby's of London in the 1960s, starting a trend which brought Christie's and Phillips's here in the late 1970s. In 1982 it was announced that Sotheby Parke-Bernet would close its Madison Avenue galleries, the result of a downturn in the art market combined with the consequences of costly expansion during the boom years. Their central headquarters is now located in a more modern building on 72nd Street and Park Avenue. You might want to go to an auction if you have time or money to spend. There is little of the reverential hush and club-like social overtones of the English Sotheby's and Christie's; here it's more frankly commercial with the auctions proceeding at a gallop and bids made more openly than the minimal nods which prevail in London. Across Madison Avenue is the Hotel Carlyle, one of the more discreet in the city, popular with senior diplomats and wealthy collectors who come to the auctions.

Turn left up 78th Street. Of the motley collection of turn-of-the-century houses on both sides of this street, the most notable is the one on the north-east corner of Fifth Avenue, now the **Institute of Fine Arts** of New York University. Built in 1912 for James B. Duke, a tobacco baron, it's a copy of the eighteenth-century Hôtel Labottière in Bordeaux. Alongside it is the more frivolous 1916 house of Payne Whitney, Gertrude's brother-in-law. This is today the cultural center for the French embassy and generally has a small exhibition in progress, allowing you to go inside and feel a trifle oppressed by the concentration of patterned marble on the floors and pillars of the circular entrance hall. The medieval fireplace is interesting but out of place, and the ceiling is worth looking up for. Back on the avenue, you can now see our main target, the **Metropolitan Museum of Art,** looming forbiddingly out of the park a couple of blocks north. (Some call it the Met, a sign of affection but also a source of confusion, because that is the pet name more commonly given to the Metropolitan Opera.)

If it were possible to justify the rape of the artifacts of the old world by American wealth, then the Metropolitan would be that justification. This stupendous museum would not be half so splendid without the bequests of art and antiquities from people satisfied to have enjoyed them privately in their lifetime but wishing to share them after death. Their motives have not always been self-effacing. Some bequests have been hedged with the condition that they be housed separately from the rest of the collections and named after the donor, ensuring him or her immortality: thus we get the Lehman Wing, the Altman Collection, the Blumenthal Patio, the Sackler Wing — none of which has artistic relevance or makes the museum easier to navigate cogently. Nor does the habit of closing galleries at random if they cannot afford the staff to keep them open. But these are insignificant flaws in a museum of which New Yorkers are rightly proud.

The idea of establishing an institution to rival the British Museum and the National Gallery in London was first aired in the 1860s by a group of citizens including William Cullen Bryant, the spiritual father of Central Park. In 1872 a batch of Old Masters was brought over from Europe and formed the nucleus of the original museum in a converted dance studio. In 1880 it moved to its present quarters in the park, since then radically remodelled and expanded. Some of those original paintings are still on display, as is a large portion of another early acquisition from overseas, the Cypriot antiquities plundered by the Comte di Cesnola, the most colorful figure of the museum's early years. An Italian count (or he claimed to be) Cesnola fought on the Union side in the American Civil War and had the good fortune to be appointed United States consul in Cyprus afterwards; at that time the island's rich trove of antiquities had hardly begun to be exploited by archaeologists. Cesnola set about retrieving as many as he could get his hands on and exporting them, in defiance of local regulations, to the United States. In 1872 the fledgling museum bought the entire collection and, moreover, appointed Cesnola its curator. The following year, back in Cyprus, he claimed to have unearthed a gold and silver treasure at Curium. Twenty years later that second collection was revealed as a fraud but by then Cesnola had risen to become the museum's director and a powerful guiding force. A quite large proportion of his initial haul is still on display, though looking neglected, in the Greek and Roman Galleries to the left of the main entrance, en route to the restaurant. After Cesnola's death in 1904, the financier J. P. Morgan rose to a dominant role on the museum's board of trustees, and made his mark in two ways. In 1906 he brought Roger Fry, the testy English art scholar, to reorganize the museum's paintings and to make judicious purchases with the bequests of funds which were now growing. Fry stayed little more than three years but laid the foundation of the present collection of European paintings. Morgan's other contribution was more tangible: much of his own collection was given to the museum by his son in 1917, though it is mostly scattered in the various galleries rather than having one to itself entirely.

Pausing to admire the linear fountains alongside Richard Morris Hunt's monumental entrance, climb the broad staircase and enter the **Great Hall**, domed and colonnaded, giving a sense of light and space which is a distinctive feature of this museum. There are shops to the left and right of the central staircase, and another upstairs, selling books and gift items, including reproductions of objects in the museum. This part of the museum's activities has greatly expanded in recent years and these are among the best gift shops in the city, though prices are quite high. At the information desk you can pick up a free map. To enter the galleries you must pay an admission fee. In theory you can give as little or as much as you like (this enables the museum to persuade the tax authorities that it is a donation rather than an admission charge) but there is a 'suggested' donation displayed. For your money you get a small metal badge which allows you to wander the galleries at will.

Where to start? This depends largely on your interests, but it probably makes logistic sense to begin with the **Egyptian Wing**, in the Lila Acheson Wallace Galleries of Egyptian Art, off the Great Hall to the right of the entrance. In the late 1970s the exhibition of objects from King Tutankhamen's tomb, which toured the United States and Europe, encouraged a new interest in Egyptian art, and burial objects comparable with (though as a group less splendid than) the King Tut treasures, are shown here. Near the entrance to the section you can walk into the tomb of Pernebi, the Lord Chamberlain of Egypt, which dates from around 2415 BC and contains some vigorous reliefs, partially painted. At the far end is the new wing built to house the Temple of Dendur, one of the Nubian temples rescued by an international effort when its site was flooded in the making of the Aswan High Dam. Because the United States contributed most to the rescue operation, the Egyptians allowed it the pick of the four temples they gave away to express their gratitude, and the Metropolitan added this glass annex, known as the Sackler Wing, to accommodate it. The setting of pools and concrete is supposed to be a stylized interpretation of its original site on the banks of the Nile; I find it cold, alienating and dwarfing. The deeply incised figures and hieroglyphs are impressive but you are not allowed inside to inspect them closely. Informative wall panels and photographs help. I like the temple best at night, when it's floodlit and makes a dramatic spectacle through the glass from outside.

While still at this end of the museum, slip into the **Chinese Garden**, a replica of one that a mandarin would have used for contemplation. A team of Chinese experts spent several months working here during 1980, to ensure its authenticity. Around it are exquisite drawings and parchments from the period, the start of a Chinese section soon to be expanded.

The Greek and Roman Galleries are back at the opposite end of the main hall, beginning with a villa transported from Pompeii, buried by the volcanic eruption of Vesuvius in 79 AD, complete with a set of wall paintings of architectural views. The well-preserved mosaic floor was found near Rome. In the adjoining gallery the highlight is the Badminton sarcophagus, its finely carved marble relief of the god Dionysus surrounded by the four seasons. Beyond are Greek carvings and statuary. The comprehensive collection of amphoras, urns, kraters, jars and vases is on the second floor, immediately above, along with some later gold and silver plates and utensils.

At the end of the Greek section, turn right to the new **Michael C. Rockefeller Wing** housing primitive art from Africa, the Americas, and the Pacific. Alongside that are the refurbished eating facilities, a waiter-service restaurant surrounded by a less expensive self-service cafeteria offering superior canteen-style food. At the entrance is a bar, a thoughtful provision for those times during a long museum tour when the mind and the ankles need recharging. There is a less expensive snack bar one floor below, in the Junior Museum.

Go back to the main staircase, though not yet up it. On the left is the **Blumenthal Patio**, named after its donor, in a reconstructed Renaissance courtyard. It came from the Andalusian castle of Valez Blanco, where the marble reliefs, incorporating grotesque animal shapes, were executed by Italian carvers in the early sixteenth century.The courtyard is adorned with other period details. You can climb on to the balcony for an overhead view and a look at the colorful patterned tiles lining the ceiling. The transfer of the whole patio from Spain illustrates the dauntless enthusiasm of the American acquisitors; if you like this kind of thing you will find much more of it at the Cloisters, the Metropolitan's branch farther uptown.

Next we arrive at the **Medieval Section**. One of its outstanding exhibits is in a glass case by the wall of the Blumenthal Patio — six meticulously crafted Byzantine silver plates depicting the life of David, discovered in Cyprus in 1902, smuggled therefrom soon afterwards and acquired by J. P. Morgan, of whose bequest they were a part. The section begins in medieval tapestry and sculpture halls, the latter divided by an imposing wrought iron (though later than medieval) screen from the cathedral of Valladolid. If you go beyond the main staircase and look back beneath it, a glowing stained glass window will draw you towards a small room fitted out as a Romanesque chapel, a calm retreat from the bustle around. It contains devotional objects and columns from the twelfth and thirteenth centuries drawn from different churches in France and Spain. The altar is a section of a Byzantine chancel screen from Italy, a few hundred years older.

Returning to the mainstream, the displays of Western European decorative arts now spread to the north and south. If you want to see them as a piece it is best first to plunge straight ahead, through glass doors, into the **Robert Lehman Pavilion.** Lehman, a banker and connoisseur who died in 1969, left his fabulous collection to the Metropolitan on condition that they found a place to exhibit it separately, a permanent monument to his good taste. So an airy, diamond-shaped protuberance was tacked on to the museum's western flank, where the paintings and objects are on show in galleries surrounding a central courtyard. Some are recreations of rooms in Lehman's own Manhattan house, with the artifacts in their original positions. Most of the early works in the collection are thus displayed, including a Botticelli 'Annunciation', an El Greco portrait of St Jerome, two Rembrandts, a Velasquez, and some magnificent majolica and Limoges enamels. The later pictures and drawings are more conventionally hung on other parts of this floor and on the floor below, including a sampling of Impressionists and post-Impressionists. Go down one of the four staircases to the central courtyard, where chairs are scattered among the eight large weeping figs in tubs. (If you go after dark and look up to the glass dome, the exhibits are reflected pleasingly in it.) Around this courtyard the nineteenth- and twentieth-century paintings, chiefly Impressionists, hang on the outer walls.

Just before leaving the Lehman Pavilion double doors on the right lead to a staircase with the notice: **'European decorative arts** . . . downstairs'. Go down the stairs to galleries packed with ceramics of the leading European houses, from the heavy, almost cloying richness of Italian maiolica (fifteenth to seventeenth centuries) to the delicate porcelains of the eighteenth and nineteenth centuries. Beyond are jewelry, clocks — a marvellous collection, most of it donated by J.P. Morgan — precious stones and metals, extravagantly conceived adornments for the powdered people who lived in settings such as we are about to see in the period rooms. Climbing the staircase in the French ceramics gallery will bring you back on the main floor behind the central staircase. Move back through medieval art, turning left before you get to the entrance to the Lehman Pavilion into the French rooms. Just beyond the down staircase is a shop front from eighteenth-century Paris containing a collection of silver from that period, followed by Rococo rooms from Paris and Vienna. Crossing again in front of the Lehman Pavilion we reach the equivalent English splendors — a carved staircase by Grinling Gibbons and some stately Georgian interiors. Proceed through galleries of British furniture and sculpture to a sumptuous bedroom from the Palazzo Sagredo on the Grand Canal in Venice, its sensuality heightened by rich reds and golds and the team of Cupids bearing the overhead canopy. Then we go backwards in time again to a seventeenth-century Swiss room with outstanding reliefs and a well preserved English Elizabethan interior from a merchant's house in Great Yarmouth, next to a small sixteenth-century chapel from France.

Now you are at the entrance to the **Arms and Armor Section**, which has 'The John Pierpont Morgan Wing' carved into the frieze on top of the pillars at the end. This comprehensive collection, in a hall hung with heraldic banners, is grouped round a set of life-size horses bearing armored heroes and enjoying thorough if cumbersome protection themselves. The most imaginative metalwork of the Middle Ages and the Renaissance was executed in the name of combat. Seek out the set of armor made for George Clifford in the sixteenth century: the blue-black background highlights the fine etching and gilding, turning Clifford into the dandiest of adversaries but also perhaps the most conspicuous, exceeded in finery only by the warriors of the Orient, whose elaborate armor is shown here also. As for arms, the prime specimens are a set of richly decorated flintlock rifles and fowling pieces made at Versailles, one of them to the order of Napoleon, and one of the earliest flintlock weapons, a wonderfully elegant silver and pearl inlaid fowling piece made for Louis XIII around 1615.

After this it is time for the **American Wing**, which should be the focal point of any visit to the Metropolitan. This is without much doubt the finest permanent collection of Americana anywhere. It was a minor outrage that for the last half of the 1970s the American collection was off limits to the public during the construction of this magnificent new wing, opened finally (but still only partially) in 1980. The second phase is due to open in the early 1980s.

Entering from the armor gallery, you are immediately in a large glass-enclosed courtyard dotted with trees, shrubs and romantic nineteenth-century sculpture, looking out on to the park. Turn left and make for the far end of the courtyard, then turn right to look at the stained glass windows from Frank Lloyd Wright's Avery Coonley Playhouse. Alongside them are two flights of stairs characteristic of Louis Sullivan, from whose Chicago Stock Exchange they were rescued: these lead to a balcony which provides good views over the courtyard and where American silver, pewter, glass and ceramics are displayed. Coming back down the stairs, walk through the limestone, ceramic and glass loggia which Louis Comfort Tiffany designed for his own house on Long Island, mounted with stained glass panels.

Walk back to the far end of the courtyard, stopping on the way at the orientation center to pick up a map, which you will need to navigate the remainder of the American Wing. The main entrance to the reconstructed rooms is through the door in the 1822 façade of a Wall Street bank, which forms one wall of the courtyard. Through the bank door is the **Federal**

Gallery, containing furniture and decorations from the post-revolutionary period (1780 to about 1830). The most important New York furniture designer of this time was Duncan Phyfe, represented by a dining table and chairs and two footstools. The rooms off the hall are reconstructed from demolished houses or made up of compatible elements from different rooms — the form of display most effectively used in the wing. Straight ahead from the Federal Gallery, through the neo-Classical Gallery, is an exhibition of late Federal furniture — more Duncan Phyfe — leading into three rooms of American folk art-paintings of moon-faced innocents, shaker baskets and boxes, and Amish quilts.

To tackle matters chronologically from here it's best to take the elevator to the top, the **third floor** of the original wing, which houses the rooms from the seventeenth and eighteenth centuries, with supporting exhibits of furniture, artifacts and construction methods. On the **second floor** we move forward a hundred years or so and notice a predictable increase in sophistication, notably in the Alexandria Ballroom. The Pennsylvania German Room (colloquially called Pennsylvania Dutch, a corruption of Deutsch), with its naive decorative techniques, is especially evocative.

To avoid going up and down the stairs too often you have to break away from the rooms here and move across to the second floor of the new wing, which has most of the painting and sculpture galleries. Go up from the Decorative Arts Orientation Gallery in the old wing and walk on through the Philadelphia Chippendale to the spectacularly ornate Van Rensselaer Hall, with two nearly contemporary rooms leading off it. The galleries are now on your left, starting with **Gallery 217,** the eighteenth-century portraits, and moving on through Sully and Bingham to the Hudson River School and Winslow Homer. (The numbering of the galleries, incidentally, has no significance in the sequence of the paintings but is useful for navigation.) In **Gallery 223** you come across, indeed you can scarcely miss, 'Washington Crossing the Delaware', Emanuel Leutze's heroic painting which, as the explanatory label rightly claims, has acquired the status of a national monument. Go back through 222 to **Gallery 224,** the balcony overlooking the mezzanine for the *trompe l'oeil* paintings of William Harnett, the rollicking Western bronzes of Frederic Remington and some fine canvases by Thomas Eakins.

On the **mezzanine floor** below are the portraits of John Singer Sargent, the impossibly elegant women in black, grey and white. With them is a small selection of more recent American paintings — Edward Hopper and Georgia O'Keeffe. Back on the ground floor of the old wing, complete the circuit of the period rooms. Notice the Richmond Room, **Gallery 110,** the over-elaborate woodwork and wallpaper with Parisian views showing how early nineteenth-century Americans derived their taste from the classical models. Much in the American Wing, you may think, is too derivative to warrant serious regard. Yet taken as a whole, the works, at least prior to the twentieth century, embody distinctively American qualities of innocence, romanticism and heroism.

With the American Wing we are done with the museum's main floor and ready to ascend the wide staircase by the main entrance to the **second floor**. The balcony provides a pleasing overview of the comings and goings in the entrance hall as well as being lined with decorative oriental pieces, mainly Chinese porcelains. The best of these are in the Benjamin Altman Collection, grouped on either side of the staircase. It was with Chinese porcelains that Altman, the department store magnate, began his career as a collector, heavily influenced by Henry Duveen, the honest uncle of the notorious Joe. Altman contributed importantly to the museum's dazzling collection of **European paintings.** At the top of the main staircase, a lavish hors d'oeuvre to the rich flavors of the rooms beyond, John Pope-Hennessy, the English curator of European art here, has filled the first gallery with the works of Tiepolo. Most were done as decorations for Venetian palaces. The three largest are scenes of Roman history, painted for the Ca' Dolfin between 1726 and 1730. He painted ten of these altogether — five are at the Hermitage in Leningrad and two others in Vienna. In the next room, around the sixteenth-century Farnese table, more eighteenth-century works include portraits by Gainsborough and Reynolds.

There are two doors in the west wall of this room. The left-hand one takes you back to fifteenth-century Flemish and French religious works, notably the 'Crucifixion' and 'Last Judgment' by Jan Van Eyck. In the rooms beyond we move forward in time through Holbein's well-fed Tudor noblemen and the strong portraits by his German contemporary, Lucas Cranach the Elder. Pressing on, we are embraced by the rippling flesh of Rubens and by Van Dyck, whose artistic preference was for sensuous robes rather than what lay beneath them. His work here includes an intriguing, dandified self-portrait. Press on through sixteenth- and seventeenth-century Italy and Spain until we get to the corner room,

Gallery 3, with a Velasquez portrait of Philip IV, less assertive than his later version at the Frick and nowhere near as deeply felt as his Juan de Pareja in this gallery.

Turn north, to **Gallery 2,** to see two gaunt El Greco portraits and his view of Toledo, a rare surviving landscape. More Van Dyck and Rubens are in **Gallery 1** and after that you will be back in the room with the Farnese table. Here turn left and left again through the other door in the west wall, taking you back to fourteenth-century Italy. Off the next gallery, the door on the right leads to a small room with ceiling panels by Pintoricchio from the Palazzo del Magnifico in Siena and, built into the walls, frescoes from Villa Mattei in Rome. Go back through the same entrance and turn right to continue the sequence of galleries. The next one has a Raphael altar-piece of 1504, one of a group he did for churches in Perugia; another of them, the 'Ansidie Madonna', is in the National Gallery in London. Now turn right (north) for majestic works by Tintoretto, Titian and Veronese. The Tintoretto self-portrait is one of two: the second is at the Fitzwilliam Museum in Cambridge, England.

Galleries 9, 10 and 11 take us up to the seventeenth-century and **Gallery 12** has a lovely selection of Vermeer's domestic compositions. Some fine landscapes by Cuyp are in **Gallery 13** and next to that is a room containing more works donated by Altman: like Lehman, he insisted they should be kept together. Rembrandt's 1660 self-portrait is more optimistic than the one we saw in the Frick, although it was done two years later. Near it are two rumbustious, pink-cheeked portraits by Franz Hals. The work of Hals in the next door **Gallery 15** is much more restrained. These are non-Altman pictures and include a shaft of Rembrandts, notably 'Aristotle with a Bust of Homer'. In the further rooms we advance to the eighteenth century — the British portraitists and the French fantasists, complementing what we have already seen at the Frick, as does Houdon's voluptuous sculpture of a bather.

The nineteenth-century is covered in the André Meyer Wing, which we shall get to soon but vault for the time being to look at the small section just ahead, devoted to twentieth-century art. The collection is sketchy because the Metropolitan has never felt it necessary to compete vigorously with the Museum of Modern Art, but it includes Picasso's haunting portrait of Gertrude Stein, and a Miro mural.

Take a break from paintings here to visit the **musical instrument**

gallery, north of the twentieth-century rooms. It's fun to hire a recorded tour from the desk on your left as you enter because it includes music of the instruments displayed. European instruments from the sixteenth-century onwards are in the section on the left, with items from Africa, Latin America and the Far East on the opposite side. There are treats for the eye as well as the ear — the bizarre shapes of some of the earliest wind instruments and the intricate carvings and inlays of the keyboard cabinets. Most lavish of all is a baroque seventeenth-century Italian harpsichord, the keyboard supported on the shoulders of three carved and gilded wooden tritons, with two pieces of flanking statuary. Look out for the Erard piano, built in England in 1840 with no thought of restraint.

Now go back to the southern end of the floor, through the Grecian urns, to complete your survey of European paintings and sculpture. When the **André Meyer Galleries** for nineteenth-century works opened in 1980 they were hailed as an object lesson in how a museum should display its permanent collections. The space is partitioned into small galleries concentrating on a single artist or period, the paintings shown in an uncluttered way which allows them to be viewed comfortably even when the galleries are crowded. The explanatory labelling is detailed and informative. There is a plan at the left of the entrance.

The Impressionists and post-Impressionists are many people's favorite schools of the period, so you may want to leave those until last. In that case, after you enter the galleries from opposite the elevator, forge straight ahead through the neo-Classicists and Romantics (David, Goya, Ingres and three choice Turners) into a gallery devoted to Courbet. Now turn left into the long gallery at the southern end of the rectangle, displaying what the museum describes as salon paintings — eastern scenes by Gerome, a portrait by Winterhalter, Millais, the animal sculptures of Barye and other works of a more literal and classical nature than the Impressionists in the central courtyard, which you are for the time being circling. Another left turn takes you through the mercifully small section devoted to symbolism and into a gallery of large sculptures dominated by Rodin — perhaps too much writhing energy to be confined in one room. Here we can finally and with relief penetrate the center, the rich collection of Impressionists, as notable for its sheer volume as for its tremendous quality.

Few will challenge Monet's right to dominate this center section.

There are twenty-eight of his paintings, some of his most luminous landscapes as well as one of the most effective of his London pictures, 'The Palace of Westminster in Fog'. Manet and Cézanne are almost as well represented, while the smaller groups of Renoir, Van Gogh and Toulouse-Lautrec make up in interest and importance for being slightly fewer. Degas has a set of galleries to himself on the east side of the rectangle — a comprehensive collection of bronze casts of his sculptures as well as paintings and pastels, a fine tour de force to round off the European section.

We are left now with the lowest floor, which is in fact the street floor. The **Costume Institute**, at the north end, houses changing exhibitions from its stock of some seventeen thousand garments. At the southern end is the **Junior Museum,** which seeks to interest children by explaining the techniques of artists and craftsmen. At weekends there are lectures in which children are taken to different parts of the museum to have something specific explained to them. They can also pick up here the equipment for treasure hunt games which take them through the galleries searching for details in the works of art. A shop selling toys and children's items is on the second floor, at the top of the main staircase, on the right.

We are roughly half way along Fifth Avenue's 'museum mile' — a rare civic understatement, for it's about a mile and a half. We shall visit the rest of the museums in the next chapter.

13

A Mansion and More Museums

BEFORE WE CONTINUE our circuit of the Fifth Avenue museums, we're going to call at the mayor's house and pass through another ethnic enclave. Take the 86th Street crosstown bus from any of the 86th Street subway stops to **Gracie Mansion** at the junction of 88th Street and East End Avenue, where Manhattan protrudes in a bump opposite the Roosevelt Island lighthouse. Because it commands a strategic view of the junction of the East River and the Harlem River — called Hell Gate by seamen on account of the swirling currents — a battery was put there by Washington in the Revolutionary War, but it failed to discourage the British navy from sailing up the East River in 1776 and destroying all the buildings on the bank.

In 1799 Archibald Gracie, a Scottish merchant, built a wooden country house there, with a colonial-style verandah on three sides. In 1942 it became the official residence of the mayor, but 'Mansion' is an overblown word for it, even taking into account the extension added by Mayor Wagner in 1960 to accommodate his large family and heavy social commitments. Mayor Koch opened it to the public for the first time in 1980. Visitors are taken on guided tours leaving hourly, with a posse of watchful officials on hand to see that none of the mayor's effects is violated. It's something of an effort to get a place on a tour, but probably worth it because this is one of the oldest houses remaining in New York and one of the few on public view which is still lived in.

Beyond the Federal front door is a spacious entrance hall and a wide elegantly curving staircase; to the left a small, cozy den where the mayor is said to watch television. The dining-room beyond it seats twenty-two; larger groups are accommodated in the more formal rooms in the 1960 wing. A narrow pantry leads to a modern kitchen designed by Mary Lindsay, the first lady of Gracie Mansion from 1966 to 1973. Mayor Koch, a bachelor, has a staff of three. The mayor's living room, to the right of the entrance, has a green motif, with love seats and petit point

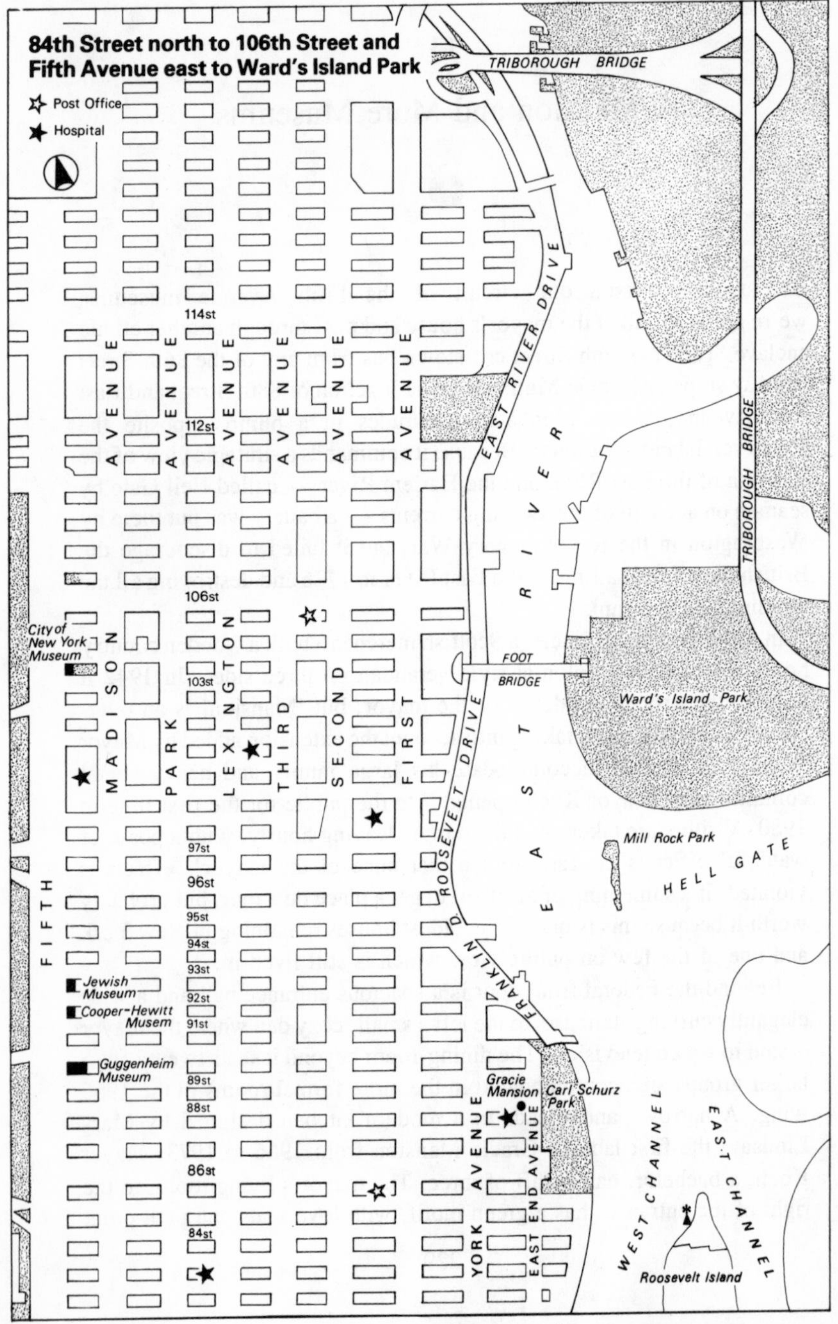
84th Street north to 106th Street and
Fifth Avenue east to Ward's Island Park
Post Office
Hospital
TRIBOROUGH BRIDGE
EAST RIVER DRIVE
FRANKLIN D. ROOSEVELT DRIVE
EAST RIVER
FOOT BRIDGE
Ward's Island Park
Mill Rock Park
HELL GATE
Gracie Mansion
Carl Schurz Park
WEST CHANNEL
EAST CHANNEL
Roosevelt Island
FIFTH
MADISON AVENUE
PARK AVENUE
LEXINGTON AVENUE
THIRD AVENUE
SECOND AVENUE
FIRST AVENUE
YORK AVENUE
EAST END AVENUE
114st
112st
106st
103st
97st
96st
95st
94st
93st
92st
91st
89st
88st
86st
84st
City of New York Museum
Jewish Museum
Cooper-Hewitt Musem
Guggenheim Museum

embroidery — a nice place to relax after a day grappling with problems concerning bus drivers and garbage disposal. Upstairs you will see the presidential suite, for distinguished guests, and two smaller bedrooms, but the mayor's own bedroom is off limits. The furniture is a mixture of antique and reproduction, some of it on loan from the Metropolitan Museum until a permanent collection of suitable pieces can be acquired.

The first mayor to use Gracie Mansion as his official residence was Fiorello La Guardia, who in twelve years in office won more affection and admiration than any of his predecessors or successors. The mayor of a large American city has wider powers than his equivalent in most European countries: his administration is responsible for billions of dollars worth of public municipal services — police, fire, rubbish collection, the streets, parks, museums and, to some extent, the transport system. With so large an amount of patronage to dispense, the office has from time to time been run corruptly, and it was a wave of reaction against that which swept La Guardia into City Hall in 1934.

Two years earlier the popular Jimmy Walker had resigned after an official inquiry implicated him in graft concerning city contracts. The playboy Walker became mayor through the good offices of Tammany Hall, headquarters of the Democratic Party machine. Big city political machines, though they often served as an efficient if crude means of organizing a democratic system, provided unrivalled opportunities for corruption and were periodically assailed by reform movements. La Guardia won the 1933 election as a 'fusion' candidate, meaning the fusion of all anti-Tammany elements, chiefly the Republican Party and rebel democrats. The son of Italian-born parents, La Guardia was the first mayor to come from the ranks of the new immigrants. After a spell overseas in the US consular service, he was appointed deputy attorney general for New York State and won a seat in Congress in 1916, at the age of thirty-four. He stayed in Washington, apart from a short hiatus, until 1932, building an impressive liberal reputation which recommended him to fusion leaders in 1933.

As mayor, the short and stocky La Guardia was ill-tempered with colleagues and he fiercely resented criticism, yet he maintained his popularity through most of his twelve years in office, partly because to a large extent he succeeded in fulfilling his campaign promises of reducing patronage, introducing a higher degree of professionalism in running the city and combating corruption everywhere; and partly by his flair for capturing the headlines: a self-styled expert in firefighting, he would dash with the engines to any major outbreak and be photographed for the newspapers. He was also the first mayor to use radio as a means of putting himself across to his constituents. He engaged in a well-publicized and sporadically successful campaign against organized crime, which had blossomed in the years of Prohibition. On the repeal of the Prohibition amendment in 1933, the mobsters needed to find other means of making money and trouble. Gambling and prostitution were two obvious fields of enterprise and they moved enthusiastically into the 'protection' of legitimate businesses, particularly restaurants. Organized crime thrives to this day but La Guardia did enjoy some victories.

The most enduring monuments to La Guardia's administration are the public works projects he began. The airport in Queens which immortalizes his name — used for short and medium-length flights inside America — is the most obvious, but the larger international airport at Idlewild, now called John F. Kennedy Airport, was also started in his time: so were the Grand Central Parkway and the Triborough Bridge which link the airports to the city. This was the time of the New Deal, when federal funds were available for works providing jobs for the unemployed. The mastermind behind most of them was Robert Moses, a compulsive builder, and parks commissioner under La Guardia and his successors.

The East River Drive, which runs below Gracie Mansion, and the adjoining **Carl Schurz Park**, were the creations of Robert Moses. Building the park above the road allows tremendous views across the river and up to Moses's Triborough Bridge to the north. The blue and yellow footbridge on the far left links Harlem with the park on Ward's Island; the decayed wharves of Queens are directly opposite and the green dome of the Sohmer piano factory farther south. Carl Schurz Park itself is small and its grass gets fearfully worn by the summer tread of cooped-up East Siders, for whom this is rare open space. Yet it's well maintained, no doubt because of its proximity to the mayor's home — a reason why it is also one of the city's safest parks. The weekend evening crowds here are mainly young men and women occupying postage-stamp sized apartments in the expensive buildings nearby. On the benches, though, you will still see a fair number of elderly people from the German and Central European community which established itself early in the century in the former village of Yorkville, two short blocks west. Carl Schurz was himself a German immigrant who lived nearby, rising to be Secretary of the Interior and editor of the *Evening Post*

Between East End and York Avenues are modern, arid apartment buildings of the middle price range. Across York towards First are more of the same, though older and shabbier, and at First Avenue Yorkville truly begins, a microcosm of almost every one of New York's distinctive features. Over the years other ethnic groups have, as elsewhere in New York, nibbled away at the edge of the Central European area, and along this stretch of the street are restaurants offering the cuisines of Japan, France, China and more. By the time we get to Second Avenue, though, we're in the thick of the Bavarian forest. Turn left from 86th Street and in a single block along Second Avenue you'll seem transported to mitteleuropa. Step into Schaller and Weber, the big food and provision shop, simply for the smell of the extraordinary array of sausages hanging from the ceiling and stacked in the display cabinet. Two doors along, at the Heidelberg Restaurant you can sample most of them without having to cook for yourself: dishes with paprika and sauerkraut and many variations on schnitzel. Beyond is the Old Dutch Delicatessen, and then the Wagner Continental Travel Agency, in case the sights and smells inspire an irresistible urge to take the next flight to Vienna. No such neighborhood would be complete without its cake shop, sacher torte in the window; for this, cross the road to Kramer's Pastries. Back on 86th Street, continuing west, there is more of the same: Kleine Konditorei is a restaurant and cake shop combined, the Bavarian Inn next door a restaurant and clam bar. Next to that, Karl Ehmer has almost as many sausages hanging as Schaller and Weber, and the Café Geiger has the most elaborate cakes of all. These shops and restaurants are distinguished by an air of permanence and solidity rare in New York: they look as though they've been there as long as the four- and five storey tenements, built for the original German immigrants, which still stand in the cross-streets north and south of 86th. That doesn't mean that the neighborhood isn't changing. Gradually the tenements are being pulled down and anonymous apartment buildings rising in their place, where more and more patrons of the singles bars (there is one of those on 86th Street too) can wedge themselves into ever decreasing living space at ever spiralling cost. All the same, the district is somehow keeping its character: long may it thrive.

Beyond Third Avenue, another swift change. Now 86th Street becomes a honky-tonk commercial section, with fast food chains, Woolworth's, camera and electronic stores, shoe shops, a couple of movie theaters and an active sidewalk life where paintings, photographs, handbags and clothes are sold from cardboard boxes. For refreshment, buy a glass of papaya juice from the colorful booth on the corner. Across Lexington Avenue, the uptown branch of Gimbel's tries to raise the tone in preparation for our progress towards Park, Madison and Fifth Avenues, where the apartment houses are older, less gigantic, more discreet and much more expensive, uniformed doormen lurking behind the potted palms in the entrance halls. At Fifth Avenue we turn right, back to our museums.

The Guggenheim Collection at 89th Street has, since its inception, been among the most adventurous of the large public art galleries. Many visitors with little interest in the modern works it displays are drawn to it by the architecture, an inverted snail's shell, the last major work of the visionary architect Frank Lloyd Wright. Purists maintain that for the fabric of a museum to overshadow its contents negates its function; the opposing argument is that if a building conforms with the spirit of what it was created to contain, then both it and the contents are enhanced. An irreverent view is that it looks like nothing so much as a giant cup and saucer.

Meyer Guggenheim came to America from Switzerland in 1848, in one of the early waves of Jewish settlement. Solomon R. Guggenheim, after whom the museum is named, was born in 1861, one of Meyer's seven sons, and he was to become the wealthiest of them. He went to Colorado in 1881 and bought into silver mines; by 1890, he and his brothers controlled mines all over the south-west and Mexico, as well as in Alaska, Latin America and Africa. With his wife, a Rothschild, Solomon began collecting art, the accepted symbol of wealth as great as theirs. In the conventional way, they began with safe Old Masters, but their (or at least his) taste changed radically after they met the formidable Baroness Hilla Rebay in 1926. This Central European lady of firm views and fiery temperament, something of a painter herself, introduced Guggenheim to the virtues of what was then called non-objective art, derided by conservative critics as pointless daubs on canvas. Under her auspices Guggenheim met Kandinsky in Germany in 1929 and thenceforth his collection was dominated by the Russian's work, though he also bought good abstracts by Leger, Klee, Chagall and others.

He lived in a suite at the Plaza Hotel and from time to time would exhibit part of his collection there until, in 1937, he established the Solomon Guggenheim Foundation with the object of creating a museum for non-objective art. Two years later it opened on 54th Street near Madison Avenue, with the Baroness as director. In 1943 Guggenheim commissioned Frank Lloyd Wright, by then seventy-three, to design a new building which in the event took sixteen years to complete and which neither Wright nor the founder lived to see opened. Wright had worked for Louis Sullivan in Chicago before starting an independent practice in 1893. He became known for his 'prairie houses', with gently sloping roofs, overhangs and terraces, precursors of the mass-produced ranch-style houses that proliferate in America's suburbs today; indeed he clearly foresaw the growth of present-day suburbia in his 1932 book *The Disappearing City*. After a fallow period which coincided roughly with the Depression, Wright began designing buildings with clear, geometric lines, in tune with the modern movement; the museum is decidedly of that period.

Guggenheim died in 1949, by which time the site on Fifth Avenue had been acquired but the daring design had still not been approved by the city planning authorities. The museum, meanwhile, was gaining a reputation for eccentricity and in 1951 the trustees replaced the Baroness with James Sweeney, a better administrator but no less difficult to get along with. He quarrelled constantly with Wright about the feasibility of exhibiting art effectively in his extraordinary building.

When the new museum finally opened in 1959 it was a huge success. Philip Johnson called it 'one of the greatest rooms erected in the twentieth century'. During the first few days there were lines to enter, to take the elevator up to the top floor and to descend the gently sloping ramp in ever decreasing circles, eyeing the works on the walls. The views of the interior itself, both from the ground floor and, especially, from the top looking down, are among the city's finest architectural offerings. Sadly, Wright died a few months before the building was completed and missed this vindication of his design. One of the museum's trustees commented: 'When your stock in trade is jewels, you need a jewel box to set them off.' The main body of the jewel box contains no permanent collection but is used for short-term exhibitions concentrating on the work of an artist or group of artists, in which the museum's holdings are augmented by loans. A sampling of the permanent collection is in a small gallery running off the ramp on the fourth floor, a short course in twentieth-century painting with forty-three works by such as Kandinsky, Chagall, Klee, Picasso Braque, Leger and Mondrian. In the gallery immediately below this, entered from the ramp on the second floor, are the exquisite works collected by Justin Thannhauser. Most of the seventy-five paintings here antedate the museum's own period of interest, being Impressionists and post-Impressionists: Pissarro's 'The Hermitage at Pontoise' stands out among the Impressionists, while Van Gogh's 'Mountains at Saint-Rémy' is the pick of the slightly later works. The forty Picassos include an especially strong group from the early part of his career, including one of his very first masterpieces, 'Moulin de la Galette' (1900). At the entrance to this gallery it's worth picking up the equipment for a free and informative audio tour of the collection. The small restaurant and book shop on the ground floor are accessible without entering the museum.

Two blocks north, with its entrance on 91st Street, is the rambling mansion, one of the most northerly of the grand Fifth Avenue houses, built at the turn of the century for Andrew Carnegie. A Scottish-born steel magnate and philanthropist, Carnegie had it built here because it was still fairly rural territory and he wanted a large garden. Today it houses the **Cooper-Hewitt Museum,** the Smithsonian Institution's National Museum of Design. Though its new function had demanded drastic alterations to some of the rooms, parts of the house are still as they were in Carnegie's time.

Carnegie came to America with his family in 1848, when he was thirteen, settling in Pennsylvania. His is another of the 'American dream' stories, where our hero accrues enormous wealth from lowly beginnings through a combination of hard work and of being in the right place at the right time. The Allegheny area of Pennsylvania was the right place because it was a center of the iron and steel industries which began to flourish in the 1870s. Carnegie's first job, at the age of fifteen, was as a messenger in a telegraph office in Pittsburgh. He soon joined the Pennsylvania Railroad, so impressing his superiors with his enthusiasm that by the time he was twenty-four he was a superintendent. He began buying stocks of railway-connected companies, including iron furnaces, and in 1865 left his job to concentrate on his iron investments, moving to New York, the financial center, in 1867. Six years later he financed his first steel mill and by 1877 his furnaces had a significant share of the growing market, a position greatly strengthened when he merged with Frick's coke company. Like many of the industrial Titans of the time, he was criticized — probably with justification — for ruthless business practices and hostility to organized labor, although he never provoked the depth of disgust afforded to Rockefeller in his prime. In 1901 he became possibly the wealthiest man in America when he sold his steel interests for $250 million to J. P. Morgan, who was amassing the huge United States Steel.

Having divested himself of his business responsibilities Carnegie was free to devote his energies and capital to philanthropy, which he pursued with as much fervor and professionalism as he had displayed in high finance, giving away $350 million during his lifetime. Like many self-made men, he was completely confident of the rectitude of his opinions, and in 1889 had written a trenchant little essay in the *North American Review* which later came to be known as 'The Gospel of Wealth'. In it, he set out his philosophy that it was the duty of the rich, having satisfied the needs of themselves and their immediate families, to devote their money to enterprises which would benefit the community, would 'help those who will help themselves', and to do so in their lifetimes.

> Poor and restricted are our opportunities in this life [he wrote], narrow our horizons, our best work most imperfect; but still men should be thankful for one inestimable boon. They have it in their power during their lives to busy themselves in organizing benefactions from which the masses of their fellows will derive lasting advantage, and thus dignify their own lives.

He summed up his views: 'The man who dies rich dies disgraced.' He fulfilled his precepts to the letter, undertaking good works in his native Scotland (which he would visit every summer) as well as in America, where education was among his chief target areas; nearly three-thousand public libraries were built with his funds. Carnegie Hall, the concert hall on West 57th Street, is the place most visitors connect with his name, but the Carnegie Corporation and Council concern themselves with funding higher education, and the Carnegie Endowment for International Peace is one of the most important private institutions for research into international affairs. Carnegie died in 1919, aged eighty-three.

His neo-Georgian house, though large, is unpretentious compared with the classical palaces his contemporaries were building; perhaps it is the red brick of the upper walls which gives it a rare cozy feeling. The entrance on 91st Street, beneath a pierced copper canopy, leads through a marble portal into a magnificent hall, panelled in warm oak from Carnegie's native land. The museum accommodates changing exhibitions of design and one is generally to be found on this ground floor, beginning in the hall and spreading west into Carnegie's panelled library. He was only 5 ft 2 in tall and the low clearance of the doorways to the library indicates that this was his private domain. It was here that he is said to have received appeals for philanthropy, so it was perhaps appropriate than many of the appellants should have had to bow their heads as they entered; while waiting for his response, they could read the uplifting mottoes around the walls.

The music room is the most westerly of those on the south side of the house, its airy French empire style contrasting with the more sombre rooms we have passed through so far. If you look at the gilt mouldings in the corners, with appropriate musical motifs, you will see that one represents the bagpipes. Next door is the garden vestibule, with windows designed by Louis Tiffany. The upper floor has been more drastically altered to accommodate its new role. Most of the old family bedrooms are unrecognizable, but the library still has its intricate teak carving, an original matching cabinet and a marquetry ceiling (if you turn right at the top of the stairs, it's the second entrance on your right).

If the Carnegie house is one of the more appealing on Fifth Avenue, the grey stone Warburg house, one block north, is among the most daunting, its high ceilings and French Renaissance pretensions giving it a cathedral-like air not wholly inappropriate to its present function. Fitted with a modern extension, this 1908 mansion is now the **Jewish Museum**. Most of its visitors, naturally enough, are Jewish, but there are interests here for everyone. In the second floor Music Room, which still contains a built-in harmonium, is a collection of elaborate religious silver and brass. On the third floor is the upper part of the entrance wall of a Persian synagogue which dates from 1550, looking more Persian than Jewish despite its Hebrew inscription. Here too is a section devoted to the archaeology of the Holy Land, including a slide show dramatizing the history of the children of Israel and a realistic life-sized model of a house used by the Israelites almost three thousand years ago.

Just before leaving Fifth Avenue for a few blocks, you can see the **International Center of Photography**, at No 1130 on the corner of 94th Street, which hosts changing photographic exhibitions. But now we're going to look at two quirkish buildings from the turn of the century. On Madison Avenue between 94th and 95th Streets, the fanciful red-brick turrets of the former fortress-like armory, with the legend 'Boutez en avant 1889-1894' have been retained and have inspired the form of the new buildings on the block, Hunter College Campus Schools. Turning left up 97th Street, back towards Fifth Avenue, you will come across the equally startling onion domes of the **Cathedral of St Nicholas**, the headquarters of the city's Russian Orthodox Church. To be properly startled you have to stay on the southern side of the street, because if you get too close you can't see the five cupolas — one large and four smaller — and, beneath them, the Russian effect of the colored brick, tiles and terra cotta. While nobody could really mistake it for St Basil's in Moscow, it does provide yet another testament to New York's ethnic diversity.

Back on Fifth again, walk past the ill-assorted buildings of Mount Sinai Hospital to 103rd Street and the **Museum of the City of New York**. It was built for the purpose in the 1930s but the bloated Georgian villa seems neither functionally nor historically appropriate. Still, this is one of my favorite museums in New York, though less appreciated than it should be because it's north of the main tourist drag (many visitors eschew the city north of the Guggenheim because they fear the encroachment of Harlem and its dangers). Those who want a lively insight into the origins and history of New York will find none better than in this small, crowded museum. The best place to start is the audio-visual display on the ground floor, along the hall to the right of the entrance. The screen folds out of a giant apple. 'The Big Apple' was the nickname given to New York by jazz musicians between the wars and has now been expropriated by the city for use in its tourism advertising. The display is a bright, twenty-minute dash through the city's past, using mainly the images on the screen but also some objects dotted about the room. The commentary is interspersed with silky, cynical and sentimental songs about New York from Broadway musicals: the whole presentation better portrays the excitement and diversity of the metropolis — in particular its native genius for showmanship — than anything else I have seen.

Back at the other end of this floor is a section about the original Dutch settlers. The centerpiece is a mock-up of one of the spurs of Fort Amsterdam, which stood on the site of the Custom House by Bowling Green. Climb on to the spur, sharing a platform with a replica of a seventeenth-century cannon, and look around at the carefully detailed, painted panorama of the city as it would have been forty years or so after the first settlers arrived; there's no better way of taking in the scale and geography of the early settlement nor of understanding why it developed as it did. Next in historical sequence, exhibits relating to New York's English period, up to the Revolution, are also on this floor, back in the direction of the Big Apple presentation. Here are two of Gilbert Stuart's portraits of George Washington, a corner of art of which you might excusably be tiring of if you've been following my itineraries conscientiously to date.

Upstairs, the pattern of the presentation switches from the historical to the topographical. Start by turning right at the top of the staircase into the series of six rooms from old homes, some actually transplanted from houses before they were demolished and some imaginatively recreated. The cycle begins in colonial times and ends with the extravagance of the early years of this century. The rooms are peopled by mannequins in period costumes and portray well the evolution of domestic life styles, as well as the city's rapidly increasing affluence in the 1800s.

A small room full of prints and maps gives part of the same story in a documentary form. Beyond that is a display of period silver and, towards the south wall, two galleries devoted to elements of the city's commercial life from which the nineteenth-century affluence sprang — the stock exchange and the port, the latter with some lovely pictures of the old clippers on South Street, as well as a few tremendous figureheads. Climb again, to many visitors' favorite part of the museum: the toys, the dolls and, especially, the dolls' houses, a fine collection reproducing the architectural styles of former times. Most intriguing is the Stettheimer House, built in 1925 as the replica of a smart country home and peopled with socialites of the 1920s: Alice B. Toklas is there, and so is Gertrude Stein. In the ballroom are miniature representations of the works of contemporary artists painted by the artists themselves. Marcel Duchamp contributed a small version of his 'Nude Descending a Staircase' and there are contributions from Alexander and Gela Archipenko. The doll collection is prettily displayed. Other toys include ingenious money boxes which grasp small coins and devour them.

On the top floor, not always open in recent years, are a bedroom and dressing room from the house of John D. Rockefeller on West 54th Street near Fifth Avenue, overpoweringly overdecorated for today's tastes, as well as surprisingly small. You could skip the basement unless you have a passion for fire engines, pumps and firemen's helmets, but before you leave, make time to look in the shop, which sells some of the most interesting and best-made souvenirs of New York. When you do leave, walk east down 103rd Street for the Lexington Avenue subway, or take a bus down Fifth Avenue.

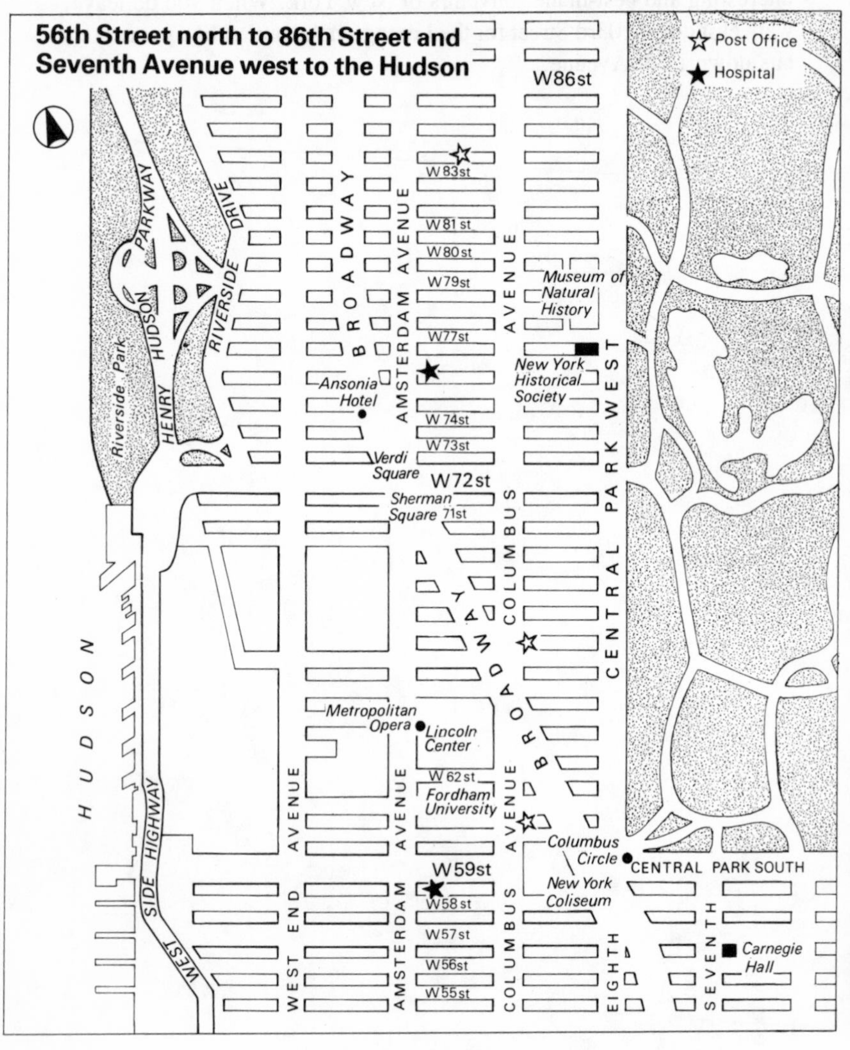

56th Street north to 86th Street and Seventh Avenue west to the Hudson
Post Office
Hospital
W86st
W83st
W81 st
W80st
W79st
W77st
W 74st
W73st
W72st
71st
W 62st
W59st
W58 st
W57st
W56st
W55st
BROADWAY
AMSTERDAM AVENUE
COLUMBUS AVENUE
CENTRAL PARK WEST
WEST END AVENUE
EIGHTH
SEVENTH
CENTRAL PARK SOUTH
Museum of Natural History
New York Historical Society
Ansonia Hotel
Verdi Square
Sherman Square
Metropolitan Opera
Lincoln Center
Fordham University
Columbus Circle
New York Coliseum
Carnegie Hall
RIVERSIDE DRIVE
HENRY HUDSON PARKWAY
Riverside Park
WEST SIDE HIGHWAY
HUDSON

14

The Upper West Side: Music, Music, Music

NEW YORK's status, now undisputed, as one of the world's most musical cities, was achieved only with difficulty. As the place grew in size and wealth its newly rich denizens decided they must rectify what they felt to be a general lack of 'culture'. In his book *Music Comes to America* David Ewen wrote:

> Famous European musicians came to this country to give concerts during the nineteenth century and returned to Europe with both well-filled purses and strange tales of American naiveté in music. There could be no denying that America, in music above everything else, was innocent; she was awkward and ingenuous and misinformed as only the very young and uneducated can be. She was sublimely oblivious of any standard of artistic excellence. What concerned her most in music seemed to be the obvious, the meretricious, the sensational . . .[14]

Nevertheless, when New York's renowned (though now demolished) opera house, the Metropolitan on Broadway south of Times Square, was erected in 1883, the primary motivation was not artistic but social. The burgeoning new rich found they couldn't get boxes at the fashionable Academy of Music, on 14th Street, because all were spoken for by members of the older aristocracy: so they simply built a new opera house, the three tiers of private boxes signalling unequivocally its chief function.

Carnegie Hall, built eight years later on the corner of 57th Street and Seventh Avenue had more legitimate musical overtones; the prime mover behind its building was Walter Damrosch, conductor, impresario and early enthusiast for Wagner. For years the hall, with two-thousand eight hundred seats, had an almost legendary aura as the pinnacle of achievement for every ambitious classical musician or singer, as well as for some more popular entertainers. But with the construction in the mid-1960s of Lincoln Center, Carnegie Hall's role in the city's cultural life was reduced to a secondary one and for a while it was even in danger of demolition. Now it's protected by a preservation order and, except for its high summer closing, keeps its seats well filled, often as a venue for visiting orchestras.

The hall is undistinguished architecturally, yet unmistakably of its period. The fifteen-storey tower of studios to the east throws it out of kilter and the ugly fire escape along the Seventh Avenue wall does nothing to enhance its appeal. Though there are no formal tours for visitors, you will normally be allowed inside if you go to the stage door on 56th Street and there is no rehearsal in progress. The auditorium is painted white with gold highlights and has red plush seats; such restraint denoted a serious purpose in an era when theatrical interiors vied with each other for the extravagance of their decor. The best of all ways of seeing the inside, of course, is to get a ticket for a concert. If you do that, reserve a table for after the performance at the Russian Tea Room, a little way east along 57th Street, at No 150. This old and deservedly renowned restaurant is a New York classic. The Edwardian decor, red and gold, is wonderfully atmospheric, the service slick and the food interesting — variations on Russian dishes such as chicken Kiev, borscht and blinis (stuffed pancakes).

The walk from Carnegie Hall to Lincoln Center takes us past a clutch of expensive apartment houses of varying vintage and quality; within walking distance of both Central Park and the Fifth Avenue stores, this has long been a desirable residential area of central Manhattan. On the south-east corner of 58th Street and Seventh Avenue, is **Alwyn Court**, which boasts the most fanciful exterior in the city, an extravaganza of French Renaissance terra cotta detailing done in 1909 by architects apparently determined that no square inch of the building should remain unadorned. If you think it's all too much, just compare it with the functional and dreary modern block, complete with resort hotel balconies, on the west side of Seventh Avenue at the corner of Central Park South. The excesses of the Alwyn are greatly to be preferred.

Walk west along Central Park South. At the corner of the park is **Columbus Circle**, the statue of the Italian navigator surrounded by a jumble of incompatible buildings, mostly modern. Facing you on the far side is the blank and characterless Coliseum, a venue for trade shows. The curious Moorish structure to the south was built as a gallery of modern art but is now the headquarters of the city's Department of

Cultural Affairs. The ground floor has a visitors' bureau where useful maps, leaflets, information and cheap theatre vouchers can be obtained. To the north, just west of the park, the slender black and white Gulf and Western skyscraper has a 43rd-floor restaurant and bar providing a first-rate view of the park.

Now walk up Broadway, which runs off at an angle at Columbus Circle. At 62nd Street and Columbus Avenue, on the left, is the beginning of **Lincoln Center**, the performing arts complex built in the mid-1960s. The idea for the center originated with the desire of the Metropolitan Opera to move out of its aging building near Times Square (plans for the opera to go to Rockefeller Center had collapsed with the Depression, thirty years earlier). At the same time the New York Philharmonic Orchestra was coming to the end of its lease on Carnegie Hall, so the idea of an arts center bringing together all New York's major companies began to take shape. Lincoln Square, one of the city's worst slums and due fairly urgently for redevelopment, seemed a natural site. John D. Rockefeller III was one of the principal benefactors for the scheme, which is why Wallace Harrison, essentially the family's house architect (he had done much of the work on Rockefeller Center) was brought in to mastermind the design, along with Max Abramovitz, his partner since 1941.

Harrison's idea was to get different architects to create individual buildings but to make sure that they blended easily with one another. Thus all are faced with white Travertine marble — the material used for the plaza which they surround. The three main halls are all modern variations of classical colonnaded design. They aroused inevitable controversy when they were built and even now architecture critics are sniffy about them, though the prevailing view is that they are at least preferable to the unimaginative apartment buildings which sprang up in the surrounding streets, on the coat-tails, as it were, of Lincoln Center.

Approaching from Broadway, you walk into the Center's courtyard, a fountain in the middle and the three main halls around it. Directly in front of you is the largest, the Metropolitan Opera House, designed by Harrison himself and seating nearly four thousand people. On the left is the New York State Theater, the work of Philip Johnson and home of the city opera and ballet companies. On the right, Avery Fisher Hall is the venue for concerts of the New York Philharmonic Orchestra. When first built it was called the Philharmonic Hall but because the acoustics in Max Abramovitz's original interior plan were so abysmal it had to go through a series of expensive modifications. Finally, bounteous Mr. Avery Fisher donated $10 million to have the inside stripped away and replaced with the oak panelling which now provides a nearly perfect sound; and the name of the hall was changed as a mark of gratitude to its benefactor. The other main building, Eero Saarinen's Vivian Beaumont Theater, is at the far end of the second courtyard, where a Henry Moore reclining figure basks in a reflecting pool. Sandwiched between the theatre and the back of the opera house is a branch of the New York public library devoted to records and books concerning the performing arts, with a small museum and art gallery above. Near its entrance is another monumental sculpture, Alexander Calder's 'Le Guichet'.

The most convenient way to see the Center is to take a guided tour. These leave every hour or so (depending on the season and the demand) from the basement of the Metropolitan Opera House. Since only twenty people can be accommodated on each tour it's a good plan, if you are on a tight schedule, to phone ahead and reserve places. The itineraries vary with daily events. If rehearsals are in progress you will get a chance to see and hear them, but from a glass control booth instead of from inside the auditorium, which you will sometimes not be allowed to enter at all. You can ask about the timing of rehearsals when you make your reservation but the information may not be precise.

The tour route may begin at the **New York State Theater**, the most lush of the interiors, designed by Johnson on a jewel box motif; the lights inside the pretty two-thousand eight-hundred seat auditorium sparkle like precious stones. At the back, the grand promenade is a large rectangle, with four tiers of galleries for perambulations, its railings formed of an unusual bronze filigree and the ceiling papered with twenty-two-carat gold leaf. At either end two plump marble statues by Elie Nadelman display appropriately festive moods. The Polish-born Nadelman came to New York from Paris in 1916 and within two years his geometric portrait sculptures, built from curves and spheres, had become fashionable in high society. Later he became absorbed in American folk art; his productivity and popularity declined but his place in the history of art is assured by the influence he exerted on Modigliani.

The tour moves to the **Opera House,** graced by Chagall murals (covered over in the morning to protect them from the sun) and by Austrian glass chandeliers, in the lobby and the auditorium, where they surprise first-timers by floating up to the ceiling just before the performance begins. The auditorium is an updated version of classic opera house design, with a colossal stage, plush seats and elaborate backstage technical facilities. In the basement, a small gallery is devoted to the history of American music and in particular of the Metropolitan Opera. A gift shop on the lobby level (the Opera Shop) sells records, books about music and imaginative souvenirs, and in the basement the Performing Arts Shop stocks items from the Center's annual gift catalogue, ranging from an inlaid music box at $2,500 to chocolates with Mozart's picture on the wrappers. The top floor restaurant affords views of the Center and surrounding streets.

Avery Fisher Hall is the social hub of the complex, at least by day, by virtue of containing the most popular catering facilities. On a fine day try lunch — quiche or a variety of salads — at the Fountain Café outside the hall: you serve yourself and sit at ease by one of the white metal tables, watching the world. Many, especially nearby office workers, bring sandwiches and eat them near the fountain or reflecting pool, or in the area to the left of the Opera House, pleasantly shaded with closely-planted pollarded planes, called Damrosch Park after a musical pioneer. The bandshell, an inverted tulip shape, is from time to time the venue for dance and folk music concerts. Rather more impromptu performances take place around the fountain, where there is a greater pedestrian flow.

Whatever you feel about the quality of the architecture, the Center as a whole works in that it creates an atmosphere of cultured calm, almost studied refinement. Just as the plaza lies slightly above the level of the surrounding streets, so is the cultural plane deliberately elevated — a symbol that the city has outgrown the huckstering approach to the fine arts which David Ewen noted. It's not that the ticket prices are especially high — for the city ballet and opera companies at the State Theater they are lower than for most Broadway musicals — but that the whole complex has an aloof quality. It was deemed necessary to make it so in order to attract the suburban middle classes to a part of town whose reputation had been unsavory. All the same there is, as so often happens, an ironic contradiction between the reality and the hyperbole which accompanied the Center's creation. In the northwest corner of the plaza containing the reflecting pool and the Henry Moore is a plaque bearing the words with which John D. Rockefeller III — not one of nature's populists — inaugurated the Center in 1963. 'The arts are not for the privileged few, but for the many,' it says. 'Their place is not at the periphery of daily life, but at its center.' However, if you go to read this plaque you'll notice that it stands on a high wall separating the plaza from the street below, one of the most criticized aspects of the architecture for the very reason that it symbolizes cultural apartheid. The road runs as a gully between the high wall of the plaza on the south and the Juilliard School for musicians and dancers on the north; a footbridge links the two arts fortifications. The Alice Tully recital hall, alongside the Juilliard School, completes the set of performance venues.

Tickets for the major ballet and opera companies are generally sold out in advance but even if you cannot get into a performance it is worth spending time at the Center at night, when the lobbies of the three main halls are lit and visible through the glass walls, the chandeliers of the Opera House giving an especially romantic and sparkling effect. At night, too, the social mix of strollers in and around the complex is spiced by the inclusion of 'mature' students from the midtown campus of Fordham University, the modern buildings just south of Lincoln Center. A Catholic University based in the Bronx, this Manhattan outpost of Fordham was built in the early 1970s just in time to cater to the growing urge of many New Yorkers to get themselves better educated. The urge hasn't gone away, and the rolls of Fordham's evening degree classes are still healthy. If there is a typical student it's a woman in her late thirties, with children in their early teens, who feels she has failed to make the most of what life has to offer. In Manhattan, where everybody bustles around so purposefully, making a fine show of being busy and involved, such feelings of being left out are fairly common and psychiatrists earn fortunes telling people how to cope with them. One way of coping is to go to college, take a degree in law, social studies, psychology or whatever, with the intention of beginning a new career. Once they have acquired their degree, many students do not in fact begin new careers: but they feel better.

Our daytime tour continues north from Lincoln Center up Columbus Avenue, penetrating the chunk of the city loosely called the Upper West Side, which stretches from Lincoln Center in the south to the edge of Harlem in the north, and from Central Park in the east to the Hudson River in the west, with Broadway its main artery. Though its social status has risen and fallen over the years, the area has retained its essential character as a home for the city's Central European immigrants, chiefly Jewish, who moved here once they had earned enough to leave the Lower East

Side. The richest moved into the apartment buildings overlooking the west side of the park and into the cross-streets running between there and Columbus Avenue, which is what Ninth Avenue becomes at 59th Street.

After Central Park West, the next most desirable West Side buildings for socially mobile Central Europeans were on Riverside Drive overlooking the Hudson. The grey and dreary West End Avenue, one block inland, was a notch further down the social scale. In the 1950s and 1960s the east-west streets between Columbus (Ninth) and Amsterdam (Tenth) Avenues became the home of newer Spanish-speaking immigrants, adding an extra ingredient to the culture mix and one immortalized in *West Side Story*. A decade or so later young single people, finding the rents less oppressive than on the Upper East Side, began to move in and stamp their own character on the neighborhood.

When I first knew Columbus Avenue it was a fairly bleak thoroughfare, lined with crumbling tenements and service establishments — food shops, shady bars, launderettes, cheap shoe shops, flop-houses, Spanish snack bars and the like. Some of these survive but more and more the avenue reflects its improved social standing. Those tenements that do remain have had a fresh coat of paint outside and have been doctored inside to match. The bars, formerly the haunt of sweaty men in shirtsleeves and women of questionable reputation, have been transformed into sleek singles bars; the shoe shops have become boutiques and the cheap eating houses are now expensive eating houses with handwritten menus and white table linen: you'll see them as you walk up the avenue from the Lincoln Center. One of the older restaurants, dating from the Hispanic influx, is Victor's Cuban Café on the corner of 71st Street. At weekends they have roast suckling pig and their black bean soup is thick and spicy all week long. Take a hearty appetite.

Turn left down 72nd Street, the chief east-west artery of the Upper West Side, also showing effects of 'gentrification' though less pronounced than on Columbus Avenue. A couple of old kosher restaurants survive, as do an Irish bar or two. On the north side of the street, not long before you reach the junction with Broadway, is the Eclair restaurant and cake shop, one of a small chain specializing in Viennese cakes and confectionery, with an unobtrusive restaurant in the rear where you can eat carefully prepared Central European food in a pleasantly relaxing setting, the whiff of fresh-baked cakes tempting all but the strongest-minded to plump for dessert with the excellent coffee. But the clientele as much as anything lends the Eclair its stamp of authenticity: the older folk sit munching poppyseed cake, talk animatedly in German and recreate for themselves and us the atmosphere of European cities some of them may not have seen for forty years.

The junction of 72nd Street, Amsterdam Avenue and Broadway used to be known as Needlepoint Park for two reasons. The first is the narrow needle-like strip of park to the north of the junction, coming to a point at 72nd Street, a statue of Verdi in its center. The second reason is that in the 1960s and 1970s this became a prime location for the sale and use of heroin, injected from usually dirty hypodermic needles. Its reputation is now a bit less unsavory although, like nearly all New York's public spaces, it harbors its share of the unhappy and the unhinged. South of the junction is a rare survivor, an above-ground subway kiosk dating from the beginnings of the system, like the other, prettier one at the Battery.

The Ansonia Hotel at Broadway and 74th Street, built in the same year as the subway station (1904), is a more obviously appealing relic, among the best surviving examples of the turn-of-the-century attempt to make parts of New York look like Paris. It was built as an apartment hotel for musicians and singers, within a demi-quaver of Carnegie Hall, so the rooms have thick, nearly sound-proof walls. It is the exterior which people adore, a tremendous collection of bulbous towers, cornices, crevices and narrow iron balconies, decorated with a flourish of imaginative terra cotta. A move to pull it down in the early 1970s, to make way for a potentially lucrative modern apartment building, provoked such an outcry — especially from those musicians who still lived there — that it was deservedly designated a landmark. It's one of those buildings where it's best, if you can, to avert your eyes from the street floor, where the demands of commerce have dictated modernization. At the south-west corner of the junction of Broadway with 79th Street stands the limestone mass of the Apthorp apartments, typical of the grandest such built in the early years of the century, less decorated than the Ansonia or the Alwyn, but not lacking in fancy scrollwork and cornices all the same. Ornate iron gates lead to the central courtyard, where once carriages would drive around the fountain to set passengers off at the entrance.

Two blocks north on Broadway is **Zabar**'s. Here, in a single shop, the diverse culture and appetites of the Upper West Side are encapsulated. Always crowded, always noisy, with customers bantering or arguing with the help, Zabar's is New York's most distinctive and best-stocked food shop. Visit it just for the smells and to watch the people, but you'll probably come away with at least a morsel of cheese, at most an armful of the latest kitchen implements. One of the cheese salesmen will advise you if you're bewildered by the variety, but don't be surprised if he does so with flip off-handedness or even brusqueness: New York delicatessen workers have a reputation, which they zealously protect, for insouciance and a caustic tongue. Once you've gone beyond the cheese and the kitchen implements you can start sniffing again at the smoked sausages, then hunt through the array of canned imported delicacies, pass by the caviar and smoked fish counter (soused herring and chopped liver are worth trying) until you reach the bakery, the home-made pasta and the exit. Zabar's tells you as much about the Upper West Side as Fortnum and Mason's tells you about Mayfair and St James's in London. The two food emporiums could hardly be less similar: the one permanently bustling, on the verge of chaos, the other carpeted, well-ordered and sleek; but that's the whole point. You can try some of Zabar's delicacies at their coffee and cake shop on the corner of 81st Street or, if you leave with something delicious, buy some warm bagels to go with it at the bagel shop across 81st, on the same side of Broadway, and take it all into Riverside Park for a picnic overlooking the Hudson.

Walk two short blocks west down 81st Street, then two blocks south for the park entrance opposite 79th Street. Laid out, like Central Park, by Frederick Law Olmsted, this thin strip of a park is a precious amenity for those who live here. When you get to the 79th Street entrance you pass under a bridge and go down some steps at the traffic circle: these take you to an arcaded walkway leading to a terrace overlooking the river and the boat basin. The view of New Jersey is scarcely thrilling but you can ogle the expensive cabin cruisers moored here. Steps on your right lead to a riverside promenade which does offer fine views of the George Washington Bridge. Follow the path north and stick to it when it curves away from the river under a bridge. Climb the steps on your right, then steer between a hillock and a children's playground and you are back level with 83rd Street.

Those not too tired or overfed to walk farther can head back south and east towards the American Museum of Natural History, opposite Central Park between 77th and 81st Streets. The best street to walk east on is 80th, lined with terraced houses largely unaltered from the turn of the century. New Yorkers persist in calling these brownstones, a term which has become a generic name for the city's Victorian terraces, but most of these are not in fact built of the sandstone which pervades farther downtown. By the time this area came to be developed, people were bored with brown and bored with Italianate architecture, and began experimenting with a number of different materials and styles, with mixed aesthetic results.

The American Museum of Natural History is the largest of its kind in the world (the *Guinness Book of Records* says the largest of *any* kind in the world) and those interested or involved in that field may want to spend a full day here. The sections on dinosaurs, mammals, birds and precious stones — displayed with a flair for the spectacular — are popular with children who also enjoy the sky shows at the adjacent Hayden Planetarium. The museum complex was begun in 1872, with extra bits added from time to time since. The main entrance is on Central Park West near the center of the building. Guided tours are usually available; otherwise the best plan is to take the elevators from the far side of the soaring entrance hall to the fourth floor and see the exhibits from the top down. This works chronologically, too, for the fourth floor is the home of the dinosaurs, as well as of a section explaining the origins of the earth. You will hardly be able to miss the tremendous brontosaurus which dominates the early dinosaur room, or the parade of mastodons down the center of the late mammals. Watch for the eerie montage of ground sloths, bathed in a dim red light, in the early mammal section.

The display technique in the animal and bird departments is to show the stuffed beasts in dramatic simulated environments: bears, lions, deer and eagles, transfixed in forests and prairies represented in skillfully authentic detail. Before the advent of television and films this must have seemed powerfully exciting, but it's a bit tame in an era when film of the animals in their habitat is so commonly available. Many of these sections, therefore, now have a musty air, which the high-ceilinged, often ill-lit exhibition halls do nothing to alleviate; some modernization is going on, however. On the third floor rooms devoted to Eastern Woodlands and Plains Indians contain some striking pieces of primitive art, as do those on the second floor dealing with Africa and Central America. The newly organized Hall of Asia on the second floor is more sophisticated, both in its content and its manner of display. Mammals and birds of New York city are also explained on the second floor. Adults finding it a bit too much may retreat to a gloomy little bar on this floor, in among the mammals, like some bizarre nightclub with an eccentric theme.

One of the most popular segments is the recently opened hall of gems, minerals and meteorites on the ground floor in the extreme south-west corner. This multi-level, carpeted area is effectively lit and dotted with audio-visual displays explaining how gems and minerals are formed; the exhibits are said to be worth more than $50 million. Most of the museum's other highlights are also on the ground floor. Just south of the main entrance, the ocean life section is dominated by a life-sized model of a giant whale, suspended from the ceiling; the cases surrounding it contain effective underwater simulations. By the entrance to that section is the Discovery Room, where on weekend afternoons, children can handle various objects (skulls, etc.) while the staff explain them. South of here again is one of my favorite segments, devoted to forests, with magnified and life-sized dioramas. The display called the Biology of Man, just before you get to the minerals, contains a model of a transparent body, demonstrating its inner workings. Near the 77th Street entrance the section on Northwest Coast Indians has many authentic totem poles as well as a canoe, 64½ ft long, made from the hollowed trunk of a cedar. The museum shop, by the 77th Street entrance, has replicas of some objects as well as interesting jewelry and items loosely related to natural history, including books and records.

One block south, on Central Park West, is another museum of somewhat specialized interest, that of the **New York Historical Society**. It contains a selection of objects and documents relating to US history. The collection of prints, maps and photographs of New York is unequalled and should be seen by anyone who wants seriously to understand the city's growth. The ground floor accommodates temporary displays while the basement is devoted to transportation, with a good collection of horse-drawn carriages. A set of photographs here shows what a blessing it was for Manhattan to be rid of the hideous elevated railway which blighted so many of its avenues for some fifty years.

Admirers of James Audubon's bird pictures will want to come here too, for many of the original water-colors are on display in a charming gallery on the second floor. On the same floor are a few period rooms from colonial times — less ambitious than the rooms in the American Wing of the Metropolitan Museum but carefully authentic nonetheless —

as well as a splendid 1766 façade and doorway from a house in Connecticut. Small collections of paperweights, ceramics and glass, including a few langorous pieces of Tiffany's iridescent gold favrile glass, enhance the displays on this floor. On the third floor the folk art section includes some intriguing home-made kitchen implements and early manufactured gadgets, evidence of the great American talent for the invention of labor-saving devices. Another native skill, advertising, is represented by nineteenth-century posters, some of them hilarious.

The fourth floor is devoted to furniture and historic paintings, including another Gilbert Stuart rendering of George Washington. Aaron Burr looks as dissolute as his reputation leads one to believe, and in sore need of a shave. When you've had your fill, walk back towards the American Museum of Natural History for the 81st Street stop on the Eighth Avenue subway.

15

Harlem and Points North

WE HAVE COME to the end of that part of Manhattan which may conveniently be tackled in day-long walks; north of Central Park the things you will want to see are too widely scattered. Yet you ought to visit Harlem, one of the city's most famous and most distinctive areas. Because of its size and because some parts are unsafe for strangers, a bus tour is a good idea, at least to get your bearings; you can always go back later and investigate more closely.

Harlem used to be a farming community comfortably distant from the city. The Dutch founded it and called it Nieu Haarlem, after a town in Holland. By the middle of the nineteenth century the farmlands had become exhausted and neat country cottages began to appear in what was the city's earliest suburb. When the population expanded explosively in the 1870s, squatters moved into abandoned fields but by the 1890s building speculators were catching up with the mounting population and, having filled most of Manhattan south of 110th Street, started putting up in Harlem apartment buildings and row houses in the same styles as those appearing almost simultaneously on the Upper West Side. The speculators had, however, been over-ambitious. They had simply built too many apartments and it was naturally those farthest from the city center which were hardest to fill, even though Harlem was by then conveniently linked with downtown areas by the elevated railway. In the first years of this century Phillip Payton, a Black real estate agent, bought some of the empty buildings and rented them out to Blacks who had formerly lived in midtown. By the 1920s Harlem, stretching from 110th to 162nd Street, was almost exclusively Black. That remains true today of its western section, the eastern part having become Spanish Harlem, the province of Puerto Ricans and other Spanish-speaking immigrants.

In the 1920s the nightspots of Harlem, in particular the Cotton Club, Small's and later the Apollo Theater, became fashionable with young white New Yorkers in search of an exotic night out. 'Let's Go Slumming' was the crude theme song of that era. Entertainers such as Josephine

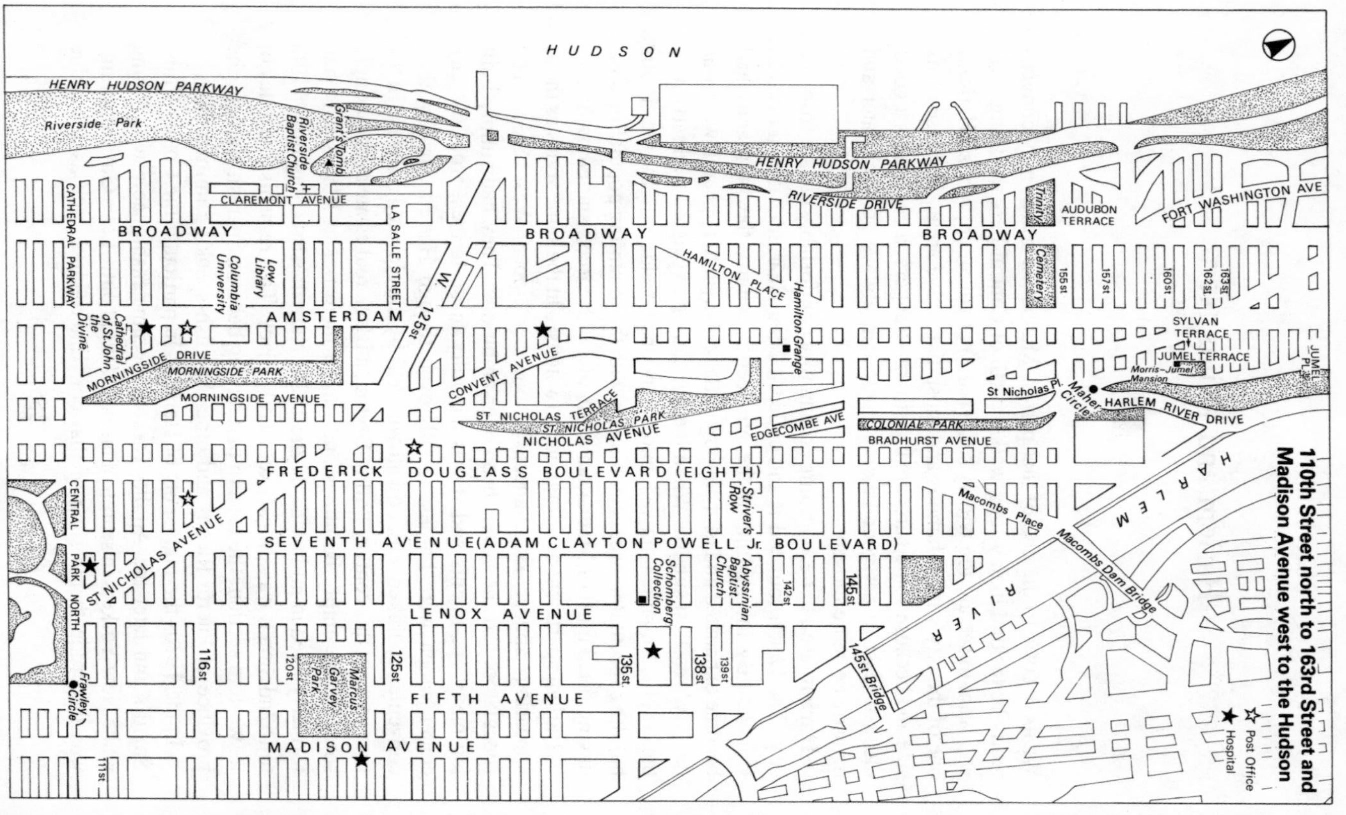

110th Street north to 163rd Street and Madison Avenue west to the Hudson
Post Office
Hospital
HUDSON
HENRY HUDSON PARKWAY
Riverside Park
Riverside Baptist Church
Grant's Tomb
CLAREMONT AVENUE
RIVERSIDE DRIVE
FORT WASHINGTON AVE
AUDUBON TERRACE
Trinity
Cemetery
CATHEDRAL PARKWAY
BROADWAY
Columbia University
Low Library
LA SALLE STREET
W. 125st
HAMILTON PLACE
Hamilton Grange
155st
157st
160st
162st
163st
AMSTERDAM
Cathedral of St John the Divine
SYLVAN TERRACE
JUMEL TERRACE
JUMEL PL.
Morris-Jumel Mansion
MORNINGSIDE DRIVE
MORNINGSIDE PARK
MORNINGSIDE AVENUE
CONVENT AVENUE
ST NICHOLAS TERRACE
ST NICHOLAS PARK
NICHOLAS AVENUE
EDGECOMBE AVE
COLONIAL PARK
BRADHURST AVENUE
St Nicholas Pl.
Maher Circle
HARLEM RIVER DRIVE
HARLEM
RIVER
FREDERICK DOUGLASS BOULEVARD (EIGHTH)
CENTRAL PARK NORTH
Striver's Row
Macombs Place
Macombs Dam Bridge
SEVENTH AVENUE (ADAM CLAYTON POWELL Jr. BOULEVARD)
ST NICHOLAS AVENUE
Schomberg Collection
Abyssinian Baptist Church
142st
145st
LENOX AVENUE
116st
120st
Marcus Garvey Park
125st
135st.
138st
139st
145st Bridge
Frawley Circle
FIFTH AVENUE
MADISON AVENUE
111st

Baker, Lena Horne and Duke Ellington made their names here and during the years of Prohibition the clubs were notorious sources of bootleg liquor. Because many white people encountered Blacks only in such a setting, the stereotype of the happy-go-lucky singing and dancing Black man was reinforced: many Blacks believe it was a factor which contributed to uneasy race relations during and after the Second World War and certainly that image was distant from the sombre reality of everyday life as lived in Harlem.

Several companies run tours of Harlem but if you want to be sure of getting a Black perspective, go with the Penny Sightseeing Company. Formed by a Black woman nearly forty years ago and employing Black guides, they run three tours a week: check in at the company's cramped office on the fifth floor of 303 West 42nd Street, on the corner of Eighth Avenue. One of the virtues of the Penny Sightseeing Company's tour is that it makes no attempt to hide the blighted areas — although the guide does ask, for the sake of the residents' pride and susceptibilities, that visitors do not attempt to photograph them. At the north-west corner of Central Park the bus enters Harlem at Frederick Douglass Circle, a desolate traffic circle named after the early Black advocate of social reform (Eighth Avenue north of the circle was a few years ago renamed Frederick Douglass Boulevard). Douglass escaped from the slavery into which he was born in 1817 to become a 'free colored man' in New Bedford, Massachusetts, a condition he found scarcely preferable. In 1841 he became a speaker for the Anti-Slavery Society, valued for his powers of oratory. 'Aliens are we in our native land,' he said at an anti-slavery meeting in 1854. 'The fundamental principles of the republic, to which the humblest white man, whether born here or elsewhere, may appeal with confidence, in the hope of awakening a favorable response, are held to be inapplicable to us.'[15] By the 1870s Douglass had become a sufficiently prominent figure to be appointed to a series of national positions. These were not posts of much importance or authority. Some were jobs for which a Black man was especially appropriate — ambassadorial assignments to Caribbean countries. He was one of America's first 'token Blacks' in the days before that phrase became fashionable.

The tour begins with some of the area's benign aspects. It stops briefly for a glimpse of the unfinished **Cathedral of St John the Divine**: this is worth more of your attention and I include it in a short walking tour of the Columbia University area later in the chapter. The bus continues north along Morningside Park and the campus of City College, an institution of higher learning which made no charge to students for tuition until the 1970s. Many successful people in the New York professions today came from poor immigrant families and were able to get a proper education only through the existence of City College on this 1905 campus, whose architecture is a cheerful mix of the Elizabethan and the Gothic.

North up Convent Avenue, beyond 145th Street, we enter the section called **Sugar Hill,** because it was where successful Black people would move into spacious detached or row houses to live what the less fortunate thought of as the sweet life. They are still some of the most desirable of Harlem's residences. As the bus passes the side streets, look down them and notice that the terraced houses are, even if in some cases badly dilapidated, closer to their original appearance than many in lower Manhattan. Most have kept the original steps and balustrades leading up to the front door, whereas downtown many have had the steps taken away to improve pedestrian flow.

The second stop on the Penny bus tour, while technically in Harlem is scarcely of it. The **Morris-Jumel mansion** at Edgecombe Avenue and 160th Street dates from 1765, when it was built by Lt-Col. Roger Morris, an English officer, on a bluff overlooking the Harlem River and across the Bronx, Long Island. When the Revolutionary War began Morris remained loyal to Britain and returned there, abandoning the house which was taken over by the Revolutionary Army: George Washington made it his headquarters after his defeat on Long Island and during the battle of Harlem Heights. When he retreated from New York the British moved in and used the house as quarters for their officers.

In 1810 Stephen Jumel, a Frenchman making his fortune as a New York wine merchant, bought the house and his American wife Eliza set about refurbishing it. He died in 1832, leaving her a wealthy widow. The following year she married the discredited former Vice-President Aaron Burr in a ceremony in the parlor on the left of the house entrance, whose suite of black and gold empire furniture, dating from about that time, makes it one of the most attractive rooms. Burr was seventy-eight when they married and Mme Jumel was twenty years younger. The union lasted only four months before the crusty bridegroom moved out.

Most of the furnishings and decoration are of Mme Jumel's period, and there are striking reproductions of contemporary wallpapers. Among these, the 'architectural' paper in the main hall, with its trompe l'oeil columns, stands out: so does the green paper in the parlor, with vertical rows of twined branches and leaves. Of the furniture, notable pieces are a sofa in the entrance hall made by Duncan Phyfe, and a 'sleigh bed', with curved ends, in Mme Jumel's bedroom upstairs, which is said to have belonged to Napoleon. This claim is also made for some of the chairs in that room and the chandelier in the parlor, but there is no convincing evidence for it. There are scattered pieces from the second half of the eighteenth century, when the house was built, but the only room fully furnished in that style is the drawing-room on the right side of the main entrance. Externally, it's a mixture of original colonial architecture and the Federal modifications imposed on it by Jumel. The Federal front door, with side windows, was one of Jumel's innovations and so was the colonnaded portico. Even if you do not take the Harlem tour you should try to see this house under your own steam. By subway, it's a few minutes' walk from both the IRT West Side local station at 157th Street (train No 1) and the IND local (AA) at 163rd Street. From both stations, make for 160th Street and walk east. The No 3 Madison Avenue bus goes within a block of the mansion but takes a long time from midtown.

By the entrance to the mansion is a quaint and rare street of frame houses, **Sylvan Terrace**, from the mid-nineteenth century. **Jumel Terrace**, at right angles to this, is a row of brownstones where, at No 16, Paul Robeson lived for the last years of his life. Though he spent his childhood in Princeton, New Jersey, and wandered the globe for much of his adult life, he lived in Harlem for a number of separate periods. The son of a minister, Robeson showed early promise academically, athletically and musically. At seventeen, in 1915, he won a competition for Rutgers University in New Brunswick, not far from Princeton. As a Black boy in the early years of the century he took for granted many instances of institutionalized discrimination, but as a lone Black youth in a white college he was exposed starkly to the reality of unreasoned prejudice. An outstanding American football player, his membership on the all-white team was at first resisted and one or two teams from other colleges refused to play against him. When he left Rutgers he moved to Harlem for the first time and entered Columbia University Law School, across Morningside Park. In 1920 he made his first professional stage appearance with the Provincetown Players down in Greenwich Village. When seeking a position as a lawyer he came up against prejudice again and, largely because he needed the money, the stage played an ever larger part in his life. He took the leading role in Eugene O'Neill's *The Emperor Jones*, which gave him the chance to use his magnificent, resonant singing voice. In 1925 he went to London with the play, beginning a pattern of splitting his life between the two sides of the Atlantic that was to last until the 1950s.

Robeson liked London because, with no substantial Black population of their own then, the English lionized rather than discriminated against him. He often returned and was for a while better known there than in his native land, though he had a New York success singing 'Ol' Man River' in Jerome Kern's *Showboat*. Paying his first visit to the Soviet Union in 1935, he became entranced by the Communist experiment and from that point his political views moved further left. On the outbreak of the Second World War he returned to the United States and there achieved probably the pinnacle of his fame when he played Othello on Broadway. With the Americans and Russians allies against Germany, his pro-Soviet views were scarcely an embarrassment, but when the cold war started in earnest he became increasingly estranged from the political mainstream. Still enraged by racial discrimination in America, he was convinced that the Soviet system held the answer. In 1949 he caused a furore at home when he told a conference of pacifists in Paris that American Blacks would not necessarily take up arms against the Russians in the event of war between the two countries. The following year, with the outbreak of the war in Korea and the growth of the McCarthyite Red scare, his passport was confiscated and he was unable to travel for eight years. In the later years of his life, as east-west tensions relaxed a little, he was reincorporated into American society. At the height of his unpopularity his name had been removed from the honor roll of Rutgers football players: it was replaced, and he was invited to sing more concerts. In 1963 he moved to Jumel Terrace, where he died in 1974.

After the Morris-Jumel break, the bus tour takes us back into Harlem proper down Frederick Douglass Boulevard (Eighth Avenue), crossing to Adam Clayton Powell Jr. Boulevard (Seventh Avenue). Ugly red-brick apartment buildings, box-like and unadorned save by graffiti, loom over streets of what were once terraced houses of considerable elegance. On 138th and 139th Streets between Seventh and Eighth Avenues are still some fine groups of houses, built at the turn of the century for white residents and designed by the most fashionable architects of the time, including Stanford White who was responsible for those on the north side of 139th Street. When the district became Black these houses were known as **Strivers' Row,** because they were the homes of the rising Black elite.

As the bus moves back down the avenues you'll see some of the sights for which Harlem has become notorious: burnt-out and exhausted buildings, with sleeping tramps sprawled in the doorways and on the pavements, clutching bottles in brown paper bags. Youths loiter on corners, scarcely bothering to be surreptitious about conducting a trade in drugs. The tour guide explains the economic conditions which produce such scars on the cityscape.

The bus stops at the **Abyssinian Baptist Church** on 138th Street, between Lenox Avenue and the boulevard named for the Rev. Adam Clayton Powell Jr., the figure with whom the church is most closely associated. Powell's father was its first minister, having moved the congregation to Harlem from midtown New York in the 1920s. In 1937 he retired and Adam Jr. became minister, combining the office with a leading role in the growing movement for Black rights. In 1936 he had helped form the National Negro Congress and two years later a committee seeking to increase employment opportunities for Blacks in New York, which by 1930 had the largest Black community in the country. It was scandalous that the shops and stores along 125th Street, the main shopping street in Harlem, were mostly white-owned and employed white assistants, although the people they served were by that time almost exclusively Black. In the same way the buses that served Harlem were driven only by whites. Powell organized boycotts of the shops and buses and won their agreement to employ Black workers. Discrimination was, however, still rife in many other areas. Protest meetings were held on street corners and in August 1943 a race riot broke out in Harlem, sparked by allegations of brutality by a white policeman against a Black serviceman.

In 1941 Powell, then aged thirty-three, had become the first Black politician elected to the New York city council. Three years later he was elected to Congress as New York's first black representative, where he contributed to numerous pieces of legislation aimed at helping Blacks and the poor. The last decade of his career in Washington was beset with controversy. The object of persistent inquiries by the income tax authorities, and then of other suggestions of impropriety involving public funds, he was excluded from Congress in 1967 by a majority vote of its members. Powell and his supporters labelled the exclusion racist. The Harlem voters showed where they stood by re-electing him both at a special election in 1967 and again in the regular election in 1968. He was defeated in 1970 and died in 1972. Throughout his stormy career in Congress, Powell remained minister at the Abyssinian Baptist Church, where he would often deliver sermons. His standing in Harlem remains

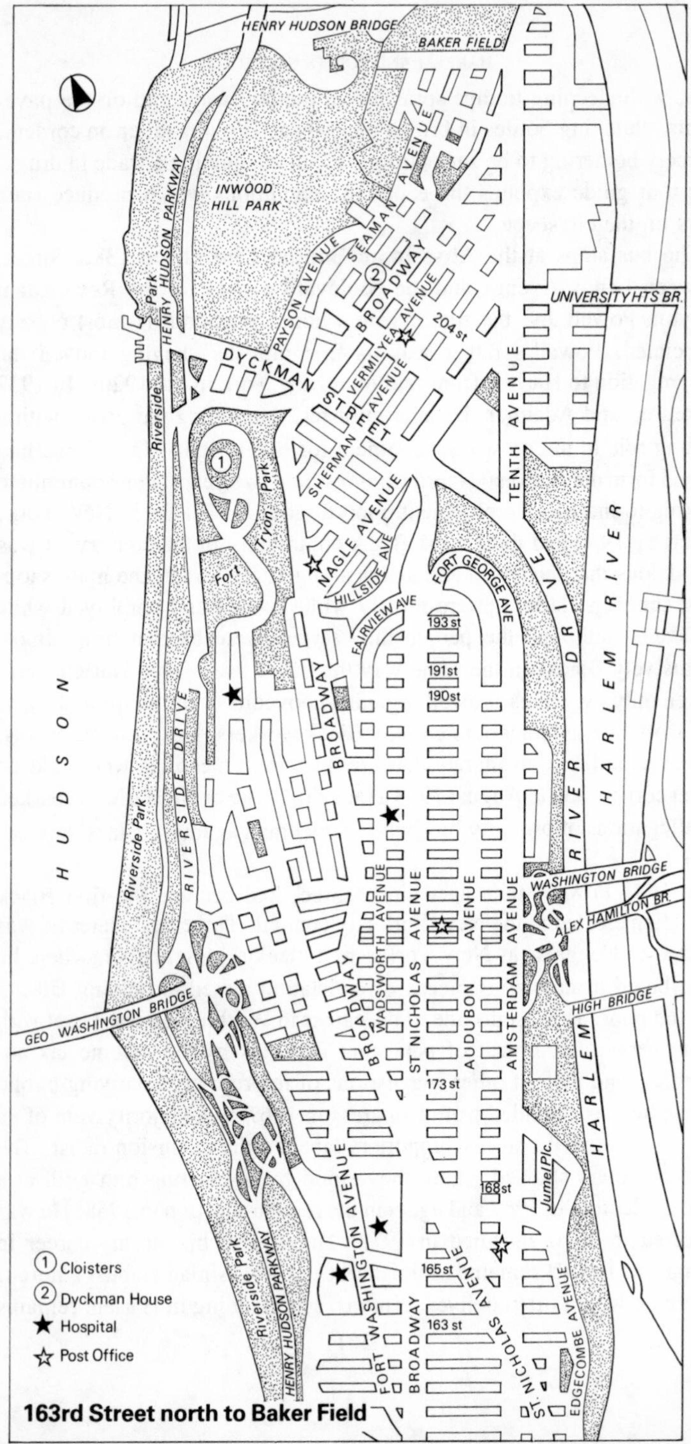

163rd Street north to Baker Field

high, as does indignation at the way he was treated by the white establishment. In the church, a small memorial room to Powell contains documents and mementoes, though there is no mention of the scandals.

When the tour group leaves the church the guide sometimes invites them to return for the Sunday service and I recommend that you do so. The regular congregation of several hundred people are courteous to strangers, offering handshakes, fellowship and an invitation to return. On Sunday morning, the buses heading for Harlem are filled with churchgoers in their best suits, polished shoes, bright dresses and wonderful hats. The choir, in sky-blue smocks, are one of the chief attractions for the visitor, giving full-throated renderings of tuneful, revival-style hymns. There is nothing solemn about the service: the long sermon is delivered with vigor and even a joke or two, and the congregation responds appropriately. For getting there, there are subway stations at 135th Street on Eighth and Sixth (Lenox) Avenues but the best way of getting there is by bus, faster on Sundays than during the week. The No 7 goes up Broadway to Times Square, then up Sixth Avenue for a stretch and Broadway again before putting you off at the corner of Lenox and 135th; No 102 goes up Third Avenue to the same point and No 2 goes up Madison Avenue to 138th Street and Seventh Avenue. As one moves out of the 90 street numbers and into the 100s, a white face becomes a rare sight on the bus as well as in the streets.

The last stop on the Penny Sightseeing Tour is the **Schomburg Collection** of literature on Black history, at Lenox Avenue and 135th Street. Now a part of the New York Public Library, this is the largest research center in America concentrating on black affairs. The angular red-brick building, opened in 1980, contains a small gallery for art by Black people. In the airy reading-room downstairs are a few sculptures and display cases for special exhibits. Arthur Schomburg, a Black Puerto Rican scholar, began the collection on which the research center is based. Until 1980 it was housed in the Victorian building next door. The bus concludes its tour by driving past the only surviving night club from the 'Let's Go Slumming' era — Small's at Seventh Avenue near 135th Street — and then down 125th Street, past the busy shops, the historic Apollo Theater and the venerable Teresa Hotel, whose notable guests, before it was converted into an office building, included President Fidel Castro of Cuba. In the 1950s, Harlem had a population of some seven hundred fifty thousand. Today it has fewer than half that and the numbers are still declining, so there may not be much time left to see it in anything like its legendary condition. White people, a thin trickle so far, have begun buying up some of the nicest brownstones.

My short walking tour in this section takes us from the unfinished **Cathedral of St John the Divine** to Grant's Tomb by the Hudson, crossing the campus of Columbia University on the way. There are interesting things to see if you can fit it in, and it need not occupy more than a couple of hours. Take the No 1 train, the IRT West Side local, to 110th Street and Cathedral Parkway. Walk a block east to Amsterdam Avenue, where the cathedral looms before you. The ambitious French Gothic west front, with its portals, pinnacles and rose window, is one of the most imposing church façades in the city; here, away from the center, land was cheap and the architect had space to express himself. The cornerstone was laid in 1892 and the first service held in the crypt seven years later; the original plan, still evident at the eastern end of the cathedral, was for a building in the Romanesque tradition. But there were delays in sinking foundations into the difficult terrain and, in the way of such enterprises, the longer the work dragged on the more disputatious became the principals. Moreover, architectural tastes began to change. In 1911 it was decided to convert the whole thing into French Gothic, then back in fashion. New architects under R. A. Cram, the leading exponent of the form, were engaged to impose the new look on the old. Cram was a man of deep religious conviction who felt that Gothic was the correct framework for worship. He was responsible for the careful if cold design of St Thomas's on Fifth Avenue, but his outstanding work is on the ivy-clad campus of Princeton University.

The body of the Cathedral of St John the Divine west of the crossing is pure vaulted Gothic, while the eastern section is a hybrid, with Gothic vaulting above Romanesque columns, beyond the Romanesque chancel arch. The arches at the very east end have remained in the Romanesque style. The crossing itself is incomplete, hung with a fine though faded set of seventeenth-century tapestries. On either side of the nave are the Mortlake Old Testament tapestries, based on Raphael cartoons in the Victoria and Albert Museum in London. British visitors will find other national connections. The curious pedestal to the right of the high altar is made of three stones from the ruined abbey of Bury St Edmunds. The 'motherhood' window, the most easterly on the south side of the nave, was unveiled by Queen Elizabeth the Queen Mother in 1954; and one of the bays celebrating the history of national churches is devoted to the English church — the third from the crossing in the left aisle. Other details to admire are the tremendous rose window, in blue and indigo stained glass, over the west door, and the eight massive marble columns around the altar. Ironically the bare, jagged-edged stone of the crossing, soaring unadorned to the ceiling and standing aloof from the stylistic quarrel, is probably the most affecting part of the whole structure. Work to complete the monster building still goes on, supervised by English stone masons (the craft had died in America). After all this time there must be scant chance of its ever being finished, but if it were it would then be the largest cathedral in the world. There are free guided tours.

If you need light refreshment go across the road to an authentic Hungarian pastry shop on the corner of 111th Street and Amsterdam Avenue. For more substantial fare the Green Tree Restaurant — also Hungarian and part of the same complex — offers inexpensive and hearty Central European meals, catering mainly to the students and faculty of nearby Columbia University. The friendly service is supervised by the proprietor, who sits beaming at the cash register, drawing on a cigar. A good, cheap restaurant of the kind New York does well.

Go north and turn right along the cathedral's northern edge at 113th Street, past St Luke's Hospital. Turn left up Morningside Drive, passing the Eglise de Notre Dame on the left. At 116th Street is a statue of Carl Schurz, the German-born philanthropist and politician, celebrated also in the park named after him near Gracie Mansion. The statue stands in a little alcove off the pavement, commanding a good view east across the rooftops of Harlem. Below, built for the most part on the side of a cliff, is Morningside Park, whose twisting, tree-shaded paths are a temptation for the energetic climber. The park is often, however, quite deserted and has a reputation for being unsafe. What's more, if you do reach the bottom of the cliff in good order you have to climb wearyingly back to the top. Better to look at it from on high and then cross the road and walk a block west, when you will find yourself entering the campus of **Columbia University.** If you're interested in touring the campus it is a good idea to go to the information office at 116th Street and Broadway, where free tours begin.

Formed as King's College in 1754, the university is the fifth oldest in the United States and a member of the 'Ivy League'. There's not too much ivy at Columbia, which moved from its old midtown campus to these spacious and formally laid out quarters, neo-Classical rather than Gothic, in 1897. It accommodates nearly twenty thousand students. The pivotal building is the **Low Memorial Library,** north of the main east-west transverse road, a stately domed structure completed in 1897 in the manner of the architect Charles McKim. No longer a library, the cool central rotunda serves as a site for ceremonies and exhibitions. If you go on the tour you'll be allowed into the Trustees' Room (Room 212) just inside the building, containing a copy of King George II's charter for the college, with artifacts and portraits relating to its early history. Room 210 is another little museum, a reconstruction of a room from the old downtown campus.

On the steps outside is Daniel Chester French's sentimental statue of Alma Mater, whose prominent site and authoritarian nature make her a natural focus for student protest: someone tried to blow her up during demonstrations against the Vietnam war. Facing the old library south of the transverse road is a more recent building which has taken over as the library and marks the fact by having the names of classical thinkers etched on to it: Homer, Herodotus, Sophocles, Plato, Aristotle, Demosthenes, Cicero, Virgil.

The nineteenth-century brick house just east of the Low Library is the only building left from pre-university days: it's now part of the department of French studies. From here, continue east and notice the cast of Rodin's 'The Thinker' on the lawn outside the philosophy department. If you find that piece of symbolism heavy-handed, wait until you have climbed the steps beyond it to a modern terrace built over Amsterdam Avenue, linking the new law school with the rest of the campus. Outside the law building is a huge black sculpture by Jacques Lipschitz intended to celebrate the triumph of order over chaos, though a cursory glance might suggest quite the opposite. The Lithuanian-born sculptor went to Paris in 1909 and fled to New York during the Second World War. When his New York studio burned down in 1952 he moved upstate to Hastings-on-Hudson. This work is typical of his allegorical pieces, showing the influence of Picasso's Cubism. At the northern end of the terrace, the 'Three Way Piece: Points' by Henry Moore was intended to revolve but has been switched off as a contribution to conserving energy.

Down the steps to the left of it, **St Paul's Chapel** is the most exquisite building on the campus, a neo-Byzantine gem in an incongruous setting, dating from 1907. Inside (it's open on an unpredictable schedule outside the academic year) are what may be the best examples in New York of the tile vaulting which characterizes many formal buildings of the period. The interlocking tiles form a pattern harmonizing happily with the Byzantine detail as well as fulfilling a structural function in supporting the domed ceiling. On Thursdays at noon during the academic year an organ recital is given here. On a raised courtyard at the north-west corner of the

Right:
Jean Dubuffet's 'Four Trees' sculpture in the Chase Manhattan Plaza.

Below:
The Lincoln Center for the Performing Arts. *Left to right:* the New York State Theater, the Metropolitan Opera House and the Avery Fisher Hall, venue for the New York Philharmonic Orchestra.

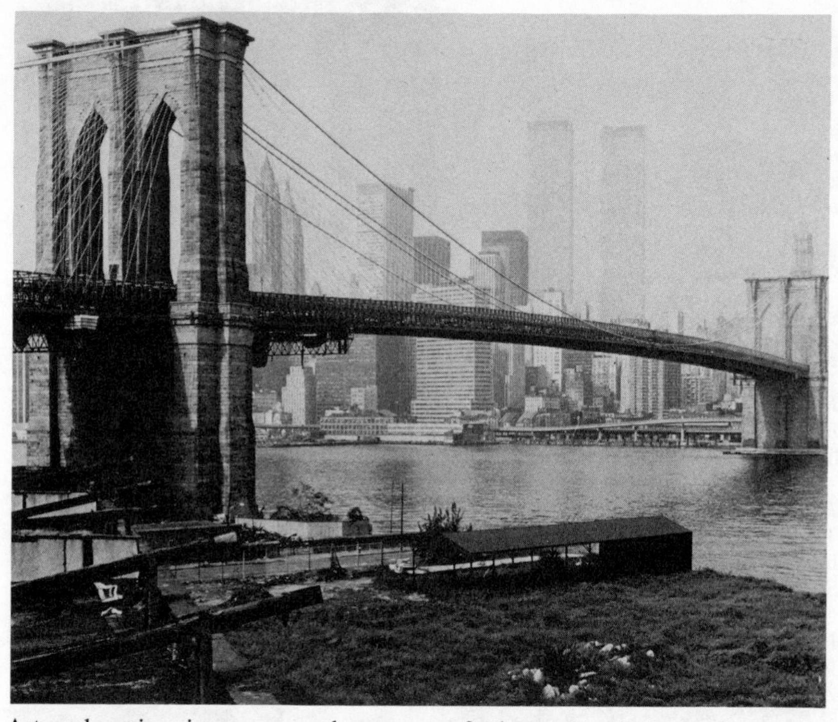

Art and engineering, grace and power, perfectly combined: John A. Roebling's Brooklyn Bridge, seen from the Brooklyn side.

campus, beyond a modern building housing the Graduate School of Business and the university's computer centre, is the truncated façade of the Pupin physics laboratories, where much of the research was carried out that led to the making of the first atomic bomb.

Leave Columbia by the Broadway entrance and turn right. From Broadway, turn left up 120th Street, here called Reinhold Niebuhr Place commemorating a much-loved clergyman and scholar, to **Riverside Baptist Church**, yet another large-scale interpretation of the Gothic Revival, this time from an even later date, 1930. Paid for by John D. Rockefeller Jr , this church never suffered from the cash problems which beset St John's Cathedral and there is a distinct if restrained flavor of wealth about it. The design is said to be based loosely on that of Chartres Cathedral but it is in reality more like a modern office building, complete with underground garage. It serves as a community center and an occasional concert hall as well as a venue for large-scale weddings and funerals of New York notables. The church and chapels are on the lower floors, the bell tower on top, four hundred feet above, with rooms between used for play groups and other social purposes. Inside, notice the delightful sixteenth-century stained glass, the delicate screen and the neo-Gothic carved choir stalls. High above the west door, dramatically lit, is a cast of Sir Jacob Epstein's 'Christ in Majesty', from the original in Llandaff Cathedral in Wales, and another Epstein, 'Madonna and Child', is outside in a courtyard on the east side of the building. You can take the elevator to the twentieth floor and walk a few flights past the massive bells (magnificently terrifying if you pass them when they ring) to the viewing platform, affording an off-beat view of the city, with a fine northern vista of the George Washington Bridge and the Hudson. Recitals on the bells are given on weekends: a rare carillon in that they encompass five octaves. There's a small museum of campanology on the twentieth floor by the elevator.

Just north and west of the church, overlooking the Hudson, stands **Grant's Tomb**. General Ulysses S. Grant, the redoubtable Civil War hero, after graduating from West Point military academy, fought in the Mexican war of 1846-8. He resigned from the army in 1854 but signed up again for the Civil War in 1861, rising quickly to the rank of general and scoring some important combat successes. In 1863 he was made supreme commander of the Union armies and inflicted the final defeat on Robert E. Lee's southern troops. In April 1865 Lee surrendered to Grant at Appomattox Court House.

Americans have, at various stages of their history, shown a preference for having a hero in the White House rather than an experienced politician, and in 1868 Grant was elected president, to be re-elected four years later. Though a poor, indecisive political leader, he was a man of generosity and moderation (he prevented the trial of Lee for treason) who worked towards healing the rifts that the war had created. He's also worth a place in history for having created the country's first national park at Yellowstone. Grant decided he wanted to be buried in New York and the city provided this site but, in the way of such projects, money proved hard to raise and the structure, a top-heavy Classical design based loosely on the tomb of King Mausolus in Turkey, was not finished until 1897, two years after his death. Though it looks shabby from the outside it's well kept inside (admission is free) where, apart from the well-polished tombs of Grant and his wife, resembling Napoleon's at Les Invalides, are two small rooms devoted to an account of Grant's career and of the struggle to raise funds for the monument.

Surrounding it, when you leave the building, are three rows of weird mosaic seats, bearing no relation whatever to the neo-Classical pile alongside. These were installed by the local community in recent years and amount to a three-dimensional version of the colorful graffiti with which their contemporaries were 'beautifying' not only subway cars and platforms but also the outside walls of the tomb itself. They stand as a monument to the devoutly held American view that any form of self-expression is in itself to be admired and encouraged; discussion is under way about moving the seats to a more suitable location.

To end this walking tour, cross the road into a small park and go down some steps at its north-east corner into Claremont Avenue, then turn left. Take the first turning on the right, La Salle Street, and turn left when you reach Broadway. You pass through a busy and noisy Puerto Rican section, in the shadow of the elevated tracks of the IRT West Side subway, before you get to the 125th Street station.

There are four sights left to see in northern Manhattan, too far apart to be combined in one walking tour, so I shall treat them geographically, from south to north.

Hamilton Grange on Convent Avenue near 142nd Street is the house Alexander Hamilton built as a country retreat for his family in 1802; he had only two years to enjoy it before being killed in his duel with Aaron Burr. Originally located two blocks away, it has been restored by the National Parks Service. The nearest subway stations are at 145th Street on both the IRT and the IND West Side lines, or you can take west side buses No 3 or 4 to Convent Avenue or the Third Avenue bus 101 up

Amsterdam Avenue, just a block away. Surrounding the Grange are some of the most pleasant and best kept terraced houses in Harlem. The avenue itself is full of trees and greenery, positively suburban.

Audubon Terrace at 155th Street and Broadway — one stop farther on the IRT West Side subway (157th Street), or you could walk from the Grange — is a collection of grandiose neo-Classical buildings accommodating three museums and two institutions. **The Museum of the American Indian** is the one visitors are most likely to find appealing, a comprehensive but crowded collection of displays illustrating the history of America's earliest inhabitants. The most important of the other Audubon Terrace museums is that of the **Hispanic Society**, which contains a small but choice collection of art related to Spain, including paintings by Goya, El Greco and Velasquez and some typically colorful Catalan tiles and earthenware. The **American Numismatic Society** has a well-ordered collection of coins; the **American Geographical Society** offers a display of maps; and the **American Academy of Arts and Letters** houses temporary exhibitions as well as a permanent show of the paintings of the American Impressionist Childe Hassam.

If Audubon Terrace is optional, our next visit is as close to compulsory as anything in this book. **The Cloisters,** in Fort Tryon Park, overlooking the Hudson, houses the medieval section of the Metropolitan Museum of Art. A highly original concept, it contains authentic medieval relics and ruins, shipped from Europe and reconstructed in a way which gives cogency to the disparate elements. In all New York, no artifacts are older than those on display here.

We owe the presence of The Cloisters to George Barnard, an enthusiast of medieval sculpture and something of a sculptor himself. Before the First World War he travelled across France and Italy, sometimes by bicycle, buying objects to ship back home. Where monasteries had been abandoned, the pillars from the cloisters had often been scattered to numerous owners who used them as garden ornaments; Barnard methodically traced and bought as many as he could. He bought them originally for resale but when he could find no buyers for the largest works he decided in 1914 to open a 'cloister museum' on Fort Washington Avenue, where he already owned a studio. In 1925 John D. Rockefeller bought the museum, the nucleus of the present-day Cloisters, for $600,000, and presented it to the Metropolitan; later he paid for its move to the present site, where it opened in 1938. The collection has been greatly expanded since, though it's still a museum of modest size. To reach it, the nicest way is to take the Eighth Avenue 'A' train to 190th Street and walk through Fort Tryon Park: the M.4 Madison Avenue bus stops right outside but takes time to get up there. You enter through a door at the lowest level and walk up a corridor and some steps to the ticket lobby, where you can pick up a free map, necessary to navigate the somewhat complex layout. Opposite the ticket desk, the Romanesque Hall contains two witty dragon and lion frescoes from thirteenth-century Spain and a twelfth-century cross from Bury St Edmunds in England, superbly carved from walrus ivory, some two feet high. The first door on the right leads to the Fuentideña Apse, with more frescoes. An entrance on the left of this chapel opens on to the first of the reconstructed cloisters, early thirteenth-century, from the abbey of Saint-Guilhem-le-Désert in southern France. This dainty cloister is brightened in spring by a show of bulbs and blossoming trees, and is also planted out for a summer garden. Its columns are in a dazzling variety of shapes, from plain round to crazily crenellated. Back in the Romanesque Hall, turn right to the twelfth-century chapel from Notre-Dame-du-Bourg at Langon, with its Italian marble tabernacle.

The southern door of the chapel leads to a passage at the end of which is another door beneath an exquisite twelfth-century stained glass window from Reims. Through this second door (locked on the coldest days of winter) are the ramparts, offering a view over the Hudson. Go back by the same door and turn right into the low-vaulted twelfth-century chapter house from Gascony: through this is the largest of the cloisters, from Cuxa in the Pyrenees. Stumpy pillars in pink and white marble are topped with energetically carved capitals supporting rounded arches. Four paths, dissecting the lawn, converge on the fountain, from the same monastery. Like the other exhibits here this cloister has nothing to do with New York save its present location, but it affords a sense of repose and, despite the incongruous setting, a feeling of how it may have appeared on its original site. Recorded medieval music reinforces the illusion.

The entrance on the right beyond the chapter house leads to the early Gothic Hall, with more notable stained glass. Through the door in the corner is a room hung with fourteenth-century French tapestries from a set woven for the Duc de Berry, depicting heroes from history. In the room beyond are the Unicorn Tapestries, best-known of the museum's treasures. In 1935 John D. Rockefeller presented the museum with these late fifteenth- and early sixteenth-century tapestries, remarkable for their bright colors and lyrical composition. Since then, countless reproductions of the panel showing the unicorn caged in a field of flowers have been made and sold, and there will be plenty to choose from at the shop by the museum entrance when you leave.

Now we have to retrace our steps back past the heroes tapestries and down the steps in the early Gothic Hall to the Gothic chapel, with its tombs and statuary. Down a few more steps is the Bonnefont Cloister from north-west France, a replica of a medieval herb garden. Beyond it, the Trié cloister, from southern France has double columns of contrasting marble supporting fifteenth-century capitals showing rather more sophistication than the earlier ones from Cuxa. Behind these two lower cloisters are the glass gallery and treasury for the display of small, rich objects, including the intricately worked silver chalice from Antioch which may date from the fourth century, a remarkable illuminated manuscript (the *Trés Riches Heures du Duc de Berry*) and some early Limoges enamels.

Go up the stairs next to the sixteenth-century carved oak door for the rest of the main floor. The Boppard Room has more fine stained glass and the tapestry hall — in fact part of the same room — is hung with French tapestries only a little less dazzling than the unicorns. The Campin Room, through a door on the right, is possibly the most spectacular in the museum, though its fifteenth-century Spanish ceiling cannot always be seen to its best advantage if the light outside is poor; the room takes its name from its most prized exhibit, Robert Campin's triptych of the Annunciation. The last hall is the late Gothic, which leads back to the entrance and gift shop. Concerts of medieval music are held at The Cloisters from time to time and regularly at Christmas. Even if you cannot get tickets for these popular concerts, Christmas is a good time for a visit. Medieval decorations and representations of the nativity are displayed and the Guilhem cloister is planted with seasonal greenery.

The most northerly sight in Manhattan is its only remaining eighteenth-century farmhouse, **Dyckman House** on Broadway at 204th Street. (Take the IND "A" train to its last stop, 207th Street.) This small wood-framed house, its roof pitched characteristically at two angles, has been restored as a museum and contains some excellent furniture from the eighteenth and nineteenth centuries, some of it original to the house. The small formal garden contains a reconstruction of a military hut, recalling critical military engagements in this northern area of Manhattan in 1776.

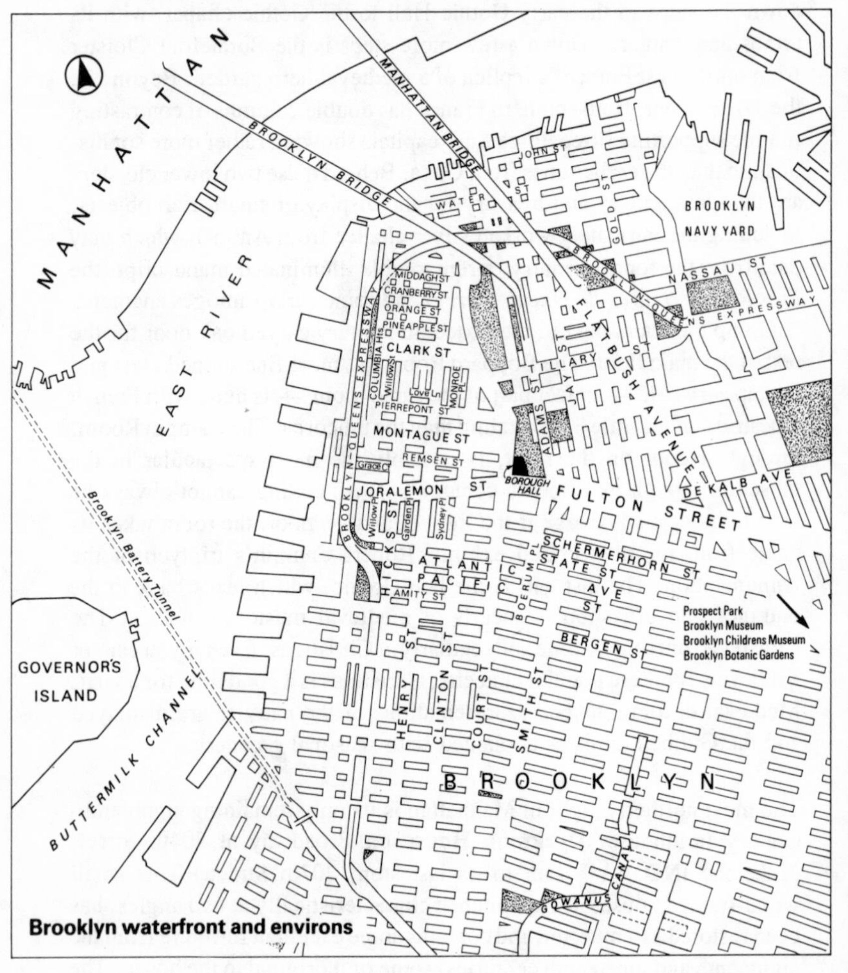
MANHATTAN
EAST RIVER
MANHATTAN BRIDGE
BROOKLYN BRIDGE
JOHN ST
WATER ST
GOLD ST
BROOKLYN
NAVY YARD
NASSAU ST
BROOKLYN-QUEENS EXPRESSWAY
MIDDAGH ST
CRANBERRY ST
ORANGE ST
PINEAPPLE ST
CLARK ST
COLUMBIA Hts.
Willow St
Love La
MONROE Pl
PIERREPONT ST
MONTAGUE ST
REMSEN ST
Grace Ct
JORALEMON ST
TILLARY ST
JAY ST
FLATBUSH AVENUE
ADAMS ST
BOROUGH HALL
FULTON STREET
DE KALB AVE
Willow Pl
Garden Pl
Sydney Pl
HICKS ST
SCHERMERHORN ST
STATE ST
ATLANTIC AVE
PACIFIC ST
AMITY ST
BOERUM PL
BERGEN ST
HENRY ST
CLINTON ST
COURT ST
SMITH ST
Prospect Park
Brooklyn Museum
Brooklyn Childrens Museum
Brooklyn Botanic Gardens
Brooklyn Battery Tunnel
GOVERNOR'S ISLAND
BUTTERMILK CHANNEL
BROOKLYN
GOWANUS CANAL

Brooklyn waterfront and environs

16
Brooklyn Heights

THE PEOPLE OF BROOKLYN are fond of telling anyone who will stop to listen that if theirs were still an independent city, as it was until 1898, it would be the fourth largest in the United States. There's nothing wrong with civic chauvinism but, in fairness, were it not for its proximity to its overbearing though smaller sister borough of Manhattan, Brooklyn would not have grown to anything like its present size. Even before the merger with the other four boroughs and before the opening of Brooklyn Bridge — the first road link — in 1883, it had been a dormitory and industrial hinterland for the metropolis. Yet because it was once a separate administrative entity, Brooklyn does have many of the trappings of an independent city — a civic center, a museum, a zoo, a beach resort, a downtown shopping area — although, sadly, it no longer sustains its own baseball team. The Brooklyn Dodgers moved to Los Angeles in 1957. This was a tremendous loss because the team — pugnacious, unpredictable and often the underdog — was an institution with which generations of Brooklyn natives, struggling to better themselves in unprepossessing surroundings, were able to identify. 'Dem Bums' was their affectionate nickname.

It was not simply the departure of a sports team: it was seen as a massive gesture of no confidence in the future of the inner city. In the year that the Dodgers went to Los Angeles the New York Giants, who played on the Polo Grounds on the edge of Harlem, moved out to San Francisco. (These were the baseball Giants: the football Giants still play in the New York area, at the Meadowlands sports complex in New Jersey.) Many contend that this double loss marked the beginning of New York's decline in morale, culminating in its near-bankruptcy in 1975. The cities were becoming the repositories of crime, filth and poverty. Anyone who had the money and the opportunity aspired to pull up his roots and head out to a detached family house and garden — if not, like the Dodgers, to

California and the sun, at least to Westchester County north of the city, New Jersey to the west or Long Island to the east.

Brooklyn residents, who inelegantly dub themselves Brooklynites, used to complain that they were the butt of vaudeville comedians. The so-called Brooklyn accent, taking alarming liberties with vowels, was used in films of the 1930s and 1940s to signify comic and uneducated characters — often taxi drivers. Today vaudeville is dead, they don't make those films any more and the joke is largely over, although a Manhattan adult education college was still, in the 1980s, offering a course in diction which it called 'How to lose your Brooklyn accent'. The demise of Brooklyn jokes probably doesn't signify any new-found respect for its inhabitants, only the decline of the borough as a separate entity.

The first human inhabitants of the area were the Canarsie Indians. In 1609 Henry Hudson landed briefly in Coney Island — now Brooklyn's raucous pleasure beach — and a few years later the Dutch colonists began to establish farms here, as in other parts of the region. As the population grew, six separate towns were established in what is now Brooklyn: the one closest to Manhattan was named Breukelen after a town in Holland. In 1640 the first ferry service was established just below where Brooklyn Bridge now makes its landfall, and that area remained the focus of commercial activity for some three hundred years, receiving a boost when Robert Fulton introduced the first steam ferry in 1814. When the British relieved the Dutch of responsibility for the New Amsterdam colony in 1664, Dutch farmers stayed on in Breukelen and the neighboring towns, doing their best to ignore their new overlords, who returned the compliment. Thus when the Revolution came in 1776, Brooklyn was still essentially Dutch, although a third of the population (still less than four thousand all told) were black slaves.

The first battle after the Declaration of Independence, the Battle of Long Island, was fought in Brooklyn. Though the revolutionary forces were defeated by the British, Washington and his men managed to retreat to Manhattan in a semblance of good order and survived to fight on. After the Revolution the population began to grow quickly, for the good harbor made it an important hub of commerce and shipping. In the 1830s the Irish became the first of a stream of immigrants to move into Brooklyn. By the time of its incorporation into greater New York in 1898 it had a million inhabitants. In 1950 the population was two and three-quarter millions but since then it has been declining as the white middle class have moved to the suburbs, to be replaced only partially by Blacks and Hispanics. Brooklyn's seventy-five square miles are nowadays split into a dozen and more neighborhoods, many consisting of row upon row of two-, three- and four-storey houses occupied by black and poor people. The East River is lined with warehouses and a dockyard: inland are their supporting light industrial premises. Our walk in Brooklyn takes us through an untypical section, the one part whose population over the years has retained a reasonably consistent middle and even upper-class character. Brooklyn Heights has always been the most pleasant part of the borough and indeed one of the most splendid in the city. Its proximity to the commercial center of Lower Manhattan made it a convenient dormitory for bankers and businessmen, which it remains.

We start the walk on the fringe of **Cobble Hill,** the district just south of Brooklyn Heights: though almost equally packed with fine nineteenth-century terraced houses, it is a shade less fashionable. By subway, take the F train of the IND Sixth Avenue line to Bergen Street. Walk one block west along Bergen to Court Street and turn right. Turn left into **Amity Street** and look out on your right for No 197, once an unassuming brick house, now tastelessly covered with veneer blocks. In 1854, long before being so defaced, it was the birthplace of Jennie Jerome, daughter of Leonard Jerome, the financier, who rented this house before he had his mansion built on Madison Square in Manhattan. In the manner of wealthy Americans of his time, he sent Jennie to England to marry into nobility. She chose Lord Randolph Churchill and bore him a son, Winston, who was to become Britain's most potent twentieth-century hero. The only part of the exterior of the house which she might now recognize are the iron railings, a pleasing feature of many of the Victorian houses here and in the Heights.

Walk to Clinton Street and turn right, crossing Pacific Street into Atlantic Avenue, turning right again. In the last ten years or so this has become an intriguing street, lined with Middle Eastern restaurants and food shops, and boutiques selling knick-knacks to the people of the Heights. The names of the shops tell the story: the Damascus Bakery, Tripoli Restaurant, Beirut Grocery. If you know your way around a Middle Eastern menu, go ahead. The spice shops should be looked into in any event, offering another of New York's distinctive range of odors.

Continue to Boerum Place and turn left. On the corner of Schermerhorn Street is a sign luring you down the steps of what was once a subway station to the **New York City Transit Museum.** By all means accept the lure if you are an enthusiast for antique forms of transport. It costs only the price of a subway token and contains a quantity of old cars, turnstiles and station trappings, as well as a relief model of the subway system, giving an idea of its complexity. A particularly charming section is devoted to pictures of the decorative tile work which still adorns many stations. A gift stall sells off-beat souvenirs, including sections of the white-on-black rolls which tell you where a train is going.

Press on along Boerum Place, then left at Joralemon Street, to come face to face with **Borough Hall**. Built as City Hall in 1849, this stern Greek Revival building is relieved by its crowning ornate cupola. Inside, one floor up, an early bell from the cupola is on display, along with portraits of such as George Washington. East of here, down **Fulton Street**, is Brooklyn's main shopping area, dominated by Abraham and Straus, a large department store bearing comparison with the best in Manhattan. At 372 Fulton Street, Gage and Tollner is one of the most charming restaurants in New York and worth a trip out for dinner one evening. It retains its original exterior from the time it opened here in 1889; the Edwardian atmosphere, complete with gas lamps, has been preserved inside as well. The food is classic American, concentrating on steaks, chops and sea food, cooked plainly. Service is solicitous and there's a good wine list. Not far away, where Fulton Street meets De Kalb and Flatbush Avenues, is Junior's, a bustling family restaurant with large portions and low prices, the best kind of unpretentious eating.

Now head west down Joralemon Street into the nineteenth-century terraces of **Brooklyn Heights.** On the right, No 135 is one of the oldest houses in the Heights, a wood-framed construction of 1833, these days sporting a pretty New Orleans-style balcony. Immediately opposite, turn left down Sidney Place, past the Roman Catholic **Church of St Charles Borromeo** on the left. This is the first of many plain yet pleasing neo-Gothic churches on this route. Nearly all are kept locked and the only way of seeing inside is to go for a service; or, if you are lucky enough to find the minister or someone else in authority when you pass, you may be allowed to wander around.

At the end of Sidney Place turn right into State Street, where Nos 103 to 107 form a set of Federal (1832) houses in something close to their original state. Glance up Garden Place as you pass it on your right: a tree-lined retreat with some good iron balustrades. We're not going to walk up it, because we want to save ourselves for **Willow Place,** a couple of blocks farther along, one of the most varied and interesting streets in the area. As you turn into it you catch sight of Nos 43 to 49, a row of two-storey houses behind square colonnades giving a deceptive impression of height. Built in 1846, they are among the very few colonnaded houses remaining in New York. Compare them with Colonnade Row on Lafayette Street, just opposite the Public Theater which, being in Manhattan, was on a grander scale. The pity is that these Willow Place houses have not been painted or maintained uniformly. Beyond them and opposite, Nos 2 to 8 are a group of bijou red-brick houses, built in 1847, with interesting iron porches and geometric designs between the upper storey windows.

Now turn right, back into Joralemon Street, where the row of plain Greek Revival houses on the north side, built in the 1840s, has been kept intact, with an unusual stepped effect on the slope of the hill. Turning left into Hicks Street, look at **Grace Church** on the left, designed by Richard Upjohn in 1847 shortly after he completed work on Trinity Church at the end of Wall Street. Opposite is Grace Court Alley, a mews of coach houses reminiscent of those on the north side of Washington Square. We turn right up Remsen Street to another, less typical church by Upjohn, **Our Lady of Lebanon**. Here he has forsaken Gothic for Romanesque, which was not to come into general fashion until some time later. The bronze doors at the south and west, bearing reliefs of Norman churches, were salvaged from the French liner *Normandie* after it sank in the Hudson River in 1942.

Turn left up Clinton Street to the next junction at Montague. Although our route takes us straight across, it is worth pausing to explore this, one of the most interesting shopping streets in the Heights. On your right, side by side, are two Brooklyn equivalents of the elaborate neo-Classical office buildings in Manhattan. The first, Manufacturers Hanover Trust, is a Renaissance palace with an interior resembling the most ambitious of the ornate stations on the Moscow subway. It's the work of York and Sawyer, the firm responsible for that remarkable bank in Manhattan, the Bowery on 42nd Street, opposite Grand Central Station. Next door, Citibank reposes in a marble temple built in 1903, which can at least claim to have been there first and not be blamed for the stylistic clash. Some of Montague Street's best restaurants and shops are just west of the junction.

Continue north up Clinton Street to the **Long Island Historical Society**, on your left at the next corner. This is a fine, powerful red-brick building put up in 1878 and, compared with the two banks, a model of restraint. It was designed by George B. Post, whose later work included the New York Stock Exchange and City College. The outside decoration involves one of the earliest uses of terra cotta in New York: some architects feared it would not survive the rigors of the climate. The research library here is contained in a fine galleried hall, panelled in black ash, unaltered in nearly a century; usually it offers a small exhibition on an aspect of Brooklyn's history. The ground floor has been much changed since the society's early days in these premises, when Sir Arthur Conan Doyle and Matthew Arnold lectured to large audiences, and now it houses a gift shop named after the wooden seated Indian outside, used in the nineteenth century to denote a cigar store. It sells an unusual selection of prints and postcards as well as authentic nineteenth-century quilts and a selection of second-hand books on New York's history.

The Church of the Savior, at the corner of Pierrepont Street and Monroe Place, is more mid-century brownstone Gothic, with five Tiffany stained glass windows. Moving west along Pierrepont Street we are getting back to the residential section of the Heights. No 82 flaunts some extravagant sandstone carvings on its outer walls, sadly wearing away. Turn right up Henry Street: on the left, beyond the junction with Love Lane, Nos 137 to 143 are four wood-framed Greek Revival houses of four stories and with colonnaded porches. Now double back and turn right up Love Lane: College Place, which comes in at right angles to the lane, is a pleasant cul-de-sac with four pretty mews houses in the corner. Notice the pattern made by the star-shaped ends of the reinforcing joists as you walk up the street. Continue along Love Lane and turn left into Hicks Street. Cross Pierrepont and, at the corner of Montague, wander into the lobby of the Bossert Hotel where, with a considerable effort of the imagination, you may conjure its stylish heyday in the 1920s. Walk west along Montague until, near its end, you come to Nos 2 and 3 **Pierrepont Place,** described bluntly by the *AIA Guide* as 'the most elegant brownstones left in New York' and well might they be. Built in 1857, they've kept their sense of style and space, redolent of fine living.

Where Montague Street meets the esplanade, looking out over the harbor and offering a famous view of the skyline of Lower Manhattan, is a plaque marking where George Washington had his headquarters in the last stage of the Battle of Long Island, supervising the retreat from what later became the Fulton ferry slip, below and a bit north. The view today is spectacular, though it was more pleasing before they built those charmless skyscrapers on Water Street, near the very tip. You can see the wharves and the old Navy Yard just below, out past Governor's Island to the Verrazano Narrows Bridge, Staten Island, the Statue of Liberty and New Jersey beyond.

Walk a block north up the esplanade before turning right into Pierrepont Street, admiring some more elaborately carved sandstone at No 6. Take the first turning on the left: this, though not marked, is **Willow Street**. On the right, Nos 155 to 159 are three very early (1829) Federal houses, with the dormers surviving on Nos 155 and 157 and all with the original lintels. No 151 is an old stable, set back from the others. Farther up, look at the iron porch and its tracery on No 113. Cross Clark Street, where on the right you glimpse the massive old St George Hotel, once the center of social life on the Heights, with a built-in subway station. In recent years it's declined and been partly converted into co-operative apartments. Continue up Willow to Pineapple Street and turn left, back to the esplanade, at this point nearly opposite the South Street Seaport and its historic sailing ships. Walk north up the promenade until it ends with a fine close-up view of Brooklyn Bridge. The street parallel with Pineapple, one block north, is Orange Street, though again it has lost its sign. Walk along it, crossing Willow and Hicks, to the **Plymouth Church of the Pilgrims**, a plain neo-Georgian edifice of 1849, with its porch added later, and again unfortunately not accessible to the casual visitor.

The church is famous not for its architecture but because it was where Henry Ward Beecher preached his highly moral sermons for forty years, from 1847 to 1887. Nowadays Beecher may be best known for being the brother of Harriet Beecher Stowe, the author of *Uncle Tom's Cabin*. In his day, he was a famous figure of substance and controversy. Their father was Lyman Beecher, a notable revivalist preacher himself. Revivalism was a powerful social force in America for much of the nineteenth century: by establishing constant standards of behavior and taste it provided a needed focus for a society which was shifting and changing.

After attending Amherst College, Beecher joined his father's ministry in Cincinnati. He attended a seminary and undertook his own ministries in Indiana, building a reputation as a powerful and persuasive orator which led to the invitation to move to the Plymouth Church in Brooklyn in 1847, when he was thirty-four. The debate over slavery still raged, and Beecher dramatized his opposition to it by holding a mock auction of a young slave girl in his church — a gimmick which proved so successful that he tried it again at least twice during his career. In his sermons on other topics he stressed the fashionable doctrine of self-improvement through effort and preached his own version of Andrew Carnegie's 'gospel of wealth' — that there was nothing wrong with being extremely rich so long as you accepted the obligation to use your money for the benefit of the community at large. These responsible yet liberal positions gained him a wide following as a preacher, a journalist and a lecturer to adult students at evening classes.

In 1874 Beecher became involved in a long-running scandal which was the talk of the town. Theodore Tilton, once a friend and colleague who had drifted into enmity (they headed rival organizations supporting women's suffrage) accused Beecher of committing adultery with his wife, Elizabeth. The air was thick with accusations, apologies, confessions and retractions. Finally the case came to court and the press reported it obsessively. The court found no convincing evidence to support Tilton's charge; Beecher was exonerated and the scandal did little to harm his reputation. The truth will never be certainly established, though in his excellent biography of Beecher[16], Clifford E. Clark Jr made the point that many people were unwilling even to consider the possibility that he might be guilty, since this would destroy the moral foundation on which they had built their lives and reveal Victorian middle-class morality to be a sham. Thus Beecher's influence was left unimpaired, and in his later years it extended into politics: his support was eagerly sought by candidates for public office, from the presidency down. He campaigned against the corruption which then prevailed in many areas of public life and advocated order in a society which was becoming increasingly disorderly. He remained a vigorous and sought-after speaker until he died after a stroke in 1887, aged seventy-four.

Sinclair Lewis, in a perceptive introduction to Paxton Hibben's 1927 biography of Beecher, wrote:

> He was a combination of St Augustine, Barnum and John Barrymore . . . In understanding Beecher we understand everything that was boisterously immature in American religion, American literature, American manners and the American relationship, ardent but sneaking, between men and women.

His striking presence is recorded in a statue in the church garden and in another near Borough Hall. Leaving the church on your left, turn left up Henry Street and left again along Cranberry, where there are some notable Greek Revival houses. Turn right up Willow for more of the same: No 22 was where Beecher lived. At the corner of Willow and **Middagh Streets**, 24 Middagh is a wooden house of tremendous charm, with its shutters and an elaborately carved doorway which demonstrates what the critics of the Federal style meant when they accused it of being 'gingerbread'. Middagh Street has a number of wooden houses dating, like this one, from the 1820s, but none in such good repair. Having looked at them, go back to the western end of the street and turn right down the steep hill (Columbia Heights), taking in dramatic views of the Brooklyn and Manhattan Bridges as you descend.

The road passes under a bridge linking two parts of the Jehovah's Witnesses' headquarters and takes you into the old Fulton ferry slip, now a small park. The former fire-house has been turned into the **Fulton Ferry Museum**, a small collection of model ships and other nautical material. The ferry was made largely redundant by the opening of Brooklyn Bridge, but it continued operating until 1924. Once as busy and frantic as the Manhattan terminal, the area now is forlorn, though some of the old commercial buildings are being converted into apartments. Among them is the former Eagle Warehouse and Storage Company, on the site of the first office of the *Brooklyn Eagle* newspaper — a fact commemorated by the model of a golden eagle swooping down at the front (though that was taken from a later office of the paper).

The *Eagle* was established in 1841 as a political voice for a group of Brooklyn Democrats. A year later it was bought by its printer, Isaac van Anden who, in 1846, appointed as its editor a twenty-seven-year-old journalist called Walt Whitman. He lasted only two years before being dismissed by van Anden because the two men disagreed about slavery: Whitman was a dedicated abolitionist and under him the paper reflected that. Van Anden offered this different explanation for dismissing Whitman: 'Slow, indolent, heavy, discourteous and without steady principles, he was a clog upon our success.' With the publication of *Leaves of Grass* in 1855, Whitman began to find his proper vocation, though it took many more years to gain popular acceptance of his poetry.

Among the campaigns the *Eagle* pursued after Whitman left was one in support of the construction of Brooklyn Bridge. Fifteen years after that was accomplished the paper was equally vigorous in its opposition to the incorporation of Brooklyn into Greater New York, failing to see it was the logical consequence of the new road link. Many attribute the eventual demise of the *Eagle* to the dilution of the borough's separate identity which flowed from the bridge and the civic merger. Ownership of the paper passed through several hands after the turn of the century and it went into a decline. In January 1955 its journalists went on strike, demanding pay parity with Manhattan newspapers and in March the owners decided the *Eagle* must close. Since then Brooklyn has had no daily newspaper of its own and is the poorer because of it.

Our final target is **Brooklyn Bridge** itself. This has been a long trek but I do urge you to make the effort to walk back to Manhattan: You'll find it the most invigorating half-hour of your New York visit. I recommend doing it in this direction because the view of Manhattan, constantly shifting, is more spectacular than that of Brooklyn. To get to the pedestrian walkway, continue up the hill away from the river. Cross the main road and bear left under the bridge (following signs to the airports) to Cadman Plaza East. Walk parallel with the bridge for a few yards and climb the staircase leading to the walkway on your right.

Completed in 1883, Brooklyn Bridge was at that time the world's largest single-span suspension bridge and the first to use steel cables; though it has since been surpassed, it remains an astonishing engineering achievement. Its creator, John Roebling, was a German immigrant who had built suspension bridges in other parts of the country before being engaged in 1867 to oversee the hugely ambitious project to link the neighboring cities. Before building had even started, the bridge claimed Roebling as a victim. With dreadful irony, his toes were crushed by a ferry boat as he stood on some piles making his final surveys in 1869. They had to be amputated, tetanus set in and he died a month after the accident, gaining posthumous revenge when his bridge eventually drove the ferries out of business.

His son, Washington Roebling, continued the work, but it wasn't long before he was overtaken by a fate almost as terrible as his father's. From spending too long in the caissons below the foundations of the towers he suffered a severe attack of the bends and was crippled for life; he had to supervise the rest of the building from the window of a house on Brooklyn Heights. When the bridge came into use it continued to exact a human toll: a few days after the opening twelve people were killed and dozens injured in the crush seeking to cross it.

There will be no such crush when you walk across today; the chief danger to life and limb is from bicycles which hurtle along the walkway, once exclusively for pedestrians. Now it has been divided by a yellow line and the northern half (on your right in this direction) is reserved for cyclists, although they don't always observe the restriction. You'll soon get used to the buzz of traffic beneath. After 5 p.m. on a fine evening, you'll pass Wall Street business people taking the air as they hoof it back to their homes in Brooklyn Heights, as well as joggers in both directions.

Do stop from time to time on your way across to enjoy the changing view, perhaps at the second seat beyond the first flight of steps (not counting the ones you climbed to get on to the walkway). Governor's Island is on the left and the Bayonne Bridge, linking Staten Island with New Jersey, in the distance. The southern tip of Manhattan is delineated by the modern office buildings of the Water Street development. To the right of these, past the cluster of Wall Street skyscrapers, the two towers of the World Trade Center look more to scale from this viewpoint than from anywhere else and, it must be allowed, add interest to the composition. The spire almost straight ahead is the fine old Woolworth Tower.

A few yards before you get to this point, the walkway will have taken you between the suspension cables, an interesting criss-cross foreground to add drama to snapshots. You get a sight of Manhattan Bridge (1909) on your right, and can see a portion of Williamsburg Bridge (1903) beyond it. On your left, look down at the fire house and the old Fulton ferry slip. The extent of the dockyard just beyond can be appreciated as you move on, with the tree-lined esplanade of Brooklyn Heights above it. The Statue of Liberty begins to dominate the view of the harbor on the left and the Verrazano Narrows Bridge comes in over your left shoulder. On the right-hand side you can identify the Empire State and Chrysler Buildings. At certain times of day, if the sun is out, Chrysler will sparkle: so will the gold pyramid atop Cass Gilbert's New York Life Insurance building on

Madison Square, to the right of the Empire State. Look for the slab of the Pan Am Building and later, from the midpoint of the bridge, the sloped white roof of the Citicorp Tower and the boxy green United Nations. Ahead, the grey rectangles of the downtown skyscrapers become easier to separate as you approach Manhattan. You can get a good view of the South Street Seaport reconstruction on the left: look down at its red-brick shops and warehouses and reflect that when the bridge was built, all Lower Manhattan was filled with structures on that scale. Imagine how colossal, by comparison, the bridge must have appeared to sightseers of the time.

As you walk off the bridge, pause near the road sign denoting a sharp right turn, to take in the panorama of the downtown skyscrapers: it amounts to a short course in New York architecture. On the far left the towers of the World Trade Center appear smaller than Cass Gilbert's Woolworth Building alongside them — a trick of perspective pleasing to enthusiasts for Gilbert's masterwork. Next, the glass monster at 250 Broadway (built in 1962) is at least a textbook rendering of the wedding-cake style, if you can imagine a black wedding-cake. City Hall is hard to make out against the background of an early-century office building but the Tweed Court, topped by a greenhouse, is more prominent. To the right of that, the golden image of 'Civic Virtue' on McKim, Mead and White's Municipal Building can be seen properly only from here. Next in sequence is the skyscraper section of Gilbert's federal court house — grim and unimaginative compared with his work for Woolworth. The modern purple-brick building on your right, with round towers at the corners, is the Murray Bergtraum High School, built in 1976, the same time as the tower of telephone company offices behind it; it cuts off most of the view of the new police headquarters. Now carry on to the subway entrance (the Brooklyn Bridge stop on the Lexington Avenue line) which is the second hole in the ground at the end of the walkway, not the first.

17

Beyond the Perimeter

THIS CHAPTER lists places on the outer fringes which, depending on your timetable, are worth making the effort to see.

Brooklyn Museum

Take the IRT West Side express to Brooklyn Museum/Eastern Parkway.

This is a decidedly lumpish pile, chiefly because McKim, Mead and White's original 1897 design was never completely built. Moreover, the monumental steps which used to lead to the entrance, on what is now the second floor, were removed in the 1930s, thus saving the breath of visitors but detracting from the composition. In front of the entrance, Daniel Chester French's figures representing Manhattan and Brooklyn, which formerly stood at the Brooklyn end of Manhattan Bridge, seem to reflect the sculptor's metropolitan prejudices: Manhattan carries the world in its hand while Brooklyn has a pronounced (and nowadays inappropriate) rustic flavor.

Inside, it is best to tackle matters from the top down, so take the elevator to the fifth floor. Here is a large collection of American pictures, less selective than that at the Metropolitan Museum and less clearly labelled. Starting with a Gilbert Stuart rendering of Washington, it takes you through a smattering of primitive portraits, some ambitious landscapes of varying quality, untypical examples of the work of Sargent and Remington, plenty of St Gaudens statuary and a fine La Farge window, up to Georgia O'Keeffe (represented by a peremptory impression of Brooklyn Bridge) and the moderns. With this and the Met's collection, no city offers a better perspective on American art.

The fourth floor houses twenty-eight American rooms from the seventeenth to the twentieth century, which again complement the Metropolitan's American Wing. The reconstruction of a 1675 two-roomed Dutch farmhouse from the Flatlands section of Brooklyn is superbly

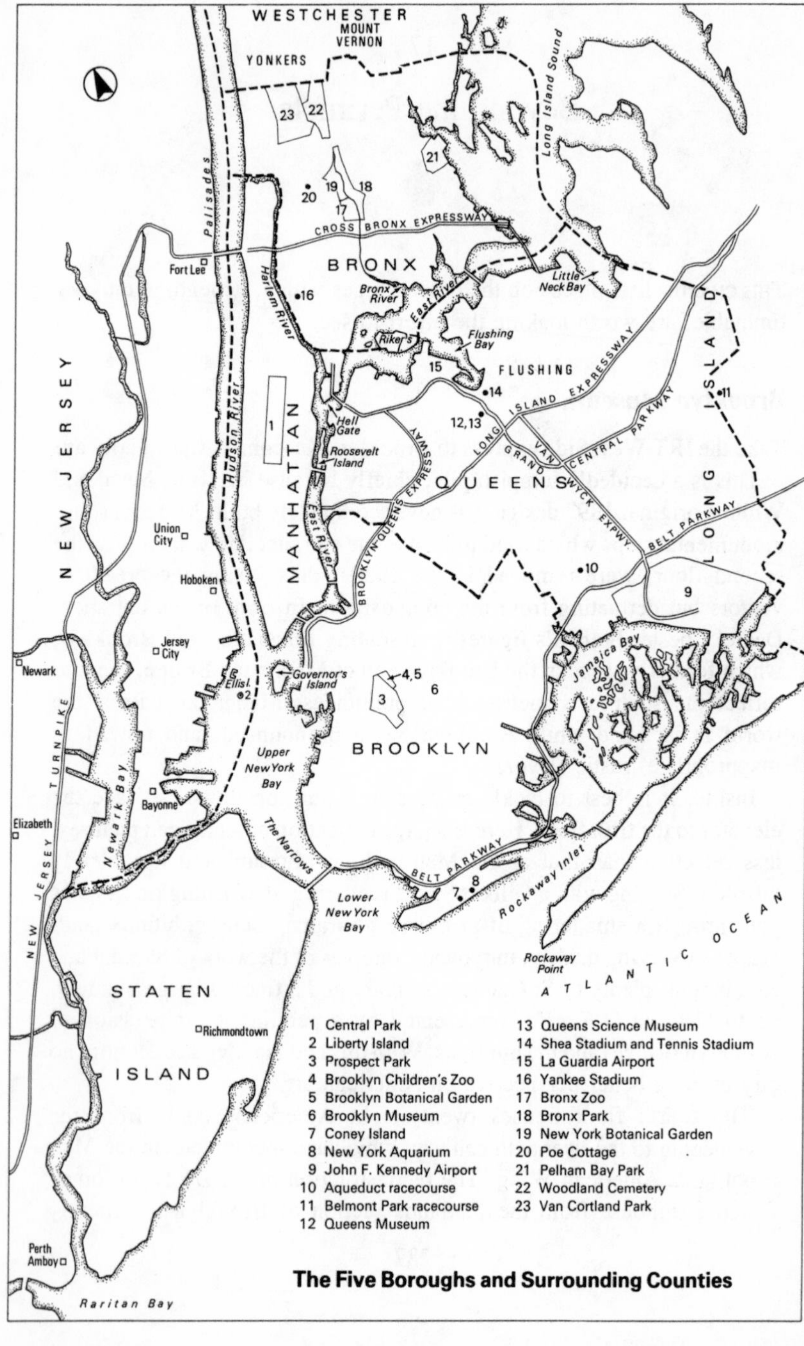

The Five Boroughs and Surrounding Counties

done. A small display of American folk art includes trade signs and toleware; there's a choice collection of American silver and a museum of costume.

Scholars of ancient Egypt prize the Egyptian and Middle Eastern collection on the third floor, its large Assyrian tablets and reliefs, its tombs, mummies and statuary, including a dignified votive cat. In the center of this floor is a fine courtyard, and around it some well-preserved mosaics. The second floor has less ambitious collections of art from farther east — China, Japan and Persia. Much of the ground floor is occupied by the museum shop, once the biggest in America, selling genuine old quilts and other nineteenth-century memorabilia, as well as inexpensive pieces of folk art and jewelry from overseas. Beyond the cursory hall devoted to the Americas is a reasonable cafeteria. Outside, the so-called sculpture garden consists mainly of bits of old buildings and street furniture rescued from the wrecker's yard, much of it threatening to disappear beneath ground cover.

Brooklyn Botanic Garden

This is my favorite open space in the city, on a more manageable scale than its more famous competitor in the Bronx, less frenetic than Central Park, and not to be missed if you make the trip to the museum; the entrance is just beside it, on the right. Notice the ornamental iron gates, representing different species of grasses. Ask at the entrance booth for a free map, then guide yourself through the Rose Garden. On the left, parallel with the roses, the cherry blossom walk is magnificent in late spring. Past the row of Norwegian maples, planted for the 1918 armistice, turn left and quickly right over a diminutive wooden bridge: this leads to a path by a lake which is part of the Japanese Garden. Follow the path to the pavilion opposite the wishing well. So authentic is the atmosphere that on two visits here I have seen Japanese couples having wedding photographs taken in the pavilion. Behind it is the Shakespeare Garden, with examples of flowers, herbs and vegetables mentioned in his works, labelled with thorough references. Past the Fragrance Garden for blind visitors, the gift shop will appeal to the green-fingered. Outside are some spectacular water lilies and on the left the greenhouses, designed by McKim, Mead and White, whose exhibits include some fascinating cacti and exquisite bonsai trees. Now head past the experimental flower beds and across the lawn to the Rock Garden, then out of the gate on Flatbush Avenue, opposite the entrance to Prospect Park.

Brooklyn Children's Museum

A first-rate outing for children under eleven, but it involves a tiresome journey by public transport. The No 2 (IRT West Side express) stops at Kingston Avenue/Eastern Parkway. Turn right and walk six blocks until the museum, built in 1977, looms unmistakably on your right. A wondrous maze of tunnels and tubes with exits on various levels, it contains few actual exhibits to look at but many engrossing things to do. It can sometimes be hard to lure children away from the enclosed stream that runs down the middle of the entrance ramp, with bricks for damming the fast-moving water and diverting the current. Other popular sections are the musical instrument gallery and the transparent plastic cubes forming a maze to climb through.

Coney Island and New York Aquarium

If you like faded old seaside resorts, they hardly come older or more faded. Coney Island was a smart resort in the early years of the century, becoming a mecca for day-trippers when the subway reached here. Now many subways come but the fastest is the Sixth Avenue line. The more garish bits of 1920s kitsch have gone, to be replaced by 1970s kitsch. The Cyclone, one of the oldest and most frightening of roller-coasters, is still here, and so is the surrealistic mushroom-shaped object which used to accommodate the parachute jump but is now idle. Walk along the wooden boardwalk and have a beer, an ice cream, a hot dog or even half a dozen clams from the snack booths interspersed with amusement arcades. On a hot summer's day you'll be part of a throng of plump, lobster-colored New Yorkers in skimpy beachwear. Go for a *real* hot dog to the original branch of Nathan's Famous eatery, still in more or less the same premises on Surf Avenue.

The aquarium, at the eastern end of the boardwalk, is good value; the pair of tremendous white whales just inside the entrance must not, indeed, be missed. In the outdoor section it almost always seems to be feeding time for the penguins. Children love that. They're also suitably terrified by the sharks and enjoy picking up the horseshoe crabs in the 'touch and feel' section.

Bronx Zoo

IRT trains No. 2 (West Side express) and No 5 (East Side express) stop at East Tremont Avenue/Boston Road, only a short walk from the southern entrance. An express bus service to the zoo (BxM11) picks up passengers along Madison Avenue at 28th, 37th, 60th and 84th Streets.

One of the world's most important zoos, with three thousand animals in two hundred fifty-two acres, it was among the first to minimize the use of cages and put animals in landscaped areas which simulate as far as possible their natural habitat, safely separated from spectators by wide and deep ravines. Among its features is the Wild Asia Express, a monorail ride above thirty-eight acres (larger in itself, the publicity material claims, than the entire London Zoo) in which Asian animals roam comparatively freely — though during the day many have the irritating habit of sleeping. The World of Darkness is a small building lit so that the animals in it believe it is night, when they are at their most active. There are three aviaries — one for colorful tropical birds, another for predators (eagles and vultures) and one for water birds. In many sections, walkways wend through naturalistic settings where the birds fly freely. Children — and adults for that matter — can ride camels, elephants and pony carts and visit the innovative children's zoo.

New York Botanical Garden

There is no convenient subway for this but a local Conrail train from Grand Central stops right outside the main entrance.

Just north of the zoo, this is one of the largest botanical gardens in America and a must for serious horticulturists though, as I have noted, less suitable for the casual visitor than the smaller one in Brooklyn. To reach all the interesting areas in its two hundred thirty acres you really need a car; and the fact that cars are allowed to drive through and to park in areas near the highlights compromises the garden's character as a haven of rustic peace. In their season the daffodils, azaleas, magnolias, cherries and rhododendrons provide a spectacular show, while the giant greenhouses in the middle, designed in 1902 along the lines of the Great Palm House at Kew in England, have recently been well restored and contain much of interest. Near them are a shop, a museum and a herbarium. You can take tea in the Old Lorillard Snuff Mill, built in the 1840s, where a terrace of tables looks out over the Bronx River.

Woodlawn Cemetery

Take the Lexington Avenue No 4 express uptown to its last stop, Woodlawn; the Jerome Avenue entrance to Woodlawn Cemetery is just beyond the elevated railway station. Since it opened in 1865, Woodlawn has been one of the most lavish cemeteries in the world, where the city's rich and famous, but especially rich, have been buried in tombs as ambitious as the neo-Classical houses they built for themselves. While the most extravagant of their Fifth Avenue homes have been pulled down, the former squires have fled north to rest, one assumes forever, in the style to which during their successful lives they became accustomed. Thus Oliver Hazard Belmont, the financier and horse racing enthusiast, took it into his head that he would like his remains entombed in an exact replica of the St Hubert Chapel at Amboise in France, where Leonardo da Vinci was buried. This immodest fancy was fulfilled and may be seen on the right of the main entrance: its prominent gargoyles and pinnacled roof stand out as you get off the train. Not far away Frank W. Woolworth, the chain store magnate, rests in Egyptian splendor, guarded by two sphinxes. Jay Gould, the financier and manipulator, has a Greek temple, modest as Greek temples go. The best plan is to pick up a free map and guide book from the office on the right of the entrance gate and work out an itinerary.

The Poe Cottage

Take the D train on the Sixth Avenue line or the No 4 on the IRT Lexington Avenue line to Kingsbridge Road. The house stands in a small park at the junction of Grand Concourse and East Kingsbridge Road, moved a hundred yards or so from a more southerly site where it stood on the very crest of the rise. It remains of interest not just as a literary shrine but as the only house left from the old rural village of Fordham, of which this was the center. Edgar Allan Poe moved here with his young wife

Virginia and mother-in-law Mrs Clemm in 1846, because he thought the country air would benefit Virginia, who had tuberculosis. It was thirteen miles north of New York City, whence the three had moved from Philadelphia three years earlier. He had married Virginia in 1836, when she was not yet fourteen, and her health had deteriorated steadily since.

Poe was a morose, tormented writer, whose poems and stories derive from a preoccupation with the morbid and supernatural. An arrogant and ill-tempered critic and controversialist, his bursts of petulance were interspersed with bouts of wild drunkenness and, his biographers suspect, experiments with drugs. Because of his instability he was seldom employed for long and was never able to attain a steady income, even after his poem 'The Raven', published in 1845, brought him as much fame as he would earn in his lifetime.

No longer surrounded by fruit trees, a flower garden and a small aviary, the wooden Fordham cottage built in 1808 is in other respects the same as when Poe and his family paid $100 a year in rent to live there, the furnishings recreated from contemporary evidence. The front door leads into the kitchen with its iron stove. On the left of it is the living-room, and beyond that the cramped bedroom containing the bed where Virginia, the move having failed to effect a cure, died in January 1847 at the age of twenty-four, bundled against the bitter cold. At the foot of the stairs is an etching that shows Poe in his cloak walking across the High Bridge over the Harlem River, one of his favorite rustic excursions. Poe used one of the two upstairs rooms as a study, the other as a bedroom. They are confined spaces wedged beneath the sloping roof of the cottage, whose modest size indicates the financial difficulties Poe suffered all his life. In the larger room, visitors can see a fifteen-minute audio-visual presentation, giving a concise account of the poet's life and his period at Fordham. Among the poems he wrote there was 'Annabel Lee', referring quite directly to Virginia's death.

After Virginia's death Poe and Mrs Clemm stayed at the cottage, but the poet's mental and physical health deteriorated. He had a nearly barren year, though in 1848 began productive work again. His emotional life continued in a state of turmoil, a series of somewhat ridiculous liaisons with literary women ending in the narrow avoidance of marriage. He was drinking heavily again but went to Richmond, Virginia, to lecture and renew old acquaintances (he had spent the early years of his life there). On his way back to Fordham, in October 1849, he disappeared in

Baltimore and was discovered delirious in the street; he died in a hospital four days later.

Van Cortland House

Get the No 1 train (IRT West Side local) to its most northerly stop, 242nd Street. Walk north from the station and you'll spot the house near the edge of Van Cortland Park on your right. It was built in 1748 by Frederick Van Cortland, from a wealthy land-owning family. A solid Georgian stone box, grander than most New York houses of the era, its most unusual feature outside are the carved faces set into the brickwork above the front windows.

On the left of the entrance, the hall or west parlor is furnished in the style of the mid-eighteenth century, though the Dutch tile fireplace might have been a bit of an anachronism even then. This room has one of the house's two fine Dutch ornamental kasts, or linen cupboards, this one in pine with painted grisaille fruits and flowers. The more formal parlor across the hall contains some rather more elegant furniture from approximately the same period, as well as a spectacular Regency mantelpiece. Some furniture has come direct from the Van Cortland family, the rest bought with an eye to authenticity. The dining room, along the corridor, has pieces from the early 1800s and one of the house's most interesting portraits, John Jacob Astor painted by Gilbert Stuart. Below the dining room is a large old kitchen with the trappings familiar to inveterate house tourists — pewter plates, large tureens, bed warmers, candle moulds and the like. Up the stairs from the kitchen, then up again, the so-called Dutch room has the other kast, fine and formidable. Just inside the Munro Chamber, the principal bedroom, is a grandfather clock bearing the date 1619. This chamber also has two fine pieces of American furniture, a walnut veneer dressing-table of 1710 and the New England maple tester bed, 1790.

Washington slept in the house when he used it as a stopping place in 1783, returning in triumph to New York. (Throughout the Revolutionary War this northern fringe of the city changed hands several times and the house was used as an operational headquarters by both British and American armies.) Washington's room has been equipped with fabrics in a striking eighteenth-century design and its lowboy, by William Savery of Philadelphia, is another outstanding piece of American furniture.

Richmondtown Restoration

Staten Island is the hardest of the New York boroughs for the tourist to come to grips with. Many visitors take the ferry from the Battery for the view of the Lower Manhattan skyline, but when they reach Staten Island they turn right around and return to the more familiar shore. One place at least is worth the trip for the visitor with an interest in New York's history, for Richmondtown is a restored village containing a group of eighteenth- and nineteenth-century houses unparallelled in the area. From the ferry terminal you can take a taxi or bus No 113.

Until the 1960s Staten Island, because of the difficulty of access, remained largely rural. It was not until the opening of the Verrazano Narrows Bridge in 1964 — the first land link with the rest of the city — that development on a big scale began. Now it is a crowded suburb; the former fields and hills have been invaded by row after row of detached and semi-detached family homes and some apartment buildings, though it is still, with its four hundred thousand inhabitants, the smallest of the five boroughs in terms of population. The name is Dutch (originally Staaten Eylandt) and is said to have been given to the one hundred-square-mile island by Henry Hudson's expedition in 1609, undertaken on behalf of the Dutch East India Company. Europeans settled here fifty-two years later.

Richmondtown was the largest town on the island during the eighteenth century and the county seat until its incorporation into Greater New York in 1898. Called Cocclestown when founded in 1685, the name was changed to Richmondtown a few years later to match the name Richmond which the British had given to the whole island. (It is still the official name of the borough but the earlier Staten Island has proved more durable.) Its restoration as a museum village involved moving some historic houses here from nearby sites and is still far from complete.

Start at the museum and gift shop, the old County Clerk's office, at the corner of Court Place and Center Street. The museum is domestic in nature: many exhibits are kitchen and garden implements from the nineteenth century. There are prints and drawings of Staten Island as it was and, upstairs, some early photographs of its grandest houses, now mostly destroyed. Here you can get a map to navigate the rest of the restoration area. Across Court Place are a carpenter's and a grocer's shop, the latter now selling old prints (both are nineteenth-century buildings moved here from other parts of the island). Next to them are the Stephens House and Store, on the site where they were built in the 1830s. The store, complete with post office, has been reconstructed in line with the period. Architecturally, this group hints at the Greek Revival style, which is illustrated at its most typical by the county court house on the other side of Center Street, immediately opposite Court Place. This solidly Classical building is not normally open to the public but the exterior is in any case its most interesting aspect. Turning left along Center Street, as you look at the court house, you come to a museum of firefighting equipment on your left.

Double back along Center Street to Arthur Kill Road. On the opposite side of the road on the left is the oldest house in the restoration and one of the few seventeenth-century buildings in the city. Voorlezer's House was built in the 1690s as a school and is on its original site. It is a charming little Colonial building which has lasted so long because of its solid oak timbers and thick foundation walls. Leaving the house, turn left along Arthur Kill Road, then right into Richmond Road. On the left, a little way back from the hill, an old barrel-maker's shop has been moved from nearby and is now used by a leather worker who, along with craftsmen in other shops, gives occasional demonstrations. A little farther on, just beyond the junction with Court Place, the Guyon-Lake-Tysen House is a transposed Colonial farmhouse (1740), well furnished and maintained, the largest dwelling on display. There are several other structures in the restoration area and, when the money can be found, the aim is to have them all open to the public, forming a smaller and later version of the extravagantly funded Williamsburg restoration in Virginia.

Hall of Science, Queens Zoo and Queens Museum

Visitors may get a rapid glimpse of the Hall of Science's prominent features — notably the early space rockets — as they drive into the city from Kennedy Airport. It is currently being refurbished and will re-open shortly. To get to the site by subway, take the No 7 Flushing train from Times Square or Grand Central and get off at 111th Street in Queens. Walk south down 111th Street. Shortly before passing under a railway bridge you will see the nozzles of the rockets pointing up into space: these are in the science museum's grounds. Just past the bridge, cross a car park (the stadium straight ahead is the new location for the U S Open tennis tournament) to reach the museum entrance. As the rocket shells outside suggest, the museum, with its curious crinkle-crankle outer wall, is strongest on exhibits relating to space travel. It is New York's only science museum and is part of a set of structures in Flushing Meadows put up for the 1964 World Fair, though the grounds were first laid out for the 1939 fair, on land which had hitherto been a swamp.

Just beyond the museum is Queens Zoo, the smallest of the city's zoos, concentrating on birds and American wild animals such as buffalo and wolves. Near it is a children's zoo in buildings which represent, though not too convincingly, a Colonial farm. Children can wander around, pet and feed the animals and take pony rides. From the children's zoo, follow the divided path across a bridge over the Grand Central Parkway. The dilapidated edifice on the right is the New York State Pavilion from the 1964 World Fair. A few yards to the left is the New York City Pavilion from the 1939 fair, which can claim a brief place in world history as the temporary home of the United Nations General Assembly in 1946. Now it houses the Queens Museum, a small gallery for exhibitions of contemporary art. For tourists its most interesting feature is the immensely detailed fifteen thousand square foot model of New York city from the 1964 fair: The panorama was such a success at the fair that it has been kept as a permanent exhibit, still regularly brought up to date with the latest buildings. The lighting effects make it turn from day to night in a matter of minutes and a miniature aircraft takes off and lands at La Guardia airport every so often. Just behind the museum you can take a close-up look at the hollow globe, a hundred and forty feet high, called a unisphere and donated by US Steel as a symbol of harmony between nations.

Flushing

This former township in the north of Queens was first settled in 1645 by a group of Englishmen, although it was still then part of the Dutch colony of New Netherland and was named after the port in Holland. Now a busy residential and commercial area, it includes the oldest house in New York open to the public, an easy subway ride on the No 7 line from Times Square or Grand Central.

Take the subway to its last stop, Main Street, two stations beyond the stop for Queens Museum. Walk north up the street, towards a prominent movie theater, RKO Keiths. Before you reach it turn right up 37th Street and walk to where the street ends in a small park. This is Bowne Street, and across it on your right you will see the low wooden Bowne House, the oldest section of which was built in 1661. You have to time your visit carefully because visiting hours are short but you get a comprehensive tour in the company of enthusiastic volunteer guides.

John Bowne emigrated with his father and sister to Boston in 1649 from Matlock in Derbyshire. Two years later he moved to the new settlement of Flushing, then part of the domain of the fiery Peter Stuyvesant, governor of New Netherland. Many of its residents were Quakers or members of other Protestant sects, and although the town's 1645 charter had guaranteed them freedom of worship, Stuyvesant had other ideas: he issued a decree that forbade any religious practice in the colony except that of the Dutch Calvinist church. Efforts to enforce this ruling led local freethinkers to present the Governor in December 1657 with the Flushing Remonstrance, asking that their former privileges of worship be restored. Stuyvesant was unmoved and the Quakers took to holding secret meetings in the woods. The young Bowne sympathized. He had come to identify closely with them in 1656 when he married Hannah Feake, the daughter of Elizabeth Winthrop, a leading New England freethinker. When he built this house in 1661 he gave permission for the Quakers to hold meetings in its principal room, which remains today much as it would have appeared then. One of the furnishings is a narrow wooden couch on which George Fox, a prominent Quaker, is said to have rested after preaching there.

In 1662 Stuyvesant ordered Bowne to stop allowing meetings in his house and tried to fine him for breach of the ordinance. Bowne refused to pay the fine, was imprisoned in Manhattan and finally sent to Holland to face trial by executives of the West India Company. He was acquitted and the company ordered Stuyvesant to adhere to the terms of the Flushing charter by allowing freedom of worship. 'The consciences of men ought to be free and unshackled so long as they continue moderate, peaceable, inoffensive and not hostile to the government,' they wrote. Bowne returned triumphantly to his family in Flushing in 1663. The following year the British took the colony from the Dutch and in 1666 Richard Nicholls, the new governor, issued an order confirming the rights of the people to worship as they wished.

The house remained in the hands of the Bownes and their descendants for generations and, remarkably, the pieces of furniture on display in it are those bought for the house over the years and used by its occupants.

Leaving the Bowne House by the back entrance, you will face a yellow wooden building with green shutters. This is the Kingsland House, a farmhouse from the mid-eighteenth Century, moved here in the 1960s from its original location about a mile farther eat. The chief interest is outside. Although Holland had ceded the colony nearly a century before the house was built, Dutch influence in this section of Long Island was still strong and the house reflects this, with its sloping gambrel roof and the curiously curved windows on the north and south sides. In the garden is a rare weeping beech tree planted by Samuel Parsons, a Bowne kinsman, in 1849.

The final landmark in this short itinerary (closed for restoration during 1982) is the Friends Meeting House, the oldest place of worship in New York, built in 1694 to enable the Quakers to have a proper meeting hall of their own, rather than borrowing private parlors. To reach this interesting wooden building from Kingsland House, walk north up Bowne Street to Northern Boulevard and turn left: It's on the left between Bowne Street and Main Street. From there, continue west along Northern Boulevard and turn left into Main Street for the subway, at the junction with Roosevelt Avenue.

City Island

Technically part of the Bronx, though miles from it in spirit, this small nautical community could almost be a little boating and fishing resort anywhere on the New England coast. It's a cumbersome journey by public transport: the No 6 Lexington Avenue local subway to Pelham Bay Park, its northern terminus, then the Bx 12 bus. Better to try to arrange to go by car. In summer, hundreds of yachts moor here and chandlers along the shore sell sailing and fishing equipment. Farther along, the main arterial avenue is lined with fish restaurants, some commanding fine sea views; the Lobster Box is one of the best, though quite expensive. At the very end of the avenue, adjoining the pier, is a large cafeteria-style eating place, where you buy your fish and chips at the counter and eat them al fresco — a cheap and cheerful venue for picking up a fast sunburn. Just north of the island is Orchard Beach, the most northerly of the city's public beaches, also served by the Bx 12 bus.

Notes for First-time Visitors to the USA

Climate

New York is hotter in summer and colder in winter than most parts of Western Europe, so dress accordingly. From mid-July to mid-September it is often unpleasantly humid and people wear very skimpy clothes, except on the most formal occasions. But if you are going to a theatre or restaurant in the evening, even at the hottest time of year, take a cardigan because the air-conditioning is ferocious. All department stores and most public buildings are comfortably air-conditioned and well heated in winter.

Accommodation

American hotels charge per room rather than per person, so the cost for two people sharing a room will be nowhere near double the single charge. Or you could rent an apartment: there are agencies in London which specialize in holiday house exchange — study advertisements in *The Times*, the *Sunday Times*, the *Observer*, the *New Statesman* or the *International Herald Tribune*, published from Paris. Since most New Yorkers live in apartments, it follows that you will be better able to appreciate how they live by doing the same, as well as sharing the mysteries and harrassments of an occasional visit to the supermarket and delicatessen. While on the subject of buildings, one tricky point concerns floors. The usual American practice is to call the ground floor the first floor. What in Europe we call the first floor is here the second floor, and so on. In this book I have used the American system, to avoid confusion with elevator (lift) buttons.

Opening Hours

Shops generally open a bit later than in London — around ten o'clock. They are open at least until 6:00 p.m. and the department stores stay open until 9:00 p.m. on two or three evenings towards the end of the week.

Most department stores are open on Sunday afternoon (12:00 to 5:00) p.m.) except in high summer. Food shops open earlier and close later and most parts of town have at least one small grocery store (delicatessen) open all night. Some supermarkets are open twenty-four hours as well, but these are mainly in the suburbs. Only the smallest shops close for lunch. This is often a half-hour or so earlier than the British lunch hour: you will often be asked to turn up for a business lunch at 12:00 or 12:30.

Post offices are normally open from about 9:00 a.m. to 5:00 p.m. but they vary. Stamps from machines are available round the clock at the post office on Lexington Avenue at 45th Street, and the main office on Eighth Avenue at 33rd Street; these are the best offices to post letters at for speedy delivery. Stamps are sold in many shops from machines but these are at a higher price than their face value.

Banking hours vary. In the central areas they usually are from 8:30 or 9:00 a.m. to 3:30 or 4:00 p.m. Savings banks open longer hours but they will not usually provide services such as cashing travelers' checks. Out of hours you can cash checks at a number of private exchange offices in the midtown area, but they usually take a higher commission than banks. Take dollar travelers' checks because American banks are often baffled by foreign currency.

Bars open from mid-morning and can stay open until 3:00 a.m.

Food and Drink

Americans are very good at breakfast. While they have allowed European and Asian influences to change the shapes and flavors of their main meals, breakfast remains distinctive and usually first-rate value. The merciless quizzing to which you will be subjected about how you want your egg fried ('over' is short for 'over easy' and means fried on both sides while 'up' or 'sunny side up' is fried on one side only) will prepare you for similar sharp questioning at every meal. You will be asked exactly how you would like your hamburger cooked, which one of perhaps a half-dozen dressings you want on your salad, and much else. Visitors sometimes find this irritating but it is done with the best of motives, to avoid disappointment.

Back to breakfast. Boiled eggs are usually served without the shell. Bacon comes thinner and crisper than in Britain. Sausages are smaller and spicier than in Britain and seldom have skins. The American taste for mixing sweet things with savory is given free rein at this meal and the sausages and bacon can, if you like, be served with syrup. Pancakes, or hot cakes, make a sweet, filling breakfast, smothered in syrup also, with a dressing of whipped butter; children should be allowed to try that at least once. English muffins — American style — are good with eggs or simply hot buttered by themselves. 'Biscuits' are scones, but are more often served in the south than in New York.

For lunch you can get almost anything served between chunks of bread — even Italian meat balls. A chain of snack-bars called Blimpie sells cold meat cuts with a choice of salad items in a foreshortened French loaf. At ordinary coffee or sandwich shops such things are called 'heroes' or 'submarines'. (In Philadelphia they are called 'hoagies' and in New Orleans 'poboys.') For around $3 they make an ample meal. If you want hamburgers and don't like the slender version served by Macdonald's or Burger King, a chain called Bun 'n' Burger makes them fatter and juicier, as do many coffee shops. Several chains with names combining the words beef, brew and burger sell larger and more expensive hamburgers, as well as reasonably priced steak and roast beef, with beer or wine. (American mustard is much milder than European varieties.) Another chain, Tad's Steaks, has a choice of a half-dozen set meals of medium quality steak, potatoes, bread and salad sold on a self-service system at exceptionally low prices, with beer or wine too. You will find several branches in the midtown area. A hot pastrami — a kind of pressed beef — sandwich on rye bread is a New York tradition you should try. Corned beef is nearly the same as English salt beef. I have recommended one or two places for this in the chapters on the Lower East Side and the diamond district.

What to drink? Beware the zippily named cocktails, which slide down the throat with treacherous ease and can make you very drunk very quickly. Beer is light, cold and thirst-quenching but, to a British palate, lacks distinctive flavor. California wine is excellent but be wary of a concoction called Cold Duck, a sweet sparkling burgundy with many of the attributes of Coca-Cola.

Entertainments and Sports

American serious drama deals with more ambitious and more universal themes than is customary in Britain. The plays are about life in general rather than particular segments of it, and the playwrights use powerful metaphors of death, madness and physical disability. Comedies are of the wisecracking, one-line joke variety, of which Neil Simon is the acknowledged master.

If you are a real film fan and do not mind staying up until the small hours, look at the television schedules. The after-midnight movies bristle with Cary Grant, Katherine Hepburn, Gene Kelly, the Marx Brothers, Abbott and Costello and the original King Kong.

There are few better ways of viewing Americans at leisure than going to a baseball game. You do not need to understand the rules (though fellow spectators will try to explain them to you) to be overwhelmed by the noise and the frenzy. The season runs from April until October and at all times except high summer you will need to take a light jacket to ward off the late-night chill, since most games are played under floodlights after dark and continue until nearly midnight. You can also glimpse one of the great traditions of American sport — arguing with the umpire.

The Cosmos play a reasonably skilled facsimile of European soccer at Giants Stadium in New Jersey (a twenty-minute bus ride from the Port Authority bus terminal on Eighth Avenue and 40th Street). The soccer season is about the same as for baseball. American football, at the Giants Stadium or Shea Stadium, is a less suitable game for the uninitiated: the rules are complex and there are frequent stoppages inexplicable to the outsider. The 'Ivy League' colleges also play each other at football. They are a group of old-established universities in the eastern part of the country and have a social and academic standing a cut above the average. The name derives from some of the league members — Yale, Princeton, Harvard — creating their campuses in a mock-Gothic style suggestive of Oxford and Cambridge.

Safety

I gave a few tips on this in the section on subways and buses in Chapter 1. As in all large cities, the rule is: don't do anything foolish. Don't walk late at night in the seedy areas around Times Square (you are quite safe until well after the theaters close). Don't take cuts through streets that look empty. Don't carry your wallet in an unbuttoned back pocket, and keep a good grip on your handbag at all times.

Manhattan Address Key

To find an address on one of the north-south avenues if you have only the number of the building, a complicated formula has been devised. You take the building number, lop off the last figure and divide what is left by two. Then you add or subtract the number shown on the following table. For instance, to locate 246 Fifth Avenue, you ignore the 6 and divide 24 by 2, making 12. After referring to the table, you add 16. Your target will be close to the junction with 28th Street.

Avenues A,B,C,D	+3
First Avenue	+3
Second Avenue	+3
Third Avenue	+10
Fourth Avenue	+8
Fifth Avenue	
up to 200	+13
201–400	+16
401–600	+18
601–775	+20
776–1286 — cancel last figure, then	−18
1287–1500	+45
above 2000	+24
Avenue of the Americas	−12
Seventh Avenue	+12
above 110th St	+20
Eighth Avenue	+10
Ninth Avenue	+13
Tenth Avenue	+14
Amsterdam Avenue	+60
Audubon Avenue	+165
Broadway (23rd to 192nd St)	−30
Central Park West — divide building number by 10, then	+60

MANHATTAN ADDRESS KEY

Columbus Avenue	+60
Convent Avenue	+127
Edgecombe Avenue	+134
Ft Washington Avenue	+158
Lenox Avenue	+110
Lexington Avenue	+22
Madison Avenue	+26
Manhattan Avenue	+100
Park Avenue	+35
Pleasant Avenue	+101
Riverside Drive — divide bldg no by 10, then up to 165th St	+72
St. Nicholas Avenue	+110
Wadsworth Avenue	+173
West End Avenue	+60

To find addresses on crosstown streets, use the plan below.

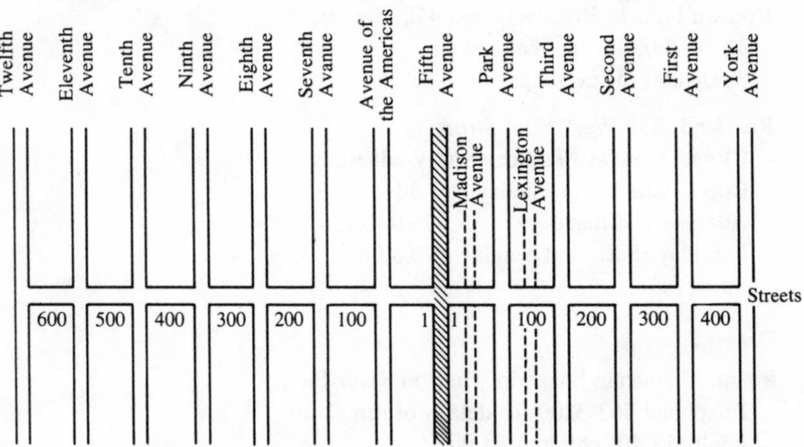

North of 59th Street, Eighth Avenue becomes Central Park West, Ninth is Columbus Avenue, Tenth is Amsterdam Avenue, Eleventh is West End Avenue and Twelfth is Riverside Drive. Because the Park occupies the blocks between Fifth Avenue and Central Park West, the numbering of the west streets begins at Central Park West with No 1; No 100 is by Columbus Avenue, and so on.

Opening Times and Admission Charges

Admission charges, where shown in the following list, were checked before going to press, but there is every chance that they will have risen by the time of publication.

CHAPTER 1

Tkts NY (theatre tickets), 100 William Street:
11:30–5:30 Monday–Friday
11:00–3:00 Saturday

Uptown branch: Broadway and 47th Street:
12:00–2:00 for matinee tickets
3:00–8:00 for evenings

Roseland, 259 West 52nd Street:
Closed Monday, Tuesday and Wednesday
Open Thursday to Sunday at 2:30
Admission: Thursday — $5.00 all day.
Friday, Sat., and Sunday — $6.00

CHAPTER 2

Round Manhattan boat trip, Hudson River Pier:
Telephone 563-3200 for details of schedules
Adults $8.50, children $4.00

Staten Island Ferry, Whitehall Street:
Telephone 248-8093 for details of schedules
25 cents return

Statue of Liberty or Ellis Island
Telephone 269-5755 for schedules
Round trip $1.50, 50 cents for children

CHAPTER 3

New York Stock Exchange, 11 Wall Street
10:00–4:00 Monday to Friday
Admission free

Federal Hall National Memorial, 26 Wall Street:
9:00–5:00 Monday to Friday (summer and winter)
Free concerts 12:30–1:30 Wednesday

Trinity Church, 74 Trinity Place:
Free instrumental concerts at 12:45 Tuesday

American Stock Exchange, 86 Trinity Place:
10:00–4:00 Monday to Friday
Admission free

Federal Reserve Bank, Liberty Street
Telephone 791-6130 for details of free tours, or write to the bank at 33 Liberty Street, New York, NY 10045

CHAPTER 4

South Street Seaport Museum Visitors' Orientation Center, 16 Fulton Street:
11:00–5:00 daily

Exhibition Ships, Pier 15, John Street:
11:00–5:00 daily

World Trade Center Observation Deck:
9:30 to 9:30 daily
Adults $2.50, children and Senior Citizens $1.25

CHAPTER 5

Museum of Holography, 11 Mercer Street:
12:00–6:00 Wednesday, Friday, Saturday, Sunday
12:00–9:00 Thursday
Adults $2.50, students with ID $2.00, children and Senior Citizens $1.00

Chapter 6

Church of the Ascension, Fifth Avenue and West 10th Street:
12:00 to 2:00 and 5:00 to 7:00 daily

Salamagundi Club, 47 Fifth Avenue:
1:00 to 5:00 daily
Admission free

Judson Memorial Church Hall, 55 Washington Square South:
10:00 to 12:00 weekdays

Chapter 7

Theodore Roosevelt Birthplace, 28 East 20th Street:
9:00–5:00 daily
Admission 50 cents
Free chamber music concerts 2:00 Saturday

Grace Church, 802 Broadway:
Free public organ recital lunch hour Thursday

Ottendorfer Library, 135 Second Avenue (St Mark's Place):
12:00 to 6:00 on weekdays

The Old Merchant's House, 29 East 4th Street:
1:00 to 4:00 Sunday
Telephone 777-1089 for details of opening hours and to arrange tours

Public Theatre, Lafayette Street:
Telephone 598-7150 for details of performances and timings

Chapter 8

Empire State Building, Fifth Avenue and 34th Street:
9:30 to midnight daily
Adults $2.50, children under 12 $1.25

Guinness World Record Exhibition:
Adults $2.75, children under 12 $1.75

Morgan Library Museum, 29 East 36th Street:
10:30 to 5:00 Tuesday to Saturday
1:00 to 5:00 Sunday
Closed Monday
Suggested donation — $2.00

Chapter 9

UN Center, 42nd Street:
Tours from 9:15 to 4:45 daily
Adults $3.00, students $1.75, children $1.25

Grand Central Station, 42nd Street:
Tours meet in front of the Chemical Bank Express Counter, east end of main concourse 12:00 Wednesday

New York Public Library, Fifth Avenue and 42nd Street:
10:00 to 6:00 Monday, Wednesday, Friday and Saturday
10:00 to 9:00 Tuesday
Closed Thursday and Sunday
Free tours at 11:00 and 2:00 Monday, Tuesday and Wednesday

Songwriters' Hall of Fame, 1 Times Square (42nd Street):
11:00 to 3:00 daily

Chapter 10

St Bartholomew's Church, Park Avenue between 50th and 51st Streets:
Telephone 751-1616 for details of tours and Sunday concerts

Museum of Broadcasting, 1 East 53rd Street:
12:00 to 5:00 Tuesday to Saturday
Open until 7:30 Tuesday evenings
Suggested donation — Adults $2.00, children $1.00

Museum of Modern Art, 11 West 53rd Street:
11:00 to 6:00 Friday to Tuesday
10:30 to 5:00 Thursday
Closed Wednesday

Adults $3.00, students $2.00, children under 16 and Senior Citizens $1.00
Telephone 956-7078 for details of old films at the cinema
Telephone 956-7070 for other museum information

Museum of American Folk Art, 49 West 53rd Street:
10:30 to 8:00 Tuesday
10:30 to 5:00 Wednesday to Sunday
Closed Monday
Adults $1.00, children and Senior Citizens 50 cents
Admission free on Tuesday night due to a grant
Telephone 581-2474 for details of current exhibition

Museum of Contemporary Crafts, 29 West 53rd Street:
10:00 to 5:00 Tuesday to Saturday
11:00 to 5:00 Sunday
Closed Monday
Telephone 397-0630 for details of current exhibition
Adults $1.00, students and Senior Citizens 50 cents

New York Experience Theater, 1221 Avenue of Americas (between 48th & 49th):
11:00 to 7:00 Monday to Thursday
11:00 to 8:00 Friday and Saturday
12:00 to 8:00 Sunday
Adults $3.90, children $2.00

Rockefeller Center, Avenue of the Americas:
Tours of the center, every half-hour from 9:30 to 4:45 daily
Adults $3.35, students $2.85, children $2.00

Tours of music hall only:
9:00, 12:45, 4:45 and 5:15 Monday and Tuesday
10:00, 11:30, 12:45, 4:15 and 5:15 Wednesday, Friday and Saturday
11:00, 12:45, 4:45 and 5:15 Sunday
Admission $3.95

CHAPTER 11

Abigail Adams Smith House, 421 East 61st Street:
10:00 to 4:00 Monday to Friday
Admission $1.00

Central Park, West 59th Street:
Tour in horse-drawn carriage: $17.00 for half an hour, $5.00 per every fifteen minutes thereafter

Delacorte Theater:
Telephone 598-7100 for details of performances and timings

Zoo hours: 11:00 to 5:00 daily
Admission free

Children's zoo: 10:00 to 4:30 daily
Admission 10 cents

CHAPTER 12

Frick Collection, 1 East 70th Street:
10:00 to 6:00 Tuesday to Saturday
1:00 to 6:00 Sunday
Admission $1.00 but $2.00 on Sunday; children under 10 not admitted
Telephone 288-0700 for details of lectures, usually: For one hour at 11:00 each morning of opening except weekends and not in summer; Chamber music concerts some Sundays

Whitney Museum of American Art, Madison and 75th Street:
11:00 to 8:00 Tuesday
11:00 to 6:00 Wednesday to Saturday
12:00 to 6:00 Sunday
Closed Monday
Adults $2.00, children under 12 free

Metropolitan Museum of Art, 610 Fifth Avenue (at 82nd Street):
10:00 to 8:45 Tuesday
10:00 to 4:45 Wednesday to Saturday
11:00 to 4:45 Sunday
Closed Monday
Suggested donation — Adults $4.00, students and Senior Citizens $2.00

CHAPTER 13

Gracie Mansion, 88th Street and East End Avenue:

Tours hourly between 10:00 and 4:00 Wednesday — reservation is essential

To obtain a reservation write to The Mayor's Office of Special Events, 42 Broadway, New York, NY 10004

Adults $1.50, students and Senior Citizens 75 cents

Guggenheim Museum, Fifth Avenue at 89th Street:

11:00 to 5:00 daily

11:00 to 8:00 Tuesday

Closed Monday

Adults $2.00, students $1.25, children under 7 free

Admission is free on Tuesday evening due to a grant

Cooper-Hewitt Museum, Fifth Avenue at 91st Street:

10:00 to 9:00 Tuesday

10:00 to 5:00 Wednesday to Saturday

12:00 to 5:00 Sunday

Adults $1.50, children under 12 free

Jewish Museum, 1109 Fifth Avenue (92nd Street):

12:00 to 5:00 Monday to Thursday

11:00 to 6:00 Sunday

Closed Friday and Saturday

Adults $2.00, students with ID $1.00

International Center of Photography, Fifth Avenue and 94th Street:

12:00 to 8:00 Tuesday to Friday

12:00 to 6:00 Saturday and Sunday

Closed Monday

Adults $2.00, students with ID $1.00

Museum of the City of New York, Fifth Avenue and 103rd Street:

10:00 to 5:00 Tuesday to Saturday

Closed Monday

1:00 to 5:00 Sunday

Donations welcome

CHAPTER 14

Lincoln Center, Broadway at 63rd Street:
Tours beginning at 10:00 to 10:30 until 5:00 daily
Telephone 877-1800 for reservations
Adults $3.75

American Museum of Natural History, Central Park West at 79th Street:
10:00 to 5:45 daily
10:00 to 9:00 Wednesday, Friday and Saturday
Admission is on a pay what you want basis but on Friday and Saturday evenings admission is free due to a grant

Discovery Room
11:00 to 2:00 Saturday and Sunday for supervised handling of artifacts
Telephone 873-4225 for details of hours

New York Historical Society, Central Park West and 77th Street:
10:00 to 5:00 Tuesday to Friday
1:00 to 5:00 Saturday and Sunday
Suggested donation — $2.00

CHAPTER 15

Harlem bus tour, 303 West 42nd Street:
Thursday morning gospel tour at 11:00, regular tour at 1:00 Saturday.
Telephone 247-2860 (Penny Sightseeing Co.) for reservations
The tours last for 3 hours, price $15.00

Morris-Jumel Mansion, Edgecombe Avenue and 160th Street:
10:00 to 4:00 Tuesday to Sunday
Closed on Monday
Admission $1.00

Abyssinian Baptist Church, 132 West 138th Street:
Sunday service at 11:00

Cathedral of St John the Divine, 1047 Amsterdam Avenue:
Guided tours at 11:00 and 2:00 Monday through Saturday
12:30 on Sunday

Columbia University Campus, Morningside Drive:
Tours from Information Office (Broadway and 116th Street) at 3:00 Monday to Friday

St Paul's Chapel: organ recital at 12:00 on Thursday during the term

Riverside Baptist Church, Riverside Drive at 122nd Street:
Viewing platform: between 11:00 and 3:00 Monday to Friday
12:00 to 4:00 Sunday
Bell ringing: 12:00 Saturday and 3:00 Sunday

Grant's Tomb, Riverside Drive at 122nd Street:
9:00 to 5:00 daily
Admission free

Hamilton Grange, 287 Convent Avenue:
Not currently open to the public as they're working on the house.

Museum of the American Indian (Heye Foundation), Broadway and 155th Street
(Audubon Terrace):
10:00 to 5:00 Tuesday to Saturday
1:00 to 5:00 Sunday
Closed Monday
Adults $1.50, children and Senior Citizens 75 cents

Hispanic Society, Broadway and 155th Street (Audubon Terrace):
10:00 to 4:30 Tuesday to Saturday
1:00 to 4:00 Sunday
Closed Monday and holidays
Admission free

American Numismatic Society, Broadway and 155th (Audubon Terrace):
9:00 to 4:30 Tuesday to Saturday
Admission free

American Academy of Arts and Letters, 633 West 155th Street:
Telephone 368-5900 for details of exhibitions and opening times
The academy is open only for exhibitions

The Cloisters, Fort Tryon Park:
10:00 to 4:45 Tuesday to Saturday
1:00 to 4:45 Sunday
Closed Monday
Telephone 923-3700 for details of concerts, especially around Christmas
Suggested donation — Adults $4.00, children and Senior Citizens $2.00

Dyckman House, east of Inwood Hill Park between West 204th and West 207th:
11:00 to 5:00 Tuesday to Sunday
Closed Monday
Admission free

Chapter 16

Long Island Historical Society, 128 Pierrepont Street at the corner of Clinton Street:
9:00 to 5:00 Tuesday to Saturday
Closed Sunday and Monday
Shop: 11:00 to 5:00 Tuesday to Saturday
Admission free

Chapter 17

Brooklyn Museum, 188 Eastern Parkway:
10:00 to 5:00 Wednesday to Saturday
12:00 to 5:00 Sunday
Closed Monday and Tuesday
Admission $2.00

Brooklyn Botanic Garden, 100 Washington Avenue:
8:00 to 6:00 Tuesday to Friday
10:00 to 6:00 Saturday and Sunday
Closed Monday
Admission free

Brooklyn Children's Museum, 145 Brooklyn Avenue:
1:00 to 5:00 Monday, Wednesday, Thursday and Friday
10:00 to 5:00 Saturday and Sunday
Closed Tuesday
Admission free

New York Aquarium, corner of Boardwalk and West 8th Street, Coney Island
10:00 to 5:00 daily
Adults $2.00, children under 12 75 cents

Bronx Zoo, Bronx Park:
10:00 to 5:00 Monday to Saturday
10:00 to 5:30 Sunday and holidays
Admission: Friday to Monday adults $2.50, children 75 cents
Tuesday, Wednesday, and Thursday admission free
Parking fee $2.00 at all times
Express pick-up by Pelham Parkway Bus Service: telephone 881-1000 for details of schedules and fares

New York Botanical Garden, Southern Boulevard and 200th Street (Bronx):
8:00 to 7:00 (dawn to dusk) daily
Cars are charged $2.50
Conservatory: 10:00 to 4:00 daily, closed on Monday
Admission to conservatory — adults $2.50, children and Senior Citizens 75 cents
Conrail train service from Grand Central (Harlem Division):
Telephone 532-4900 for details of schedules and fares

Woodlawn Cemetery, Webster Avenue and East 233rd Street (Bronx):
9:00 to 4:30 daily

Poe Cottage, Grand Concourse and East Kingsbridge Road:
1:00 to 5:00 Wednesday to Friday and Sunday
10:00 to 4:00 Saturday
Telephone 881-8900 for group visits
Admission 75 cents

Van Cortlandt Mansion Museum, Broadway and West 246 Street in the Bronx:
10:00 to 5:00 Tuesday to Saturday
2:00 to 5:00 Sunday
Closed Monday

Richmondtown Restoration, Staten Island:
Telephone 351-1617 for information about opening hours
Adults $2.00, students with ID and Senior Citizens $1.50, children $1.00

Hall of Science, Flushing, Queens:
Telephone 699-9400 for details of opening hours
*Museum is closed for renovations

Queens Museum, New York City Building in Flushing Meadow Park, Queens:
10:00 to 5:00 Tuesday to Saturday
1:00 to 5:00 Sunday
Closed Mondays
Suggested donation — adults $1.00, children 50 cents

Bowne House, 37-01 Bowne Street (Flushing, Queens):
2:30 to 4:15 on Tuesday, Saturday and Sunday
Adults $1.00, children 25 cents

Friends Meeting House, Flushing, Queens:
Call 762-9743 for opening hours

Source Notes

1. *Hudson River Landings* Paul Wilstach. Tudor Publishing Co., New York 1933, new edn 1937
2. *A Bintel Brief* Isaac Metzker. Doubleday and Co., New York 1971
3. *Humbug: The Art of P. T. Barnum* Neil Harris. Little Brown and Co., Boston 1973
4. *Gould's Millions* Richard O'Connor. Doubleday and Co., Garden City 1962
5. *The Great Crash: 1929* J. K. Galbraith. Hamish Hamilton, London 1955; Penguin Books 1961
6. *The City of New York: 1789* Thomas E. V. Smith. Chatham Press Inc., Riverside, Connecticut 1972
7. *Wall Street: A Pictorial History* Leonard Louis Levinson. Ziff-Davis Publishing Co., New York 1961
8. *The Time That Was Then* Harry Roskolenko. The Dial Press, New York 1971
9. *Seventy Years of Life and Labor* Samuel Gompers. New York, A. M. Kelly, 1967
10. *Brendan Behan's New York*. Hutchinson and Co., London, 1964
11. *The Scandalous Mr Bennett* Richard O'Connor. Doubleday and Co., New York 1962
12. *The City Observed: New York* Paul Goldberger. Random House, New York 1979; Penguin Books 1982
13. *Palaces for the People* Nathaniel Burt. Little Brown and Co., Boston 1977
14. *Music Comes to America* David Ewen. Allen, Towne and Heath Inc., New York 1947
15. *My Bondage and My Freedom* Frederick Douglass. Johnson Publishing Co. Inc., Chicago 1970 (first published 1855)
16. *Henry Ward Beecher* Clifford E. Clark Jr. University of Illinois Press, Urbana 1978
17. *Henry Ward Beecher: An American Portrait* Paxten Hibben. George H. Doran & Co., New York, 1927

Bibliography

This list includes some works of general interest to a visitor to New York, as well as books referred to or quoted in the text. It is followed by a short list of books that children might enjoy reading before or during a visit to New York.

American Institute of Architects, New York Chapter *A.I.A. Guide to New York City*. New York: Macmillan, 1967. Revised edition edited by Norval White and Elliot Willensky, 1978

Behan, Brendan *Brendan Behan's New York*. London: Hutchinson, 1964

Black, Mary *Old New York in Early Photographs, 1853–1901, 196 Prints from the Collection of the New York Historical Society*. New York: Dover, 1973

Brooklyn 1976 Symposium, Brooklyn College *Brooklyn U.S.A.: The Fourth Largest City in America*. (Brooklyn College Studies on Society in Change No. 7.) New York: Brooklyn College Press, 1979

Burke, John *Duet in Diamonds: The Flamboyant Saga of Lillian Russell and Diamond Jim Brady in America's Gilded Age*. New York: Putnam, 1972

Burt, Nathaniel *Palaces for the People: A Social History of the American Art Museum*. Boston: Little, Brown, 1977

Canfield, Cass *The Incredible Pierpont Morgan: Financier and Art Collector*. New York: Harper & Row, 1974

Capeci, Dominic J. *The Harlem Riot of 1943*. Philadelphia: Temple University Press, 1977

Churchill, Allen *The Improper Bohemians: A Re-creation of Greenwich Village in its Heyday*. New York: Dutton, 1959

Clark, Clifford E. *Henry Ward Beecher: Spokesman for a Middle-Class America*. Urbana: University of Illinois Press, 1978

Clark, Tom *The World of Damon Runyon*. New York: Harper & Row, 1978

Cook, Adrian *The Armies of the Streets: The New York City Draft Riots of 1863*. Lexington: University Press of Kentucky, 1974

Dickens, Charles *American Notes and Pictures from Italy*. London: Oxford University Press, 1957

Edmiston, Susan and Cirino, Linda D. *Literary New York: A History and Guide*. Boston: Houghton Mifflin, 1976

Ewen, David *Music Comes to America*. New York: Allen, Towne & Heath, 1947

Freedland, Michael *Irving Berlin*. New York: Stein & Day, 1974

Friedman, B. H. *Gertrude Vanderbilt Whitney*. Garden City, N.Y.: Doubleday, 1978

Galbraith, John Kenneth *The Great Crash, 1929*. London: Hamish Hamilton, 1955

Garrett, Charles *The La Guardia Years, Machine and Reform Politics in New York City*. New Brunswick, N.J.: Rutgers University Press, 1961

Goldberger, Paul *The City Observed: New York: A Guide to the Architecture of Manhattan*. New York: Random House, 1979

Gompers, Samuel *Seventy Years of Life and Labor, an Autobiography*. New York: A.M. Kelly, 1967

Harris, Neil *Humbug: The Art of P.T. Barnum*. Boston: Little, Brown, 1973

Haskins, James *Adam Clayton Powell: Portrait of a Marching Black*. New York: Dial Press, 1974

Hershkowitz, Leo *Tweed's New York: Another Look*. Garden City, N.Y.: Anchor Press, 1977

Hibben, Paxton *Henry Ward Beecher: An American Portrait*. New York: George H. Doran Co., 1927; New York: Readers Club, 1942

Hower, Ralph M. *History of Macy's of New York, 1858–1919*. Cambridge: Harvard University Press, 1943

Irving, Washington *A History of New York*. Edited for the modern reader by Edwin T. Bowden. New Haven, Conn.: College & University Press, 1964

James, Theodore *The Empire State Building*. New York: Harper & Row, 1975

Kouwenhoven, John A. *The Columbia Historical Portrait of New York: An Essay in Graphic History*. New York: Harper & Row, 1972

Kutz, Meyer *Rockefeller Power*. New York: Simon & Schuster, 1974

Lasker, Joy and George, Jean *New York in Maps*. New York: Ballantine Books, 1971

Levinson, Leonard Louis *Wall Street: A Pictorial History*. New York: Ziff-Davis, 1961

Lockwood, Charles *Manhattan Moves Uptown: An Illustrated History*. Boston: Houghton Mifflin, 1976

Lomask, Milton *Seed Money: The Guggenheim Story*. New York: Farrar, Straus, 1964

Loth, David *The City within a City: The Romance of the Rockefeller Center*. New York: Morrow, 1966

Metzker, Isaac *A Bintel Brief: Sixty Years of Letters from the Lower East Side to the JEWISH DAILY FORWARD*. Garden City, N.Y.: Doubleday, 1971

Mitchell, Joseph *The Bottom of the Harbor*. Boston: Little, Brown, 1960

Mooney, Michael Macdonald *Evelyn Nesbit and Stanford White: Love and Death in the Gilded Age*. New York: Morrow, 1976

Morris, James *The Great Port: A Passage through New York*. New York: Harcourt Brace & World, 1969

O'Connor, Richard *Gould's Millions*. Garden City, N.Y.: Doubleday, 1962

O'Connor, Richard *The Scandalous Mr. Bennett*. Garden City, N.Y.: Doubleday, 1962

Purtell, Joseph *The Tiffany Touch*. New York: Random House, 1971

Rogers, W.G. and Weston, Mildred *Carnival Crossroads: The Story of Times Square*. Garden City, N.Y.: Doubleday, 1971

Roskolenko, Harry *The Time That Was Then: The Lower East Side 1900–1914: An Intimate Chronicle*. New York: Dial Press, 1971

Rushmore, Robert *The Life of George Gershwin*. New York: Crowell-Collier Press, 1966

Schoener, Allan *Harlem on My Mind: Cultural Capital of Black America 1900–1968*. New York: Random House, 1969

Silver, Nathan *Lost New York*. Boston: Houghton Mifflin, 1967

Simon, Kate *Fifth Avenue: A Very Social History*. New York: Harcourt Brace Jovanovich, 1978

Smith, Thomas E.V. *The City of New York in the Year of Washington's Inauguration, 1789*. Riverside, Conn.: Chatham Press, 1972

Stevens, Mark *"Like No Other Store in the World": The Inside Story of Bloomingdale's*. New York: Crowell, 1979

Tomkins, Calvin *Merchants and Masterpieces: The Story of the Metropolitan Museum of Art*. New York: Dutton, 1970

Van Loon, Hendrik *Life and Times of Peter Stuyvesant*. New York: H. Holt, 1928

Wilstach, Paul *Hudson River Landings*. Indianapolis: Bobbs-Merrill, 1933

Books for Children

Du Bois, William Pène *Call Me Bandicoot*. (Tall tales on the Staten Island ferry trip; for young readers.) New York: Harper & Row, 1970

Children's Writers and Artists Collaborative *The New York Kid's Book*. (A miscellany of fact and fiction, for all ages.) Garden City, N.Y.: Doubleday, 1979

Griffin, Judith Berry *Phoebe and the General*. (An adventure story for young readers, set in Fraunces Tavern at the time of the Revolutionary War.) New York: Coward, McCann & Geoghegan, 1977

Konigsburg, E.L. *From the Mixed-Up Files of Mrs. Basil E. Frankweiler*. (Two runaway children and a mystery in the Metropolitan Museum of Art; for ages eight to twelve.) New York: Atheneum, 1967

L'Engle, Madeleine *The Young Unicorns*. (A fantasy thriller set in the Cathedral of St John the Divine; for older children.) New York: Farrar, Straus, 1968

McHargue, Georgess *Funny Bananas: The Mystery in the Museum*. (The museum is the American Museum of Natural History; for ages eight to twelve.) New York: Holt, Rinehart & Winston, 1975

McHargue, Georgess *Stoneflight*. (A fantasy about the statues of New York, set on the Upper West Side and in Central Park.) New York: Viking, 1975

Sasek, M. *This Is New York*. (A lively picture book for young children.) New York: Macmillan, 1960

Selden, George *The Cricket in Times Square*. (The adventures of a musical cricket who lives in the subway station; for ages eight to twelve. The Upper East Side is the locale of Selden's *The Genie of Sutton Place*.) New York: Farrar, Straus, 1960

Spier, Peter *The Legend of New Amsterdam*. (A picture book story of the earliest days of New York; for younger readers.) Garden City, N.Y.: Doubleday, 1979

Thompson, Kay *Eloise*. (The adventures of a six-year-old who lives in the Plaza Hotel.) New York: Simon & Schuster, 1955

Index

Because the maps for the most part follow closely the itineraries in each chapter, map references (M) are given in the index only for the most important sights and institutions. Numbers in italics refer to illustrations.